WORKING IN THE MAGIC CITY

THE WORKING CLASS IN AMERICAN HISTORY

A list of books in the series appears at the end of this book.

WORKING IN THE MAGIC CITY

Moral Economy in Early Twentieth-Century Miami

THOMAS A. CASTILLO

UNIVERSITY OF ILLINOIS PRESS
Urbana, Chicago, and Springfield

1 2 3 4 5 C P 5 4 3 2 1
♾ This book is printed on acid-free paper.

Library of Congress Cataloging-in-Publication Data
Names: Castillo, Thomas A., 1971– author.
Title: Working in the magic city : moral economy in early twentieth-century Miami / Thomas A. Castillo.
Description: Urbana : University of Illinois Press, [2022] | Series: The working class in American history | Includes bibliographical references and index.
Identifiers: LCCN 2021055205 (print) | LCCN 2021055206 (ebook) | ISBN 9780252044458 (cloth) | ISBN 9780252086533 (paperback) | ISBN 9780252053450 (ebook)
Subjects: LCSH: Working class—Florida—Miami—History—20th century. | Social conflict—Florida—Miami—History—20th century. | Service industries workers—Florida—Miami—History—20th century.
Classification: LCC HD8085.M5293 C37 2022 (print) | LCC HD8085.M5293 (ebook) | DDC 305.5/62759381—dc23/eng/20211201
LC record available at https://lccn.loc.gov/2021055205
LC ebook record available at https://lccn.loc.gov/2021055206

Contents

Preface

In many ways, this book began when I was twelve years old. Past-due mortgage payments and the demands of a five-child household kept my parents economically anxious. One significant moment was when my dad was left in the lurch when his only employee, Roberto, quit his one-man-run Castillo Painting Company. My father earned a living painting people's houses in early 1980s Greater Miami. It was barely a small business. His effort to join the local painting union yielded inconsistent work, a function of the whittling of construction union power over the years. The anxiety of getting enough work to pay the bills likely intensified my dad's lack of tact and rough nature, leading to a hostile work environment. Roberto certainly had cause to leave, but my dad was a struggling worker, too, desperately seeking to survive America's increasingly antiunion environment. It is unclear to me whether my dad asked or whether I volunteered, but I ended up working for him that summer and the next (and sometimes over weekends during the school year). I continued working for my dad on and off for the next several years.

It was during the period between 1979 and 1984 that a declension narrative emerged in my family about our recent past. Amid the economic struggle, my dad would express deep regret for making the decision not to follow a General Motors parts factory that was moving to Bensalem, Pennsylvania, at the end of 1978. GM was consolidating three plants, including Englewood, New Jersey, where my father had started working in 1966. Because my dad was a United Automobile Workers (UAW) unionist, the workers in the plant were offered funds to relocate and retain their jobs. Instead, my father decided to go south in 1978 and create a life for his family in south Florida. According to my mother, he continued to dream that he would return to Colombia and transplant his American children. He long wished to return to his home country especially after having been successful in establishing a family. I did not know this fact until my mother told me about his intentions sometime after his death in 2005.

In any case, our consistent economic woes forced my dad to hold two jobs at times and my mother to begin her own work life in retail. That did not prevent us, during at least one period, from having to go on food stamps. Food-stamp coupons looked like Monopoly money back then, and it carried enormous stigma. It broke my parents' hearts.

In many ways, my youth ended when I was twelve years old, and I have ever since been shaped by the hard lessons of forty-eight- to fifty-hour workweeks. We were often restricted from picking up the telephone because of the threat of the bill collectors calling. All we ever could afford were used cars, which required us to develop our olfactory and auditory senses so as to detect the seemingly inevitable mechanical problems of our vehicles. Too often needed home and car repairs were postponed, or my dad did the best he could to correct immediate problems. My mom worked her magic to make ends meet with creative budgeting or cooking that helped spread meager quantities while also soon getting work in retail. My mom's entrance into the workforce really hurt my dad, and his conservative value that his wife should be focusing her energy on keeping up the home. Of course, maintaining the home was a full-time job and childcare was a costly non-alternative.

For my dad, dental care was usually done by an unlicensed immigrant who had practiced back in their home country; I do not recall more than one or two visits to the dentist in my youth and certainly nearly none during my teenage years or twenties. My older brother and sisters were forced to find work as soon as they were legally able to (at sixteen years where we lived at the time) in order to mitigate our collective struggle. The day after my sixteenth birthday, I filled out an application to work at Bojangles Chicken, where my siblings had worked years before me. Our ever-present anxiety, although rooted in the economic, permeated all other realms of my and my family's existence in Greater Miami.

In conversations around the kitchen table during the 1980s, my dad would wax nostalgic about how well we had had it in New Jersey, how he had made it in the United States as a Colombian immigrant without ever finishing high school. This success was defined by his luck in meeting my mom, an immigrant from El Salvador, on a San Francisco trolley in the early 1960s. Labor union history, though, was critical to the actualization of this American Dream story. His memories of Englewood were imbued with narratives of dignity and respect. His eyes would glitter with such life about how he did not have to take "any shit from the foreman, especially if he looked at you in a funny way" because all he had to do was go to the shop steward and lodge a complaint. My dad was remembering how he was treated with dignity, earned a living wage, had benefits, and was not human capital to be used and tossed when no longer needed. The UAW got GM to pay for his relocation, if he so chose. That sort of articulated respect demonstrated my father's value as a human being and as a worker and the benefits of collective action. I am not sure whether he knew any labor history—probably not much. But those rights he had had as a worker in Englewood were the result of many hard-fought battles and much pain and suffering. He stood on the shoulders of many workers before him.

Nor could he have known how those victories were tragically being reversed. What he ended up getting in the 1980s and after were hokey Ronald Reagan platitudes about "Morning in America" and a faith that he was a member of the middle class. No doubt, his memories of Englewood dignity shaped his perceptions. The dissonance between reality and fantasy crystalized into a deep-seated alienation. Since life is lived in the here and now, few have the luxury of engaging deeper structural dynamics. The rhythms of work and play take too much time. An onslaught designed to discipline worker unwillingness to accept neoliberal precepts had just began. That story has to await another book. This one reaches back to one place and time that happens to be a location where I once lived (and still have loving family and friends residing) and whose class history I just happened to research. It is perhaps unsurprising that I found many of the roots of the Reagan era precarity simply by chance.

Acknowledgments

I wrote this book with the belief that the dignity of the human body and spirit should never be compromised. Along the way in researching and writing it, I have benefited immeasurably from family, friends, intellectual discussions with authors dead and alive, peers and colleagues, mentors, and institutions. Each has given me more than I could ever repay. I remain humbled and in awe of the luck that has allowed me to research and write this book.

Several historians have been very helpful. I want to first thank David Sicilia for all his support over the years. His sound advice and strong mind have helped me countless times. At Florida International University and since my days there, Alex Lichtenstein helped center my thinking and also set a standard of impeccable scholarship. The late Brian Peterson inspired me to first take on Miami as a research topic, but his influence went much further. From nineteenth-century and twentieth-century European and Russian history to the study of great intellectuals and artists such as Friedrich Nietzsche and Bertolt Brecht, Brian introduced me to a world of higher learning that continues to influence me. I thank Felice Lifshitz, my first college-level history professor, for setting a high bar for mentorship, scholarship, and enthusiasm for learning. At the University of Maryland, Gary Gerstle, the late Ira Berlin, and Julie Greene offered much useful insight, especially on labor history.

Several archivists, librarians, and institutions have been invaluable to the project. I would like to thank especially Dawn Hugh of the Research Center at HistoryMiami Museum and later Ashley Trujillo for providing helpful assistance. But there were many others who were very helpful as well. I would like to acknowledge the various institutions and the useful staffs that helped the research of this project: the George Meany Archive (now at University of Maryland); the Wirtz Library in the Labor Department; Special Collections at the University of Maryland; Interlibrary Loan at the University of Maryland; Interlibrary Loan at Coastal Carolina University; Special Collections at the University of Miami (especially the help of the late William Brown); the Florida International University Library; Black Archives History and Research Foundation of South Florida; the Florida State Archives; the National Archives in College Park and Washington, DC (especially Tab Lewis and Eric Van Slander); and the Library of Congress Manuscript Room and Microfilm Room. Thanks to all those who answered my questions over the telephone and via email.

I can't imagine a better experience in writing a first book than what I have had with the University of Illinois Press. I thank James Engelhardt, who helped shepherd the project in its early stages, and Alison Syring for seeing it through. I thank the anonymous readers, Nelson Lichtenstein, and the entire editorial board for their feedback and helpful suggestions. The amazing work of Ellie Hinton, Geof Garvey (a great copy editor), Tad Ringo, and so many others was critical. I have been warmly welcomed and supported here by the Coastal Carolina University community—students, colleagues, and administrators. Financial assistance was given to me from Coastal Carolina University research and professional development grants, as well as from a subvention for the publication of this book. I thank Brandon Palmer, the chair of the History Department at the time, and Dean Claudia Bornholdt, dean of the Edwards College of Humanities and Fine Arts, for making the latter support available to me.

Other friends and colleagues played crucial roles in the development and growth of this book: at Miami, Mayra Beers, David Callejo, John Clasca, Gilbert Lleonart, Evelyn Miranda, Roberto Pacheco, and Pablo Toral; at Maryland, Herbert Brewer, Jeff Coster, the crew at Letters and Sciences, Claire Goldstene, Pete Hoefer, Kate Keane, Ricardo Lopez, Larry Nagl, Linda Noel, Shari Orisich, Yali Pan, Erika Rapier, and Eric Van Slander. A special acknowledgment goes to my former football teammate and Hialeah compatriot and a damn sharp scholar, Tony Lopez. Joe Armenio, a dear friend and one of the smartest people I know, provided enormous help through the writing and revising of this book by reading, editing, and offering all kinds of support.

My family have been at the heart of this book's journey. Although no longer in this world, my older brother Oswaldo Anthony Castillo and my father Oswaldo Ramon Castillo were central to what defined my curiosity and sense of social justice. My mother Julia Lisette Castillo has been unconditional in her support and I am deeply grateful. My siblings' loyalty, love, and commitment to family have been inspirational. Thank you, Gabe, Lisette, and Sandra for just being there for me. Much love to my entire extended family (cousins, nephews, nieces, aunts, in-laws). My wife's family (especially Ayşe, Ilyas, and Salih) and friends in Turkey have offered timely support and encouragement.

Sevgi Erdoğan, my wife, has helped this project in so many ways. Words can't express my debt to you. Thank you for introducing me to your world. Thank you for your feedback and listening over and over again about class harmony and moral economy. Thank you for setting such a high standard for intellectual excellence. I am just damn lucky we met.

INTRODUCTION

Working-Class Community

The development and growth of US cities in the nineteenth and twentieth centuries often took the appearance of a business venture. Each addition, from buildings and parks to infrastructure, constituted a progressive march for social betterment and a sacrifice to the god of economic growth and abundance. While the urban-rural tensions persisted, the city won out as the dominant power between the two regions. Farmland and the outskirts of the urban would serve the demands of the city—the bastion of modernity, acting as the brain to the body and revealed in the landscape of finance, manufacturing, and the service trades.

Developed in early-twentieth-century industrial America in a relatively pristine and sparsely populated area, Miami built on this longer history of the city. Its founders and boosters pushed for growth, begged for investment by selling its potential for economic profit, and packaged its climate, natural landscape, and geographic proximity to the Caribbean and Latin America as unique competitive advantages. South Florida's history of Native American, slave, and Atlantic world past would be mostly forgotten or selectively remembered.[1]

Miami endured an identity crisis of sorts in the first half of the twentieth century over what kind of city it would become. Two visions emerged of how the city would develop. Many were satisfied to keep the city simply as a resort town with agricultural development in the hinterland and business focused on sales of consumer goods and services filling the urban landscape. The rural outskirts would complement the tropical resort where aristocrats basked in the pleasures of sports recreation and leisure, a path that assumed tourism would remain the primary economic engine. This viewpoint expressed a concern about Miami becoming an industrial center. One revealing example of the concern took place with the debate over the effort to develop a cigar-manufacturing sector. While local newspapers in their typical urban booster spirit advocated anything that would grow the city, including making cigars, Miami's business elite were more selective and exclusionary—at least through the first few decades of the century. The Miami Chamber of Commerce appears to have deterred and stunted the growth of the cigar-manufacturing sector. Only a few cigar factories emerged (three to twelve workers per establishment), but they only totaled about fifty to seventy-five workers in the early 1920s and grew only to about three hundred by 1934. Miami never came close to reproducing Key West's or Tampa's Ybor City cigar-manufacturing dominance. The Miami Chamber of Commerce (CC) claimed in an October 1924 meeting that "Miami had decided that they will not want to make this a center such as Tampa, on account of its adverse effect on the tourist business." E. G. Sewell, president of the CC, and others "cautioned against bringing in any industries which would attract a *cheap class of labor* . . . [since this] will have an adverse effect on our tourists, especially at the bathing beaches" (emphasis added). Sewell expressed here an economic vision that entailed shaping development along particular lines and excluding certain types of workers. Sewell and other CC members had little interest in developing a manufacturing sector that would include immigrant laborers. In the case of cigar work, the model of labor struggle and diversity of Ybor City where Cubans, Italians, and Spaniards resisted employer power while also establishing unique communities likely represented the opposite of what Sewell hoped to build in Miami.[2]

Others argued logically, in a second vision of city development, for Miamians to also invest in agricultural development and not to be so dependent on tourism.[3] They advocated growing an industrial sector and later in the century a financial sector in banking and in trade. As a potential economic gateway to the southern hemisphere, these proponents of a more diverse economy argued that Miami would enjoy a natural competitive advantage because of its geographic proximity to Latin America. But the attempts to create a manufacturing landscape ran up against physical limitations such as Miami's distance from the northern United States (improved over time with air travel) and the lack of adjacent small towns and cities depending on a great port city; the lack of deepwater harbor accommodations;[4] flooding along the Everglades' eastern boundaries that required the reclaiming of the wetlands through drainage and canal construction;[5] and the absence of any significant extractive mineral attracting investors for quick turnaround of profits. Vegetables and fruits would slowly become more important over time as flooding and transportation problems were resolved; farming in the rural regions of Dade County did not pose a threat to the tropical tourist landscape as manufacturing development would.[6] The idea of making Miami an economic leader in Latin America was reinforced culturally by the imperialist assumption that the United States benefited from its racial superiority to darker and foreign peoples—aided and abetted, of course, by native Latin Americans complicit in the exploitation and "development" of their homelands. These two visions of progress—Miami as tropical tourist destination and winter playground and as Latin American industrial-commercial capital—constituted tense countervailing arguments at the root of Greater Miami's political economy.

Into the 1950s, the adjacent city of Miami Beach did its best to safeguard the exclusivity of the first vision by keeping out Black residents from either living on or visiting the beach for leisure; restricting Jews from use of clubs and hotels; and remaining cost-prohibitive for low-income workers more generally. Fear of worker theft led hotels, bars, and restaurants to force the seasonal transient workers, and even those who commuted to work from Miami, both white and Black, to submit to fingerprinting and criminal background checks.[7] The winter season witnessed an increase of the local police force and the migration of northern detectives to Miami Beach and Miami to secure the perception of safety in the winter playground—a term used widely by boosters and promoters of Greater Miami that often referred more specifically to Miami Beach.[8] Increasingly over time, the acute seasonal ebbs and flows of unemployment characteristic of an economy overly reliant on the short winter tourist season (roughly December to April) made for an unstable and insecure environment, one that could not be sustained as the area's growing resident population struggled to make ends meet throughout the year. The origins, or at least dreams of, a year-round economy revealed a commonsense reaction to the seasonal dynamic of irregular work. It was not until after 1945, when air conditioning became widespread, that summer tourist trips to Florida increased, thereby offering a bit more year-round employment.[9]

Complicating the two visions of economic progress was the precarious business of community building, particularly for the workers of the city. The rhetoric of boosterism—as embedded in the two visions of progress—only served to silence much of Miami's working-class history. The story of workers was at best a sidebar to heroic accounts of hardworking founding pioneer entrepreneurs or the benevolence and intelligence of wealthy magnates.[10] The winter playground emphasis prioritized the need of the winter resident and tourist. Despite their apparent inertia, the workers and small-business owners who built and kept Miami operating needed and demanded more stability. The consistent push to hire home labor, residents of the area, and particularly unionized workers revealed the effort for a moral economy.[11]

House painter, one-time editor of the weekly city labor union newspaper, and poet Stephen Cochran Singleton observed in December 1928 that Miamians were determined that their city "become a home and not a road-house." He continued, "We are beginning to realize that the components of our future prosperity will be products and not tips . . . that one citizen who will insist on good schools and who will make something to sell is worth 100 visitors."

Singleton called for more men "who can wear overalls efficiently and men who can pay wages to these overall wearers sufficiently." Singleton's words revealed a vision of class harmony where workers—limited here to a masculine image of the ideal laborer—held jobs that paid living wages. While Singleton clearly aligned with the vision of a diversified economy, his concern for creating a stable society amid a political economy geared toward "carnival" put him in opposition to the logic of tourism economics. It would be wrong, however, to focus only on his social conservativism.

More significant was the tone of Singleton's insights. His concern was with the creation of a moral economy or, as he described it, a partnership in "our municipal corporation." Singleton demonstrated an impatience with the antics of boosterism—such as luring visitors to Miami with the city's daughters in "nearly nude" photos. His airs of prudish Victorian morality and patriarchal assumptions could easily distract the reader as he also added his equal impatience and frustration with jazz, the dance hall, and bootlegging.[12] When read beyond these obvious interpretations, however, Singleton's observations offer a serious criticism of the precarious, insecure, and deferential nature of tourist economics, particularly the low pay, short-term work, and expectation of docility from workers. He demanded more substantial work, wages, and community-building endeavors such as school construction. In the context of the short tourist season, such comments represented a moral compass for development that challenged the economic precarity typical of the working class. The incessant calls for year-round tourism—that is, including the summer—in the interwar years probably did not alleviate Singleton's concerns.

Miami boosters were unsure how to balance the demands of a resort town with its characteristic flows of people with that of a growing, more permanent working-class community. Many workers certainly were interested in settling or were simply less willing to circulate like pieces of capital forced to move for the interests of investors or wealthy tourists. The city's oldest newspaper, the *Miami Metropolis*, argued in 1920 that the city had to draw small-business entrepreneurs and workers: "Something must be done to offset the idea that Miami is a rich man's town. It is that, and it is more—it is the town for the man who may not be rich but who can contribute as much in brain and genius and labor toward the town as does the man with only his money bags."[13] The possibility for growth and development depended on a permanent population, one that hoped to make a life in south Florida.

Yet the reality that "laborers are toiling away to make a paradise for the rich man's pleasures" was a public testament and expectation that revealed the reproduction of class hierarchy. It also highlighted how paradise on earth needed to be humanly constructed. This quote, taken from a 1915 *Miami Metropolis* article discussing the building of Vizcaya, John Deering's extravagant 185-acre villa on prime waterfront property in southern Miami, offers an important lens through which to view the past. Referring to what was then known as the Deering Estate, the article boasted how "one out of every twenty-five of Miami's 20,000 residents" was working daily in its construction. The paper highlighted its extravagance resulting from its use of "an Italian Renaissance style," which it authenticated by listing the materials used to build it. Here is a small sampling: stone from Miami's own scarce and precious limestone, as well as from the Florida Keys and Cuba; red Spanish roof tiles from houses in Cuba Deering bought for the sole purpose of extracting the tiles; royal palm trees purchased fully grown from Cuba to decorate the causeway between Miami Avenue and the estate's boathouse (Deering had a channel dredged in the bay to facilitate the transport of these materials to the worksite).[14] The construction project was a literal representation of laboring for the rich man's pleasures. The underlying principle of this exchange was that south Florida land was designed—as was the land and property in Cuba and the Caribbean—for the wealthy white American to enjoy for their leisure and play. Property yielded not only pleasure for them but also financial value for the real-estate speculator, the critical booster in Miami's history that preached how real estate was "better than gold mines."[15] Work for the well-to-do served as a symbol of Miami's tourist economics. Displays of social hierarchy and performances that reinforced this class relational logic defined the cultural backbone that shaped the economy.

But the view that saw deference and service as essential to economic survival conflicted with notions of equality as expressed in the Declaration of Independence and as promised by American Exceptionalism. If all humans were created equal and if what made America unique was the absence of a feudal past and messy class conflict, then how did society reconcile the apparent contradiction between the demands of social hierarchy and the visions of greater social equality?[16] This book explores this class dynamic. I argue that class struggle operated along the discursive axis of class harmony.

Class-harmony discourse was a language that navigated the tension between two visions of social order: one inegalitarian, the other more egalitarian. The former embraced a social order of clear class hierarchy, in which laborers worked for the rich. Work was exoticized in hokey platitudes and moral caricatures and mocked in playful performances of deference, some quite undignified. In essence, the rich were busy directing others and living the leisured life while workers labored in happy cadence. The egalitarian vision of social order was dominated by the drive toward moral economy. While dignity in work was a given, just as important was the idea that all had the right to a competency. In Miami, the right to a pleasurable life, with access to recreation and decent living conditions, also shaped this twentieth-century version of moral economy. The vision of class harmony clashed with the rigid sense of social hierarchy.

The language of class harmony—instead of classlessness or class conflict—served to hide struggle within the tourist economy and capitalism more generally. Miami's political economy, perhaps more than most others, necessitated a peaceful social setting to ensure the promises of the winter playground; that Miamians came mostly from other places raised the stakes for creating a culture that appeared welcoming.[17] Class-harmony discourse obscured struggle in the historical memory in part because of the demands of tourism and community. It represented a discursive framework on which workers struggled in their efforts to create community amid their persistent economic precarity.

While nowhere formally articulated by any of the historical actors in this study, one may find class-harmony discourse by analyzing an array of historical documents: newspapers, private papers, organization minutes, government records, and letters, among others. Class-harmony discourse negotiated class conflict and debated competing notions of social order and power among the classes. It engaged the realities of class hierarchies by arguing for class cooperation rather than class conflict. Many employers tried to foster an oversupplied labor market and, consistent with this structural goal, tried to create as pliant, docile, and loyal a workforce as possible. For their part, workers sought a stable labor market able to supply jobs over longer periods (as opposed to temporary and seasonal work) while also pushing to alleviate the hardships of work, the insecurity of low pay and inconsistent work, and the financial vulnerability emerging from such conditions. In Miami, class-harmony discourse was a function of a culture of growth and development, of the business of boosterism, and of the political economy of tourism. In opposition to the apparent concession to classlessness that such a language suggests, this book will demonstrate how class-harmony discourse provides a theoretical framework that challenges notions of US classlessness and broadens the boundaries of class conflict and class consciousness.

Despite the vast changes that south Florida would endure in the post–World War II period, the social, economic, political, and cultural history that defined earlier Miami had an enduring influence on the later city. In order to understand class struggle and the nature of class relations in spaces of US leisure such as south Florida's tourist-based economy in the early twentieth century, one has to unpack the language and political dynamism of class-harmony discourse—an expansive language that expressed class tension, conflict, repression, and even progressive grassroots politics. Hospitality practices in tourist work and the urban boosters' push for rapid growth and development shaped this class language. The effect of the resulting hegemony has been a distortion of how we have remembered class struggle and its interrelationship with race in spaces such as Miami, outside industrial and mineral extracting locations; that is, places that lacked major labor upheaval such as prolonged strikes and violent clashes.

Discursive practices emerged in a context where racial segregation, industrial labor conflict, and welfare capitalism existed as social realities, solutions, and limitations to shaping class relations.

Working in the Magic City analyzes the history of class and race by exploring the nature of capitalism as it developed in Miami, Florida, in the first half of the twentieth century. More specifically, it focuses on how class and race relations reflected and reinforced the nature of power in that locale and how those dynamics reflected larger national patterns. Miami's continuous growth, changing population, and economy rooted mainly in low-wage, service-oriented jobs and employment seasonality poses a challenge to understanding class and race relations. The constant change and persistent obstacles that workers faced both in living their lives in low-wage and seasonal work strained the efforts to organize collective responses to ameliorate such systemic problems. This study contributes to the vibrant and penetrating work of historians who have explored the central importance of class in shaping civil-rights struggles, and who remain careful not to write about race and racism in isolation or to elevate whiteness as the important shaping force defining race relations. Histories of pervasive white privilege have too often narrowed the history of capitalism by making the working class the main culprits in the reproduction of class-racial power. The degradation of the working class, more generally, is ignored or silenced through overly positive assessments of their apparent power. Instead, more focus is needed on the shared struggle and cultural and political obstacles preventing cross-racial class solidarity.

The juxtaposition of the words *harmony*, *struggle*, and *conflict* may appear strange, particularly in the absence of the words *consent*, *legitimacy*, and *authority*. The latter words express finality or at least imply political exchanges over the nature of power. Too often liberal democracies, such as the United States, assume consent, legitimacy, and authority, which then translate into simplistic interpretations of class consciousness or the lack thereof. In this common framing, on one end of the ideological spectrum stands individualism and on the other stands collectivism. Individualism and collectivism were not and are not mutually exclusive. Hierarchy and competition have coexisted with mutuality and sharing, sometimes in conflict and sometimes in healthy balance.

Class-harmony discourse suggests a different discursive spectrum of political class. In contrast to classlessness and American Exceptionalism, class-harmony discourse centers process, contingency, and the all-too-human desires for social balance, dignity, and peace. In this light, process and contingency become synonymous with struggle and conflict. The language of class harmony, instead of demonstrating hegemony, consent, or false consciousness, reveals how contestation was involved in defining and enacting competing notions of class harmony. More specifically, class-harmony discourse points to the limits of worker power and the reality that one could not live in constant conflict or war. Housing, nourishment, health, and peace of mind were (are) needs too difficult to sacrifice, at least for too long, without the risk of losing them altogether. The importance of this insight is that it allows for wider inclusion of class conflict without having to demonstrate the degrees of commitment to social-democratic unionism versus occupational or craft unionism.[18] The former often translates to measuring the prevalence or degree of commitment to racial liberalism and left idealism (anarchism, socialism, or communism) in historical actors. No litmus test measuring the degree or extent of individualism or communalism will do. When the analytical focus becomes the historical context and the nature of power, not preconceived notions predetermining political conservatism or radicalism, the complicated nature of moral economy is revealed. The social democratic project of unionism often operated in the context of scarcity and competition, placing workers with difficult decisions and, sometimes, unfair outcomes.

Some historians have mediated efforts at worker disempowerment by arguing tenuous conceptions of working-class agency. They argue that workers embraced paternalistic values and adopted consumerist expectations rooting them firmly in individualism and the politics of reciprocity. But this conception can be too linear and unproblematic. A multidimensional story of the nature of power and work is foreordained to fulfill a self-fulfilling prophecy that depicts workers as merely individualists and middle class in outlook, that is, as assumed in the absence of evidence and with a liberal bias to read expansive and inclusive notions of free will even into capitalism's worst manifestations. The scarcity of evidence on one count—scattered anecdotes proving these assumptions—is strengthened by the absence of a robust record of radicalism or other prominent dissent from the existing political economy.[19] The noble radical straw man, such as William Z. Foster, is the exception that proves the rule. Consumerism historiography has only reinforced the tendency to find a simplistic rendering of John Commons's and Selig Perlman's wage-conscious worker. Unfortunately, this work has contributed to the drive to abandon the arena of production and issues of worker's control on the shop floor even while it has expanded our engagement with economic justice.[20] The quest for greater economic security and overall happiness, which often underpinned unionization drives, is understated in the whiggish history of capitalist triumphalism and in the dubious agency rooted in the literature of the cultural turn.

Working in the Magic City seeks to recast the idea of class harmony as an arena of conflict as opposed to a sign of worker accommodation. The idea of class harmony, at least as played out in welfare capitalism and company unionism, has gained attention only in certain sectors of the economy, mainly in mass-production industries and factories or in extractive work such as mining. The construction industry, service work (hotels, restaurants, etc.), and other small worksites have mostly remained outside the scope of historical studies. More generally speaking, historians have failed to identify manifestations of class-harmony discourse as arenas of class struggle, particularly in less-organized economic sectors and locales. Scholars have, nonetheless, demonstrated how workers often argued for and acted toward attaining greater power.

The book argues that scholars need to reframe the idea of power and focus the essence of worker struggle as a drive toward greater social harmony and as an expression of moral economy. The push for shorter hours, higher wages, economic security, better working conditions, and other means to improve the quality of life has defined this longer history. Sometimes such movements dissolved into violence, often as a result of employer and state action. These movements were held in check by the employers' power and state authority as defined by legal opinions, legislation, and police power. The reality of this stout resistance and worker lack of financial resources frequently left few good options.[21] In general, workers' concerns focused primarily on wider distribution of wealth and thus fairer distribution of power; but workers also were concerned about economic justice and fairness. Their concern extended to living lives with meaning and an opportunity to attain happiness. The concern was often articulated in moral terms, as when class harmony expressed moral economic demands. The idea of moral economy—the protection of individual competency and the right to a livelihood amid fair working conditions—defined the morality.

The history of the application of the concept of moral economy is too broad and deep to engage here. Scholars from across the social science and humanities spectrum have offered much to the historical understanding of the term.[22] The book adds to the resurgent interest in moral economy. It argues that moral economy was often expressed in harmony discourse vernacular. In addition to efforts to protect work (home labor, union job site), fighting for living wages, and arguing for just prices (cost-of-living struggles), one may add the drive toward what historian Benjamin Hunnicutt has discussed as the forgotten American Dream: a dream of freedom from the demands and burdens of the marketplace. Hunnicutt identifies this as "higher progress," which he defined as "the democratic advance of freedom beyond political liberty and economic struggles." Having its origins in the American colonies and further developing in the nineteenth century, Hunnicutt traces this history into the twentieth century and focuses primarily on the struggle over shorter hours.[23] Adding this scope when viewing worker struggles over wages and hours raises the significance of such efforts. To attain lives with meaning, working toward self-awareness, and safeguarding spaces for individual growth and development were at the heart of worker activism, ambition, and efforts to survive. The struggle for a living wage and shorter hours thus highlights this fight for humanity.[24]

Because the city of Miami emerged at the height of Jim Crow and in the South, how harmony negotiated class and racial hierarchies is central to this book. As a history of class relations, it focuses on the working class and how they struggled for financial security and community amid an economic climate that praised the existence of abundance but that applied an ideology of scarcity. As a history of race relations, it tells a familiar story of cultural division and racism. When the study of class and race are combined, the outlines of the causes and pernicious consequences of social hierarchy become more apparent and the differences between the two analytical categories less blurred. Unfortunately, historians have too often given short shrift to class in their study of capitalism, elevating race, gender, ethnicity, or other identity and ideological categories as the primary agents shaping inequality and subordination. The common "class, race, and gender" focus of studies has too often neglected class to the detriment of critical structural analysis and sharp social history.

The discursive landscape of whiteness studies, for example, has explored the racial components if not roots of capitalism. Cedric Robinson's *Black Marxism* (1983) used the term *racial capitalism* to denote the interconnectedness between racism and capitalism; several historians since have used the term but not necessarily the same social-scientific methodology or style of sweeping generalizations that characterized parts of Robinson's book. Such terms needlessly segment the experience of the working class at the cost of understanding class commonalities among groups. As much as one may embrace the goal of eliminating the divisive ideas of race and the destructive results from racism on society, ideas such as racial capitalism risk becoming intellectual caricatures. Racial capitalism explains inequality too neatly and also risks perpetuating racist, nationalist, and other cultural essentialisms.[25] In the place of critical, analytical, and dynamic class histories, historians have offered the hegemonic framework of white privilege, where the wealthiest to the poorest whites embrace a racial bond with bottom-line economic and social benefits.[26] The direct and indirect results of such hegemonic arguments are damaging to the larger political project of attaining an egalitarian democracy and debase its intellectual rigor. Ideological assumptions of capitalism—whether they are the narratives of natural "man" or economic "man"—are seldom questioned or engaged. All too often the tenets of liberal democracy are unknowingly adopted and thus the framework of capitalism is left unquestioned.[27] Racism is too often linked merely to psychology.[28] As the historian John Munro reminds us, too much is at stake to not consider class and race in all their fullness.[29]

Working in the Magic City will outline the commonalities within the working class in one place and at one moment in history. A careful analysis of the commonalities will allow for a starker account of the causes of the divisions between workers and explain the struggle of power that they had with their employers. The book will unpack a fuller narrative of how class and race unfolded together in lieu of a longer theoretical discussion here. It relies on a vast number of insightful historians such as E. P. Thompson, Herbert Gutman, David Montgomery, Barbara J. Fields, Eric Arnesen, Alex Lichtenstein, and Brian Kelly, to name but a few. All emphasize the centrality of class, the need for critical, local histories, and the importance of connecting local narratives to larger processes of capitalism. Race for them is ideologically constructed whereas class, in Barbara Fields's words, refers to "the inequality of human beings from the standpoint of social power." In perhaps her most famous phrasing, Fields wrote, "class is a concept that we can locate both at the level of objective reality and at the level of appearances. Race is a concept that we can locate at the level of appearances only."[30] This book is concerned with exploring these historical processes: class as objective reality and appearances and race as appearances.

My profile of the objective reality will demonstrate the similar types of arduous labor, power, and powerlessness that Black and white workers experienced; this entails outlining the power of the ruling class and the strategies of attaining and keeping power. The analysis of ideology will examine how narratives of race and class hierarchy divided and united groups—employers and employees, Black and white, rich and poor. Barbara Fields reminded us years ago that "an understanding of how groups of people see other groups in relation to themselves must begin by analyzing the pattern of their social relations."[31] This book is a study of the pattern that defined Miami's social relations.

Working in the Magic City will explore through class analysis the history of the formation of community amid the flux of early city development and analyze the political economy that gave it sustenance. It begins with an overview of the history of race and class in the interwar years, and subsequent chapters unpack the history of working-class organizing. Chapters on the chauffeur conflict, building-trades unions and open-shop conflict, and the story of how workers reacted to the high rates of unemployment in the late 1920s and 1930s constitute the outline of the book. The peopling of Miami and the efforts to create community were persistent throughout the interwar period. Such efforts often manifested as movements against economic scarcity and for economic security. Analysis of the language of harmony contributes to class, labor, and working-class history by demonstrating how classlessness and class-conflict frameworks divide too neatly a complicated social history driven by a deep desire for dignity against the alienating forces of exploitation.

CHAPTER 1

Class and Race in the Interwar Years

It is unquestionable that Jim Crow was firmly rooted in Miami, Florida, at the beginning of the twentieth century and that outright racists permeated all parts of the city. With Ku Klux Klan parades, mob-rule lynching, and overzealous police imposing law and order unequally and unfairly, Black Miamians faced constant reminders that their lives existed in a different paradigm than whites—that they were less free than whites. The racism did not exist in isolation or reflect mere bad attitudes, psychological dysfunction, or the earning of a psychological wage of white privilege. Its sustenance was harvested from a political economic system that profited from cheap labor and the reproduction of a reserved army of laborers. Workers, white or Black, would struggle mightily in their efforts to attain moral economy within such a precarious and at times hostile environment.

One way this precarity was articulated was through the discrimination against the impoverished and marginalized more generally. A case in point was Miami's notorious street tax. First introduced as an idea by Miami Mayor John W. Watson in February 1913 but not passed by the city council until October 1914, it empowered the city to collect a yearly tax of $3 cash from "all able bodied male persons over the age of 21 and under the age of 55" who resided in the city and did not pay real or personal property taxes. Only a few traces of this institution remain in the historical record. From newspaper reports, the tax collectors appeared to more often target American and Bahamian Blacks, though unemployed whites were also charged.[1] To avoid harassment, one had to carry a receipt of payment of the tax or face arrest and serve ten days in jail unless paid in full. Mayor Watson had actually wanted to impose a potential alternative payment plan that required six days of road-construction work but that provision did not make it into the final city ordinance. The ordinance created a clearly untenable situation lending to abuse and likely fear and contempt of city officers.

In one rare moment, an entrepreneurial Black impersonated a police officer by borrowing an actor's police uniform, which he used unsuccessfully to collect the street tax. It was unclear whether the suspect was a Bahamian or American Black. The article's class-denigrating title—"Negro Had Bright Idea for Getting a Living without Much Trouble"—lampooned the suspect while also using a sexual double entendre in describing him as a "big burly negro . . . swinging a billy of enormous proportions." Stereotype here reinforced class hierarchy, arguing, in effect—not unlike Mayor Watson—that social control was needed to discipline the unruly (in this instance the hypersexed and lazy) masses. In another instance of subtle racism but with a Caribbean imperial tinge, the *Metropolis* noted how the municipal court in one session "resembled a meeting of the Haitian parliament" in that not one "white case was on the docket." The readers learned that most of the "twenty negroes" in court were guilty of not paying the street tax. The tax was not only collected on the streets, but in residences, resulting in at least one instance of a street-tax collector officer shooting a noncompliant Black. The officer was later acquitted and the city paid his legal fees. Black protest of the tax amid World War I labor shortages allowed them to leverage employers desperate with threats of mass out-migration to end the street tax. It appears, though, the "work or fight" rule during the war did its part in controlling the unemployed and disciplining labor. The four years of enforcement of the street tax served as a reminder that the Black and white propertyless would face regular harassment.[2]

Racism and the commensurate exploitation that so often accompanied it would seem to explain the street-tax institution. Racist stereotypes and the targeting of an apparent Black underclass marked its implementation. One's imagination has hardly to stretch to identify how the street tax could easily be corrupted regardless of the most progressive intentions to expand the young city's coffers for likely needed projects and other local government costs. Such a tool also served to control the propertyless, which indicates, of course, the existence of such a class. The extant evidence of the institution is rather thin. No other history of Miami has ever referred to it. Yet what does exist indicates that poor whites were forced to pay the tax. Neither racism nor classism offers an adequate explanation. The immorality of prejudice has less explanatory power than the deeper power struggle shaping Miami's political economy. Employers pressed hard and, at times with the backing of local police, forced workers to follow their mandates and particularly to become a form of labor tool or piece of capital. The political economic context offers sharper insight than poor attitudes and bigoted thinking.

Miami, a city built on tourism and dreams of greater economic power, resembled a frontier landscape but with a dash of tropical decor. The city's investors sought to take advantage of south Florida's climate. Agriculture offered promise, tourism even more, and, of course, speculation in real estate, the sort of business that Karl Marx described as fictitious capital. That is not to say that many did not hope that manufacturing would develop, but that sector never quite grew. Migrating workers also sought economic opportunity. The sweat of their labor could possibly be a path to social mobility or greater economic security. The potential abundance of the land and the warmth of the climate represented a fair enough environment to sojourn for a living and for others to settle and make a life. The task of building and maintaining a city clearly required their hard work, skill, patience, and cooperation. High or at least fair wages could lure some to come but, more important, workers were attracted to the availability of work and the possibility of living a life with dignity, leisure, and security. Others worked under a more rigid disciplinary context in which labor was more openly exploited. Regardless, precarity defined a worker's existence.

This chapter provides an overview of interwar Miami. Early Miami, from its founding to about World War II, experienced enormous growth both in population and the construction of buildings and structures. Despite several insightful studies of this period, its working-class and political economic history has been less studied. The focus on race and less on class dynamics partly explains the incomplete picture. Another is the nature of Miami's labor history archive. Not many archival records exist documenting the worker's perspective. Yet historical trails do exist even if the collective memory of Miami's working-class history has slipped through the cracks. Subsequent chapters offer close contextual analysis and deep readings of various records, whereas this chapter offers exploratory framing and insights.

The Peopling of Miami: A Bird's-Eye View

Incorporated in 1896 in sparsely populated Dade County, Florida, Miami's population grew from a few thousand at the beginning of the century to 5,471 in 1910, 29,571 in 1920, 110,540 in 1930, 172,172 in 1940, and 249,000 in 1950. This represented a growth rate of 520 percent between 1920 and 1950.[3] The population for Dade County consistently expanded as Miami's expanded: 11,933 (in 1910), 24,536 (1915), 42,753 (1920), 111,352 (1925), 142,955 (1930), 180,998 (1935), 267,739 (1940), 315,138 (1945), and 495,084 (1950). A few points stand out about the dynamics of the huge percentage increases. Greater Miami experienced its slowest growth rates between 1925 and 1945, with an uptick between 1935 and 1940 followed by its slowest growth during World War II (1925–30, 28.4%;

1930–35, 26.6%; 1935–40, 47.9%; 1940–45, 17%). It went through its largest percentage increases in the 1920–25 interval (160%), and its largest aggregate jump occurred after 1945, when its population increased by 179,946 (57.1%)—that is, by nearly what its entire population had been in 1935.

Evaluating the composition of the population and the way it changed over time can become a bit confusing, particularly when one considers the US Bureau of the Census's changing practices, shifting data categories, and expanding geographic scopes. Florida's state censuses, taken in the middle of each decade until 1945, are useful supplements in understanding Miami's demographics. Together they offer a bird's-eye view of Miami's population growth, which resulted primarily from migration from other parts of Florida, the bordering southern States, the Northeast, and the Midwest. Throughout the early twentieth century, Miami's small foreign-born population and northern migrants represented the roots of a cosmopolitan city. Not until World War II and the postwar years did Miami see its largest immigrant population increase. The development of Latinx Miami, for instance, started to occur after World War II as many historians have noted.[4] Modern Miami, however, dominated by Spanish speakers, did not truly begin until after the Cuban Revolution in 1959. While Bahamian Blacks had once represented a majority of the area's Black population (with miniscule numbers of other Caribbean Blacks residing in the city), southern Blacks became the overwhelming majority by the mid-1920s (see table 1–1). Viewing change at the county level helps account for the expansion of Miami as a metropolitan area even though the US Census Bureau did not define the standard metropolitan area as a geographic category until 1950, when it included all of Dade.[5]

Through about the late 1930s, about half of Miami's white residents came from other parts of the South, primarily from Florida and Georgia but also South and North Carolina, Alabama, Tennessee, Kentucky, and Virginia (see table 1–1). Along with the increasing number of southern Black migrants, the southern feel that Miami engendered was as much a function of the heat and geography as it was the customs of the people who resided there. No doubt, the southern twang was a dominant cadence in town through the mid-1940s. While outside the focus of this book, it is important to note that no scholar has systematically studied the southern roots of Miami's population. Historian James Gregory has noted how the topic of internal migration has been "one of the seriously underanalyzed issues of twentieth-century historiography."[6] Yet we can make some reasonable deductions about Miami's southern population.

Miami-Dade had very few residents up to 1910 and then experienced an explosion. The increase in Floridians, Georgians, North and South Carolinians, Alabamians, and other southerners indicates a large migration into an initially insignificant base. Natural increase, for example, cannot explain the 160 percent increase between 1920 and 1925. Not much is known about the nature of migration flows before 1950: the length of residency, the number who left, and, generally, the overall circulation. The growth of Miami's Floridian population (the largest single group throughout the period, for both whites and Blacks) likely consisted of many migrants from other parts of the state and, thus, the increase was likely not just a function of natural births, even when considering the number of Florida births from non-Florida migrants or immigrants.[7] What is absolutely clear is that population movement shaped Greater Miami's landscape. People regularly came and went by boat, train, car, and later by plane. At the heart of what defined Miami was the continuous circulation of people: the influx of hopeful potential residents or just sojourners or speculators who had no intention of settling down; the seasonal ebbs and flows of tourists and workers; and, finally, the outflow of migrants when things simply did not work out.

Sometime in the late 1930s and early 1940s, Miami experienced a large in-migration of white nonsoutherners, both native and foreign-born. The influx, according to the 1945 Florida State Census, indicates that northeasterners (especially migrants from New York, New Jersey, Pennsylvania, and Massachusetts) about doubled their previous 1935 high; midwesterners arrived in large numbers as well. The changing categories and practices make tracing the shifts difficult, since individual nonsouthern states were not listed in the Florida State Census compilations prior to 1945. As table 1–1 indicates, a huge jump in the white population occurred between 1935 and 1945 (an 80% increase). A number of these migrants may have been immigrants from their original northern entry points and others second-generation immigrants. A study sponsored by the US Bureau of Census in the 1950s, *Immigrants and Their Children, 1850–1950*, drew this conclusion, identifying California and Florida as favored destinations for "the internal migration of the resident foreign population," though both states experienced increases in second-generation immigrants as well—this latter pattern is evident in the increase between 1920 and 1930 (see table 1–1). The study found a "relative increase" in the "relative concentration" of first-generation immigrants between 1920 and 1950 in the following locations: New England (except Rhode Island), New York, New Jersey, the District of Columbia, and Florida. At least in the case of Miami, the increase in concentration occurred mostly after 1935. As table 1–1 highlights, the movement of first-generation immigrants saw a spike between 1935 and the early 1940s, then a huge increase after World War II. Table 1–2, listing country or regional origins for Miami's immigrant population, indicates that the first-generation immigrant population increased particularly from Russia and Central Europe (especially for Germany, Austria, and Poland, 2,163 in 1935 to 4,694 in 1940). Not much else is known, unfortunately, about second-generation immigrants because the US Census stopped including these data in their compilations after 1930. It is interesting that the number of white Latin Americans and Caribbean people remained relatively small for the period

TABLE 1–1. White/Black native/foreign demographics

Dade County	1920	1925	1930	1935	1940	1945	1950
Native whites	22,072	75,880	101,992	132,293	194,790	177,678	377,138
South*	N/A	41,863	N/A	71,065	N/A	126,939	N/A
North*	N/A	33,526	N/A	61,228	N/A	102,303	N/A
Second-generation	4,526	N/A	17,362	N/A	N/A	N/A	N/A
Foreign-born	3,385	6,544	10,893	12,390	23,119	33,869	51,554
(% of whites)	(12.7%)	(7.9%)	(9.6%)	(8.56%)	(10.6%)	(12.97%)	(12%)
Total white	26,593	82,424	112,885	144,683	217,909	261,233	428,692
Black* († includes only Miami)							
South	4,455†	14,064†	19,507†	30,232	32,794	48,476	N/A
Foreign-born	4,815†	7,982†	5,512†	5,072	4,063	4,612	N/A
(% of Blacks)	(51.9%)	(36.2%)	(21.9%)	(14.1%)	(11%)	(8.6%)	
Total Black	9,270†	22,046†	25,116†	35,924	36,857	53,905	64,947
Total Dade	42,753	111,332	142,955	180,998	267,739	315,138	495,084

*North includes nonsouthern states; south includes US Census Bureau definition cited by James Gregory, *The Southern Diaspora: How the Great Migrations of Black and White Southerners Transformed America* (Chapel Hill: University of North Carolina Press, 2005), 8: AL, AR, DC, DE, FL, GA, KY, LA, MD, MS, NC, OK, SC, TN, TX, VA, and WV. Notes on southern Black numbers: 1920 and 1940 represent estimates derived from subtraction of foreign Blacks from total; for 1930, 11,072 born in Florida, 8,435 other states (presumed to be southern); for 1935, 16,902 from Florida, 13,031 other southern states; for 1945, 25,300 FL, 23,176 from other southern states. Notes on foreign Black numbers: for 1920, 1925, and 1930: numbers are available only for Miami; only 1925 indicates specific national identity, Bahamians = 7,505 (455 West Indies); 1940 numbers for Miami include adjacent areas (not yet defined as a Statistical Metropolitan Area); 1935 includes 5,047 Bahamians (22 Cubans, 3 Puerto Ricans).

Sources: US Bureau of the Census, *Fourteenth Census of the United States, 1920*, vol. 2, *Population* (Washington, DC: US Government Printing Office, 1922), 760, 795; US Bureau of the Census, *Fifteenth Census of the United States: Population 1930*, vol. 3 (Washington, DC: US Government Printing Office, 1932), pt. 1, 412; US Bureau of the Census, *Negroes in the United States, 1920–32* (Washington, DC: US Government Printing Office, 1935), 33; US Bureau of the Census, *Sixteenth Census of the United States: 1940*, vol. 2, *Population* (Washington, DC: US Bureau of the Census, 1943), pt. 2, 44, 142; Nathan Mayo, *The Fifth Census of the State of Florida, 1925* (Tallahassee, FL: T. J. Appleyard, 1925) 105 (white nativity), 115 (Black nativity); Nathan Mayo, *The Sixth Census of the State of Florida, 1935* (Winter Park, FL: Orange Press, 1935), 98 (white) 110 (Black); *The Seventh Census of the State of Florida, 1945*, 13 (Dade figures), 93 (white nativity), 108 (Black nativity); *Census of the Population, 1950*, vol. 2, pt. 10: Florida (Washington, DC: US Government Printing Office, 1952), 27, 29.

under study in this book. By 1950, however, one can begin to see pockets of a developing Latin American population, likely Cuban, around the Miami River and along the later-famous Calle Ocho. The census categorized these 4,413 immigrants as originating from the "Other America."[8]

Race, Class, and Memory

Migrants coming to Miami arrived in a city committed to maintaining the class hierarchy, in the way space was organized, in the nature of employer-employee relations, and in how the poor were treated. Take, for example, the codification of racial and class segregation. The 1921 city charter, written by local business leaders and responding to World War I racial strife, empowered Miami's government to maintain a segregated community, that is, "to establish and set

TABLE 1–2. White foreign-born country or region

Dade county*	1925	1930	1935	1940	1945
British Isles	1,548	2,419	2,321	3,738	N/A
Canada	1,234	1,788	1,915	2,587	2,668
Russia (USSR)	322	778	1,357	4,186	N/A
Central Europe	942	2,186	2,393	6,237	N/A
Scandinavia	713	841	958	1,570	N/A
Northern and Western Europe	250	277	1,017	871	N/A
Mediterranean Europe	547	779	885	1,564	N/A
Cuba and other West Indies	966	1,078	1,492	1,354	2,292
Mexico/Central-South America	60	N/A	90	186	382

*See table 1-1 for sources. Area composition and other notes: British Isles = England, Wales (listed except for 1925, 1930, and 1945), Scotland, and Ireland (northern and free state); Central Europe = Germany, Poland, Austria, Hungary (represented the four largest groups), Yugoslavia, Czechoslovakia, Bulgaria, Romania, and three others (countries included changed each year); Scandinavia = Sweden, Norway, Denmark, and Finland; Northern and Western Europe = France, Belgium, Switzerland, Holland, Luxemburg, and various others (countries included changed each year); Mediterranean = Greece, Italy, Spain, and Portugal. The 1925 Florida state census listed 0 Cubans, 725 Bahamians, and 275 West Indians (specific countries not listed); its 1930 census listed 266 white Cubans; all other years listed only Cuba and West Indies or just the latter without indicating any breakdown. For 1945, the Florida state census listed 2,562 for England and 16,587 for Europe. US Bureau of the Census, *Sixteenth Census of the United States: 1940*, vol. 2, *Population* (Washington, DC: US Bureau of the Census, 1943), 73. The foreign-born origin numbers listed for 1930 are different from those used in table 7–1 by Shell-Weiss, *Coming to Miami: A Social History* (Gainesville: University Press of Florida, 2009), 105. Shell-Weiss erred in listing census data from native whites with foreign parentage (425) instead of foreign-born (424). A minor error in an otherwise fine book.

apart . . . separate residential limits or districts for white and negro residents" (sec. 3, pt. ii, Charter of the City of Miami). This stipulation remained in the charter through the 1940s, a surprising holdover after the 1917 Supreme Court ruling of *Buchanan v. Warley*, which made it unconstitutional for states and local governments to legislate residential segregation. Not only was Miami's community to be defined in racially segregated terms (the Black district was known as Colored Town through the early 1920s or Central Negro Section in the 1930s and 1940s), charter writers also empowered the local government "to prevent persons with no visible means of support, paupers, and persons who may be dangerous to the peace or safety of the city from coming" to Miami (sec. 3, pt. v). Neither of these provisions existed in the 1913 Miami charter. The changes represented innovations on how to control the working class. In such transparent terms, Miami's ruling citizenry mandated the exclusion of the poor (and the subtle association of poverty with criminality) from the city while also establishing rigid boundaries of segregation.[9] Keeping Miami a safe and pleasant tourist destination meant strictly controlling and at times excluding the poorest members of the working class from the city, thereby signaling to the rest that ostracism awaited all who pushed too hard for change or who failed to succeed economically. The codification of class hierarchies represented the inhumane social practice of stigmatizing an entire group of people, an art and science of human inequality.[10]

This juxtaposition of race and class in the Miami city charter reflected a cruel reality about the nature of capitalism in the Magic City. The ruling citizenry embraced class hierarchy as much as it preached economic mobility, property ownership, and freedom for family development and growth, the rhetoric of the American Dream. Like the street-tax institution discussed in this chapter's opening, antivagrancy laws represented law-and-order efforts to discipline the working class. Transient workers and sojourners were particularly targeted. Migrants, white or Black, entering the city from the late 1920s through the 1930s faced systematic harsh treatment if they could not show they had financial means for housing or a job waiting for them, or were visiting family. Police harassed them if they lacked these certifications, often arresting them for vagrancy. This dubious crime could lead to unfair punishment such as being put to labor on local farms, street construction or other infrastructure work, or expulsion from the county via police wagon. Local newspapers and observers dubbed this latter practice the Hobo Express, at work since at least 1928 and sanctioned by the city charter. Limitations clearly prevented the city's complete control over the inflow of migrants to the city, namely, an overstretched police force and the need for labor to accommodate the local economy. "Fruit tramps," for example, were migrant laborers traveling the East Coast in search of agricultural work, such as harvesting Dade's tomato crop. Even building-trade workers with jobs and money in their pockets could be rounded up by police, as in August 1925, when sixty-eight white craftsmen, forced to sleep "on the porches of public buildings for a lack of quarters," were arrested. In trying to safeguard tourists from unsightly and undesirable visitors, city officials and citizens ensured a negative attitude toward the poor and working class.[11]

It is important to remember how the poor, white hoboes, sweatshop and factory workers, "lintheads," "white trash," and other groups designated for denigration were marginalized and ridiculed in bigoted terms. The historical record from across the country is replete with evidence for this type of treatment. Toby Higbie emphasizes, for example, how midwestern white hobo laborers fell into a quasi-racial caste. They were looked down on merely for making a living through seasonal labor in lumbering, mining, and agriculture, all critical industries in a region dependent on such a casual reserve army of labor. Historian Mark Pittenger's study *Class Unknown* broadens the scope of analysis to include the studies of the lower classes since the late nineteenth century conducted by researchers going undercover to investigate "how the other half lives." The social scientific and journalistic obsession with the process of degeneracy into poverty indicated a paradoxical dynamic. Impoverishment was often explained as a function of culture that ended up becoming quite deterministic in its conclusions, not dissimilar from Lamarckian hereditarianism then in decline by the early twentieth century but "still in circulation." Pittenger writes, "It certainly seems ironic that the culture concept, usually seen as having helped liberate American thought from racialist and hierarchical assumptions, should also have functioned to frame the impoverished as a primitive and degenerating breed."[12]

The flipside of this cultural coin was the underlying idea that the dominant culture of capitalistic, competitive values was a good thing. Often ignored in this assumption was how capitalism tended to make workers into a commodity, a form of capital in the same category as work animals or animal husbandry to be exploited for profit. Indeed, a biblical verse (Joshua 9:21) sanctioned cursing a class to serve as "hewers of wood and drawers of water," a phrase Peter Linebaugh and Marcus Rediker remind us originated in the early era of modern capitalism. Constitutive of these larger cultural and historical dynamics was the role of racist imagination. Karen Fields and Barbara Fields point out in their insightful book, *Racecraft: The Soul of American Inequality in American Life*, that "Americans wove racist concepts about inequality that made 'Black' the virtual equivalent of 'poor' and 'lower class.'" Race and culture, as the historian Judith Stein asserted, served as metonyms for class. Members of the lower class, often including the working class more generally, were subjected to maltreatment, including the mockery and condescension characteristic of articulations of racism. The tendency has persisted and has been identified across time and place. Perhaps in the context of leisure-rich-and-speculative Miami, the light of positivistic and hopeful visions of the promise of America burned a little brighter and the scorn for the less fortunate more intense.[13]

The system of racial segregation therefore helped maintain the cultural, social, and economic impediments against the poor and working poor and kept in step with the deeper traditions of segregation culture. This is evident in how the memory of Miami's founding was shaped. City tourist brochures advertised the vital role that Black workers played in the city's history and economy, an unconscious gesture that reinforced class hierarchy. As the narrative went, Miami pioneers John and Everest G. Sewell arrived in Miami in the late nineteenth century as representatives of the Flagler railroad interests to help remove trees and brush and to build roads. According to the city's publicity pamphlet published from the 1930s through the 1950s, "the Sewell brothers, from Georgia, *worked negroes as their specialty*. With hundreds of them, they [the Sewell brothers] accomplished wonders clearing land so that buildings could be erected" (emphasis added). Unabashed and stating a common occurrence, this history of Miami's growth and development calculated that knowledge of how the Sewell brothers "worked negroes as their specialty" was significant to highlight until city publicity agents in the 1960s omitted that statement, perhaps because race no longer effectively hid the cruel nature of class exploitation. Pioneer history emphasized the heroics of bosses, rather than labor, to engage arduous work—that is, the "negroes" were not getting credit. Rather, pamphlet writers celebrated the Sewell brothers' skill at working others for Miami's growth, which demonstrated the dynamic of class hierarchy exoticized in a tapestry of frontier Americana and triumphant capitalist history.[14]

Much of Miami's post-civil-rights local history celebrated the work of American and Bahamian Blacks in building the city and placed their effort on an equal plane with the Sewell brothers and other pioneers. While well-intentioned, this ahistorical corrective obliterated the significance and persistence of class hierarchy by indirectly embracing a modernization and bootstrap narrative. Jim Crow racism was the culprit in this literature because it delimited Black opportunity but gave little if any critical analysis to the structure of class hierarchy or the shared experience of work among the working class. While often insightful and sensitive to various threads in Miami's social history, the local history contributions tend to flatten the history of work and class while moralizing that of race. The violence and exploitation that defined segregation certainly merits attention. Miami's working-class history and general worker precarity, however, remain less explored, especially in the pre–World War II period.[15] Someone had to do the arduous labor of clearing the land of brush and trees, of land reclamation and dredging shallow harbors, of lifting, unloading, and moving cargo, raw materials, and products from trains, ships, trucks, and at jobsites, and of generally doing the work that constructed and drove the city's economy (building construction, hotel staffs, retail work, etc.) in order for Miami to develop. The critical question about power—under what conditions—has been left unanswered. Accepted uncritically or indirectly are the assumptions that class hierarchy was acceptable, low pay for difficult work was justified, economic insecurity was (is) a natural state, a managerial class must oversee a working class, and the entrepreneurial spirit built the nation, not the actual workers. As a result, racism and racial violence become anomalies of a particular time and place or the result of particular ideas or attitudes.[16] Morality tales highlight individual accountability and deviant profiles. Liberal democracy and the triumphant march of capitalist growth and development remain unscathed by such primitive divergences as segregationist America. Another critical historiographical interpretation, whiteness studies, notes how the nasty legacies remain by complicit, witting or unwitting, benefactors of white privilege.

Reinforcing this line of analysis is how the occupation distribution among white and Black workers reveal that a clear racial-class hierarchy existed in Miami. White workers held jobs in more diverse occupations than Black workers. Taking 1940 as an example, more than 69 percent of employed white men worked in the following occupational categories: clerical, sales, and kindred work (9,614/25% overall); craftsmen, foremen, and kindred work (7,607/19%); and proprietors, managers, officials (6,639/17%), professional and semiprofessional work (3,248/8%). In at least the construction trades, white skilled crafts workers enjoyed a virtual monopoly over jobs. Of the 3,818 employed construction skilled workers, 3,604 were white and 214 were Black. Seventy-nine percent of construction laborers, however, were Black (1,696 versus 443). The pattern held true as well in other trades and for women. Jobs with more exposure to the public or office jobs were reserved for them: 92 percent of waitresses were white, and for stenographers, typists, and secretaries, less than 1 percent were Black.[17] The appendix gives the occupation-distribution pattern for the years 1930 and 1940. White workers held more diverse jobs, in part because they and their employers relegated Blacks to the bottom of the economic totem pole. The practice, of course, was not unusual in the South or the United States more generally.

The pattern was rigid and consistent over time. For example, well over 76 percent of employed African American men held jobs as laborers in 1930, 1940, and 1950 in various capacities such as janitors, laborers, and servants in both domestic and nondomestic work. Nearly all dockworkers were Black during this same period: in 1930, 217 of 221; in 1940, 348 of 359; and in 1950, 268 of 293.[18] At least 90 percent of employed Black women worked during these same years primarily as domestic and nondomestic servants, as laundresses, and in other service work. One could go further into the century, say to 1970, and the pattern of low-income labor would remain consistent for Miami Blacks, even in the midst of a vibrant civil-rights environment.[19] The predominance of low-income occupations and the reality of underemployment would remain true for many whites as well, especially because retail, restaurant, hotel, and similar service jobs remained numerous and often represented the only options for many Miamians.

Employers and city developers acted on the mandate to keep production moving forward. In a growing city built on tourism, the urban setting became a factory of sorts with various divisions and seasonal demands pressuring a diverse group of workers to complete the tasks of corporate Miami, Winter Playground for the USA. The service economy—much of it local in nature—was built on selling Miami as a semitropical vacation destination, where tourists were promised fun, leisure, and pleasure. While much of this representation was the product of boosterism and concerted advertising drives throughout Miami's history, the question of how the result was translated into the quotidian life is less clear. Or, put another way, how was Miami as a tourist experience created and reproduced and how did it affect the working class and class relations more generally?[20]

On the surface, the pattern of employment distribution just noted would suggest that white workers benefited from the privileges of whiteness. That insight, however, would fail to account for the particular class texture of work and Miami's service economy. Most people worked in working-class jobs and had relatively little power, especially in relation to their employers. As the economist Michael Zweig notes for recent America, the working class resides "in a place of relative vulnerability—on the job, in the market, in politics and culture."[21] Many in Miami were service workers and often were participants in constructing particular experiences. Whether the job entailed skilled craftwork in the building trades constructing hotels or other structures, music entertainment, service behind a counter, waiting tables, driving people places, or cleaning tourists' clothes, many workers in Miami were involved in constructing a place and often shaping the experiences of others, both residents and tourists. How workers, Black or white, experienced their relative vulnerability and shared the endeavor of producing the Miami tourist and consumer experience are questions that have been little studied. Low-wage work, seasonal employment, and general economic vulnerability defined much of Miami's service economy. Skilled and unskilled workers may occasionally have earned higher wages than normal during periods of labor shortages, but the seasonal and cyclical variability of the economy led to great insecurity.

From its earliest days, white capitalists such as Henry Flagler profited from bringing Black laborers into the region and paying them low wages. Whether from the Bahamas or other parts of the South, south Florida drew Black workers because of bad economic conditions and job opportunities at home.[22] City developers maintained a low-wage labor market as a function of existing values employers placed on unskilled work; they also pushed to limit skilled worker demands. Racist discourses legitimized and rationalized hierarchical relationships while articulating working-class precarity. Classist and racist assumptions justified forcing Black vagrants ("negro loafers") to work on nearby farms or other jobs. In the aftermath of the 1926 Great Miami Hurricane, Blacks faced forced conscription to help pick up debris resulting from the devastating storm. Yet such examples of racist motivation can easily negate its underlying class dynamic.[23]

Black and white workers from southern and northern cities were frequently "recruited" to work in Miami to assure the flow of production and supply chains. When Bahamian Blacks were difficult to obtain during a labor shortage in 1925, shipping companies recruited Black dockworkers from northern Florida, North and South Carolina, New Orleans, and even Philadelphia, to name a few of the points of origination. Companies also imported several white dockworkers. R. W. Parker of the Merchants and Miners Shipping line articulated the most succinct assessment of the political economy of class struggle. He commented that "the negroes should be paid enough for a decent living, but the wage should be small enough so that they will have to work six days a week for that living," which he concluded would lessen the labor shortage problem by 50 percent. Parker's vision does not seem to have materialized, at least not in the course of the next ten months.

Labor shortages on the docks inspired several wildcat strikes among Black dockworkers. One forty-four-word *Miami Tribune* story noted that a "Negro Agitator" speaking to "a number of negro laborers" attempted "to arouse dissatisfaction" but was stopped by the police. Other newspaper coverage of these labor actions devoted even fewer words. The Clyde-Mallory shipping line was particularly notorious for paying poorly and having horrible working conditions. They faced persistent worker action from early September 1925, suggesting that the "agitator" simply highlighted real grievances. Even though the Clyde-Mallory line may seem progressive since they hired Black foremen, the shipping lines nonetheless kept wages low among its mostly Black workforce. Recalcitrant, motivated workers and extreme competition forced several of shipping companies to accede to higher wages, which were still very low. The Clyde-Mallory line eventually imported a "crack" crew of more than 150 white Italian dockworkers from New York in October, following through on a threat they had made to Black dockworkers in early September. This importation allowed them to circumvent the labor-market competition and Black worker action. The first contingent to arrive came on the SS *Robert E. Lee*. They were "fed and housed" by the company in "special barracks: at first they lived on the SS *Chippewa* docked in the Biscayne waterfront but later moved to barracks built for them. The practice apparently was not uncommon. One railroad company even had workers bunk in their cars. Such conditions likely kept workers under their employers' control. When some of the Italian dockworkers were alleged to have stolen from the shipping warehouse, they were sent back to New York. The period of better wages ended in the summer of 1926 when the shipping companies unilaterally and arbitrarily reduced wages by 20 percent. When dockworkers refused to work at the lower scale, they were replaced the same day. Readers of the newspaper report announcing the wage reduction learned that no delays occurred.[24]

The brief sketch outlined here is a small piece of a more elaborate story. Few historians, it is interesting to note, have written on the real-estate boom of the 1920s, let alone the labor-history context. What these episodes and this book more generally uncovers is that the city operated like a factory, and many of its workers functioned as capital inputs. The workers struggled to earn a living yet contested the effort to make them mere human capital. The fight for dignity at work combined with the drive to form community. Each were expressions of their humanity. While workers were often pitted against each other in competition over jobs, and sometimes resorted to racist and classist language in their protectionist battles, the vision of a moral economy and greater equality often inspired and directed the fights for greater equity and perhaps even the dream of equal opportunity. They are keys to understanding Miami's political economy as well as the relationship between race, class, and memory.

Coming to Work in Miami

Work opportunities drew many to the city. In the case of construction workers, the pull factors were directly linked to the number and size of building projects. The boom years of the early and mid-1920s witnessed a huge influx of construction workers to accommodate the labor demands of employers. White and Black resort workers, in retail, restaurants, and hotels, migrated to the city for job opportunities particularly during the tourist season, December to April. Black workers, particularly women, tended to work more behind the scenes doing very arduous labor, a situation that mirrored the tourist towns of Saratoga Springs, New York, and Newport, Rhode Island, as documented by historian Myra B. Young. Most Black women, for example, worked as domestics and laundresses for the entire period of this study (see Appendix).[25] Movement to and from south Florida defined the nature of many workers' experiences, especially those struggling to find steady jobs.

The vast majority of Blacks moved to present-day Overtown, labeled through the 1920s as Colored Town, though "negro settlements" were scattered throughout Greater Miami in such places as in Coconut Grove (south of Miami) and near Lemon City (north of Miami and roughly site of modern-day Little Haiti), areas where Miami's oldest Black Bahamian residents lived. Both locations were annexed by Miami in 1925. Sometime during the early 1920s, Liberty City, an unincorporated Black village, developed near another Black neighborhood known as the Brown division. The *Miami Daily News* soon labeled it "the aristocrat of Miami's colored sections," housing groceries, restaurants, churches, dry-goods stores, billiard halls, lodge halls, a dance hall, and even a swimming pool. In 1925, Miami annexed it as well. A little over a year after this 1925 report, the 1926 Great Miami Hurricane destroyed many homes of this nascent community of about 1,500. Local histories date Liberty City's founding to the 1930s, but it is clear that a history predates this timeline. The name Liberty City likely revealed several overlapping dynamics: Black Miamian celebration of the history of emancipation; the 1920s Jazz Age cultural energy found in such phenomena as the "New Negro" and the United Negro Improvement Association movements; and the area's potential as an alternative to overcrowded Colored Town; it probably tapped into good old Miami marketing panache.[26]

Colored Town, nonetheless, remained the largest "negro settlement." Its residents lived primarily in shotgun houses and in crowded and congested conditions—notoriously the poorest section of the city. Several local scholars have noted the vibrancy and agency within Colored Town, where a lively cultural life existed with an active nightlife and devout religious fabric that shaped the bonds of community. Life, though, was a tough path in Miami's exploitative context. Efforts to alleviate Colored Town's dilapidated conditions emerged in the 1930s. Numerous newspaper reports and grand juries reported on its unsanitary conditions; the 1930s movement for the public housing project, Liberty Square, in Liberty City, northwest of Colored Town, made such reports even more common.[27] Whites frequently discussed their concerns about the movements of Black workers within the city and occasionally raised alarms about how Black domestics and workers represented potential public health nuisances as carriers of diseases such as tuberculosis they brought from their homes or the Black establishments they visited. Blacks worked primarily for white employers, for long hours and for low wages, so large supplies of workers were readily needed and whites sometimes facilitated transportation, but more often than not Black workers relied on Black taxi and jitney drivers. On occasion, direct bus lines between Black and white residential areas ran only at the beginning and end of workdays. Indeed, their role as laborers made them essential to the city's economy as their central geographic location suggested, but their importance did not eliminate the racism and classism that help marginalize them.[28]

In general, there are few reports on how workers came or where they lived. Wealthy tourists may have brought their own servants with them during their winter stays in Miami Beach and Miami. In 1918 and 1919, amid brewing labor union conflict, the Miami Beach hotel magnate Carl Fisher made sure to provide "for the housing and care" of white and Black workers during construction projects on Miami Beach, including the erection of his Flamingo Hotel. Fisher planned for servant quarters in winter bungalows he constructed on Miami Beach during the twenties—accommodations were also made in hotels. In the mid-1920s he built a set of cottages for "a little village of workmen" whom the City of Miami Beach, the Fisher Properties, the Miami Beach Improvement Company and Beach Construction Company employed. Aside from one 1925 newspaper report, no other record exists discussing who composed this "little village." It is likely that it was the origin of what became known as the Smith Cottages in South Beach, where white workers of diverse backgrounds (of various national origins and possibly Jewish) lived for low rates in poor housing during the tourist season. It was razed in 1951 and replaced with a housing project.[29]

Fisher also had a hand in building a small village of about fifteen houses "suitable for negro laborers" near Forty-first Street and Pine Tree Drive in Miami Beach. Fisher ordered builders to "surround the entire *plantation* with a fence . . . so that the place will not be an eyesore to the rest of the property." The use of the word *plantation* evoked both the undeveloped conditions of Miami Beach as well as the memory of slavery and absolute power over labor. Dr. Enid Pinkney, a local Black preservationist, recalled how her Bahamian father and mother worked on Miami Beach in a location that appears to be at this Pine Tree intersection. She notes how "her parents worked and lived in servant's quarters" and how her brother was born there. "The Bureau of Vital Statistics . . .

refused to put Miami Beach on his birth certificate because he was black." Hers is the only firsthand account or oral history I have found that documents the existence of this location or servant's quarters. The area was destroyed in 1927 before development of new housing started. Other wealthy owners of winter residences, such as J. C. Penney and Harvey Firestone, made accommodations for servants, but it is unclear whether the servants were Miami residents or part of the owners' entourage.[30]

The history of servants in Miami is difficult if not impossible to uncover, but a review of real-estate advertising throughout the period from World War I through World War II reveals the persistent inclusion of servant quarters in new housing and hotels. It indicates that real-estate and hotel developers were cognizant of the need to cater to an obvious demand, at least from the well-to-do. The quarters consisted of at least three varieties: houses for rent for the season, servant quarters adjoining hotels, and servant quarters annexed to whites' houses. At times, the quarters were on top of garages or on second floors. Often advertised during the winter tourist season, the advertisements told buyers that servant quarters were located in rooms above the garages that were tucked away in the rear of residences. The Nautilus Hotel announced in 1923, for example, that its "servant quarters" were going to be built "north of the hotel." Some of the other Fisher hotels had guest cottages with adjoining servant quarters as well. Thousands of such advertisements appear throughout the period.[31] The servant quarters and even chauffeur quarters were advertised for exclusive neighborhoods in the entire area, including not just Miami Beach, but also Miami, Coral Gables, and others. It is unclear whether or how many servants actually roomed in these spaces or whether many of these advertisements merely displayed leisure as a function of sweated labor. Certainly, few phenomena in capitalism made more sense than the marriage of marketing and real estate or the propping up of leisure by a servant class.

From the mid-teens through the early 1930s, a seasonal pattern held true for many establishments, especially in Miami Beach, when boarded-up windows and closed-for-the-season signs announced the economy's dependence on tourism. Floods of tourists and workers arrived during the short tourist season (December to April), some deciding to make South Florida a home. Northern workers often arrived to run businesses (hotels, retail stores, and restaurants) that were open only during the winter season. Migrating hotel workers likely took up quarters in their places of work, especially those who worked in the owners' northern establishments. Residents strongly criticized the practice of hiring nonresident workers as detrimental to community life and as a contributor to local unemployment. As later chapters will discuss, an ethic of home labor protectionism emerged in the interwar period. Construction sites hiring northern and nonunion labor were sometimes struck or faced other types of labor action. Such antagonism increased as the year-round population grew and when the economic downturn of the late 1920s and 1930s hit Miami.

Where workers ended up residing while in Miami is not clear. Housing shortages were chronic throughout the interwar period as population growth increased the housing needs. The housing problem was particularly acute at the height of the mid-1920s real-estate boom. On occasion, employers built living quarters for their employees, as the Fisher and dockworker examples suggest. In the summer of 1925, Miami's Chamber of Commerce (CC) arranged to build wooden barracks in the "colored part of town" (NW First Avenue and Seventeenth Street) for the recruitment of "negro common laborers" from outside Miami to relieve the labor shortage problem. Chief of Police Leslie Quigg promised to arrest Black vagrants in an attempt to help the CC acquire cheap labor. The Miami City Commission and CC highlighted the need to find accommodations for workers, including numerous tent cities and employer-built temporary small houses and even "portable homes"—flimsy housing of "wood construction" that would "provide spacious quarters for up to eight persons," located on undeveloped tracts, and where builders asked for construction and even fire ordinances to be waived. The call to build and buy "homes and apartment houses for their employees" revealed the dependent and vulnerable position workers often found themselves in when employed in Miami. Several employers, including Burdine's department store, built apartments for prospective employees. One recorded instance occurred when the Coral Gables Corporation built the San Sebastian Apartment Hotel—a three-story building that contained seventy-two apartments. Workers on the project were temporarily housed in a tent city.[32]

Tropical Landscapes

Much of Miami's landscape was intentionally designed for a tropical and a tourist leisure effect. The cumulative effect of such interventions was the formation of a peculiar Miami culture, rooted in tourist economics built on the practice of shaping representation and performance for greater consumption and a particular tropical style of leisure. Such a setting, where hospitality and the pleasure of others were dominant ethics, necessitated a language of harmonious class relations. The reality of class conflict, though, often meant that class struggle would be translated to harmony discourse.[33]

The building and development of south Florida became an effort to create a tourist product and a marketing scheme to lure the wealthy and the free-spending middle class. Gregory Bush and Paul George, among others, have written on the packaging of Miami. Bush argued that the process was part of a larger phenomenon of promoting spectacle in the late nineteenth and early twentieth century. The marketing effort, Bush wrote, "reflected a growing consciousness about the need to engineer people's attention to the large-scale market and 'magic' of the modern technological world." Historian Julio Capó suggests that Miami was sold as a fairyland. Bush and George say little about the nature of class and how workers contributed to or reacted to the spectacle; Capó's focus on pre-1940 queer Miami mostly sidesteps political economy. The working classes, Black and white, came to Miami primarily not as tourists but to work and earn.[34] They did the necessary work of building and maintaining the city. The marketing of Miami entailed creating exclusive spaces and, what is more important, setting cultural norms of what was in and what was out; when they cared, workers imitated as best they could or simply made adaptations, putting their own stamp on the city's culture. It is difficult to trace the patterns, but one can locate the cultural grist that fueled them.

The city leveraged its geographic location. Lacking a natural mineral resource to exploit, city builders capitalized on the area's special resources of sunshine, seashore, and subtropical climate. Local organizations such as the CC guided the boosterism. Led by the enterprising and ambitious E. G. Sewell during Miami's boom years between 1915 and 1925, the annual influx of tourists neared one million, as Paul George has noted. Tourist accommodations were sometimes inadequate, however, as when hotels apparently turned away an estimated ten thousand visitors during the 1918–19 winter tourist season (sometimes incorrectly listed as 1917). Housing shortages affected not only tourists but also the workers who struggled to find a place to reside during their sojourn or for eventual conversion to permanent residence. Nonetheless, the tourists who arrived in Miami experienced one end of the production process, while workers who constructed that experience attempted to make a life in the winter playground.[35]

We know that certain cultural motifs emphasized the Spanish colonial past of Florida or simply the exotic and extraordinary. Architects used Mediterranean styles, from Spanish to Arabic, to denote the wealth and leisure possible when living in Miami; the legend of Black Caesar taught tourists about south Florida's ties to the infamous pirate Caribbean and encouraged yachting in south Biscayne Bay for sports fishing and voyeuristic adventure; the Musa Isle Indian Village (Miami River and Twenty-seventh Avenue) packaged Seminole culture and south Florida fruit and vegetables, reminding its visitors of yet another tamed frontier land ready for agricultural exploitation.[36]

As a result of early attempts and ongoing efforts at developing Dade County agriculture, coconut palm trees spread throughout the south Florida landscape, as did other tropical fruit trees such as papaya, avocado, grapefruit, and mango trees. Into the twenty-first century, many homes across the class structure continued to have these trees in their yards, especially mangoes and avocados. The many varieties of palm trees became a staple feature of south Florida, planted near resort spaces (hotels, beaches, golf links, horse racetracks, shopping districts, etc.), residential districts, and roads; their images permeated the iconography that defined Miami as a tourist destination. In the context of Miami USA, palm trees associated a tropical landscape with tourism within a safe, tamed, and apparently exotic place without the apparent annoyances of a foreign land.[37]

Mediterranean-style barrel roofs pervaded the architectural landscape, from the wealthiest corners such as the John Deering estate discussed in the introduction to working-class neighborhoods, though the spread occurred over time. Apparently, the practice of extracting barrel roof tiles from Cuban homes was a common practice among the wealthy in Miami at least through the mid-1920s. But other exotic pieces also made it onto or into homes of the wealthy: huge jars that had allegedly once been used to transport olive oil from the Canary Islands to Cuba, marble floor blocks, iron hasps, "marble and bronze pieces from the old city hall at Santiago," marble doorknockers, and iron window grilles. As architecture critic Beth Dunlop has written about Mediterranean Revival as developed in south Florida between 1917 and World War II. The purpose of such styles was to "evoke antiquity, generally of a romantic Spanish nature," though often drawing from Italy, so as to "express ideas about a place with no long history to draw on, no common culture, [and] no unique aesthetic." The concern "to make the new look old" revealed how the anxious nouveau riche defined south Florida architecture. Added to this aesthetic project, of course, was the leisure motif of open spaces, swimming pools, cabanas, and tropical landscaping, including fruit and palm trees. While the Mediterranean Revival style became less common over the 1930s as the efficient aesthetic of Art Deco emerged and, later, mass-produced houses came to dominate the south Florida landscape, the practice of marking class distinctions through architectural style continued as a well-rooted tradition.[38]

Workers, white or Black, built their homes on the basis of past practice and convenience. They bought or rented ready-built (manufactured) houses throughout interwar Miami. Some Bahamian Blacks built houses in Coconut Grove and Overtown in the Conch style common in Key West and the Bahamas, though some American and Bahamian Blacks adapted styles from their hometowns to their new abode. As noted earlier, most Blacks, African American or Bahamian, bought or rented homes built shotgun style. It is less clear where white workers lived. A 1980s history of Dade County architecture, *From Wilderness to Metropolis*, may tell us something about white workers' preferences even though it avoided using the term "working class " and only used "middle class" or "lower middle class" when discussing housing. We learn that "mission style houses, along with the bungalows, became the most popular building types for the moderate income subdivisions that spread throughout the metropolitan Miami area." The small, compact structure of both bungalows and mission-style houses translated to lower construction cost and thus more affordability to workers. Most homes were indeed small because most housing in the interwar period was for single families. Interestingly absent from the history as well was any discussion of apartments in which workers also likely lived. In 1925, more than 50 percent of families lived in apartment houses. The percentage decreased to 27 percent the following year, which was still up from the 14.1 percent in 1921. The omission of the term "working class" from the history revealed more a general inability to discuss class outside the classless framework of the American Dream rather than any racist tendency. Many of its contributors were (are) outstanding local historians quite sensitive to the diverse history of the region.[39]

Despite the best efforts of local historians, a clearer picture of how class was organized by neighborhoods is lacking in the historical record. Much more is known of the wealthy areas than about where the working class lived, in part because no systematic analysis exists for the 1930 and 1940 handwritten census schedules. More is known about the history of Colored Town or the Black areas of Coconut Grove than about other locations where workers lived. White workers lived across the city but seem to have congregated further from downtown Miami and, over time, spread across the county. They lived in neighborhoods such as Riverside, Little River, and Allapattah. These neighborhoods' racial and ethnic profiles changed after the 1950s as the population grew to include more diverse groups, but they remained primarily working-class. In general, less is known about how working-class neighborhoods changed over time: even less clear is how they started and developed over time, what kind of work its inhabitants did, and possible class divisions within them. The absence of records or chroniclers of this history points to a process of silencing the past. Specifically, a dynamic that has negated narratives of class struggle.[40]

The biggest differences between working-class neighborhoods and exclusive ones were at the level of scale and proximity to waterfronts. The wealthiest, whether winter residents or Miami's own elite, resided in Miami Beach, on landfill (artificial) islands in Biscayne Bay, on Miami's waterfront (such as Millionaire's Row on Brickell Avenue), in Miami Shores, in Coral Gables, and in Coconut Grove. Coral Gables, adjacent to southwest Miami, had some working-class neighborhoods but was built for more affluent residents. George Merrick, its visionary promoter, sold Coral Gables as a center of civilized living amid "native tropical and sub-tropical trees and shrubs" with ingenious landscape architecture and an ideal paradise setting accommodated with abundant parks, golf courses, and playgrounds. As the "heart of the American tropics" and with "40 Miles of Water Front," it used Spanish names to mark its streets (Ponce de León and Granada Boulevard, for example), general Mediterranean architectural revival style in the construction of its homes and buildings, and beautiful gateway entrances to residential neighborhoods to highlight their exclusive nature. Over time, excessive development in south Florida (usually further north and west from Miami) led to the proliferation of human-made lakes and a sometimes-dingy canal-water drainage system. More homes were around some watering hole and thus a reminder to their owners about the advantages (and disadvantages) of living in tropical Miami.[41]

In typical advertising bravado, most real-estate developments and tourist boosterism sold Miami's tropical landscape and the paradise that south Florida could represent for recreation and leisure living. And so, it is not surprising that the stories of workers and where they lived is missing for the most part from the literature and iconography of the interwar period. What is clear is that over the course of the twentieth century the initially exclusive nature of some of Miami's real-estate developments often could not be sustained. Miami Beach, for instance, witnessed enormous growth in the 1930s in part because the area south of Lincoln Road, today's South Beach, opened to a broader array of classes and ethnicities, including Jewish residents (whom most hotels continued to exclude). Favorable US housing policy that began during the New Deal, and to a lesser degree Florida's 1934 homestead tax exemption law, certainly had its effect in drawing people to the state and helping more working-class and middle-class people in their efforts to acquire houses.[42]

The tropical landscape of south Florida had different meanings for workers, tourists, and the wealthy largely because the material conditions of their experiences differed. Despite differences in conditions, some things remained common besides the climate. Some degree of exposure to the aesthetic of the imagined tropical style was likely for tourists and residents even in a highly segregated society. In the flora, the architecture, and the thousands of lines of advertising print and photography and art (in postcards, brochures, and local newspapers, for example), residents and tourists alike were inundated with the ideas of recreation, leisure, and good living. The many options for entertainment allowed all classes to escape reality, though the forms were likely segregated by class in style and access. Some required active engagement: fishing, golf, tennis, sailing, swimming in pools or ocean, shuffleboard, bowling on the green, horseshoes, cards, checkers, chess, bridge, dominoes, tennis, basketball, football, and baseball. Residents formed local sports leagues, particularly for baseball and bowling and usually associated with particular occupations that ran at various points of the year but especially in the spring, summer, and fall. Spectator sports, which often integrated gambling, included: polo (especially limited to the upper classes), horse and dog racing, jai alai, baseball, boxing, and even professional wrestling. Nightlife entertainment included live music (performed by union and nonunion musicians), dancing, dining, vaudeville, and simply lounging around during the mild and usually good winter weather. Other frequent forms of entertainment included picnics, parades, and outings to beaches or pools, though racism and general poverty limited or prevented many Blacks from engaging in water recreations.[43]

Workers clearly had positive reactions to the Florida setting. In addition to the hope for jobs, temporary visitors and old and new residents embraced the recreational opportunities Miami offered. The warm weather, lush vegetation, and access to Biscayne Bay and the Atlantic Ocean offered the possibility of a good life. Stephen Cochran Singleton's poem "My Florida" offers insight about why a worker would find happiness in the region while demonstrating the creative possibilities of the working class. "My Florida" captured the beauty of Florida's natural environment and the centrality of movement and work. The idyllic landscape ("low-swung stars, the "tide-swept bars") await the traveling worker but only if they can find "some way to earn," "some work," "some errand." Singleton's "My Florida" suggests the significance of the natural landscape to workers. Life was not defined solely by work, despite work's usurpation of so much time and energy. It is in this context that the push for shorter hours, better working conditions, and higher pay gain even more meaning. Workers struggled for a fuller humanity, one that directly contradicted the alienation so often forced on them when laboring in winter playground USA and capitalist America more generally.[44]

Conclusion

Miami's cultural landscape embraced class hierarchy and thus helped reinforce existing power relations. Despite cultural hegemony, workers confronted the hardship of getting by, occasionally bursting through the narratives of harmony. They too sought class harmony along moral economy lines: each person had a right to a competency. But the lure of instant riches, of the easy life promised in fun and leisure, often helped to blur the similarities between white and Black workers. Reverend Robert Newton Ward's June 1923 sermon in Miami's First Congregational Church suggested the absurdity of class hierarchy. Ward pointed out that the Christian call to love thy neighbor rested on the fact that all were the children of God. But, he argued, "so long as God has made human-kind as he has, there will always naturally be what is called classes." Educated men naturally seek the companionship of other educated men, Ward pointed out, as do mechanics other mechanics and Blacks other Blacks. His logic derived from his divine insight: "Christ does not expect me to make a companion of an animal or to carry myself to the level of one." Ward highlighted how a community was held together through faith, that all should remember to keep their place, and that "the poor stand no more chance of getting into Heaven than do the rich." Ward's amazing defense of paternalism and hierarchy speaks volumes about the resonance of class harmony as an idea with conservative tendencies as well as a potential rallying point for progressive change.

Ward's sermon stood in stark contrast to the various calls for social equality. Reverend Philip Irwin, a white Episcopalian preacher giving a sermon in a Black church, was tarred and feathered by a "band of ruffians" in 1921 for preaching social equality between the races, even advocating intermarriage. Irwin denied these charges, though he admitted to teaching a more hopeful message from the New Testament than Ward's later sermon. He highlighted the powerful potential of the Declaration of Independence. The juxtaposition of the social equality advocated in both texts and the alleged preaching of racial equality has important significance. Whenever Blacks challenged the status quo, they represented such a threat to capitalist power relations as to disrupt the social order even if they adopted the egalitarian mythology of the American nation-state. The social control that segregation represented affected both whites and Blacks, silently binding both to the class hierarchy endemic to capitalism. Three years later, an ominous marble monument was placed near where Irwin had been attacked. One side told how a person teaching racial equality had been tarred and feathered; the other side wrote, "If you are a reckless negro or a white man who believes in social equality, be advised that Dade County don't need you." Even just the appearance of racial equality could lead to major grandstanding, as in 1929 when the Florida state legislature passed a resolution condemning Herbert Hoover's wife's White House tea date with the wife of African American Illinois representative Oscar De Priest.[45] Racism and classism revealed the most perverse contortions of the human spirit. How workers were limited and broke free from such restraints is the subject of the subsequent pages.

CHAPTER 2

Driving and Chauffeuring in Miami

In the early twentieth century, Miami was divided into two cities, one white and one "colored." Divided by residential segregation, Miami was also divided by rigid boundaries in the job market, which sometimes even defined the nature of spatial mobility.[1] Despite the city's slowly expanding economy, employment opportunities remained scarce, especially during eight to nine months of the year outside the very short tourist season. Such a volatile context, combined with the racist historical context, increased the likelihood that white and Black chauffeurs would clash. The white violence and intimidation used to deter Black drivers from driving and, what is perhaps even more significant, drive for a living, point to the realities and day-to-day anxieties of living in a country dominated by racist regimes.

Workers' struggle to survive is a key aspect of this story. The struggle was not merely a function of the unstable and harsh capitalist economy that offered little security to workers, or just an outcome of its industrial or extractive sectors. Miami's sunny climate and penchant for leisure and play can magically make those surface differences all that matter. Appearance becomes reality and class struggle a phenomenon occurring only in specific economic sectors. But Miami's tourist-based economy, as it grew and developed, pushed workers to gain protection and led them to expect a moral economy not unlike that of other workers who organized unions throughout the country. The meaning of moral economy was different for white and Black chauffeurs. White chauffeurs hoped segregation would function as a wall to keep Black drivers out of chauffeuring. Such segregation principles, a consistent and logical expectation in a racist society, seemed a reasonable tactic in their effort to work for a living wage. The effort, of course, resulted in absurd and unjust outcomes.

Tourist protest of the ban against Black chauffeuring pushed Miami's white elite to adjust their segregation expectations. Their protest provided an opening for Blacks to make their case for moral economy. They argued for their right to a competency and the basic right to use the new automobile technology. They benefited as well from their deference to the demands of the market and the principle of employer power. The violation of an employer's right to hire whom they pleased trumped white worker hopes for protectionism and moral economy. White chauffeurs ultimately relented and accepted a compromise to help maintain a harmonious running economy. Tourist economics demanded that white pleasure-seekers maintain their comfort and convenience and act out their imaginative desires for Black docility and service. Black protest, combined with tourist complaints against the city's anti-Black driving custom, led to a negotiation to extend the color line during this period. Black agency, the economic context, and the political discourse of class and race harmony helped African Americans gain the right to drive, albeit within the confines of a segregated city.[2]

Rooting the historical analysis in the economic and political context helps clarify the complicated issues of race and class. Outlining the power wielded by white, union chauffeurs points to the role of unionism in keeping the color line in the job market. It also highlights how the scarcity of work opportunities, resulting in part from seasonal unemployment and oversupplied labor markets, allowed for the worst discriminatory instincts to flourish. The context caused many of the scarce jobs to become highly coveted. The union movement sought to infuse value in jobs often devalued by employers. Further, the racist stereotypes of the era fostered easy condescending and paternalistic associations with certain types of work such as chauffeuring among employers. In addition, the politics of growth in Miami's tourist economy, as expressed in harmony discourse, set the terms of the debate. A conservative context was undermined by the demands of the everyday dynamics of a tourist economy: Black workers needed to get around and white tourists wanted to be accommodated to enhance their leisure experience.

Black workers' persistent challenge to white chauffeurs' rules and to hardline segregationists suggests an active and ongoing tension among workers and between employer and employee over control of the job market despite the political context of class harmony. While white chauffeurs may have been unsuccessful in attaining complete control of the local labor market, their moral economic appeals did not fail because they were unable to convince other whites about their racial superiority. Rather, unlike skilled craftsmen, their work fit a culturally hegemonic, servile profile in a service job especially suitable for leisure-play economics. Tourists could ultimately bring their own driver to the city or choose a local driver according to their particular biases and prerogatives and remain consistent with the racism of the day. The relatively easy entry into the chauffeur business made it a fluid arena, but the reality of segregated space likely forbade Black drivers from white sections of the city. Nonetheless, attaining the right to drive unmolested represented a huge victory.

Defining the Chauffeur

Miami's incorporation in 1896 coincided with the period characterized by historian Rayford Logan as the nadir of US race relations. The subsequent and continuous violations of Black civil rights would define the political, economic, and social context of the first half of the next century.[3] Such impediments made life difficult if not nearly unbearable. Black Miamians certainly resisted countless daily indignities, yet their efforts faced rather rigid ceilings, especially in where one could live. The segregated character of Colored Town reinforced practices then common in America, which only highlighted the marginal value employers attributed to "unskilled" work whatever the skin color or ethnicity of the worker.

Complicating the narrative was the struggle to define service jobs as high-wage labor and efforts to make service work available only to local residents through training programs, giving locals preference over migrants. This dynamic revealed a desperate effort to attain a livelihood in a relatively low-wage economy. Much of labor history has been defined by workers arguing for higher wages for devalued work, often determined by arbitrary measurements of skill. The process of defining skill, evaluating effort, and attributing value are inherently contested terrains. Of course, employers had a say in defining the nature and quality of the skills they wanted their workers to demonstrate. As early as 1931, organized labor accommodated employers' expectations when they helped push the Dade County School Board to sponsor vocational training in hotel work so as to help relieve local unemployment. The vocational program trained workers to be housekeepers, maids, waitresses, food checkers, linen-room workers, and front-office workers.[4] Even employers such as Burdine's department-store chain headquartered in Miami, a Miami institution in existence through the twentieth century, implemented since 1926 their own training programs for resident workers. Burdine's hired graduates of Boston's "Prince School for Store Service Education" to supervise the teaching of a fifteen-part course, "each taught under a specialist in each division of the store." By the 1940s and afterward, Dade County Schools operated a vocational education program that trained residents in various skilled jobs, as well as hotel work and even retail jobs.[5]

Blacks, in any case, moved to Miami in pursuit of job opportunities in the tourist industry and service work in general. Their arrival led to an increase in the permanent population, but temporary seasonal growth occurred as well. According to the Works Progress Administration's research on late 1930s Black Florida, Miami's Black population doubled during the winter months, a time when tourism also peaked. It is unclear when this pattern of migration started or how the circulation flows actually operated because of its transient nature and the lack of records. As noted in chapter 1, the inclusion of servant quarters in housing—whether in hotels, apartments, or rental housing—suggests that winter residents brought their servants with them or expected to hire domestic workers and chauffeurs when in town.

Throughout this time, the exclusion of Blacks from jobs that were considered skilled is particularly notable. As I demonstrate in the next chapter, white male workers actively sought to exclude Black men from skilled jobs in Miami. The practice was most effective in the building trades. The success of the strategy depended on the degree of control over the occupation that union workers could muster without causing too much of an imbalance in the city's economy. Defining chauffeuring as a skilled job, however, proved difficult—which did not prevent white chauffeurs from trying. Their endeavor was partly an attempt to define the work as skilled and to eliminate its servile profile—a castelike dynamic loaded with classist, gendered, and racist connotations. As an occupation, driving had less prestige than the handcrafts in the building industry. Whereas employers relied heavily on craft workers for successful completion of construction jobs, chauffeurs never convinced the public or their employers that their occupation required as much deference despite the white supremacy discourse they used. And, unlike workers in the building trades, drivers for hire also had to contend with general competition from transportation alternatives in the urban context. Miami chauffeurs' dreams of winning a bigger piece of the transportation market faced continuous challenges from walking, biking, the short-lived and limited trolley network, jitneys, personally owned vehicles, and car rentals. Of course, the knowledge of place for incoming visitors and the attractiveness of convenience derived from the strategic location of hacking stations, as they were called, were critical selling points for providing the service of driving.[6]

Besides the basic requirement of having to drive an automobile, what defined a chauffeur was not always clear. What did a chauffeur transport? If he moved goods, was he still a chauffeur or simply a trucker, a personal driver, a teamster, or a taxicab driver? What if he worked for a particular company to transport goods or a particular family as a domestic chauffeur? Occupational names assigned in the 1920 census for drivers—that is, anyone who earned a fee or wage by transporting people or goods by automobile, truck, or horse- or mule-drawn cart—highlight the confusion.[7] The terms *chauffeur*, *driver*, and *hackman*, for instance, were often unclear in regard to whether the person transported people or goods, particularly when the chauffeur reported that he earned his wages on his own account but did not provide any other information. Was he an independent contractor? Did he solicit tourists to drive them? The terms *chauffeur* and *driver* were used interchangeably through the 1920s, applying to anyone who drove for a living. By the 1940s, however, *chauffeur* took its present occupational designation as being distinct from other drivers, such as teamsters or taxi drivers.[8] In every case, however, the jobs were open exclusively to men.

The 1920 census compilation for occupations did distinguish between domestic chauffeurs and others, though the numbers were not recorded for cities with fewer than fifty thousand residents. And the census did not account for the type of vehicle or what was being transported. Freddie Andrews, the Black Miamian whose resistance to the color line in chauffeuring helped lead to its renegotiation, described himself as a hack driver who owned a vehicle, but what that meant to the census compilers was not indicated. Newspaper accounts showed that he did own an automobile (labeled as "car" or "auto" in the census rolls). The 1920 census rolls, though, demonstrate that Blacks succeeded in working as all kinds of drivers. Out of 151 men who labeled themselves as chauffeurs or drivers, Blacks constituted 22 percent (33). Out of 41 domestic chauffeurs, Blacks made up 39 percent (16). They dominated in other driving fields that required horses, such as carriage drivers (27 of 35), teamsters (35 of 37), and draymen (34 of 35), many of which were associated with construction work of some sort.[9]

Similar problems in accuracy persisted in the 1930 census compilations. More clarity did emerge in the job designations than in the 1920 census schedule, but census compilers did not note the finer distinctions between chauffeuring individuals under different arrangements. Bus, transfer, and taxicab companies were accounted for in the census, for instance, but a reader would not know from these data how many chauffeurs worked for private families, whether they were white or Black, or whether their work was permanent or they were employed only as temporary servants. A quick review of the census rolls indicates how prevalent it was for Black chauffeurs to work for private families. The 1930 census listed 428 Black chauffeurs and truck and tractor drivers from a total of 1,341 (constituting 32 percent) and 14 owners and managers of truck, transfer, and taxicab companies (15.2 percent of 92).[10]

The problem of labeling represented more than just a semantic conundrum. Malleability of the labels used to describe driving work reflected the newness of driving automobiles as an occupation. It also reflects the racial flexibility the work afforded and the ease of entering into the field. Reduced to its simplest terms, anyone who purchased an automobile could become a chauffeur for the transport of people; white union control of teamster work prevented easy entry of Blacks into this transportation field. Even with the high cost of purchasing an automobile, entering the profession proved relatively open, despite the impact of licensing and insurance laws emerging in the period, which may have added some institutional barriers. Certification and other professional capital costs of chauffeuring needs to be studied but does not appear to have hampered the entrance of Blacks into this line of work before 1920.[11] The prevalence of Black men serving as domestic chauffeurs in 1930 suggests that they drove Black and white clients around town, work that was perhaps seen as an extension of more servile roles, especially when serving white tourists.

Whatever employers thought, however, native white chauffeurs across the nation identified Black and immigrant men as direct competition for their livelihoods. This was particularly clear in the early twentieth century. New York chauffeurs in 1912 complained that Europeans "willing to work for smaller wages than Americans" and "the negro" were lowering wages and reducing the supply of work. "Everybody wants to be a chauffeur," related one white driver. "So, of course, wages have been going down." Black chauffeurs in New York faced sabotaging of their vehicles, such as finding mothballs in their gasoline tanks, their ignition systems short-circuited, and their carburetors thrown out of adjustment. White chauffeurs were right to perceive changes in the racial and ethnic makeup of the available labor pool. Blacks increasingly entered chauffeuring between 1900 and 1910 and continued to do so in the following years. From a national total of 4,639 (10.3 percent) in 1910, Blacks made a leap to 38,360 (13.5 percent out of total of 285,045) in 1920, which demonstrated the increasing importance of automobiles and job opportunities. Pressure from Blacks, therefore, increased competition throughout the country.[12]

Expectations of a chauffeur's duties also changed over time and varied with place of employment. Early on, chauffeurs tended to be skilled mechanics. Unpredictable mechanical breakdowns and the lack of infrastructure needed to accommodate them made skilled driver-mechanics necessary. A perusal of the situation-wanted advertisements in the *Miami Metropolis* indicates having such skills as a selling point for chauffeurs. One advertisement stated that the chauffeur was "experienced" and could "make [their] own repairs" and another pitched "nine years experience [*sic*] driving and repairing [and was also] handy with plumber and carpenter tools." Knowledge of how to fix cars continued to be a useful attribute whether one served as a domestic chauffeur or as a private chauffeur for hire, but technological advances made automobiles easier to repair (and handle), decreasing the need for specialized knowledge. In addition, with the rise of garage mechanics as a separate and distinct occupation, chauffeurs soon became differentiated by what they drove and who employed them. A domestic chauffeur worked for a private family. Chauffeurs for hire were either independent contractors or hired by a particular company, such as a hotel or a garage.[13]

Employers also expected chauffeurs to provide services beyond driving, as the one advertisement cited suggests and countless others confirm. "People want him not only to be a servant but to know that he is a servant," commented the manager of a garage in New York. The garage manager noted that additional chores were expected of the chauffeur, such as washing car windows. One writer argued that paying extra for a private, skilled chauffeur would save money because an employer would not be subject to the exorbitant prices charged in garages. He emphasized that chauffeurs hired in garages tended to be young boys "drawn to automobile-driving by the attractiveness of the work and the comparative ease with which automobile-driving is learned" but who lack "mental balance" and were irresponsible. On the other hand, the writer argued, the "high-priced chauffeur"—indicating a private one who was skilled, experienced—offered reliability and would not engage in "joyriding," taking the car without permission either for recreational use or to supplement one's income by offering taxi service. Garage owners protested being identified as "high-priced" and blamed the chauffeurs for charging commission fees for their patronage. Whether garages were high-priced or not, chauffeurs pitched reliability and responsibility, emphasizing they did not have "bad habits," were competent, or were married in addition to their willingness to do additional work.[14]

Debates among employers, chauffeurs, and garage owners defined the "chauffeur problem," which peaked in the first fifteen years of the twentieth century. Protests by white chauffeurs suggest that white men resisted wealthy employers' desire to exact more servile behavior from them. Racially defined skills and roles played no small role in these discussions. Thus, Miami's chauffeur conflict developed in the dynamic context of ongoing labor troubles, racial tension, and debates over the prestige of chauffeuring at a time of rapid change.

The 1915–19 Chauffeur Conflict

On February 28, 1915, a Black chauffeur from Palm Beach was run out of Miami for driving three white women passengers. The *Miami Herald* reported that the Black chauffeur had "wagered with a white man that he could come here, drive about the city and 'get away' with it." He "did not realize that a strong sentiment prevails in Miami against colored chauffeurs," the newspaper reported, and was soon "closely pursued by several cars containing Miami chauffeurs, realizing that unless he vacated the car he would be handled roughly, [he] abandoned the car and beat it afoot for the colored section." The Black chauffeur later appeared at the police station to ask for protection. He was put on a train to Palm Beach, while the car remained in Miami for the owner, a Mister Metcalf, to retrieve the next day. The chauffeur was "convinced that while it's healthy to drive autos in Palm Beach, a Negro has no business acting as [a] chauffeur in Miami." The *Metropolis* reported that the Black chauffeur shared ownership of the vehicle with three other Blacks and had come to Miami despite knowing the prejudice against Black drivers. Instead of criticizing the white chauffeurs, both newspapers brushed off the incident as the Black chauffeurs' failure to respect the boundaries of the color line. Business and labor, it is interesting to note, colluded in maintaining strict segregation rules. The collusion reflected the implicit class understanding of how to accommodate a scarce job market. Racism inevitably produced awkward social outcomes. To avoid class conflict and also maintain a racist social order, Miami's white working class needed placation within the logic and callousness of segregationist culture.[15]

Debate over the chauffeur situation lasted for the next several years, intensifying in the summer of 1915 as a result of the February incident and heightened interest in how segregation in driving would ultimately affect the city's tourist industry. Supporters of Jim Crow legislation first accepted the racial practice of restricting African American chauffeurs from doing business, though some whites did point out that the segregation dialogue bordered on hypocrisy, noting that Blacks were hired in service work. Disagreement especially centered on the practice of allowing tourists to bring their own Black chauffeurs with them when visiting the city.[16]

How many times white chauffeurs prevented Blacks from driving in the city is not known. Newspaper reports suggest that it did not occur often, though knowledge of the prejudice against Black use of automobiles likely deterred many from purchasing an automobile. The high price of automobiles was an equally important obstacle. Still, the *Miami Metropolis* questioned whether allowing white chauffeurs' threats to shape the city's customs was actually in Miami's best interest. Letters from tourists to the *Metropolis* complaining about the February incident sparked further interest in the topic. In an editorial entitled "Shall Mob Law Rule Miami," the newspaper indicated its own stance on the issue: the newspaper felt it unwise to prevent tourists from bringing their Black chauffeurs to the city. Taking a law-and-order position, while conceding to racial etiquette, the newspaper's editorial staff suggested that if Miamians agreed to forbid tourists from using their Black chauffeurs, then the city needed to inform the tourists of the regulation. If not, then the city of Miami should accommodate tourists and their chauffeurs, despite the boycott of garages or intimidation from white drivers.[17]

The *Metropolis* did not defend the right of Blacks to drive. But it did recognize the damage that the complete elimination of Black drivers would have on Miami's tourist industry, its economic engine. "We want the business of these touring parties, and the value of one machine to Miami, with occupants, who are usually liberal persons, means much to the city. . . . It would cost more than could be overcome in the way of hostile publicity." The completion of the Dixie Highway, designed to increase the number of tourists who flooded into the city each winter, would only exacerbate the problem, they argued. Booster ideology led to comparisons with the customs of other southern cities and merged with the classist sentiment common to the era. "In practically every southern city owners of cars have colored chauffeurs," the *Metropolis* reported. "In Atlanta, for instance, a majority of the owned machines are driven by negroes, the same as southern carriages of the Southern gentlemen were driven years ago." This image remained a key strand in the argument for allowing tourists to bring their Black chauffeurs with them to Miami. The segregation status quo, the newspaper argued, allowed for Black drivers to be employed in a servile, docile position, particularly when at the prerogative of white employers.[18]

The leadership role played by the *Metropolis* in Progressive Era Miami was not insignificant. Simpson Bobo Dean, part owner of the newspaper from 1904 and its sole owner from 1914 to 1923, served as a muckraking voice in early Miami. Dean lived a life in newspapers. Born in Alabama on March 21, 1871, Dean began work as a reporter for the *Journal and Tribune* in Knoxville, Tennessee, when he was just nineteen years of age. In the 1890s, he moved to Florida. Soon thereafter, he started the *Palm Beach Daily News*. By 1909, Dean had become a strong populist voice against Henry Flagler and the Florida East Coast Railroad. The most famous of his criticisms of Flagler focused on the high freight rates he charged growers. When local businessmen petitioned Dean to ease his opposition to Flagler—which they feared would sour business relations the powerful FEC—Dean turned around and published a list of their names in the *Metropolis* on April 1, 1910. Several Miamians wrote letters of support for the newspaper's position, and soon after "the advertisers and subscribers who had dropped their support of the newspaper through [Florida East Coast] pressure came back. The railroad finally readjusted its rates."[19] The *Miami Metropolis* was also among the city's strongest supporters of Prohibition. As a "dry" newspaper, the *Metropolis* served as the city's gadfly. Its journalistic style contrasted sharply with the more conservative coverage of the city's other newspaper, the *Miami Herald*. Therefore, when wealthy tourists began to complain about their inability to travel with their Black chauffeurs, Dean and his newspaper pushed for a resolution that would be in the best interest of the city, while the *Herald* hesitated, expressing skepticism about whether a problem actually existed. From the *Herald*'s perspective, northerners visiting Miami merely had to accept the local segregation custom in chauffeuring.[20]

Even more important, the *Metropolis* and *Herald* disagreed about whether to publicize the city's race-based chauffeuring regulations. The former believed the Chamber of Commerce, "representing the progressive thought and action of the community," needed to investigate the matter and take a formal stand to protect Miami's tourist industry. The *Herald* did not believe the city had a significant chauffeur problem. Thus, they saw no need for publicizing the guidelines or for the city's political leaders to take steps to investigate it. The *Herald* continued to refer only vaguely to the ongoing debate, even as a major public forum was convened by the Chamber of Commerce to address the issue. News of the forum itself was kept extremely brief and relegated to the middle and end of the newspaper. The *Metropolis*, on the other hand, provided extensive front-page coverage, evoking criticism from the *Herald* that the *Metropolis* was only "creating trouble" for an issue that was "not a burning question." The *Herald* simply did not believe that many white tourists cared to bring "colored chauffeurs" to the city, it insisted that the segregation of chauffeuring was a well-established rule, and any change threatened Miami's color line.[21] Later, even the *Herald* would be forced to concede that a problem existed given the increasing instances of conflict and disruption to the tourist industry. But in the summer of 1915, they continued to offer little coverage of the chauffeur debates while ostensibly deferring to the sensibilities of hardline segregationists who did not want Blacks to drive.

A typical and especially revealing commentary on the rationale for opposition to Black men working as chauffeurs was offered by George Okell, owner of a Miami garage. His insights pointed to how class and race operated in tandem. In a letter to the *Metropolis*, Okell described the February incident as an exceptional case and the fault of one Black driver who was "looking for trouble." According to his retelling, the Black driver from Palm Beach had stepped out of his socially accepted place and knew Miami's racial custom but nonetheless chose to defy it. Arguing on behalf of the white chauffeurs, Okell turned to a discourse focused on standards of living. Miami's white chauffeurs, he wrote, were family men who "organized a union for the mutual protection against low wages and demoralized labor conditions. . . . They realize that when the door is thrown open and the negro chauffeur tolerated that the negro will work for lower wages and under conditions that a white man can not compete." Floyd McNeil of the chauffeurs' union concurred. Moralizing a bit further, McNeil argued that accepting Black chauffeurs would be like "asking them to come to the level of the negro, and that is not pleasant." As racist as McNeil's comment was, it did contain a naive observation of the causes of the material reality defining so much of Miami's social and economic landscape. The low wages paid to Black workers (African American or Bahamian) and the squalid conditions of Colored Town seemed to suggest they consented to live in impoverished conditions. Yet even such absurd analysis did have a sliver of insight within it. A particular class (employers, business) sought to benefit from oversupplied labor markets, devaluation of work, and justification of asymmetrical race- and gender-based wage scales. Opponents to Blacks working as chauffeurs also criticized the extensive boosterism that the city's businesses engaged in because it flooded the local labor market with workers. The juxtaposition of class and racial threads in such criticisms was no accident. The underlying logic of moral economy called for the protection of individual competency, something continuously threatened in capitalist economies.[22] More than race alone, the class dynamics of the growing chauffeur debate were increasingly plain.

Permeating this discourse was the idea that once one concession was made, complete integration would be the result. In a letter to the *Miami Metropolis*, the union carpenter P. L. Ryan argued against allowing Blacks to compete with white chauffeurs, stating that no white man wanted competition from Blacks. He questioned the racial values of advocates of a more liberal chauffeur policy when he said that some whites "would welcome even [boxer] Jack Johnson had he a Negro chauffeur." In a hopeful prediction, but one marred with a deep racial hatred, he wrote, "I do not believe there is a man, woman, or child in Miami today that will live long enough to see a Negro chauffeur on the streets of Miami." (Of course, he would soon be proved wrong.) The *Herald* elaborated on the point, stepping away from its normally more reserved stance. As one 1915 editorial intoned,

> If negro men are to take up the work of chauffeurs it will be followed by garages operated by colored men in the white portion of the city, and the color line once being broken, there will be nothing to prevent other colored business from coming in the white part of the city, and for colored residents to chose [*sic*] any part of the city they desire for their homes. The question resolves itself to this, do we want any change made in the regulation that has prevailed from the beginning?[23]

Such reports were intended to play on the race fears of many among Miami's more vulnerable classes, depicting a dystopic racially integrated urban landscape. Of course, the sad fact was that this effort to unite the white community against any change in the racial status quo actually described the reality of Jim Crow Miami. Such public confessions that Miami was indeed a white man's town were borrowed from language used by whites throughout the South. The degree to which this attitude was laced with classist fears could be overlooked. Racial hyperbole functioned as a defensive barrier to feared encroachments and served to appeal to the larger white public's racism. Yet Ryan's argument against competition represented a stab at a critical component of capitalist labor-market principles. Still, Miami's Chamber of Commerce refused to take a position on the matter, claiming it had no authority to do so.[24]

More moderate positions accepted racial segregation but criticized the rigidity of hard-line segregationists for not being more sensitive to the finer sensibilities of the wealthy, an obvious source of increased revenues for the city. C. L. Sheeler, a resident from Buena Vista, a suburb just north of Miami, argued that Miami should imitate Baltimore, "the metropolis of the South," in allowing Blacks to drive. Sheeler criticized the white chauffeur's argument on two counts. First, he argued, employers should have the right to choose their workers; closed shops should not be allowed. And, second, he noted, Black chauffeurs were willing to work at cheaper rates than many whites and were biologically suited to service. "The negro is a servant, by nature a humble and obedient servant, and a faithful one. I know such in service 20 years," he wrote. Who were these white chauffeurs to challenge the preference for such labor? Some of these white union "chauffeur kickers," Sheeler added, "have a 'nigger mammy' cooking their dinners, nigger girls serving the guests at the table and a nigger nurse taking care of their children. . . . Then somebody wants to howl about a Black man driving his celebrated Ford car on the streets of Miami, and down Dixie Highway." To individuals like Sheeler, barring Black chauffeurs made no economic sense and directly violated not only accepted racial customs but also the guiding principle of a free market. Sheeler went as far as to suggest that the white chauffeurs who interfered with Black chauffeurs' right to ply their trade, or the rights of white or Black citizens to hire them, should be arrested. This would not be the first or last time in the history of class struggle when the forces of law and order were called on to control the working class; nor that their interests for good working conditions and wages were ignored or their submission to labor-market commands were confused as consent or to signal their cultural peculiarity or inferiority.[25]

T. V. Moore, a successful pioneer farmer, highlighted the hypocrisy of garage owners who refused to cater to Black patrons. His criticism demonstrated how segregation allowed for interaction between the races in the context of formal economic exchange. Violating this right, Moore argued, created a double standard. Moore made it clear that he was not a supporter of integration in any form. Blacks' driving rights constituted an issue of basic economic fairness. No difference existed between Miami clerks accepting the money of Black patrons and the potential exchange between Blacks and garage owners, Moore concluded.

Editors at the *Metropolis* also supported this argument. They found it absurd that complaints would be raised about whites and Blacks engaging in the exchange of goods and services when "every store in Miami has in it white men and women who wait on negro customers every day [and] are glad to have the opportunity." The newspaper also argued that Blacks enjoyed mobility throughout the city despite the recent protest. Potential safety concerns as a result of incompetent drivers—another argument used by white chauffeurs to argue against allowing Blacks to enter the trade—was also refuted. "Every train arriving in Miami is met at the depot by vehicles, drawn by horses and driven by negroes, and there is no provision that these negro drivers shall not take men, women and children to any part of the city. Nor has there been any complaint that those who use these hacks are not safely driven or that they are subject to any annoyances because of the color of the driver," *Metropolis* editors wrote. According to the city directory, the number of Black drivers in Miami also was increasing, from 49 in 1913 to 76 in 1915.[26] Driving an automobile, however, remained a problem. At least one Black physician, according to Floyd McNeil from the chauffeurs' union, had to ask for permission just to drive his own car.[27] To hard-line segregationists, it was all the same: driving, for whatever reason, was a white male right and one that they did not feel should be extended to Black residents.

The chauffeur issue remained a concern through the peak tourist season in 1915–16, with similar discourse driving the debate. The Highland Improvement Association endorsed "anti-negro chauffeur propaganda" claiming that, while they could not vouch for the morals of each white chauffeur, "we are still of one mind that the worst of them is far superior to the best negro chauffeur." Editors at the *Herald* continued to insist that the number of Black chauffeurs entering the city was so minuscule that either business lost by offending tourists would be insignificant or most visitors to Miami would comply. The white chauffeurs, however, decided to hedge their bets and moved to mitigate any negative associations by offering free service to any white visitors who arrived with Black chauffeurs, thereby adding an incentive for white patrons to accept their demands of racial exclusion. Still, the first reported example of a Black chauffeur being replaced with a white one that season demonstrated just how ridiculous the policy remained. White chauffeurs approached a white family who had arrived with their Black chauffeur and explained the local custom, offering to drive them free of charge if they would consent to preventing their own Black chauffeur from taking the wheel as long as they were in the city of Miami. The white visitors accepted their demands. The Black chauffeur changed "his seat to one of the rear seats and the Miami white chauffeur climbed in and took charge of the car." The tourists were driven around the city, apparently with the Black chauffeur still in the back seat, where the tourists spent the day shopping. Later, however, the visitors commented that, if they had known of Miami's custom, they would never have come. The white chauffeurs' attempts to control the market hung on a tenuous line bound to break with the city's continued, steady growth and the lack of prestige associated with their occupation.[28]

Not until Blacks actively resisted did Black Miamians get the right to drive automobiles for a living. Freddie Andrews, a twenty-three-year-old native Floridian, attempted to start his own chauffeur service in July 1917. To his dismay, white chauffeurs physically threatened him, prompting Andrews to retaliate. He was then arrested. Later that day, the *Metropolis* reported that Andrews stabbed Randolph Lightburne, a white chauffeur, whom Andrews believed was among his "persecutors." Andrews was eventually sentenced either to pay a $50 fine, the equivalent of two or three weeks' salary, or to serve sixty days in jail. Andrews seems to have paid the fine, because, two weeks later, he was arrested a second time for driving a car in one of Miami's white neighborhoods. *Metropolis* editors continued to defend Andrews, depicting the white chauffeurs as wrongdoers, noting that they "attempted to make trouble for the negro" and to engage in his "persecution."[29]

The Black community's response further encouraged editors at the *Metropolis* to actively protest the city's policy of exclusion. On July 14, 1917, the *Metropolis* published an article entitled "Negroes Not to Use Violence to Gain Privileges." It simply consisted of a letter from Miami's Colored Board of Trade, a significant statement by the paper to offer the Black perspective. The Colored Board of Trade announced that they did not advocate the use of violence to resolve the chauffeur question, but that they did expect "Negro rights [to be] respected." Resorting to symbols of a peaceful and harmonious community, the board explicitly "denounced any resort to violence as both imprudent and lawless." Choosing their words carefully so that it was clear they were in no way favoring racial integration, the board was quoted as saying: "We have no controversy with any individual or body of individuals which call for a resort to violence but we do insist, that negroes as citizens of the commonwealth have certain definite legal and moral rights." Both white and Black community leaders believed in maintaining a segregated city as long as basic standards of fairness were maintained.[30]

The Colored Board of Trade appealed to the civility of the community, pointing to the need for "protection of the courts and all law-abiding citizens." They hoped to tap into the sympathies of the white community. "We have faith in the judgment of the best white citizens and we welcome any effort looking forward to a better understanding between the races," the board wrote. The board assured white Miami that they had no clandestine plans and encouraged ongoing dialogue, noting that they did "not bar the public from attendance at any of [their] meetings." This shift in the terms of the debate from free-market exchange to principles of civility underscored just how much the actions of white chauffeurs threatened peace and harmony across the city. Therefore, the Colored Board of Trade argued, the policy of excluding Black drivers could no longer be accepted as either a legitimate white working-class strategy or as central to maintaining racial segregation.[31]

On July 16, 1917, racial tensions reached a peak with the bombing of Colored Town's Odd Fellows Hall. The bomb wreaked incredible damage, breaking most of the building's windows, breaking off large chunks of plaster, and cracking its concrete walls. In one place along the front of the building, it knocked a hole in the structure's façade, leaving it open to the street. The bombers, whom the *Metropolis* believed to be white chauffeurs or individuals serving on their behalf, had targeted one of the city's most important buildings. Not only was Odd Fellows Hall one of the largest structures in the neighborhood, it also symbolized the Black community's success in establishing a separate state in the "commonwealth" of Miami. For writers at the *Metropolis* and for white community leaders, the hall also represented the social order and cohesiveness that Miami's biracial society had attained in the roughly two decades since its incorporation. Odd Fellows Hall was a cultural center in Colored Town that served as the meeting room for lodge groups. The hall was also a place for entertainment. As local historian Dorothy Jenkins Fields has noted, "On Saturday nights the piano players at Odd Fellows Hall filled the air with music" and Blacks engaged in the latest dances. Hence, the intentions of the bombers were clear: by hitting Colored Town's largest building and damaging a concrete symbol of the community's independence, they attempted to hurt the Black community's sense of accomplishment in a violent demonstration of white might.[32]

Editors at the *Metropolis* tried to ease fears of an impending race riot by reporting that conditions were under control. They blamed a few "white rowdies" for the bombing and noted that ten police officers had been sent to Colored Town to "prevent further disorder." "The fear of negro reprisals and of race riot, which had been generally entertained by leaders of both the whites and negroes" had "fairly well dissipated," the *Metropolis* claimed. The newspaper also urged the Miami community to take action for peace, underscoring that the racial tension present in Miami was the result of criminal activity, not of a larger breach between the city's Black and white communities.[33]

Comments by the many participants made at town meetings held at the central school and, later in the same day, at a church in Colored Town, also were published. The first meeting included white authorities and Black leaders, including a local judge, the chief of police, the acting mayor, and members of the Colored Board of Trade. The second meeting included the same actors and a packed house of Blacks that overflowed onto the streets. The newspaper reported that the Black community did not "want any trouble" and assured readers that there would be "no trouble if the authorities will control the lawless element among the white population." Black leaders continued to appeal to Miami's "best white citizens," calling for community peace and asking for whites to control those who would perpetuate this kind of violence and harassment. One Black pastor went as far as to appeal to white authorities to "exercise the same control over your lawless element that we do over ours." He added, "We have been segregated and do not object, but we want the line guarded and we want to be protected in our rights in our own section."[34]

Miami's Black community also tapped into whites' anxiety about maintaining social order by alluding to their willingness to protect themselves if continually threatened. Comparisons between Miami and East St. Louis, where a race riot had broken out just one week before, also were made. There, it was Black competition for jobs that sparked the riot just two weeks earlier in which nine whites and about forty Blacks died. Building on the fear that tensions were such that much the same could happen in Miami, some Black residents went as far as to note that they were prepared "to protect themselves" and were worried that "their sense of wrong might overcome their better judgement." Apparently, rumors were circulating that Blacks were stockpiling ammunition, leading to

Florida's local National Guard contingent, Company M, camping in Miami to ransack the Black undertaker's business searching for such stockpiles. But these comments were also tempered by uplift and patriotic discourse such as noting how they had no complaints about segregation, only wanted to build up their "part of town," and were active in supporting the World War I effort through Liberty Bond drives and Red Cross subscriptions.[35]

A deferential tone generally marked communication between Blacks and whites at the town meetings, representing Black leaders' clear understanding of how to balance an implied threat with an affirmation of commitment to nationalism and civic duty. When Black community leaders met in a church in Colored Town to discuss the bombing with white leaders present, they opened the meeting with Black singers singing "America." In the context, the song was an apt choice. The poetic vision of liberty in "America" ("from every mountain-side/ let freedom ring," for example) evoked a moral call for justice that fit well with Woodrow Wilson's call to make the world safe for democracy. Blacks had struggled for decades to gain the freedom promised by Reconstruction, if not by the Declaration of Independence. While Wilson's policy of segregation in the federal government made the daily indignities of Jim Crow that much more offensive, a glimmer of hope existed in the patriotic rhetoric of democracy and liberty. Several Black leaders, including W. E. B. Du Bois, would call for patriotic support for the war through service. Miami's Black community embraced the war effort, as the Reverend Jarrel Drake emphasized in the meeting. Not only would more than three thousand of the community's men register with the local draft board to fight by the war's end, the community also contributed volunteer service in the Red Cross and promoted Liberty Bonds in the spring and summer of 1917. At some level, Black leaders understood the value of performing the song "America." The context of World War I, meeting in a church, and the threat of violent race rioting sent a powerful message that Blacks had a right to drive and that Jim Crow needed to accommodate.[36]

Black leaders also understood the importance of Black labor to the city's economy. They used the threat of out-migration to leverage further protection from Miami's white business elite, spurring the city's business leaders to take action to protect Miami's economic prosperity. Local newspapers had been reporting labor agents from other parts of Florida had begun infiltrating the city, seeking Black workers for their own communities. Florida historian Jerrell Shofner has observed that "between 1916 and 1920 about 40,000 Blacks left the northern Florida counties," making Miami a prime target for labor agents because of its population growth. On June 9, the *Miami Herald* reported the arrest of C. H. Bryant, a labor agent from Taylor County in northwest Florida, for enticing labor away from Dade County. This enticement law had been enacted in 1889 in an apparent attempt to prevent feuds among turpentine employers fighting over workers. In any case, the *Herald* commented that the shortage of unskilled labor in Miami was the result of this recruitment, which was causing Black out-migration. Two weeks later, the newspaper remarked that "the negroes of the south are migrating to the north in large numbers, leaving the fields uncultivated and the crops unharvested, and the future an unsolved problem." The Black leadership tapped into this anxiety in the July 16 meeting. Some of the most prominent members of the community, including the most successful Black businessman, Dana Dorsey, threatened that "If negroes could not be given rights and protection in Miami they have elsewhere, they would leave Miami." Charles Thompson, a Black real-estate broker, observed that "many of the better class of negroes . . . had already left because of conditions here." The exodus should matter to everyone in the city, they argued: If the better class of Blacks left, who would maintain order in Colored Town?[37]

Editors at the *Metropolis* also played up this idea of "respectability." Noting that it was the city's most industrious Black residents who opposed the monopoly white chauffeurs claimed in the city, they again appealed to the values of hard work and free-market exchange while underscoring the threat to white prosperity. They also cast aspersions on the city's progressivism, noting, "Miami is probably the only city of any size or importance in the United States where negroes have not been allowed to drive automobiles under any circumstances." Noting that "there was no restriction on the age, condition or qualifications of white chauffeurs" whatsoever, and that "until recently, the police court has generally found a reason for fining the negro and discharging the white men when infrequent arrests have been made," writers for the *Metropolis* painted a sharp contrast between Black residents' lawfulness and industriousness and white men's unregulated monopoly on driving.[38]

Ultimately, though, it was the argument that granting Black men the right to drive in Miami was central to maintaining segregation that held the most sway with many white city leaders. In an editorial published on July 16, 1917, "Wise Heads and Sober Judgment Needed," the *Metropolis* declared that the people of Miami had finally "awakened to a realization of the trouble that they have permitted a bunch of irresponsible white men to stir up for their peaceful city." Reminding readers that the editors had "warned Miami of the probability of trouble" more than a year ago, they compared white chauffeurs to hounds and their victims to rabbits and foxes. What were "white rowdies doing in Colored Town at two o'clock in the morning?" they wrote. "Why are white men at any hour of the day or night permitted in Colored Town unless they can show legitimate reasons of being there?" Blacks visiting "White Town" at night would be quickly "locked up as suspicious characters," they wrote. So why were not "the white scum that visit Colored Town all hours of the night put in jail?" "The city, county, and state officials are white men. The courts are presided by white men," the *Metropolis* continued. "The 'justice' that is meted out is all for the White Man, and it is only wonder that negroes of Miami have kept patient as long as they have." The burden of maintaining peace and harmony, then, rested on white community leaders. Only by "securing a common justice for the negro" within the bounds of a racially separate society, could there be progress in Miami.[39]

These sentiments were taken up by a group of white and Black business leaders at a community conference held the following day.[40] The white committee asserted that by "unwritten law," only white men were allowed to drive automobiles in Miami. "Miami had been built as a white man's town," they noted. As such, the prohibition against Black driving was simply "in accord with the prevailing sentiment of the white voters of the city." Nonetheless, they consented that it was "only fair" to Blacks to set a more reasonable policy of segregation in driving. The white committee proposed three conditions: (1) Blacks would be protected when driving their own cars, (2) they would be allowed to drive buses and cars for hire, but only for transporting other Blacks, and (3) "the solicitation of negro patronage by white car and bus drivers" would be discouraged as much as possible. City officials at the conference, including the sheriff, the chief of police, the acting mayor, and two councilmen, supported the resolution. Black leaders reluctantly agreed. At some point over the course of the following week, Mayor Parker H. Henderson issued a curfew restricting both Black and white drivers from working in any city neighborhood after 6:00 p.m.[41] It was the first official statement to openly acknowledge the right of both Black and white men to earn a living by driving or to place equal restrictions on what could be done in Black and white neighborhoods.

With an agreement reached, members of the North Miami Improvement Association increased their calls for the police department to apprehend the bombers of Odd Fellow's Hall. The *Metropolis* seconded this call and noted that they could produce a "long list" of other unsolved crimes. The chief of police eventually resigned, although he denied being pressured by the community's criticism. The individuals who bombed Odd Fellows Hall were never found.[42]

By the fall of 1917, a new equilibrium was reached that went beyond the summer arrangement. Mayor John W. Watson persuaded white chauffeurs to agree to be "law-abiding" and let white owners of private cars, tourist or resident, to hire Black chauffeurs. The chauffeurs still objected "to negro hack drivers being allowed to solicit white patronage in the white section of the city," thereby protecting the segregated landscape ideal. By doing so, white chauffeurs prevented Black drivers from cashing in on the lucrative white tourist business. Perhaps white chauffeurs and the white working class more generally finally realized that their racist utopic dreams transcended the realm of reality. Miami's tourist economy would defer to accepted Jim Crow etiquette even while there likely remained recalcitrant white chauffeurs who reluctantly agreed to even this compromise.[43] Black chauffeurs, however, may have figured out ways of circumventing the inconveniences of being unable to solicit white tourist clients. The report of the new compromise motivated at least one Black chauffeur to place an advertisement in the "Situation Wanted" section of the *Metropolis* just three days later that read "COLORED CHAUFFEUR wishes position with a private family [and] can make [his] own repairs [and] also furnish references from a prominent New York family." The addition of Black chauffeur job advertisements represented an unprecedented change, including pushing many white chauffeurs, for the first time, to list their race as "white" in their own advertisements. The perceived need to differentiate one's color is suggestive, though clearly both Black and white drivers insisted on pitching their responsible demeanors (listing age, marital status), competency (years of experience, mechanical skills), and general professionalism (references).[44] It is unclear whether other forms of solicitation, fixed arrangements (hotel services), or grapevine communication emerged to sidestep the white chauffeur effort to monopolize Miami's white tourist driving sector. At the very least, Black drivers were able to drive Black clients. The 1920 and 1930 census indicate they constituted a healthy percentage of the total number of drivers, and so many were able to make a living out of driving.

The struggle to control the local labor market had, by September 1917, turned to the effort of gaining city council support for protective legal measures. White chauffeurs compromised in November, in part, because they sought the city council's support by passing ordinances designed to make driving nonresident chauffeurs prohibitive, thereby helping their efforts to maintain a just price. According to one report, 125 northern chauffeurs plied their trade in the 1917 winter season, indicating that Miami's chauffeurs, in their effort to maintain a moral economy, fought at least two battles in controlling the chauffeuring trade, competition from Black resident drivers (Bahamian and African American) and from nonresident white chauffeurs. They had succeeded in permanently blocking the Black hacking business from the white tourist trade through intimidation and violence even with the summer compromise and the new fall concession. Miami's white chauffeurs complained nonetheless that nonresident drivers undercut resident chauffeurs by offering rates at uncompetitive levels. Their larger plan sought to block nonresident chauffeurs through high licensing fees. The initial proposal, introduced by Chauffeurs Union Local 196 in September, would charge nonresidents $200 and residents (defined as six months of residency) only $3, both of which would be added to the $2 state licensing fee (changed in early November to $150 and $5). It is interesting that complaints from at least one "auto livery" (taxi) business protested because it hired many nonresident drivers during the tourist season. A new version of the ordinance in November excluded "persons who pay taxes on a $2,000 valuation [and] persons having an established business and their employees." These proprietors would have to pay only the resident fee for each driver. The public discussion over protection was absolutely fascinating for its openness and clarity.[45]

The goal was clearly "to give resident chauffeurs a monopoly of the hacking business, and to keep out transient drivers." Aside from the constitutional implications of such efforts, the attempts at protection clearly reflected the ideal of moral economy, one especially responding to the particularly unique contours of tourism and Miami's development as a young and growing city. A winter resident, Edwin F. Boss, argued in December 1917 during a heated council meeting that efforts to protect "the home talent" reflected the "good old republican yell of protection that we have been fighting for years. Of course the chauffeurs want protection," he observed, "but they are not entitled to it any more than carpenters or anybody else." Two council members (E. L. Brady and L. T. Highleymen) argued that local year-round residents should be favored and "be protected from the 'fly-by-nights.'" A third (Hickson) pointed out that "Oh, we were all fly-by-nights when we first came here. That's what everybody is when he first comes to Miami."[46]

Perhaps the most interesting turn in the debate was over the very nature of tourist economics. One individual in a white coat who preferred to remain nameless stated that Miami was getting a reputation of being a "hold-up town and this chauffeur ordinance was "in favor of 'hold-up men.'" Councilor E. L. Brady tersely responded that "all tourist towns are holdup towns. . . . It's their business to hold people up, and the people who visit them expect to be held up." Councilor L. T. Highleymen pointed out how Asheville, North Carolina, charged resident chauffeurs $25 and $75 for nonresidents. Boss suggested that "real" cities like Chicago, New York, or Indianapolis did not "do it that way." Highleymen retorted, "Miami is rank amateur compared to New York. I paid fifty cents for a sandwich there last summer, and if they charged me fifteen cents here I'd howl about it."[47]

The exchange was a rare window into the dynamics of the asymmetries of price and how price reflected local economies. The tourist experience may have entailed the expectation of paying more, as suggested by Councilor Brady's crude framing. It highlighted how tourist transactions reflected a fiction. The shaping of the landscape as a paradise of pleasure, marked by spaces of leisure, fun, and play, included not only the manipulation of the symbols and narratives of class, gendered, and racial hierarchies. The struggle over licensing fees represented an opportunity for year-round residents to attain a livelihood. It raised an interesting question of how city officials could foster a stable, responsible community within the limits of tourist economics. The need to support a home population who struggled for work the rest of the year therefore seemed logical for Brady and Highleymen. Why should hometown folks not gain an advantage over itinerants in the town's most lucrative business, tourism? Like the chauffeurs, they sought to regulate competition for moral economic reasons precisely because the winter season drew not only tourists but also a temporary working class or, perhaps more annoying to union chauffeurs, petit bourgeois entrepreneurs. This city council meeting ended with the agreement to lower the exorbitant fees from $150 for nonresidents to $75; this would then be further reduced in January to $25 and $5 for residents. The result was disappointing: no chauffeur, of the 194 getting licenses during the 1918 season, paid the nonresident fee. All filed affidavits claiming residence. This led, later in the year, to a decrease in the licensing rate to $10 for nonresidents and no change for residents. So, what had started as a hopeful strategy crumbled with the realization that Miami's population growth and fluctuations made such licenses nearly impossible to administer effectively. Everybody who came to Miami apparently were originally "fly-by-night" migrants who eventually settled permanently or succeeded in seeming that they would settle.[48]

One other effort led by the white chauffeurs' union in winter 1919 attempted to establish a local commercial chauffeuring license examination. It would have entailed an examination by a panel of three examiners, one likely being a member of Local 196 of the chauffeurs' union. The chauffeurs' lawyer who crafted it, D. J. Heffermen, had already appeared nine times before the city council to make the chauffeurs' case. He argued that its purpose was for the "assurance of safety to the visitors to the city in that their valuable pleasure cars would not be damaged by careless drivers of the big trucks" or other drivers for hire. It was overwhelmingly rejected by Miami's city council. J. T. Blackman, city council member and president of the carpenters' union, cast the only vote favoring it.[49]

The race-labor peace established by 1917 was apparently short-lived and may have been short-circuited by the chauffeurs' union's inability to pass protective labor ordinances. Two years later, in November 1919, a new round of alleged violence and harassment occurred. The historical context had changed in that Miami was in the midst of a threat of a general citywide strike, which led to an effort by the *Metropolis* and business interests to depict organized labor as lawless. This pattern of coverage, as well as the history of Miami's labor struggle, will be discussed more carefully in the next chapter. It does appear that the chauffeurs' union may have been honest when they vehemently denied the charges that they had scared away a tourist family from Tennessee driving into the city with their Black driver. The *Metropolis* story, embedded in an editorial, merely republished a very short report from the *Palm Beach Post*. (I was unable to locate this report in the *Palm Beach Post*.) The editorial emphasized the potential loss of tourist investment, the need for law and order, and a plea for "the better element in union organizations" to control their rough element.[50] The details of the incident remain unclear, but white racist intimidation of the sort is not unlikely.

There is little doubt that Miami faced a charged atmosphere during the fall of 1919. Yet whether white chauffeurs reverted back to the pre-1917 policy is uncertain if not dubious. Throughout 1918 and more sparsely in the winter of 1919, Black chauffeurs placed situation-wanted advertisements in the *Herald* and *Metropolis*; several white chauffeur advertisements indicated their race during this period as well. No reports of chauffeur violence or intimidation appeared in 1918 or throughout 1919, whether in newspaper stories, editorials, or tourist letters. If the policy did resume, then it would be quite unusual for no historical trace to be left, particularly in light of the extensive discussion and engagement in the period between 1915 and 1917. The timing of the *Metropolis* story reproducing a *Palm Beach Post* report was certainly suspicious.[51]

Four separate news items published in the *Miami Metropolis* over two days apparently verified the Tennessee tourist incident and feigned objectivity. The first article (November 5) contained the union's statement of denial, which also gave details not indicated in the newspaper's report. Details included how the tourists "drove into a local garage and asked a night man in attendance if it was a fact that she would not be allowed to use her colored driver" and was told that Miami was a "white man's town." Yet the newspaper introduced that statement with a synopsis of a Chamber of Commerce (CC) meeting condemning alleged intimidation by the chauffeurs' union. The newspaper reported that CC members had discussed that the incident was not isolated, that there had been "a number of instances" of tourist intimidation.[52] The minutes of the CC meeting contains details not appearing in the *Metropolis* story, some inconsistent, others unstated anywhere else. At least once, the CC president, E. A. Roberts, erred when he stated that the tourists were from Cincinnati.

The new details not appearing in the *Metropolis* article included that the tourists expected to stay at the Berni Apartments during their winter stay (apparently starting much earlier than the typical December–April season), the Black chauffeur had been refused car-washing service at a local garage, and he had been "intimidated by an upper of the local chauffeurs' union and threatened." Charles Leffler asserted that "it was common knowledge that this kind of carrying on was being conducted," offering as evidence his contempt for the power of Miami's unions over the labor market followed by an accusation that "eighty percent of the [white] chauffeurs are under age boys." He claimed he believed the "upper of the local chauffeurs' union . . . was H. G. Hill, walking delegate." He likely meant Horace T. Hill, one of the union's business agents. Leffler added an anecdote to further bolster his case. A "colored doctor [named] Frazure" (likely Solomon Frazier) had at some point "an iron bolt thrown through his wind shield," which nearly injured "a passenger of his car." It is difficult to believe the claim of underage chauffeurs under the state laws and age restrictions for chauffeuring, which required drivers to be at least eighteen years old. The 1920 census rolls also contradicted those observations. The relevance of the Frazier incident, though likely accurate, seems of questionable relevance, since the minutes provided no date or period when it occurred—that is, no time frame such as "recently," "the other day," "last week," "a month ago," or "last year." Leffler's memory of a bolt-throwing event seemed superfluous in the context; and his unsubstantiated claims and statistics were not questioned. The white racist act may very well have been unrelated to the chauffeurs' union. Leffler's agitation over union power suggests his bias and perhaps clouded memory. Finally, E. A. Roberts mentioned that another tourist party had inquired whether they could bring their "colored chauffeur to Miami" and was advised by a local real-estate man that they could. The entire discussion did not allude to the 1917 compromise even when, from at least one report in late November of that year, they had alerted tourists inquiring about the use of personal Black chauffeurs in the city. Were no more letters sent in 1918 or 1919? Was Miami's new 1917 policy successfully disseminated but now was endangered by a raving mob no longer able to abide by the compromise?[53]

The next day (November 6) the *Metropolis* published three more items. The first, an article that included the CC's resolution condemning the chauffeurs' union's action, urged city authorities to "prosecute anyone intimidating a chauffeur, white or colored." Affidavits filed by the journalist attesting to the accuracy of the report followed the resolution. In it, the West Palm Beach journalist who had first reported the case admitted he had inferred that the chauffeurs' union was involved in the incident. That point was buried in the story. The newspaper's presentation offered an air of procedural formality that bordered on the dramatic. The reporter, Howard Sharp, also interviewed the tourist family who repeated the story while also correcting that they did not know the identity of the white chauffeurs who accosted their driver. One letter appearing in the *Metropolis* editorial page, the second news item, vouched for the veracity of the Tennessee family. That letter offered further hearsay "that a few days previous a lady from New York found her chauffeur beaten into insensibility." The fourth and final news item was a report of another tourist family forced to leave the city. No details were provided except that the family's plans to invest heavily in Miami would likely change because of the white chauffeur policy. Mr. Calloway, the family's head and a Confederate veteran, "stated emphatically that in leaving Miami" he did "not surrender his conception of the right to employ his own servants."[54]

This barrage led to swift action from Mayor W. P. Smith, who promised to maintain "law and order." After the recent reports, the Chamber of Commerce's advertising-boosting investment needed protection from lawless behavior, for, from their perspective, such incidents clearly undermined the effort to lure investors. Smith, determined to offer such protection, announced his bona fides that he was not a politician nor was he a partisan for either union or nonunion workers. His explicit racism and apparent open-mindedness confirmed his authenticity. The newspaper quoted Smith as saying, "if a man comes to Miami with a Chinaman whose ears are wrongside on, he is going to be treated fairly. I am no 'nigger lover,' was born in Georgia, have no chauffeur myself, but if a man comes down here I am going to see that he gets square treatment."[55] The chauffeurs' union argument that its members were "peaceful, respectable citizens in times of peace and also in times of commercial war" fell on deaf ears. The tide of public opinion, as indicated by the CC's and the mayor's actions, had apparently turned against the union members. They were unable to garner much sympathy and seemed opportunistic targets during the heated fall labor trouble. A *Metropolis* editorial heartedly approved the apparent end, once again, of the "negro chauffeur" intimidation problem. The newspaper noted that, as "a descendent of the Old South," Smith merely used the phrase "nigger-lover" to indicate beyond a shadow of doubt that he was no "social equality" "scoundrel." Smith's commitment in assuring a "square deal" meant defending racial hierarchy and disciplining organized labor to accept its mandates.[56]

The speed of the reaction suggests the staged nature of the outrage, an effort to delegitimize unions and help justify the use of police action against organized labor. Apparently, the chauffeurs' union was correct when they assessed that they would be depicted as "unprincipled, coldblooded, heartless rogues [willing] to resort to any mean or ruthless tactic in order to gain a point." Threats of labor strikes by Miami's Central Labor Union loomed large that fall. The struggle, however, resided within the building trades sector and not in other arenas. Motivation certainly existed to pressure local officials to use police power to end worker protest, and that project entailed building a case. Whether chauffeurs sought to expand the fight to include a revision of the 1917 compromise seems unlikely. It would have indeed represented a bad strategic move. The chauffeurs did claim in their statement that they "knew nothing of the affair until we saw it in your paper." In light of all the circumstantial evidence offered here, it appears they very well may have been telling the truth. If so, perhaps they were correct to assert that "it is only our enemies that see us in the false light."[57]

Conclusion

The *Metropolis*'s support of the Black community and the white community's concession to them in the 1917 segregation policy is indicative of what was perceived as progress in race relations at the time. The color line had been redrawn to meet the needs of both the Black community and the white business leadership. In the process, community leaders, both Black and white, pointed to the resolution of the chauffeur conflict as evidence that Miami's drive for economic prosperity and growth was secured in the spirit of compromise. Miami's white leaders, ever cognizant of the prevailing sentiments of their racial and economic class, were acutely aware of the benefits of making the city's Black community content—namely ensuring peace and harmony and maintaining the racial status quo. Those concerns outweighed demands by white, working-class chauffeurs to grant them a monopoly over driving in the city.

Yet the white chauffeurs' union objective in controlling driving was larger than the apparent low fruit of preventing white tourists or residents from hiring private Black drivers. Their November 1917 concession revealed their strategy. The question of controlling the urban spaces where taxicab or private car solicitation could occur was not addressed by Mayor Smith's law-and order-stance. The Chamber of Commerce made no recommendation, nor did Smith suggest he would ensure Black drivers a place in the hacking stations in the white segregated areas. Segregation of white businesses, apparently, would not be challenged. The concession to Black demands and protecting Black men's right to drive, for either personal use or economic gain, represented only incremental change. The lines of segregation remained sharp, even if somewhat redrawn.

The socially condescending and racist view that Blacks belonged in service occupations thus enabled Blacks to enter chauffeuring despite continuous violent threats from white drivers.[58] Black worker insistence, as evidenced in their actions, combined with the real economic threat that if Black chauffeurs were not allowed to drive, white tourists would stop coming to Miami. But the debate was not one-sided. Black leaders, including businessmen, professionals, and Protestant pastors, took advantage of the opportunity to insist on racial uplift and the unreasonableness of the Jim Crow rule that some were advocating. This in no way should devalue working-class Black agency. Indeed, it is in the opportunities offered within this oppressive social system for economic improvement that one may discover hidden transcripts of resistance as well as open attempts by Black Miamians to fight for their dignity through economic self-improvement.[59]

These battles were also far from over. Blacks for a short period took advantage of the new right to drive around town to go to the beach but soon faced a concerted quasi-legal barrier to the sea. The short victory on this front did not mean an end to the push to expand other basic rights, especially those pertaining to economic survival. Thanks in no small part to continual efforts by Miami's Black community between 1917 and 1923, the city's curfew was slowly extended from six to nine in the evening. While the presence of any curfew at all in this thriving tourist metropolis still surprised some northern visitors, as in much of the South, Miami leaders continued to insist that having clear boundaries offered a better solution to racial conflict than the violence that defined mob rule.[60] Black residents also continued to mount challenges to attempts to control their economic and physical mobility in other ways. By the early 1930s, African Americans controlled fourteen bus, transfer, express, and taxicab companies in Miami. By 1936, the number of Black jitneys had jumped to twenty-five. The number of Black-owned and Black-operated taxicabs grew apace. And while whites likely continued to periodically challenge the right of Black men to be able to drive, Miami's Black community continued to fight to preserve this basic economic and social right.[61] For all these reasons, the chauffeur debates proved a pivotal chapter in Miami's civil-rights and labor history, foreshadowing continual controversy about taxicabs and buses, and ultimately the attempts to desegregate public transportation itself.[62]

CHAPTER 3

Fighting the Open Shop

In the midst of Miami's biggest labor conflict as of September 1919, a curious and fascinating request was made by the newly founded business organization, the Greater Miami Association (GMA)—an alliance ironically founded on Labor Day consisting of building contractors, wholesale dealers, architects, lumber-yard companies, bankers, real-estate people, and automobile dealers, essentially the heart and soul of Miami's business class. In the conference they had with organized labor's Building Trades Council (BTC), the GMA requested that the white unions eliminate "negro unions from the labor situation in Miami" as one of their six demands. The white unions, as an interesting note, responded that they had no authority over Black unions because the International Hod-Carriers, Building, and Common Laborers' Union, Local 402, was affiliated with the AFL and therefore was a legitimate and sovereign labor union. Indeed, on several jobs where workers walked off, Black hod carriers walked off alongside white skilled mechanics. Later, when the Central Labor Union (CLU) threatened a general strike in October and November, the white unions sought the solidarity of these Black laborers again. The CLU articulated here the idea, which Miami's delegates to the 1920 State Federation of Labor convention would later assert, that "industrial security" was desired by all workers.[1]

The employers' specific request for "the elimination of negro unions" revealed their concerns about the cost and the ideological limits of the employers' calls for "equal rights to all," a National Association of Manufacturers (NAM) rallying phrase for the open shop. With labor troubles threatening Miami's $2 million building boom (more than $29 million in 2019 dollars), the GMA argued in early September against closed shops,[2] though they avoided using the term "open shop," at first opting instead for the more neutral sounding "equal rights to all." The short transition in phraseology ("open shop" would be embraced by business by the end of October) suggested their deeper strategy. The *Miami Metropolis* did not hesitate to use "open shop" in identifying the GMA's goal, soon correcting themselves when the GMA asked them to. Marcus Milam, of Railey-Milam Hardware and spokesperson for the GMA, preferred to avoid the term's divisive meaning since it was "contrary to the impression" they desired to give to the people of Miami. Indeed, "equal rights to all" subsumed class conflict and spun out tapestries of class harmony. Class struggle merely represented impediments to economic growth and violations of rights (specifically, the employers' right to employ whomever they pleased). Such rights language built on Teddy Roosevelt's Square Deal realism. Milam's open admission revealed how the GMA, like the NAM, sought to shape public opinion in patriotic terms linking "a right to a living" to perhaps the most important of all American myths, the idea of equal opportunity for happiness.

Yet the NAM's vision entailed undermining worker power. Their interest in gaining white worker support in repressing the hod carriers' union revealed their true intent. Equal rights for them did not include the right to unionize. Rather, they hoped to divide workers between union and nonunion and, in the laborers' case, gain white skilled worker support to efficiently disable their Black brothers from the benefits of organizing and acting collectively. The *Miami Metropolis*'s interpretive instinct built on its observation of the city's labor turbulence since at least the start of World War I. The GMA sought to discipline workers and organized labor and also signal to potential investors that Miami was open for business. They remained anxious over their ability to overcome labor-union control of the labor market, an anxiety brewing since the start of the war.[3]

This chapter adds a new dimension to our understanding of Miami's early-twentieth-century history by exploring union resistance to the open shop. The growth of the city depended on the construction of buildings and other structures, and unions capitalized on the vital role skilled workers play in construction. A pragmatic understanding about the nature of power underlay the approach of craftworkers—sometimes labeled with the negative moniker "aristocracy of labor." While craftworkers were often narrow in their approach for power over the labor market, the precarity of their economic status and the power advantages of their employers (increasingly more precarious through their own collective organizing efforts) served as major obstacles in allowing greater worker solidarity. Miami's fast growth, combined with effective union organizing, established the city's unions as uneasy partners in the New South city-building project.[4]

Business and organized labor divided not just in their conceptions of power in the workplace. A line had been drawn in the sand over the deeper struggle between individualism and communalism. Both employer and employee had stakes in individualism and communalism, for different reasons but for the same general goal: each wanted to attain social harmony and abandon the precarious state of conflict and economic insecurity. Employers wanted their businesses to run smoothly, efficiently, and at the lowest possible cost. The formula of harmony often could be reduced to the absence of conflict irrespective of the nature of the work process or the distribution of wealth within the business. Too often the concerns and grievances of the employees became relevant, from the perspective of the employer, only if they became detrimental to the goals of the business. Firing was the easiest solution, that is, if other workers stood in line to replace the outgoing employee. More systemic problems needed more effective resolution, whether in labor shortage conditions or if the employer failed to convince or coerce at least some workers to take the job. The more skills the workers possessed, the more power they usually had in the workplace, especially when few workers with their skills were available. Unions, such as those in the building trades, attempted to maintain markets in which labor was in short supply in order to maintain a high value for their labor and thus lessen their own commodification. Restricting the labor supply meant establishing a more stable labor market, controlling the pace of work, and yielding living wages. Their primary concern was to create a moral economy. The more capital reduced workers to commodities, the greater the disharmony. Hence, workers at the lowest point of the political-economic totem pole felt the greatest social disharmony, and those at the top felt the greatest harmony.

Unions developed their argument of moral economy within the terms of capitalist America. Unionism helped create a sense of community among workers, offering them a better bargaining position with Miami's employers. Historians of southern labor have made great strides in studying agricultural labor, domestic workers, and manufacturing industries such as tobacco, textiles, mining, shipping, and railroads at various moments and places in the South. The conclusion, nonetheless, remains that unions in the South were relatively weak. The collusion between state and business to suppress unionization efforts—as well as division among workers resulting from race, gender, and disputes over unionization—helps explain the inability of unions to make lasting inroads into the South. Despite such obstacles, Miami's open-shop battles in World War I and after demonstrates how unionists succeeded in framing work in moral terms despite the continual employer efforts to discipline them and control the labor market.[5]

Framing the Historical Context

The effort to divide workers through a patriotic framing, as employers would do during the war, demonstrated class-harmony discourse in action. Employers attempted to win over the public and confuse workers through appeals to their individual self-interest in its crassest manifestation. Racism's contorted logic and consistent dissonance allowed for a clear double contradiction: employers were not desiring equal rights for all (especially if it meant promoting unionization) nor were white workers supporting a robust Black unionization effort or at least direct competition in the skilled trades or in lowering the value of unionized work. The threat to union control of the local labor market, however, did create an opportunistic and synergistic moment. On at least two occasions before 1919, Black carpenters sought to unionize and gain support from the Local 993 (the white carpenters' union), once in 1904 and again in 1914, but were rejected in both instances. Despite this record, Black carpenters remained persistent in their efforts to gain sanction from their white union brothers, again seeking approval multiple times for a Black union local in 1919 and early 1920. In one instance, the white union recording secretary was ordered to throw the "negro carpenters" request into a wastebasket where it apparently belonged.[6] This labor action excluded Black skilled workers from jobs in the white sections of the city. This rule in effect prevented the sharing of economic prosperity, for the largest economic investments occurred in white areas. It was not merely a function of racism that explains the exclusion. Perhaps as significant, the protectionism reflected deeper economic anxieties stemming from irregular work, high cost-of-living realities, and employers' skepticism in their quest for greater control of the labor market.

Established in March 1902, Local 993 enabled carpenters to bargain for higher wages and fight for shorter work hours or at least for a consistent work schedule. Throughout the late 1910s and 1920s, Miami carpenters earned wages that compared well with those in other cities in Florida and in the country. The union mandated double-time pay for overtime (not time-and-a-half) through at least 1931, revealing a recognition of the special conditions of labor in a hot, humid environment, thereby furthering protecting workers from employer abuses and demonstrating their power in the labor market. Miami carpenters also enjoyed an eight-hour day, forty-four-hour workweek (half-day Saturdays), which seems to have been the national standard, but the double-time standard for overtime seems exceptional to Miami's conditions. The push for higher wages in the construction sector, of course, depended on market conditions—that is, the amount of construction underway, the availability and cost of building materials, and the supply of workers.[7]

Significant unionization in the building industry, a dominant sector in the local economy, suggests Miami enjoyed a strong union culture. Craft unions perhaps benefited from their long history of successful organizing. Skilled construction trades had organized national unions affiliated with the American Federation of Labor (AFL) in the late nineteenth century, and locals of these unions formed early in Miami's history. By 1915, cement workers, bricklayers, stonemasons, tile setters, lathers, roofers, and plasterers, electricians, plumbers, operating engineers, and sheet-metal workers had established union locals in Miami. The carpenters of south Florida organized the East Coast District Council in January 1914, expanding the carpenters' union's influence over the area from Fort Lauderdale to Homestead. After 1920, with the increase in building construction amid the great land boom, carpenters and painters formed multiple locals.[8] Though acquiring firm numbers is difficult because of Miami's constantly changing population and gaps in the archive, combining the 1920 census figures with union records suggests that 90 percent (892 of 993) of the city's carpenters were unionized in 1920.[9] Other AFL craft unions for musicians, barbers, printers, railroad workers, streetcar conductors and motormen, and butchers added to Miami's union environment.

Despite the history of exclusion, newspaper accounts indicate Black common laborer unionists offered their support to white building-trade unions in the late summer and fall of 1919. They engaged in a sympathy strike regardless of the ceilings in the skill trades. The Black carpenters' efforts to once again gain access to skilled jobs, while ultimately rebuffed, suggest they acted to take advantage of the labor trouble. It may very well have been an organized, collaborative strategy between Black laborers and carpenters to finally get a firmer footing in the biggest industry in Miami. Or it merely reflected the fluidity among Black workers having to take any job available despite their skill level. The laborers' union's actions demonstrated their keen insight that a sympathy strike represented a strategic alliance that could maximize their power and those of others in their community. In May 1919, Miami Black businessmen and Negro Uplift Association committee member Kelsey Pharr highlighted how "Miami is the last place for members of our race in the state" to find adequate work. In an editorial two weeks later, the Negro Uplift Association (Pharr and four other signatories) argued for "the right to labor as free men," which includes the opportunity to "work in whatever places [Black worker] abilities will sustain them and for whatever persons who may choose to employ them, *regardless of the part of the city in which those persons may live*" (italics added). And while skilled Black workers failed to persuade white unionists to include them in the economic growth in the white sections of the city beyond the job of hod carrier (common laborer) and the contested arena of chauffeuring, the strike reveals a deliberate approach to improving the laboring opportunities and to righting "a very great injury" suffered by them. The attempts at racial solidarity had a minimum effect. The laborers soon pushed for higher wages, which motivated Black carpenters to make inroads into the white labor monopoly. That the white-led Building Trades Council and CLU would appeal to the Black laborers' union later in the fall reveals that a small degree of class solidarity, however flawed, was possible, at least in the context of the city's biggest labor crisis to that date.[10]

The most critical power dynamic of this episode, however, was not the issue of racism but rather how Miami's business elite sought to undermine labor union power. This effort seems to have formally begun in April 1917, just about at the start of US entry into World War I when local building contractors and some building-trade master craftsmen (plasterers, carpenters, plumbers, etc.) contractors organized the Master Builders' and Contractors' Association (MBCA). Soon in the summer of 1917 and in subsequent years, the Association would lock into a continuing struggle with labor over rationalizing and controlling the construction sector. The local building contractors wanted to disrupt prevailing labor market norms, ones rooted in moral economic terms, for a system that gave them sole power over hiring decisions.[11]

The historical context of this struggle occurred in Jim Crow conditions and not simply because of the racism of white workers. Racism was a shared sentiment among most whites of all classes and it entailed at least two forms of exclusion. The first was social and cultural separation that was rooted in distorted views of African Americans, yet that opened up occasional spaces of interaction such as in providing labor (servile service, sweated labor, etc.) or market exchange (housing, goods, etc.). The second involved employer efforts to lower labor costs through cutthroat competition and other cost-related measures (avoiding overtime and costs incurred by workers such as transportation or irregular employment).

A long-standing thread in labor historiography offers a problematic framing of civil rights by charging labor unions as the culprits in preventing minorities from attaining equal opportunity. Despite its progressive intent, we should be wary of framing white working-class racism as the driving cause of inequality and inequity. Such a cultural understanding would distort the nature of political economy and the self-interest of employers who wanted, above all, to maintain a labor hierarchy in the production process. It also tends to obscure the precarity endured by many in the working class.[12]

Too often the liberal political commitment to equal opportunity necessitates maintaining the fiction that economic mobility is a process of ladder climbing. Those who block workers' progress up the ladder are seen as merely self-interested parties engaging in the perpetuation of economic inequalities for no reason other than racial hatred and obsession to protect their white-skin privilege. Thus sullied, the market is deemed less free and hence unable to ensure equal opportunity and economic security. What remains is the perspective that markets are natural arenas for equity. The unchallenged assumption is that profit, working conditions, and the overall security of workers are not inherently contentious issues within capitalism. The economic precarity of individuals is understated, ignored, or—worse—assumed to be a function of poor behavior, inadequate skill, or lack of merit, thereby helping replicate capitalism's logic and class asymmetries. Social justice arguments of the type are an understandable reaction to frustration with injustice as experienced by marginalized groups, yet they reveal a hidden mystification of power as articulated in the workplace and labor market.

The open-shop struggle in Miami in the World War I period and 1920s, and the later political battle over Florida's right-to-work amendment during World War II, demonstrates how workers, white or Black, faced the reality of constant economic vulnerability and economic insecurity. An emphasis on the notion of white privilege too often negates or minimizes the nature of worker vulnerability and how the divisions among workers (white union versus white nonunion, ethnicity versus ethnicity, white versus Black) benefited the employers' bottom line.[13] Economic success for employers increasingly was driven by the reduction of labor to a commodity, a capital input, which gave little regard to workers' well-being in the workplace or as citizens in the republic. Lest we forget, it was workers and their unions fighting living-wage and working-conditions struggles throughout the country and in Miami that made economic security a moral choice. Workers assured economic growth by, in real and metaphorical senses, sacrificing their bodies through the sweat of their labor. The sacrifice entailed, of course, the time to travel to work, the actual laboring, and then a period for mental and physical recovery from labor. Workers, in effect, took on many bodily and emotional costs (much of which is too often ignored) while enjoying little if any financial security. The desire for labor-market protection—access to regular work, decent working conditions and wages, defense against employer power excesses—articulated a deeply moral understanding of economics that challenged capitalism's tendency to treat workers as commodities.[14]

National labor leaders on occasion spoke grandly, though perhaps indirectly, about the moral economic motivation behind union organizing. Despite a long record of business and government collusion against workers' organization, national union leaders' most hopeful idealism envisioned governmental recognition of labor protection. Longtime AFL president Samuel Gompers celebrated as "epochal" the 1914 Clayton Act's declaration that "labor is not a commodity or article of commerce." It marked "the end of the old period where workers were under the shadow of slavery." Only through organization, Gompers argued, could workers attain "industrial freedom," meaning they would not be compelled to accept whatever an employer "chooses to offer," particularly when forced by "immediate necessity" to accept "terms that are unfair." Andrew Furuseth of the International Seamen's Union would criticize the 1919 labor provisions of the Treaty of Versailles for weakening this labor-as-commodity language, even as this founding document of the International Labor Organization (ILO) sought to provide international standards for labor protection. One key provision stated that "labour should not be regarded *merely* as a commodity or article of commerce," which, Furuseth emphasized, changed "an absolute negative to an equally absolute positive." He ridiculed such a play on language by offering an illustration of the logic: "Somebody says Andrew Furuseth is a scab; somebody else does not like that and proposes a resolution that he is not a scab; somebody amends it to read that he is not 'merely' a scab; and that is what you get." It was not until 1944, when the ILO revised its constitution in the Declaration of Philadelphia, that the word *merely* was dropped.[15] Union worker resistance to the open shop and later the right-to-work amendment represented a commitment to challenging employer power and revealed a strategy to safeguard a moral economy. Such resistance persistently faced near insurmountable odds against the power of business, the biases of the state, and the workers' lack of wealth and their economic dependency on employers.

The MBCA, organized sometime in April 1917, sought to control the building industry, making it more predictable and cost-effective, thereby further rationalizing it. The MBCA drove to unify contractors under its aegis of collective business power in opposition to organized labor. Such collaboration would counter labor unions' power in the labor market, though a hope existed that such worker entities as the BTC, with which most of the building trades maintained affiliation, would help discipline the workforce to a more bureaucratic and organized form of labor standards. What the role of the individual craft labor unions would be in such a process was unclear except that the MBCA wanted more predictable wage commitments and the lowest acceptable rates. At the very least, contractors viewed unions as organizations that would effectively control workers in an ordered labor market. Organized labor's greatest benefit, in the employers' most positive understanding, was in helping to provide a steady and dependable workforce. Capital's critical reservation was that organized labor submit to rules of when to ask for wage increases, limit the amount of these raises, minimize work rules, submit to employer efficiency expectations, and under no circumstances engage in sympathy strikes or demand that union-made materials be used on job sites (which would further bind greater worker solidarity across the state, region, and nation). The demand to operate as an open shop—that is, with employer freedom to hire whomever they pleased regardless of union affiliation—would become an added expectation in some worksites and under some contractors and was likely a consistent employer utopic vision of having the ability to pluck from the tree of labor whenever they desired. Successful unionization impeded that or raised standards high enough to positively affect open-shop worksites. Class divisions, in any case, emerged early on in spring and summer 1917 between skilled worker unionists and a small number of unionists who had become contractors and had decided to join the MBCA. The carpenters requested that a union member listed in the minutes as "Brother Martin" "retire" from Local 993 because he had decided to join the MBCA in early May and, later in August, amid a pending building-trades strike, the union moved "that all members affiliated with the Master Builders' Association be dropped from membership."[16]

The contractors' move to organize reflected a reaction to labor's power and the martial spirit of the times. The MBCA sought to impose greater discipline on the laboring classes. While Miami had been regionally recognized as a closed-shop town (at least among skilled construction workers and other craftsmen such as typographical workers, musicians, and butchers), the expanding war economy, growing worker unionization, and an accommodating national government likely lent to the perception that action was needed. Within the logic of the bottom line, any effort to control cost made economic sense to the contractors, but it did run up against vocal and organized opposition. The MBCA's purpose was to create local construction standards and limit when unionists could demand pay increases. The move was interpreted by unionists as too inflexible and a usurpation of power, one made more ominous with the rising cost of living, World War I realities, and the threat of lowering labor standards with greater labor competition and arbitrary or unfair forms of labor discipline. The ability to control the labor market was at the heart of what justified labor unions, which meant at least two things: (1) the right to control the supply of the labor pool to ensure a competency for all and undermine the employers' ability to use labor competition to weaken workers' negotiating power, and (2) the right to make the case for a living wage and sound working conditions especially if the case demanded immediate action to accommodate changes in the market and living conditions.[17]

The High Cost of Living and Home Labor

Entering the summer of 1917, local newspapers reported the prospects of an intense building season and the need for more skilled and unskilled workers to meet its labor demands—essentially, a regular theme through at least the 1926 Great Miami Hurricane. The anticipated construction boom paralleled a heightened concern for the rising cost of living. The *Miami Metropolis* began extensive coverage on Miami's high cost of living as early as March 1917. It strongly encouraged consumer awareness about local speculators and price gouging. While some local grocers protested the implication that they hiked prices by withdrawing their advertisements from the newspaper, many Miamians responded to the *Metropolis*'s informative and muckraking efforts with ongoing rigor. Special home-economics courses were being taught at the Woman's Club and local high schools on various strategies to lower the cost of living. Various groups such as the Union Label League were getting together to discuss cost-cutting strategies. A buyers association formed to help consumers navigate cost-of-living issues. And discussion started in early May 1917 to form a housewives' league as a standing committee within the Woman's Club dedicated to dealing with the high cost of living.[18] The housewives' league does not seem to have ever successfully formed, which may have had something to do with (as the newspaper identified her) Mrs. George Cook's favorable report on forming a cooperative store to lower the cost of foodstuffs.

As an active member of the Woman's Club and heading its committee exploring the possibility of organizing a housewives' league, Amy Cook had attended a meeting of the Housewives' League of the Socialists, where she learned of the cooperative store they had been planning for the previous three months and had finally just started. It was an idea that the three railroad unions (engineers, trainmen, and conductors) were also experimenting with. As the wife of a realtor, Amy Cook likely committed a social faux pas when she was quoted in the *Metropolis* as saying "I was much impressed by the earnestness of thought and study given to the situation by the [Socialist] leaders. The meeting was most instructive in every way to me."[19] As far as I can tell, Cook's cooperative store idea never came to fruition; I have also been unable to locate any evidence of how or how long the socialist's housewives' league operated. The cooperative store idea, however, remained influential in the Woman's Club battle against the high cost of living. It appears that the cooperative store discussion was the genesis of the weekly City Curb Market that formed a year later and would become a regular Miami institution. Organized by the Woman's Club, the market sought to knock out the retail store as intermediary and thus reduce consumer prices, and protect local farmers from out-of-county competition as well. These efforts reflected an ongoing informal moral economic sentiment of buy-at-home initiatives that often translated among working-class residents into what I call home-labor protectionism. Such initiatives sought to prioritize the livelihood needs of local economic interests, particularly workers but also business owners, over outside competition. One interesting occurrence was that Amy Cook rose to the World War I position of county food administrator just prior to the Curb Market's launching, being recognized for her "splendid theories of conservation" and for leading "several woman's club movements" in the struggle to reduce the high cost of living. Ongoing discussions about the high cost of living would persist through 1919. As for the socialist cooperative store, not much is known of its history.[20] The upbeat prospects of a robust building-construction outlook, and thus the appearance of a favorable labor market for skilled workers, paired with the somber realities of rising prices and World War I, framed the historical context for the subsequent labor struggles.

Critical here was the contested terrain of buy-at-home rhetoric. The *Miami Herald* led a buy-at-home movement (as an advertising campaign) between April and early June 1917 to promote local merchants that equated patronage of local businesses with community and hometown loyalty. The "trade at home" movement, as the *Herald* called it, featured one full-page advertisement per week (published each Monday) for ten consecutive weeks. The advertisements pitched a local buying patriotism, listing forty-nine merchants to patronize, yet they were mostly silent on the cost-of-living concerns being raised by the *Metropolis*. Only one advertisement (April 9) commented indirectly on consumers' cost concerns, highlighting how local merchants had "integrity and [were engaging in] methods of honest merchandising"—so much so that they were "whittling down profits." Only a "few merchants" were asking customers to take on the costs but, in the end, the advertisement informed readers to "carpe diem" (enjoy the present day). Throughout the campaign, the *Herald* carried advertisements of the forty-nine businesses and published a few brief stories and editorials on the "trade at home" movement. The forty-nine included ice-cream parlors, pharmacies, groceries, and butcher shops; furniture, hardware, paint, and musical-instrument stores; jewelry, clothing, shoe, and department and dry-goods stores; and banks and gas and electric companies. The list was a who's who of Miami pioneer establishments, including Sewell Brothers clothing store, W. M. Burdine & Sons department store, E. B. Douglas Department Store, the Bank of Bay Biscayne, and Railey-Milam Hardware Company. The weekly full-page advertisements varied little and argued that realizing Miami's economic health and growth potential necessitated patronizing local businesses. The first advertisement stressed that if "the profit on merchandise bought by our citizens from stores in other cities" or "mail order houses" during the last ten years had been spent "at home," the additional resources would have circulated back to local investment. It would have allowed the construction of "a mammoth factory or mill employing 2,000 men at high wages." The message was a powerfully moral and practical one. The most "progressive and reliable merchants" were making their plea to Miami's citizen-consumers to support the local economy and did so by linking that request with the positive outlook that such consumption would translate to the expansion of employment opportunities. The resulting economic growth would help boost the attractiveness of Miami as a city in which to live. This prosperity would help everybody.[21]

The ideal of establishing steady employment and a functional local economy carried obvious utility. Consistent with Miami boosterism (often framed as the "Magic City" or "Miami spirit"), workers logically embraced the arguments for economic growth, yet with an important codicil: the need to protect workers' standard of living through steady employment, fair wages, and humane working conditions. And so, what did workers think of this buy-at-home campaign? As usual, not much of a record is extant. A letter to the *Herald*, however, from J. T. Blackman, the president of Carpenters' Local 993 and BTC, represented an immediate and direct response to the campaign from at least one well-connected worker. As an engaged and active citizen, who would later be elected to Miami's city council, serve as its president, and even briefly become acting mayor, Blackman was strategically positioned to understand workers' needs and concerns. Entitling his letter "A Plea for Local Labor," he agreed with the gist of the merchants' argument for economic growth through local purchasing. He simply took issue with the duplicity and convenience of focusing only on consumption and the empty "slogan of getting together" (that is, a conservative class harmony)—a theme, he wrote, that "we are always reading in our Miami newspapers." "Let us at least be consistent along all lines," Blackman wrote, and stop "the very bad practice of importing so-called 'skilled labor' to do the important work of our city." Blackman criticized how Miami's "mechanical class" had been passed over too often for outside contractors and (apparently nonunion) workers to complete various construction jobs such as dredging, bridge, street, and sewer work. "Give the important skilled labor to our own household, and thus keep all the money, possible, right here at home, and then the merchants will have no cause to grumble, for the mechanics will then . . . spend among them what they have earned." Once this was done, Blackman argued, "then we will have an ideal city," where citizens and artisans can take care "of every situation that may arise." His was an argument for moral economy, insisting on a radical conception of class harmony and a demanding localism. It entailed an active effort to foster competency and the economic improvement of local workers. Speaking on behalf of Miami's working class, Blackman asserted that, while they "heartily sympathize with the merchants and business men," workers' own economic interests were a critical part of the city's future that was not being fully considered in the buy-at-home campaign. Merchants, and the public more generally, needed to be reminded that home labor also needed to be protected.[22]

Male and female retail clerks followed this drive for moral economy by announcing their intent to organize and hopes to attain better working conditions, including a "living wage for women clerks." The Retail Clerk's Protective Association succeeded in organizing Local 779, though its proposed agreement with city stores was hardly radical nor ever accepted. Even W. M. Burdine & Sons, a store that later joined the open-shop Greater Miami Employers' Association (GMEA) in 1920, was intrigued enough to invite union representatives to speak to his workers. It appears that the genesis of Burdine's company union, the Burdine's Employees Protective Association, may have originated at this moment. Two years later, the company employee magazine, the *Enthusiast*, would appear. The New York department store, another future open-shop advocate, offered to pay the initiation fees for eighteen of its employees. They likely desired a dependable workforce and loyal customers who shopped at a union shop while hoping to control the labor organization. Succeeding in getting a draft of their proposed agreement published in the *Miami Metropolis*, the men of the local made no specific wage demands for themselves, but they insisted on improving the conditions for women. The retail clerks' proposed weekly minimum wage of $8 for women would have been a significant improvement over the $3 to $5 that stores were paying. The union demanded that Sundays, July 4, Labor Day, Thanksgiving, and Christmas be holidays, and that closing time be 6:00 p.m. (except for 10:00 p.m. on Saturdays), with an exception for the six nights prior to Christmas, when 10:00 p.m. would be the rule. They also attempted to set limits on which customers they would attend after closing time: only those who had entered prior to closing, suggesting that employees were regularly forced to extend their work hours for last-minute customers. The proposed agreement demonstrated deference to employers insisting that workers would be obligated to be punctual and that employees must "use every effort to aid in the building up the business of employers." The union seemed prepared to trade fairness for worker discipline, insisting on a union shop (requiring employees to join the union within thirty days), submitting to mandatory arbitration, and a near prohibition on striking. Not much else is known of the union's history, but it was able to sign up about one hundred and seventy-five members by September 1917. Their inability to get employers to sign a contract, despite their success in attracting worker interest, indicated the difficulty workers faced in organizing independent unions in the sector. Only in the early 1930s did hotel and restaurant workers start to organize in those fields.[23]

As a counterpoint to the weaker position of retail service workers, J. T. Blackman's insistence on protecting home labor reflected the raison d'être of building-trade unions. As I have emphasized in my article "Miami's Hidden Labor History," not only did the carpenters and other trade unions in Miami seek to control labor markets, they also worked to create a sense of community. They did so through pressing fair consumerism, union label efforts, providing death benefits for members, and organizing charity efforts and social events like dances, often with the help of active lady auxiliaries. They helped organize and direct Labor Day parades and participate in other Miami events to boost the city's economic potential. In one 1915 boosting parade, Local 993 of the carpenters won first prize for "best Industrial prize float for organized labor." Their float demonstrated their demands for high living standards in support of family life. Carpenters worked on a little house atop the float "while Mr. and Mrs. C. C. Maxwell stood on the little porch with their suitcases in the front ready to move in the moment the carpenters were through." The union existed, the demonstration argued, as an organization working on behalf of workers concerned with moral economy as articulated through the symbol of family life—that is, carpenters contributed to the well-being of society by doing the essential task of building homes for families. Despite these efforts, workers, skilled and unskilled, remained vulnerable, particularly in a climate of continuous competition and population movement.[24]

While not analyzed closely in this book, a critical structural dynamic defining US working-class history—one often difficult to trace and study—was how workers had to travel within states, regions, and even across the country to find work. One of the most crucial purposes of labor unions was to minimize the harm such peripatetic patterns could present and the resistance that business assembled against unionization. The history of agricultural workers stands out as a powerful example. As many historians have demonstrated, the impoverished and deeply precarious nature of farmworker life was often a function of not being rooted in specific communities. Farm owners often devalued the skill required in harvesting and emphasized harvesters' lack of rootedness (hence, the preference for migrant laborers).[25] The construction-trade unions sought to avoid a similar fate in at least three ways. One, they emphasized their unique craft skills; the safety demands of urban structures helped support that sort of argument. The craft apprenticeship standards reflected this understanding. The eventual licensing and skills certification of each craft bolstered and validated the educational value of the craft. Two, solidarity through unionization ensured the maintenance of pay and working-condition standards. This required consistent vigilance and worker action when confronted with employer recalcitrance or simply collective action to ensure individual benefit. Or, framed in another way, labor unions understood that the market was not a fair or consistent arbiter of acceptable living standards. Organization and solidarity were needed to do so. As dangerous and abhorrent as striking was—sacrificing immediately needed pay and risking job loss—it had tactical and symbolic value expressive of worker intelligence and dignity.

Three, and as noted in the earlier discussion of the carpenters' union, the efforts at labor-market control undermined employer power. Unions served as employment agencies and national networks of labor communities when they published stay-away notices in union publications or corresponded with other locals. The carpenters' records abound in this practice.[26] It is important to note that the correspondence between locals across the country, which often offered current information about local labor markets, is largely lost (as are countless other labor union records). The building of Miami from a small town into a big city was literally the function of amassing enough human power to build and then maintain it as a living community. The dangers of being unemployed and the possibility of being exploited were very real. Construction unions, serving as employment agencies, protected against such outcomes. Consider the example of lathers, a trade related to carpentry but represented by a separate labor organization until 1979, when they affiliated with the carpenters' union. The lathers' occupation entailed mostly nailing the frameworks (wooden laths) for plaster walls and ceilings (for which they were paid by piecework rates), but they also did other types of work around construction sites known as day work or jobbing (such as nailing metal laths and setting up of scaffolding, for which they were paid an hourly rate). Miami Local 345 of the Wood, Wire, and Lathers' International Union placed advertisements in the local newspapers directing contractors and builders to contact them if they needed any lathers through the winter of 1917. In November 1915, they published a stay-away notice in the union's national journal, the *Lather*, warning traveling lathers that few job prospects existed. The upcoming winter tourist season promised the construction of only 'a few small bungalows. According to the notice, job-seeking lathers the previous winter were "picked up" and forced to work on the construction of Dixie Highway. As the story was related in their national journal, the, when they were unable to find employment, these lathers were compelled to fish for provisions and so became targets as apparent unemployed vagrants. "The ever watchful sleuths" (i.e., local police or company private detectives) put a stop to this apparently undisciplined behavior of living off the land and forced them to work on the Dixie Highway project. Such passing anecdotes were reminders of worker precarity regardless of the level of craft skill one possessed and particularly in the context of the construction sector's ebbs and flows. It also explains the underlying logic of the *Lather*'s subheading, echoing the Knights of Labor motto: "the injury to one is the concern of all."[27]

Roots of the Open Shop

Several skilled construction workers declared their intent to demand higher wages in the summer of 1917, collective action that was independent of the contractors' organizing efforts. It appears that workers more generally were responding to the high cost-of-living concerns and the regular periods of extended unemployment. Carpenters Local 993 took the lead, announcing in January that they "would demand an increase of 12½¢ or $5.00 per 8 hours" to begin on May 1, a move soon followed by the Coconut Grove Local 1149 in March. The start date of the increase seems to have been entirely coincidental with May Day and selected after consultation with contractors in December 1916. J. T. Blackman, in a letter to the *Miami Metropolis* in January, insisted it was to put carpenters on a par with other skilled workers and to deal with rising living costs.[28] Later, on June 23, Local 806 of the painters' union declared that they would be demanding 50¢ more a day, increasing their wages to $5 a day ($5.50 if they furnished their own brushes), which was to go in effect on July 16. As far as the local newspapers indicate, the bricklayers', masons', plasterers', and plumbers' unions did not request similar raises, but they were already making more than carpenters and painters. Plumbers and stonemasons earned $6 a day, brick masons $7, and plasterers $5.50. The MBCA accepted these wage scales, but they resisted the lathers' union as their inaugural initiative to control the labor market.[29]

At some point in the late spring, the lathers' union announced pay rates would rise beginning in July, though the specific date is unclear (either July 1 or July 16). They were seeking an increase for piecework from $3.50 per thousand laths nailed to $4.00 and day work from 62¼¢ an hour to 75¢ an hour or from $5 to $6 for an 8-hour day. The vast majority of lathers' work consisted of piecework. Rough estimates ranged between 80 and 90 percent or more, leading wage discussions to focus entirely on the piecework rate. The best assessments offered by the lathers was that no more than the equivalent of forty days of the year was paid at the day-work rate. The carpenters' union, it is useful to note, mandated in their by-laws an hourly wage to assure a "higher standard of skill" and therefore to protect against speedups and the intrusive control of their craft.[30] The MBCA seems to have chosen to resist the lathers' union because they were, according to newspaper reports of the conflict, seeking to recruit more contractors into their organization. The lathers' union's small membership (around twenty members) likely made them an attractive target, especially since the painters, who had more than two hundred unionists, represented a tougher battle despite their equally objectionable wage demands.[31] It does appear that the Miami union lathers were 100 percent organized and that several of them had left town in search for work during the July–August labor dispute, leaving only about eighteen in the vicinity. They stopped working for the contractors who had refused to pay the new wage scale yet remained at work for the smaller contractors who had accepted it.

The MBCA gained concessions from the lathers' union in mid-August after weeks of disagreements that included a misunderstanding between the BTC and lathers' union. The lathers sought the assistance of the larger BTC as an apparent show of strength against the newly formed MBCA. Unfortunately, the BTC went beyond the lathers' mandate and tried to negotiate a resolution that conceded more than the lathers were willing to give up. The BTC concession was apparently not enough. The MBCA went forward with a two-day general construction work lockout that included all the other skilled trades and that reportedly cost more than $7,000 in lost wages. The MBCA attained a reduction of the piecework rate demand to $3.75 and the day-work rate to $5.50, though they had initially sought to lower the daily wage to $5.25. The building-trade unions voted overwhelmingly to support their brother lathers, forcing the contractors to negotiate and ultimately accept a larger wage increase than they had hoped to concede. The MBCA nonetheless forced the lathers to accept that the new wage scales apply only to new building contracts. The projects that started prior to the agreement would remain at the old rates. Unaffiliated contractors, as noted, had been paying the new rate since the effective date of the initial wage increase.[32] It is unclear whether they continued to pay the scales of the lathers' original demands or converted to the newer wage scale. It was not unusual for some contractors to pay more than the minimum local union rates because of the tight labor market and competition between employers to acquire and keep skilled craft workers. Later, in the 1920s, open-shop employers were forced to pay high wages in order to fend off unionization and make their point they were not antiworker, indirectly proving that labor unions raised working conditions. In any case, Miami avoided a prolonged labor disturbance that had threatened to expand and include the entire construction-trade union movement. A labor battle that had begun in mid-July reached an apparent successful resolution by mid-August.

The lathers' union's struggle against the MBCA offers much insight into the conditions construction workers faced in Miami's political economy, as well as the nature of newspaper bias. It represented an opening salvo in the labor turbulence that would mark the city's landscape for the next several years. If Miami was on the path to become a laborers' paradise slowly expanding to include more workers under the union umbrella (as the retail workers and later hod-carriers organizing efforts suggest), the MBCA and other business interests soon revealed their displeasure in sharing power with the city's worker-citizens. Capitalism required a docile workforce that was individualistic and atomistic. Cost predictability in the construction industry, and for that matter, other economic sectors as well, was the business wish of the day. From the capitalist's perspective, if unions were to be tolerated, they needed to deliver workers, ensure efficient work, prevent work stoppages, and keep demands for wage increases to a minimum. References to the economic and overall well-being of employees were at best annoyances conveniently ignored. Whereas workers in the building trades had relative success in controlling the value of the skill by creating a robust national presence (though facing persistent employer challenges), other workers, such as common laborers or in service trades (hotel, retail, etc.), struggled to do the same. The newspaper coverage of the lathers' labor conflict became the model for the power struggles occurring in the subsequent years. Therefore, it will be useful to dissect this one episode more carefully to uncover the labor union approach, the public-relations tactics of the contractor-employers, and the reporting styles and editorial positions of the *Metropolis*—whose coverage left the most robust historical trail.

Lathers made the case that their demands were just and reasonable because of the high cost of living. Unaffiliated contractors agreed and, of course, the MBCA did not, arguing that such an increase would raise building costs. The MBCA, in its public statement, published on page one of the July 16 *Miami Metropolis*, accused the lathers of not being efficient workers, claiming that, if they were, they would have been earning \$6 a day at the \$3.50 piece rate (per 1,000 lathed), a wage higher, they claimed, than what carpenters were getting

($5 per day). Only the wage scale was provided; the contractors did not break down the productivity rates for the public, preferring to keep the value of the lathers' skill perplexing. Deducing from the piecework rate, one may arrive at the contractors' productivity expectation. The contractors' claim that lathers could earn $6 a day meant their idea of a "competent workman working 8 hours" translated into about 1,714 nailed laths a day, or a little over 214 nailed per hour (more than 3 per minute).[33] The lathers' union humorously disputed these projections in their own statement to the newspaper published the next day on the last page. They refuted the MBCA's conception of a fair or realistic day's workload, scoffing at the contractor's estimating powers. Either it reflected "the makings of a novelist" or it revealed the shady practices of overcharging prospective builders to gain a more favorable contract. They thus countered the contractors' notion of productivity and morality. The lathers' union argued that the most they earned in a week was $21, and that included five eight-hour days and a half-day on Saturday. Lathers' union representative Wilbur Wadsworth would later note that they were earning $22 a week. If we estimate at the higher weekly earning capacity of $22, that would convert to $4 per day or about 1,142 nailed lathes (more than 142 per hour or just over 2 per minute).[34] The lathers' assessment, based on their actual experience, was, in fact, lower than what the carpenters were earning. The contractors' projections thus represented a difference of 572 per day or 72 per hour or 33 percent productivity increase.

How the contractors arrived at their production estimates remained unevaluated by the newspaper. Labor value remained a mystery. Their claim that the lathers were underworking was indeed a laughable proposition in light of the contractors' miraculous work rate per minute and per hour. Lathers argued that they contributed a "relative quota to the growing wealth of Miami by the skill and artistry of our craftsmanship." They lampooned the MBCA's productivity estimates, though they did not seek to explain the nature of their work. The lathers simply noted that the artistry of their craft was a valuable "commodity we bring to the market place to barter for the privilege of living in your midst." The use of the term *barter* was significant because it pointed to a homespun yet concrete attribution of worth that asserted fairness or moral economy. It implicitly reflected a distinct viewpoint from capitalist notions of human capital and value. Perhaps mistakenly, the lathers assumed that the public would understand that such work speeds were not feasible whether because a typical lather was unable to produce such outputs or such speedups endangered worker safety and/or jeopardized the quality of the work. They were handling hammers and nails in south Florida's humid and hot weather. They emphasized instead the moral issue prevailing at the time.

The high cost of living was preventing lathers from "a reasonable accretion of the decent things of life." "Decent things" included "the right to sanitary housing, sufficient food for our families and the possibility of rearing and educating our children." Yet, they claimed, "the modest advance we are asking . . . is still miles behind the acute rise of living." As an illustration of how reasonable their wage demands were ($4 per 1,142 laths), they pointed out that a typical bungalow's cost would increase by only $2.50 (5,000 laths per typical home). The real culprit of spiraling building costs existed on the material supply side, not their wage rates, which of course reflected the critically important labor they contributed to the production process. It is interesting that the lathers' union's published statement was silent on the outrageous headline the *Metropolis* used for the contractors' press release: "Contractors Not Willing to Pay Lathers $8 a Day" (that is, $4 per 1,142 lathed, based on the eight-hour workday). Within the formula of using only the piecework rate, the *Metropolis* headline assumed that lathers would nail 2,000 laths a day (250 an hour, or more than 4 per minute), exceeding even the contractors' own inflated productivity potential. If they had followed the lathers' own actual work rates (1,142 per day), they would have realized that far from $8 daily wage, the new scale would only result in $4.57 daily earnings, or 57¢ more per day than the old wage rate and still less than the carpenter wage.[35] The headline may have been intended to get a reaction from the public or may simply have been a typographical error, for nothing in the contractors' statement suggested a rate of $8 a day. Possibly the lathers' union did offer a response to the headline title but the newspaper did not print it, or it simply has been lost in the historical records. Nonetheless, the placement of the contractors' statement on page one and the relegation of the lathers' response to the last page in the next day's issue, does suggest an inherent bias for the contractors' position despite the newspaper's apparent gesture of fairness in also publishing the workers' press release.

The lathers' union seemed to hit the nail on the head when they charged that the contractors sought "to arouse public sentiment against the justice of their [the lathers'] cause." The contractors' argument about productivity challenged the very notion of unionism, subtly applying square-deal logic that the public welfare would be hurt. They were arguing in effect that workers, unable to earn more through hard or deft work, would raise building costs because of their greed and lack of ability; higher construction costs would deter investors and therefore impede economic development.[36] This double-whammy public-relations tactic targeted both the work ethic of workers and the skill and expertise that unionism was meant to guarantee. These arguments undermined the core justifications of unionism: high-quality work for a fair wage. If lathers or other unionists were holding back their labor while still expecting a living wage, then they were essentially robbing the employer of a good day's work. The darker, unspoken class bias inherent in such a framing was that certain sorts of labor had less value and individuals performing them deserved to get less and thus live worse. The class logic was consistent with a May 22 *Metropolis* article which reported that M. F. Comer, a contractor building a few bridges in the city, refused to pay his "negro labor" $3 a day because they simply were "not worth" it. (They were being paid $2.50.) When these common laborers struck for higher pay, the newspaper reported that Comer "promptly fired the whole bunch" and immediately got busy "breaking in a new set." The objectification and indirect reference to animal training evoked associations with slavery. In the context of free labor and market relations, in the process of seasoning, an unruly laborer was fired instead of physically punished or sold down the river. This contractor clearly was able to take advantage of a labor market predicated on desperate workers forced to accept minimal wages for critically important but devalued work.[37]

The sophistication of the MBCA's attack in their press release was particularly subtle in that the contractors claimed—as they and other business interests would often state publicly throughout the next several decades—that they had "no general complaint of the position of trade unions" and merely expected their cooperation. This was par excellence conservative class harmony. The MBCA simply fought against a wage increase and did so by arguing that workers only had themselves to blame for not earning more. The case being made was lazy at best, but who would notice? It revealed an effort to exploit antiunion tropes and the public's general lack of knowledge about the nature of work being performed. How to attribute a fair value for the necessary task of lathing—the construction step required for plastering—remained unexplored in the *Metropolis*'s coverage of the labor conflict. They cared little to do so as they genuflected to the masters of business and the gods of economic growth, yet it is critical here to highlight that their bias in the handling of the labor conflict was far from clear. Despite the suggestive evidence indicated by the discussion of the piecework rates and productivity or the page on which the stories appeared, the newspaper's class-harmony discursive style easily hid their class prejudice. Their editorials offer a window into their ideology, yet their reporting suggests that a tension existed between the official position of the newspaper and their reporters' efforts in capturing the story.

The *Metropolis*'s coverage made a show of presenting both sides, quoting labor leaders, one even by name. In the newspaper's reporting, we learn much. It was revealed, but denied by the MBCA, that the entire point of their resistance was to recruit more contractors, and evidently several did not care to join. Even the young MBCA experienced dissension within its ranks. Contractor Elmer E. Shaw was removed from the MBCA negotiating committee when other members learned he "was favorable to granting the demands of lathers." The newspaper also reported that "one member of the bosses' association" highlighted that "the general lockout is contemplated as a method of disciplining the lathers." Such explicit articulations of the contractors' motivations and intentions are enormously valuable. Seldom are such open admissions of the dynamics of class power available. Only one report quoted extensively from the lathers' representative, Wilbur Wadsworth. Yet even this one interview yielded a picture of what the workers faced. He reported the statistic that lathers earned at most forty days' worth of day-work pay a year, which the contractors' own assessments verified. We learn, for example, that lathers paid 25¢ a day to a solicitor or lathing boss, who was a union member in charge of finding lathers work. While the reporters did not reveal whether they had learned more about the reason for or significance of the solicitor position, the offhand fact provides a trace of evidence of how the labor market actually operated. The solicitor's duty of finding work entailed going to each contractor to identify available work and then distributing the jobs equally among union members. The moral economy of the arrangement indicated that (1) the lathers' union represented the individual through the strength of the collective, thereby helping to maintain high work standards, a living wage, and fair working conditions; and (2) the effort to distribute work equally safeguarded each lathers' competency in the market. Wadsworth also noted that "it had been impossible for lathers to live on their earnings" a phrasing that indicated workers were enduring a difficult time making ends meet and had agreed to take action.[38] In sum, the actual news reporting offered useful details to the public, though the *Metropolis* published two MBCA public statements while not giving the lathers, the BTC, or the Central Labor Union an opportunity to respond in kind.

One of the contractors' statements consisted of the lockout notice given to the BTC and lathers' union. The text highlights the contractors' condescending view of the lathers' work and hope that the public would defer to their expertise. The opening paragraph of the notice is particularly revealing:

> For the purpose of advising you what action our body has taken to arrive at an amicable settlement, we wish to state the scale demanded by the lathers, namely, $4 per thousand for piecework, and *$6 per day for day work, being an increase of $1 per day for day work* and 50 cents per thousand on piece work, we consider excessive as compared with *other trades requiring more skill*; also taking present conditions into consideration, it was felt that this was *not the time for further increases in the cost of building*, rather was it *the duty of everyone concerned in the building trades* to strain *every effort to economize* and *keep the industry within attractive limits to speculators* and home builders; for these reasons the demands of the lathers were refused.[39]

The MBCA clearly claimed authority for its organization and yet engaged in legerdemain when highlighting the $1 day-work increase first before presenting the 50¢ piecework rate increase. The switch was not merely a slip in parallelism—50¢

should have preceded $1 for the sake of clarity. Though this was not easily detectable, the contractors seemed to want to confuse the public by employing a shell game of sorts by pairing $6 with $1 even when, by all accounts, piecework entailed nearly all the work of the lathers. The statement reveals that the argument over incompetence entailed a judgment that the lathers' work did not require much skill. That point was hardly transparent in previous admissions (the July 16 statement) except that the contractors clearly did believe, as their productivity expectations show, that the lathers' work should be done under sweatshop conditions. The duty to economize fell on the shoulders of workers, and that entailed accelerated, more intense work. The workers' burden had to be endured, not only because these servants depended on the goodwill of their masters' discretion, but the contractors wished to attract speculators to invest in Miami. These capitalists, according to the contractors' judgment, required the right signaling—labor could be disciplined and kept in line—in order to draw their money to the city. One suspects that the unionists expected such attitudes and helps explain the need for organization as an effort to limit the extent of exploitation.

Perhaps they were also not entirely surprised by the *Metropolis*'s editorial stance on the labor conflict. The newspaper's three editorials dealing with the labor situation uncritically took the contractors' side and followed a crescendo of progressive alarm, as their headlines indicated, the last of which lacked only an exclamation point for final dramatic effect: "Fair Dealing Is All That Is Wanted" (July 27), "All Miami Concerned in Strike Situation" (August 7), and "A Hold-Up Will Not Be Tolerated" (August 11). The first editorial responded to a carpenter's letter, written anonymously, complaining about a Chamber of Commerce discussion (July 24) seeking that building-trade workers and material suppliers reduce their prices for a period of five months in order to stimulate a building boom. The Chamber of Commerce hoped "that renewed building activity would recompense them at least in part for the sacrifice . . . [and thereby give] Miami a big boost." In a nutshell, the Chamber of Commerce sang how economic growth promised rising tides would raise all ships. And was it not the patriotic duty for most Americans to sacrifice during this time of war? The *Metropolis* may not have been advocating a reduction of wages in the high-cost climate, but it did repeat the contractors' bias of slacking workers: the contractors' "only objection [is] paying good wages for jack-leg service . . . [because] incompetent workmen are [being] protected by Union rules." Allegedly, union rules protected incompetency "by insisting that the jack-leg carpenter and the bungling stone-mason, and *the slow-moving lather*, and the inefficient plasterer or electrician be paid for a day's work that a good workman could accomplish in a third of the time" (italics added). And how did the newspaper arrive at these damning conclusions? Readers learned that "The Metropolis was told" and that "substantial businessmen" object. Why would anyone pay a "high wage" to workers who insisted on being unfair and dishonest "by holding the good workman down to the pace of the incompetents"?[40] The mind of an attentive reader must have been contorted and absolutely dumbfounded by the potential economic crisis facing the city. So, businesspeople did not object to paying high wages to employees who work hard and fast, or at least for highly skilled work; but high building costs were preventing projects from moving forward; meanwhile, Miami's newspapers often sounded alarms of labor shortages, yet workers often were unable to find work in an economy experiencing ebbs and flows in all sectors. What was real and accurate? Whom to believe?

The newspaper's next two editorials (one at the start of the lockout and the other just after) continued this deference to the contractors' position. The new twist was to associate unionism with gangsterism in specifically practicing its moral economic mission, though the *Metropolis* just repeated the business accusation of inefficient workers. The weak conservative class-harmony cadences referred to how most "union men in Miami are the good citizen type," "believe in square deal principles," and "deplore the tactics of the gangster." Business, within this class idealism, could not expect workers to accept "less wages than he needs to support his family." If he does, "then capital is dead wrong and every honest capitalist knows it." While they did believe that the lockout was an unsound move and were afraid that it would "engender bad feelings," the newspaper deemed unionists at greater fault. They were stubborn, refusing "to have anything but their own way in the dictation of prices and privileges for the work they do." Ultimately, the determination of value was a skill deferred to the capitalist with minimal moral obligation but one still consistent with implicit capitalist logic: the concession that capitalism necessitated the reproduction of labor through paying just enough for human survival and reproduction. The final editorial continued the theme of unionists as gangsters when they repeated rumors that the lathers' union was going to demand pay for the period they were not working (since mid-July) at MBCA-controlled jobs and another worker action from plumbers seeking a wage increase to $7 a day. As its headline pointed out, a "hold-up will not be tolerated."[41]

By August 1917, the *Metropolis* had drawn a line in the sand. It would not support a strong working-class movement if it appeared such an effort would jeopardize growth and development. Regardless of what life entailed for the working class, the newspaper would go only so far in its support of workers. Neither the *Herald* nor the *Metropolis* offered sensitive in-depth analysis in its coverage of working-class life. No special report of what it was like to start a life in this developing city nor any profile of the working-class settler in south Florida was ever published. At least, if it exists, I have yet to find it. The newspapers focused on boosterism, which entailed the selling of the entrepreneurial potential of the region. Sure, there were stories about climate, morality, social events, sports, development, and anything that highlighted vibrancy, potential, and harmony. The common sentiment was to focus on that which would yield investors and their working-class builders and producers. The message was loud and clear for workers: Come one, come all. Stay or leave but please be docile, efficient, and productive while here—and don't forget to bring enough money to hold you over during lulls in employment or for a return ticket to wherever you came from. For those who stayed, please refrain from causing much ruckus. Attend church, play some, shop, work, and avoid class consciousness. That last reflected more hope than reality.

The local newspapers' worker-union coverage was problem oriented, and that meant focusing on issues such as labor shortages or strikes. The underlying assumption of the latter was that workers were essentially being unreasonable and unions were covering up for several problems. The newspaper's position mirrored that of the contractors and business more generally. Unions apparently did not address the issue of inefficient workers—the unfair productivity rates expected of lathers notwithstanding. Unions allegedly did not address worker "greed" to earn more and their unwillingness to accept lower wages for the common good. The papers were resoundingly silent on business's economic interests and portrayed businessmen as selfless, benevolent wise men. Unions allowed agents to roam the land with the power to stop any job for failure to abide by union rules; the power of contractors to fire his employees, to reject workers' arguments of fair wages or working conditions, or impose a lockout remained their undeniable prerogative. They backed the incompetent workman. Such dangers to production were simply unwieldy and preposterous for masters ruling servants to accept. Unions did not accept their place in the hierarchy of power. As such unruly entities, they represented radical challenges to the status quo. Labor unions disrupted order, especially when bearing witness to exploitation and demanding a better standard of living—meaning good working conditions, better wages, security, and a reasonable workday and workweek.

"Square Deal City" and Moral Economy

Labor troubles ratcheted up again at the end of the year and culminated in the early part of 1918. Miami building-trade unions asserted their high level of worker control when they remained resolute on maintaining the local double-overtime rule and in their resistance to the open shop. Contestation over overtime pay occurred at the US Coast Guard's Dinner Key Air Station (in Coconut Grove) construction project in November and early December 1917. In a sympathetic strike with workers in Key West, Miami's building trades protested that the W. P. Richardson Company of Jacksonville, Florida—contracted to complete work at both sites—was running an open shop in Key West. Miami's unionists also took offense at maltreatment from a job superintendent at the local YMCA job, whose work was also being led by the Richardson Company. Disagreement over the painters' work jurisdiction with the D. J. Conroy Company paint store and contracting firm over the painters' union rule that only unionized painters mix paint led to a painters' union strike in late December. The Conroy Company was the only painting contracting firm in the MBCA. After the Conroy Company hired nonunion painters in various jobs around town, including the Red Cross building project in January, the strike quickly expanded to include a renewed conflict between the building trades and the MBCA. This time, the MBCA openly declared their goal of being recognized by organized labor as having the authority to speak for Miami's contractors.[42]

The MBCA and the building-craft unions' battle over control of the local labor market advanced to a higher stage of conflict, with the former leading an effort to win the hearts and minds of the public. The MBCA attempted to turn the community against labor's power by branding labor-union policies and actions as unpatriotic. Unionism, according to the MBCA, was having a negative effect on the public, the third leg of the apparent square-deal triad. When in January union painters and carpenters in sympathy walked off the Red Cross Building, a project controlled by the MBCA, the contractors sought to stigmatize the building-trade unions by appearing committed to its completion despite the unions' withdrawal of labor. They hired nonunion painters and donated their own labor time to finish the uncompleted work. The MBCA made the implicit argument that even with work related to such a neutral, patriotic, and critically war-related resource, unions stubbornly refused to compromise and therefore proved a threat to the community and, implicitly, the nation. The themes of union leadership representing outside forces and guided by selfish motives, of union worker inefficiency, of hurting potential economic investment, of failure to sacrifice for community and nation—picked up from the previous summer's lathers' union conflict—would recur, and they carried particular sting in the wartime context.[43]

In response to this assault on their patriotism, the BTC published a letter in both the *Herald* and *Metropolis* arguing that the MBCA was guilty of "fake patriotism" or "cheap claptrap patriotism." The carpenters' and painters' unions resented the implication that they were unpatriotic, noting their many donations to the Red Cross, which included an offer to furnish free labor to complete the building on condition that the nonunion workers be taken off the job. Local 349 of the International Brotherhood of Electrical Workers (IBEW), who had earned praise for their offer to finish work amid nonunionists on the site, were rebuffed by the contractors and finally published a twelve-hundred-plus word letter critical of the contractors. As far as the Red Cross leaders were concerned, the BTC argued they were "allowing themselves to be used as a tool of the Master Builders' association." E. B. Douglas, a Red Cross volunteer and leader of the effort to erect the new building, expressed what one would expect from someone not affected by the power issues at stake: disinterest in the details of the labor conflict and an expectation simply for the project to be completed as soon as possible. Mrs. T. V. (Mary) Moore, a Red Cross worker and wife of the local business pioneer T. V. (Theodore), noted that five women were ready to volunteer to help finish the building, stating "I can pound nails and paint. . . . Our solider boys are in great need of the materials which we are supposed to furnish. We cannot get these materials out and shaped up without proper room and facilities." The BTC, however, pointed to how the employers sought to weaken unionism in the city using the Red Cross project as a way to "inaugurate a system of scabism in Miami." The Red Cross leadership contributed to the demoralizing moment by not criticizing the Conroy Company's hiring of nonunion labor and failure to meet the painters' work-standard expectations as well as the MBCA's refusal to accept organized labor's offer of free labor.[44]

The contest for patriotic authenticity only colored the MBCA effort to obtain labor standardization in the building construction market. Over the next few months, Miami's unions reacted to this attempt to wrest control of the message by actively demonstrating their patriotic fervor and concrete connection to the local community. In the summer of 1917 alone, they had organized a home guard unit consisting of labor union members (Company A). This unit and separate contingents of unionized workers would later march in the big April 7 Liberty Day parade. They called attention to their Liberty Bond contributions, including the full-page advertisement they paid for in the local newspapers soliciting increases in the purchase of war saving stamps. Organized labor also volunteered their time to the following projects: the painters' union painted the Women's Relief Association's New City Day Nursery; the carpenters' union built the county's home guard's armory for free; and the painters' union contributed a painting to the post office building—"fourteen feet high and twenty-five feet long"—that reproduced a recent *Collier's* magazine cover depicting Columbia, with marching soldiers in the background, urging workers to buy war saving stamps.

On February 9, the MBCA issued a fourteen-point ultimatum that essentially sought to undermine union power nearly entirely. All the points expressed a concern for controlling labor costs and expressed a desire to make the labor situation in Miami attractive to investors. It included such provisions and criticisms (some overlapping) as worker inefficiency (5 points); passing more costs to workers such as transportation to adjacent Miami towns (2 points); severe restrictions on labor power, such as limiting union communication and control on jobsites, including business agent[45] influence (7 points); strict standardization of collective bargaining rules such as contract end dates being the same for all trades (December 31), a minimum of ninety-day notice prior to wage-increase demands; and the prohibition of the strike through a mandatory arbitration system (5 points). The BTC and each individual craft union rejected the ultimatum, which led to a lockout, though it appears that the demand for work was relatively lax, as usual, and so minimal hardship out of the ordinary was felt. Both contractors and trade unionists openly expressed concern about scaring investors away by having such an open conflict in the midst of the tourist season, even in the midst of the war.[46]

The MBCA's public-relations tactics, while obvious stabs at the legitimacy of unions, did not quite succeed, in part because the building-trade unions collectively had a quick and consistent response. By mid-March, all the various craft unions arrived at agreements with the MBCA, though no details are extant. It appears from the subsequent conflict in the fall of 1919 that most of the ultimatum demands did not succeed in shaping new contracts. The one point that the building crafts attempted to be sensitive to was advance notice of wage increases, but such matters were usually dealt with toward the end of a bargaining agreement, and unions appeared to offer as much notice as possible. Unionists reacted passionately to the MBCA ultimatum in part because they feared the degradation of working conditions if they lost leverage against their employers and they resented how the contractors tried to manipulate the public in ways such as caricaturing workers and offering confusing information (not unlike the lathers production rates the previous year). The MBCA's statement that introduced the ultimatum offered a quite insightful perspective on the conditions workers faced in Miami: they noted that "this being a tourist city, we cannot regulate work to provide a regular and continuous employment for any certain number of mechanics." The seasonal nature of construction work was a national phenomenon. Yet it is clear that Miami's unionists sought conditions that would mitigate the hardship of unemployment and the intensity of work required to finish construction projects in expedited fashion (the race to completion by the tourist season). The unionist stance was reflected in their arguments about the value of their work and time, though doing so at times also entailed denigrating nonunion workers, particularly Black workers. Of all the comments that were being made, however, only two, one by M. E. Fidler, the newly elected Central Labor Union president, and J. L. Bridges, a railroad engineer unionist, made racist allusions. Fidler, who had named his eldest son Eugene Debs, suggested that white labor would leave Miami because the poor working conditions in a nonunion city would force the work to be done by "the Nassau nigger . . . who is some intelligent gentlemen . . . some mechanic." J. L. Bridges warned that a nonunion city would lead to the "employment of negroes and other unskilled labor posing as skilled labor at starvation wages." Yet even these two racist comments point to a deeper concern for the degradation of work and a lame effort to appeal to the public's own racist fears and the wish to keep Miami a white man's town.[47]

Nonetheless, unionists primarily took offense at the implication that Miami's workers were particularly lazy, inefficient, less skilled, immoral, or some combination of the four. While the lathers mocked the contractors' work speed expectations in the summer of 1917, painters and others also criticized the contractors' arguments that workers were not working hard enough. The IBEW boasted about their "brains, skill, and brawn," a sentiment that mirrored the lathers' own claim about the "artistry" of their craft. Painter C. S. Hansen thought the arguments of inefficiency and soldiering[48] were slanderous. He pointed out that the wages demanded by Miami's unionists were fair and compared favorably with wages in other cities in the country, even though, in his opinion, they worked more intensely than workers in those cities. This line of defense included emphasizing the respectability and professional sensibility of union organization. In a meeting organized by the Good Government League, labor activist and teetotaler J. D. Hendricks ("a former drinking man") highlighted how Miami's unionists were homeowners, churchgoers, morally upright (not "saloon bums"), and organized to keep up high work standards, not unlike lawyers. C. S. Hansen echoed the skilled tile setter's, printer's, and painter's claim to specialized knowledge and expertise. Making a radical assertion of equality, Hansen argued that "it ought to be as much interest to a community to keep good plumbers as [it is to keep] its good doctors." Hendricks and Hansen argued that scabism seriously threatened labor's moral economy and therefore the well-being of the community. Some Miamians observed during these weeks of labor turmoil that the working class, or laboring people as Reverend Ira Adams preferred to call them, constituted more than 90 percent of the population. Contractors who hired nonunion labor would be designated as unfair, a label that employers loathed but that reflected the ethics of moral economy.[49]

Labor shortages, increased by the wartime demands for skilled and unskilled workers, likely only intensified the MBCA's frustration with the power of unionized labor. Several of the building crafts requested wage hikes right at the time that many of them were departing for wartime opportunities, including African American workers. Emblematic was when the US government began to recruit skilled and unskilled workers to build both docks and ships in Charleston, South Carolina, in July 1918. White skilled workers were going there and other port cities such as Jacksonville, Florida, and Penniman, Virginia, leading to a strain on the local labor market. Equally challenging to employers was the 1917 Immigration Act, which imposed a literacy requirement. The law severely restricted Bahamian immigration to the area, increasing the shortage of laborers, particularly farmworkers, in Dade and nearby counties. When Bahamian workers were recruited to go to Charleston in a special wartime exception, local employers complained loudly. The Charleston recruitment crisis afforded Black leaders the opportunity to successfully lobby for the end of the notorious street tax, a social-control practice discussed in chapter 1.[50] The founding of the CLU's newspaper, the *Miami Central News*, in April 1919 added to the perception of labor's growing power. And so, workers of all stripes gained during the war, a development that likely made employers a bit more anxious. The wartime labor-market conditions and the greater employer organization set the foundation for the labor crisis in 1919 and labor conditions in 1920s Miami.[51]

Tensions over wages and worker-control issues slowly intensified between organized labor and business during the war. As noted, the high cost of living was concerning workers.[52] Anxiety over labor problems emerged in early May 1919 with rumors that construction workers might push for new wage hikes. C. D. Mackey, president of the BTC, claimed no wage demands would be made in "the near future." Architects, contractors, and builders expressed their disappointment with Mackey's vague prognosis and had hoped to have a definite date for any push for higher wages. In addition, J. T. Blackman, who was currently serving as the president of the City Council (but no longer president Local 993 or the BTC), addressed the architects' and builders' concern over labor shortages. He noted that "we want to avoid the bad business, especially for the skilled workmen, of having men come here with their families, probably without the prospect of a job, only the prospect of the big volume of work going on in Miami, and have to bear the heavy expense of waiting for a job to turn up." He was a champion of the workers' need for steady work and protection of the union standard that kept the half-day on Saturdays, something he explained was "an essential thing" and "an established institution . . . not likely to be changed." The Woman's Club continued their ongoing battle against the high cost of living in the late summer and appointed committees to investigate the city's costs in comparison with costs in other cities. They also organized meetings with city officials, business interests, and unionists to resolve the problem of rising prices. The issue would remain a concern for several months to come. Employers realized early the frustration about the high cost of living, a situation that had defined the World War I economy and continued to affect the postwar economy. They were correct to anticipate agitation from workers over wages, especially in light of Mackey's and Blackman's public statements. Painters and chauffeurs would push for wage increases later in the summer. Miami's employers were better prepared and in a more favorable climate than in 1917, benefiting from two years of the MBCA organization experience and a national backlash against unionization and leftism.[53]

The labor conflicts in 1919 stemmed from white skilled workers' strength and business's desire to disempower them. In mid-August, first painters and then chauffeurs and teamsters demanded higher wages, triggering labor troubles in the fall of 1919. Employers particularly protested painters' demand for immediate wage increases. Painters went on a short strike before builders bitterly made the wage adjustments. Soon the city would twice escape a wider-scale strike. The hiring of nonunion Black teamsters in the end of August precipitated the first conflict. White chauffeurs refused to unload materials from the teamsters' trucks on grounds of both the union shop and the color line. Local 196 of chauffeurs preceded to place more than twenty firms on the unfair list. Business interests responded with an effort to institutionalize the open shop in the city, and thus they hoped to capitalize on the national open-shop trend at the time. Businesspeople declared that labor's practice of using only union label materials and advocacy of the closed shop was a threat to their freedom. They attacked unions as being inefficient and expecting unfair labor conditions, an argument existing since at least the summer of 1917. Business interests, from contractors to retail, particularly wanted to institute the open shop, which they described as a principle of "equal rights for all." Their activity would lead to the formation of the GMEA and the declaration that Miami was an open-shop city.

Organized labor countered with declarations of their Americanness ("no trace of bolshevik tactics," as reported in the *Metropolis*), solidarity for the union shop, and support of segregation at the workplace. The building-trade unions attempted to preempt possible criticism of communist connections when they declared their Americanness, a point they felt should have been self-evident from their patriotic efforts. The historical record does not indicate that communism or socialism ever became issues in Miami during World War I or the postwar period as in other parts of the country. Miami's unionists were aware of the red-baiting tactics and acted quickly to squash any hint of such an association. More specifically, business (with collusion of the local newspapers) attempted to associate violence and intimidation to union activism and recalcitrance against the nonunion shop. The flare-up of the chauffeur conflict in November, as discussed in chapter 2, pointed to this dynamic. With the exception of a few instances of minor alleged union intimidation, however, charges of radicalism linked to the work of "unthinking agitators" never did stick, despite the efforts of business and their disapproval of labor's business agents. As noted in one of their demands in the winter 2018 ultimatum, employers sought to reduce the power of business agents, who were seen as challenging their conservative vision of class harmony because they often directed worker actions.

In addition to their business unionist style and little or questionable use of violence, the BTC and CLU used the race card and adhered to an urban ethos to shield them further from charges of radicalism. The BTC turned the rhetoric of business against them by stating that "equal rights for all" meant a desire to place white skilled labor on the same plane as Blacks and, therefore, threatened Miami's status as a white man's town. In the first strike, business folded and gave in to the union workers' demands for better wages and the removal of the Black chauffeur replacements. They created the Greater Miami Association, however, which would later add "employer" to its name. From 1919 onward, unions would struggle to keep Miami a union town, perhaps less so for the building trades but certainly in service work (as the retail workers stillbirth suggested). Contractors faced a strong union presence unwilling to give up the fight for dignified work. Amid this turmoil, the *Metropolis* finally openly articulated a point it had long held but never quite stated: it argued that Miami ought to become a "square deal city," which essentially boiled down to an open-shop town. They arrived at this position by accepting one contractor's argument that he was unable to find competent skilled union workers. In addition, to bolster his antiunion stance, he expressed concern about an unruly workface based on one act of worker intimidation.[54] The BTC backed down from a citywide strike in early November in the interests of protecting the success of the upcoming tourist season. Clearly, unionists were not insensitive to the economic realities of the city, acting on their own need to earn as much income as possible in Miami's volatile seasonal economy. Though they acquiesced to business, the BTC realized that keeping the best interests of Miami first would serve their interests more in the short term (by keeping workers earning a living), though also in the long term (by maintaining positive public relations).

Despite union labor's apparent acquiescence, organized labor hunkered down in the following years in an apparently permanent struggle over power in construction work and over the workers' right to unionize in the city. The modernist emphasis on economic progress, growth, and development encapsulated by the booster rhetoric that shaped Miami's history, however, helped obscure the story of workers and their struggle for power. *One Year of Open Shop*, a pamphlet published by the GMEA in October 1920, was emblematic of the process of historical obliteration. In order to attract investors, the GMEA sought to dispel notions that the city had a strong labor movement, reflecting the national mood toward unions after World War I. It presented a simple linear history of the city's development and growth, pasted with short anecdotal accounts, newspaper clippings, and testimonials from local businesses on the success of the open shop. In its telling "The Story of the Open Shop" (the article's subtitle) depicted a city, once stunted by closed-shop conditions, advancing under open-shop terms achieved by heroic businessmen. "The city had been for a long time under the complete domination of the Labor Unions," the pamphlet pronounced. "All building operations were conducted on the Closed Shop basis. Every employer of labor was absolutely subject to the rules and regulations of the Labor Unions and was compelled to yield every point to the whims and arrogance of the Walking Delegate [i.e., business agent]." There may have been a grain of truth to this accusation, but it was a distortion of the workers' plight.

It is unsurprising to note that the narrative discussed only the fall 1919 labor struggle. Apparently, historical context was anathema to public relations. It loosely charged that union leadership was radical. Its primary evidence for the charge was that Miami's building-trade unions had sent out a letter to unions in other cities to have their members "stay away," a common practice that warned unionists of the lack of work or of existing labor troubles. This effort to prevent the flooding of the local labor pool was twisted, employers seem to say. Without any context and discussion of the workers' perspective, employers argued unions were against a free labor market. This unionist effort at controlling the supply of workers in the region was inaccurately blown up and reframed as a denial of nonunion workers' right to work and thus an undermining of equal opportunity.

The GMEA portrayed itself as the rightful protectors of class harmony—that is, along technocratic and paternalistic lines. Union labor could work in the city, *One Year of Open Shop* argued, as long as it accepted the free enterprise principle that business had the right to choose its workforce regardless of union affiliation (a position anticipating Florida's right-to-work constitutional amendment that passed in 1944). Employers sought to depict unions as dictatorial, undemocratic, and inefficient. It is important to remember here that the GMEA wanted to attack unions as an institution, but they were careful not to target individual workers. From accusations of soldiering to corruption, antiunion politics across the country stressed the threat that organized labor represented to the American Dream. Unions, from the perspective of many employers, were obstacles to efficiency (particularly in determining value). The employers' entrepreneurial instincts would be stifled if unions were allowed to have "complete domination" of the workplace. *One Year of Open Shop* thus argued that, in defeating the closed shop, the GMEA had protected the opportunity to work and attain riches in a legal and honorable manner. The GMEA patriotically and heroically protected the harmony of interests against the worst collective instincts threatening individualism.[55]

Unions resisted this portrayal of their role in Miami and in workers' lives and they contested conservative notions of class harmony. They too argued that they were protectors of class harmony but along moral economy lines: in the advocacy of the union label, of fair wages, and of other working condition issues. Unions sought to protect the livelihoods of their members. Businesses that gave fair wages, followed the arranged work rules and conditions, and purchased when possible union-label materials were embracing organized labor's conception of class harmony. In addition, Miami's unions argued that business needed to hire home labor (that is, residents) and to work through the union to get workers. Implicit in these demands was the idea that through collective action—a formal expression of community interests—workers could keep at bay the worst aspects of individualism and greed gone mad. Union carpenters responded to the GMEA's pamphlet with their own notice in their national journal, the *Carpenter*, announcing that Miami was still a closed-shop city. W. R. Robbins, a member of the Composition Roofers, Local 57, and in 1921 first vice president of the Florida State Federation of Labor, commented on the propagandistic nature of the term "open shop." He urged unionists at the 1921 State Federation of Labor Convention to desist from using the term because, in his opinion, it only strengthened the cause against organized labor. "There is no such term," Robbins argued, because what business was fighting for was actually the "closed shop to every man who wants to stand for the protection of his fellow worker." Robbins's concern with language reflected both his astuteness about the role of presentation and memory in creating a positive public image and the uphill battle faced by unions against a relatively organized and better-financed business community.[56]

The struggle over the control of the labor market was persistent throughout the period. In addition to continuing their efforts to organize and maintain worker solidarity, local unions mounted their own public-relations campaigns in the early 1920s, continuing a practice they started in the 1918 battles over patriotism. Reacting to a 1920 GMEA advertisement for the open shop, organized labor put out its own advertisement making the case for union and home labor. Getting several small businesses and citizens (nearly four hundred) to support their efforts, a full-page advertisement with their names made the case for an enlightened class harmony, boldly stating (repeating the GMEA's use of the phrase) "here is where we stand":

> We, the undersigned business men, property holders and citizens of Miami, believe that the future prosperity of our city depends upon harmony between capital and labor and a pulling together of all classes of its citizens. We are opposed to the importation of outside labor to take the places of our people who have become citizens, home owners, taxpayers, and who have helped so materially in the building of this great city to its present size and beauty. We further believe that any differences that may arise should be settled by consultation between two parties affected or by arbitration.[57]

These exchanges continued over the next few years with labor consistently using class-harmony language and repeatedly returning to the theme of moral economy.[58] Two years later, the International Typographical Union paid for a series of advertisements in the local newspapers celebrating their tradition of welcoming all religions, creeds, and nationalities and accepting "equal rights to women," including "equal pay with the men." Perhaps the most powerful image used in this series, simultaneously published in the *Sheet Metal Workers' Journal*, was a cartoon depicting the cost of not choosing a union (see image 3–1):

FIGURE 3–1. Moral economy as a path to economic security and happiness. (*Miami Daily Metropolis*, September 9, 1923.)

economic security now and in the future. Organized labor argued that workers risked being left in destitution particularly in old age if they did not act collectively and resist the open shop.[59]

Miami's unions organized the Miami Union Labor Association (MULA), led by Lewis Hertig of the painters' union, specifically as a public-relations campaign against the open shop. Its emphasis was moral economy, using the language of cooperation and class harmony. Organized labor, it argued, worked to keep the labor market running smoothly and to prevent low or excessive wages while assuring high-quality work. MULA published twenty advertisements between January and June 1924. The most confounding advertisement asserted that "labor is a commodity." On the surface it seemed to contradict workers' efforts to avoid exploitation, suggesting workers had adopted the employers' viewpoint. The text of the advertisement demonstrated how class harmony, as a means of finding common ground between employer and employee, often required major rhetorical contortions, particularly in the context of Magic City boosterism. It argued that organized labor's skill and competency was superior to that of nonunion workers. More efficient and better-quality work would be the result of hiring union labor. Yet MULA also criticized the employer tendency to exploit unorganized workers. "Our generation is almost insane in its desire for speed," MULA noted. "Business is a lemon squeezer. Get the juice, get it fast, then throw the remains of the lemon away and reach for a new lemon." They clearly attempted to win over the public with moral arguments while appealing to the unorganized. The advertisement went on to say that "wise employers" ought to understand that only unions, acting as certifiers of skill and protectors of a fair labor market, could provide competent and efficient workers. The large letters asserting that LABOR IS A COMMODITY likely did its trick of drawing the reader in, but the argument for moral economy put things in perspective. MULA's platform recognized the mutuality of interest between employer and employee, but they wanted economic growth to center workers' interests such as fair wages, safe working conditions, and home ownership. They also expressed their commitment to resolving labor disputes peaceably, rejecting violence, intimidation, and radicalism (such as the "I.W.W. and Bolshevism," which they deemed "un-American"). They proudly claimed their membership in the AFL.[60]

In reality Miami was never entirely closed or open shop.[61] Organized labor maintained a prominent presence throughout the city's early history and interwar period, but the rapidly growing city challenged the success of unionization with a continual influx of new workers, in addition to business leaders' antiunion attitude. At the very least, the efforts of unionists to gain a stronger presence demonstrated a significant level of worker agency and faith in unionization. The story of the open shop was neither linear nor as neat as the GMEA wanted to maintain. The war over the open shop continued despite their claims in the press or pamphlets like *One Year of Open Shop*. Their conservative class-harmony idealism, though, was simply a public-relations spin. The GMEA, for example, operated a free employment bureau that sought to supply open-shop employers with a steady flow of workers. The numerous advertisements the GMEA placed in the newspapers through the early 1920s pitched its arguments. The very existence of the free employment bureau, however, revealed its persistent struggle to create an open-shop city. As it happened, GMEA and its employment agency vanished by the middle of the decade. The building-trade unions remained a strong force, and its unionists continued to deal with the reality of irregular work in the construction sector, though the building boom, and the entrance of national firms with established union connections, helped bolster their position. The carpenters' union maintained high membership numbers, and one would suspect that the same remained true of the other building trades.

Conclusion

William Jennings Bryan, the Great Commoner, had just recently announced that he planned to move permanently to Miami, Florida, when he spoke at the 1922 convention of the Southeastern Builders' Supplies Association being held at Miami's Hotel Halcyon. The delegates at the convention "praised the spirit of the Magic City," many being impressed with the numerous construction projects underway even during a national economic downturn. Bryan appealed to their vanity by highlighting the vital social role of their industry when he stated that "the building of a home is next in importance to the feeding of the people." He took the occasion to argue what he felt most important to ensure this public welfare: "the need for harmony between contractor and builder, employer and employee," as the *Miami Daily Metropolis* reported. Bryan pointed to the Magic City as an example of how to ensure such an enlightened goal by noting the provision in the new city charter that "empowered the government to appoint a board of conciliation." As the 1921 city charter (sec. 3, pt. dd) outlined it, if formed, the "Municipal Board of Conciliation" would have "authority to investigate and report on disputes between employers and their employees" in order to inform the public, but it did not bind either party. No record exists that this board of conciliation ever convened. The progressive spirit and hope for square-deal negotiations embedded in the provision clearly was a product of its time.[62]

It is unlikely that business interests were able to ever create an entirely "square-deal city." Workers continued to struggle for a moral economy using class-harmony language. Miami's local market economy empowered workers to some extent, but successful union organizing relied on rigorous effort, on the national network of union membership, and on the longer tradition of unionization. The establishment of Local 993 and other building-trade unions early in the city's history seems to have played an important part in this success. The specific leadership styles and union decisions during the period under study, however, are often less clear. From the rate of unionization and labor activities such as Labor Day parades, one can deduce that workers continued to organize into unions. Nonetheless, some worksites remained union shops while others experimented with open-shop conditions—hiring union and nonunion labor.

After the land boom bubble burst in 1926, the building trades faced a major downturn, which led to contractors gaining a reduction in wages in 1927 and 1928 from the building-trade unions. Harry O. McClurg of the Bridge, Structural and Ornamental Iron Workers, and organizer of the Central Labor Union's Citizenship Committee discussed in later chapters, noted that many unionists had not worked since December 1926. These "aristocrats of labor" (his words) often worked only about three to five months in any given year, therefore reducing their apparent high wages by about half. It is unclear how he arrived at this estimate, but his criticism of a seasonal economy and irregular work powerfully highlighted a major defining issue of interwar Miami. So the reduction of wages certainly hurt and fueled the desire to make Miami an "all the year around city." The downturn meant that now they had to make what they earned stretch a little further—that is, if they were lucky enough to get work. The Magic City, and the deeper dream of establishing a moral economy, faced this challenge of economic crisis as it entered the Great Depression.[63]

CHAPTER 4

Winter Playground Blues

Unemployment, Home Labor, and the Hobo Express

Miami newspapers from the late 1920s and early 1930s offer an interesting picture of the city's history. Local stories celebrate economic growth, and wealthy visitors comment on the leisure they were enjoying in their visits to south Florida and the sunny outlook this southern abode offered. Tobacconist Charles D. Larus Jr. noted in his March 1933 visit that Greater Miami was heaven and the rest of America like hell. In his view, unlike the rest of the nation, Miami had plenty of work, maybe too much for its residents: "The hotels . . . are crowded; taxis are running day and night. I talked to drivers who complained they were being worked to death. The stores are crowded and the beaches crammed with people. . . . People there have money and they are spending it." Humorist George Ade agreed with Larus's general outlook stating one would not believe a depression was underway "if you visited the beach just now. Every hotel in the wide area known as Greater Miami is packed and jammed; huge crowds in line at the betting booths, at the horse races, people waiting in line at every good picture theater; motor cars from every state of the union parked solidly, block after block, and the open lanes a never-ending parade of cars and still more cars." One can easily be induced to rub one's eyes and ask: did the Great Depression not hit Greater Miami? This historical exploration of the local newspapers such as the *Miami Daily News* or the *Miami Herald* would lead to hundreds and hundreds of lines of print and plenty of pictures of bathers or people just having fun, stories of gambling raids, weddings, and testaments to the steady march of growth and development. The answer could very well be that things were not so bad and that Miami escaped the worst of the Depression blues.[1]

In between and nearly invisible wove stories of quiet desperation and exclusion. Hidden in the back pages on March 1, 1933, the *Miami Daily News* printed a story of a jobless worker committing suicide. Headlined "Despairing Man

Takes His Life," it told its readers how August Albreicht, a thirty-eight-year-old stationary engineer from Ocean City, New Jersey, was visiting Miami with his wife and, "trying to obtain work here ever since his arrival[,] . . . had grown despondent because of diminishing funds." Albreicht was lucky enough to visit with a reserve of money and thus was able to sustain them during his search for work in south Florida; the transient poor were often unable to do so. We do not know how long he had been searching for work or the deeper psychological reasons that led August to kill himself. Awkwardly juxtaposed next to this story was a photograph of another visitor to south Florida, fishing lure manufacturer Bob Weisenfeld, posing with a large sailfish shown as evidence of his skill and the effectiveness of his Calamity bait product. Just two pages over, the article "Catholic Agency Aids Needy" told of the charitable work done by the Associated Catholic Charities in helping "the underprivileged and giving assistance to those who are destitute." As a member of the network of Community Chest welfare agencies (in an aggressive drive soliciting donations), its primary aim was "to keep the family together whenever possible" by providing food, clothing, and shelter, never turning away "an applicant of any other religion." Both George Ade and Charles Larus failed to comment on the numerous charitable events marking the landscape at the dog and horse racetracks and Miami's Bayfront Park, simultaneous with the tourist extravaganza they witnessed, and a challenge to the accuracy of their impressions.[2] Nor did they write about the harsh system of exclusion that kept the transient poor away from their view—evidently heaven was not for everyone. The exclusion contributed to the possibility of a guilt-free vacation.

Amid this cacophony of joy and progress and the background of destitution and economic struggle existed a complex social and cultural history; namely, the politics of growth and the challenges of work and survival in a political economy rooted in cheap labor and the performance of servility, hospitality, and business boosterism, which placed a premium on the idea of harmonious class relations. This busy business of appearances can play tricks on the historian's eye, since the demands of tourist pleasure and city growth often hid the struggles in the shadows. Miami's tourist industry and the city's booster interests constructed a narrative of perpetual city growth, framed in contradiction between the forces of modernity and the promised pleasures of a subtropical resort town. The parallel realities of pleasure and suffering, of the rich and the down and out, created the potential for class tension. The tension did not lead to a break, in part, because a class perspective that emphasized harmony among the classes dominated Miami's class relations. Workers as much as business interests (and tourists) embraced growth and development, which put a high demand on compromise and quick resolution of labor conflict. The class-harmony framework endured real-world challenges over wages, job conditions, and labor-market dynamics.

Unemployment, underemployment, and labor competition provided an important space for class-harmony ideology to percolate and take shape. This chapter explores that space through an analysis of how three key interrelated issues shaped the politics and economics of unemployment through the 1930s in south Florida: regular seasonal unemployment, home-labor protectionism, and a set of deficient private and public welfare and work programs reliant on state exclusionary practices. These three issues defined the contours of unemployment as a problem and the limitations faced by the unemployment movement in fighting the plight of poverty and joblessness. The political economic context of scarcity reinforced localism and indirectly bolstered the sensitive tourist economy despite how unemployment seemed to threaten to the social order.

Tracing Unemployment

Miami's workers faced regular seasonal unemployment because of the city's reliance on the construction trades, retail and restaurant businesses, and the tourist industry. The *Miami News*, the city's labor union newspaper, commented on the seasonal work phenomenon in an April 1937 editorial celebrating the Works Progress Administration's decision to restore and expand job opportunities in the district: "In no other place in America, save perhaps California, are there such enormous variations in seasonal unemployment as are to be found in Southern Florida."[3] Reliant on a primarily local economy with a small manufacturing sector, workers did not have many job options. The ebbs and flows in construction work led to inconsistent employment and so increased the pool of the unemployed and underemployed. Yet unemployed construction workers, while experiencing economic distress, had more alternatives from the continuous building projects that marked Miami's landscape and the relatively powerful position that the building trades held in the local economy. Despite adding to the numbers of unemployed workers at any given moment during the year, construction workers were sure to find work as long as building continued in the city.

The service jobs that defined the local economy and the tourist industry were much more problematic. In addition to being low-paid, workers in these occupations faced constant fluctuations in joblessness. The short tourist season from December through April, in particular, caused a consistent pattern of unemployment from the late spring through early fall, often with the highest rates of joblessness during the hot summer months. In general, the duration and frequency of unemployment and the number of unemployed during the year, especially in the summer months, remains unclear as a result of an incomplete historical record.

Few statistics chronicle the fluctuations; the most concrete and definitive numbers offered at best a static picture of unemployment. According to the

TABLE 4–1. Unemployment in major Florida cities, 1930 census (parenthesis indicates total number of unemployed)

Cities	Male	Female
Miami	12.9% (4,692)	10.93% (1,702)
Jacksonville	7.6% (3,058)	6.47% (1,235)
Tampa	9.48% (3,341)	9.65% (1,490)

Source: Data in this table is derived from the US Bureau of the Census, *Fifteenth Census of the United States: 1930; Unemployment*, vol. 2, *General Report* (Washington, DC: GPO, 1932), 154–55 (Jacksonville), 166–67 (Miami), 223–24 (Tampa). Class A (unemployed looking for work) and B (those with jobs but out of work due to layoffs).

1930 US Census, Miami had more unemployed than the other major cities of Florida, Jacksonville and Tampa. Miami unemployment among men was 5.3 percentage points higher and 3.42 percentage points higher than in Jacksonville or Tampa, respectively; the differences among women were slightly lower than men: more than 4.5 percent and 1.3 percent for the same cities (see table 4–1). And so, in that one moment in April 1930 when the census data was gathered, Miami had the highest unemployment rate among the major cities in the state, even though the census was taken at the tail end of the tourist season and not in the doldrums of the summer months. A downturn in tourist visitations and fewer construction projects likely contributed to the lull.

These numbers, in any case, reflected conservative estimates. The statistics in table 4–1 pertain only to workers reporting that they were unemployed and searching for work or who had been laid off and were waiting to be rehired. The census indicated that unemployed workers may have misunderstood census enumerator questions and then proceeded to be counted in other unemployment categories that excluded them from the general calculations. The statistics shown in table 4–1 constituted more than fifteen thousand unemployed for the entire state (men and women), and my calculations combined those who listed being individuals unemployed and searching for work (class A) with those claiming to hold a job but currently laid off (class B). That represented more than 40 percent of the unemployed for the entire state. Unemployment numbers for other parts of the state for smaller towns or cities were not calculated by the Census Bureau. Also unavailable was the number of individuals excluded by reason of choice or error from just being missed by enumerators, which may very well have included the burgeoning number of transient unemployed. Excluded, as well, were all individuals, aside from children under the age of fourteen, who were not counted as gainful workers. This population constituted more than thirty thousand people and included women deterred from looking for work for various reasons (culture and lack of job opportunities likely leading the list), youth attending school, and others for a variety of reasons. Unfortunately, the

US Bureau of the Census did not select Miami as an area to investigate in its special census of unemployment conducted in January 1931; that information would have offered a more complete picture and update of existing data.[4]

As with the rest of the country, Blacks suffered greater official rates of unemployment, among both men and women, than did whites. The same caveats about census methodology apply, which suggests that the rates may have been even higher. Nearly 17 percent of all Black Miamians in 1930 were unemployed and whites endured just over 11 percent. Black men and women experienced similar rates (17.1% and 16.5%, respectively), but whites experienced a larger gender difference (12.25% versus 7.1%, respectively). These data reflect the reality that more Black women worked than white women as a percentage within each group of women. More than 56 percent of Black women were in the workforce as opposed to only about 19 percent of white women, a reflection of the general low pay, inconsistent work, and therefore Black family needs for more sources of income. The large number of Black women in the workforce meant that they risked experiencing greater rates of unemployment during economic downturns because they worked unskilled trades (working primarily as laundresses, as maids, and in other service work).[5]

The next authoritative statistics appeared in the November 1937 when the US government conducted an unemployment census. Continuing to use 1930 as a base year, Miami's unemployment increased for men to 14 percent (5,365) and for women to 24 percent (3,820). This change was better than the declining conditions in Jacksonville (for men 8,486 = 21% and for women 6,198 = 32.5%) and Tampa (for men 6,892 = 22.48% and for women 4,117 = 27%). Tampa's static population between 1930 and 1935 (only a 1% growth rate) suggests that the city may have endured the most stagnant economy. In these same years, Miami's population growth of 15 percent and Jacksonville's nearly 10 percent growth suggests the unemployment rates based on 1930 statistics may be off, but it is unclear by how much if one were to adjust for individuals not seeking work and for population growth. Nonetheless, combining the number of unemployed with the number of partly unemployed—that is, those who recorded some hours worked recently but were looking for more work—Miami's rates of underemployment shot up to 33 percent for both men and women, Jacksonville's would rise to 29 percent for men and 40 percent for women, and Tampa's would increase to nearly 29 percent for men and 32 percent for women.[6]

The category of partly unemployed represented an example of how confusing the statistical categories can be and how fluid and incomplete the actual numbers were. The awkward and imprecise phrase "partly unemployed" used by US census takers misstated the problem by not reframing the issue as underemployment or inconsistent employment. "Partly" suggested some work as opposed to not enough employment for survival—a slight semantic difference that suggests a tendency to avoid more negative assessments. The census survey evaluating hours worked by the partly unemployed during November 7–13 confirms this interpretation. More than half reported working fewer than sixteen hours in that week (almost half, 1,392 of 2,871, reported zero hours) and more than two-thirds worked fewer than twenty-four hours. Because no population statistics of the gainfully employed exist for 1937 and because Florida and its major cities continued to experience population growth between 1930 and 1940 (with a greater increase in the second half of the decade), it is unclear how the unemployment rate changed from month to month or year to year, though Miami, Jacksonville, and Tampa continued to hover around 10 percent unemployment in 1940.[7] One must also assume that omissions existed in these census numbers similar to those that occurred in the 1930 census, especially with regard to the transient unemployed. It is likely that employment conditions at best remained the same or at worst declined. Again, the question of seasonal employment suggests ups and downs for a significant proportion of the population.

Anecdotal observations made during and after the 1930s confirm the slipperiness of the unemployment statistics and the persistence of seasonal unemployment as suggested by the census data. Perrine Palmer, who will be discussed more carefully in the next chapter, offered evidence of changing unemployment numbers. He was a civic activist and social gadfly who spent lots of time traveling around the city and county and then writing letters to government officials and the local papers about his observations on the economy and the need for an expansive social welfare net. His insights on local conditions provides much suggestive evidence about unemployment, though the historical record is incomplete on how he arrived at his statistics. He noted in February 1931 that more than ten thousand unemployed walked the streets, a number that indicated a significant increase (about three thousand) from the previous year. Notably, this evaluation occurred during the height of the tourist season.[8] In December 1931, W. H. Green, chair of Miami's Unemployment Fund Committee and later head of the local New Deal Civilian Works Administration, responded to Senator Robert La Follette Jr.'s inquiries about local relief needs by stating that "approximately 5,000 heads of families" were out of work (clearly excluding nonheads of households), but these numbers had been materially reduced because "our winter season has begun, vegetable canning factories operating, and the farming industry has picked up." He indicated an upward trend in unemployment rates, noting an increase of 40 percent since 1929 and 30 percent since 1930. Finally, Green insisted that if federal aid were extended to Miami, it would be most useful from March to December, an absurd framework that excluded only three months.[9]

Palmer revealed a continuation of this upsurge when he reported in September and October 1933 between 25,000 to 40,000 unemployed in Miami and

Dade County, which then had a population of 140,000, and many more were dependents of those unemployed enduring difficult economic hardship. The numbers remained similar in July 1934 but improved slightly by August 1935 to include about 14,000—though the number of underpaid and underemployed remained high.[10] For many workers, irregular employment forced survival strategies such as overworking during times when jobs were available. Bernice Sawyer, the daughter of prominent Black resident William B. Sawyer, would recall years later that people had to work two jobs during the tourist season. "You had to make that 'season' because in the summer there wasn't very much work in Miami. So usually during the winter months you worked two jobs—if you were so lucky in such a competitive environment—and then in the summer you would be able to live."[11]

The cycles of unemployment were undoubtedly exacerbated by the constant influx of migrants arriving in Miami. What drew workers to the city? As discussed in earlier chapters, Miami's big land boom and city boosterism helped introduce south Florida into the national imagination. Beginning at the end of World War I and increasing thereafter, the real-estate boom and advertising promotion lured tourists and land speculators to Miami. Get-rich-quick dreams hid the underlying instability of an unbalanced economy. Workers seeking jobs in construction, hotels, restaurants, and other work in the bustling city were lucky to find employment. Others were not so lucky. They encountered a different reality than what boosters sold. Hope and optimism shaped their motivation as much as desperation or impoverishment. The barrage of advertisements selling the climate and good life in Florida and Miami surely had its effect. At the very least, new migrants to the city, such as the down-and-out, speculators, and tourists, wished to partake in the promised abundance that Florida seemed to offer. The visions of abundance were sullied, however, by the economic realities of the maldistribution of wealth and a decrease in business investment after the collapse of the Florida real-estate boom of the mid 1920s, followed by the economic downturn of the Great Depression.

Home Labor

Seasonal and irregular employment combined with continuous population flows into south Florida had the potential to create a divisive class context. The persistent boosterism to attract summer tourists as a way to promote year-round employment—evident throughout the first half of the twentieth century—demonstrated how local business leaders, labor leaders, and the general citizenry recognized the need for a stabler economy. Yet permanent residents held an ambivalence about migration to the city. Their own likely recent arrival to the city and the economy's dependence on tourism to generate growth and development did not prevent an ambivalent feeling—often of deep disgust—to emerge about migration to Miami. In the labor competition, in encounters with unorthodox travelers, and in the ostentatious displays of wealth, Miami's residents expressed mixed feelings about who came to Miami.

Because permanent employment would remain a challenge for many year-round residents, and because the presence of the wealthy, because free-spending tourists displayed great disparities of wealth, and because workers pouring into the city flooded the labor market, local residents used various monikers, sometimes opprobrious, to designate the various populations arriving to the city. The term *year-round resident*, individuals and families living in Miami throughout the year, marked the division between visitor and permanent resident. *Winter residents* constituted a wealthy class who owned second homes or occupied other winter residences in Miami or Miami Beach. Since they did not represent competition with workers, local businesses could openly welcome them and other well-off tourists, while others ogled at their accumulated wealth. Their upper-class status and leisure seeking rarely received open criticism, though their presence during the economic downturn may have grated on the sensibilities of the down-and-out and others with visions of greater economic equality. The Committee of One Hundred, an exclusive rich men's social club made up of wealthy magnates from the Midwest and Northeast and a few prominent Miamians founded in the mid-1920s, and the Cocolobo Cay club, a fishing, boating, and party club on Adams Key that included some of the wealthiest men in the country, were interlocking south Florida institutions that reminded Miamians of the hierarchical US class structure.[12] Stories of their activities filled the newspaper pages during each winter season through the 1920s and 1930s. The arrival of other rich or famous people made good boosting news as well.

Other, less-desired, visitors received open disapproval, and such moments could warn workers of their own vulnerability. Mobsters like Al Capone, for example, faced a *Miami Daily News* antimob campaign and the passage of a strict vagrancy law targeting organized crime. The ordinance originated after Al Capone and three of his friends were quickly released after being arrested without warrants. The Miami City Commission sought to increase the penalty of vagrancy to $500 (it had been $100) or imprisonment of no more than sixty days (a decrease of thirty days).[13] Such efforts to control movement and prevent crime likely resulted in the local practice—beginning as early as 1933—of fingerprinting hotel, bar, and night-club workers.[14] In any case, labor unions protested during the week of efforts to pass the ordinance (it failed in the first two readings and finally passed on May 23 in the third City Commission vote). They feared that the ordinance would be used against labor during strikes and lockouts. One newspaper reported that a labor union representative was surprised that the city charter even had a provision to keep out "undesirables" and thought it and the ordinance were likely unconstitutional. It certainly represents an interesting window for the historian to see how many citizens remained clueless about the details of the law, as well as an example of a civic education occurring in real time. When the provision passed, one commissioner noted "the new ordinance would no more affect labor than the one now on the city books, which has withstood the test of years without objection."[15]

Historians have given less attention to *tin-can tourists* (an early manifestation of trailer-camp tourists) and *snowbirds* or *out-of-state employees*. Tin-can tourists were working- and middle-class and often older travelers interested in exploration, freedom of movement, and low travel costs. Not having to pay for hotels because of the convenience of traveling with camping and other living accommodations, tin-can tourists acquired opprobrium especially when residing in what some residents deemed unsightly tourist camps. Their status remained ambiguous in any case. Some viewed them as impermanent, but others argued that they sought permanent residence. In either case, they became or represented potential competitors in the job market or eyesores in residential neighborhoods or in real-estate developments where their camps emerged. The Lemon City Improvement Association argued in 1930 against the presence of a tourist camp in their area of the city (northern Miami), stating that tourist camp residents "work for such small wages that our own wage earners cannot compete." While initially, in the early 1920s, tin-can tourists sometimes evoked the image of the frontiersmen seeking adventure, they soon evolved to just another group of tourists but of a more middling sort.[16]

While technically anyone north of Florida who arrived in the state during the winter months could be called a snowbird, those transients who ended up working in the city (often in the construction trades and the retail, hotel, and restaurant sector) became particular objects for criticism. The term *snowbird* denoted a transitory and ephemeral relationship between migrant or tourist and south Florida that acquired a negative connotation if the snowbird became an out-of-state employee. Employers who deliberately brought out-of-state employees to south Florida to staff their jobs earned equal criticism from local residents. Their arrival contributed to class divisions and class tensions among workers and between businesses and workers. The 1941 WPA guide for Miami, researched in the late 1930s, indicated the regular seasonal influx of at least a thousand Black chauffeurs, domestic workers, and hotel employees during the winter season, but an even larger number of whites arrived searching for work. Various city leaders, small-business owners, union leaders, and the unemployment movement, among others, pressed Miami's government to hire the city's or the state's home labor first and to encourage local employers to hire locally.[17] Such appeals during the Depression demonstrated how various social classes attempted to protect local workers from starvation and unemployment, thus creating a strong localism that promoted the provision of work and a reduction in the demands on relief efforts.

Home-labor protectionism was an essential component of Miami's localism and reinforced the idea of class harmony. As noted in earlier chapters, labor unions pioneered the effort to control the labor market by communicating with union locals across the country about economic conditions, warning fellow unionists to avoid coming to Miami. Employers never fully supported that kind of labor-market control by unions because it undermined managerial prerogative. But context was everything. The Great Depression made such efforts an ethic to be celebrated, by workers and businesses, as a way to improve the local economy and to maintain good relations among the classes. Workers—union and nonunion—judged employers' localism on whether they hired home labor first; employers, in keeping the appearance of harmonious class relations and the loyalty of consumers and workers, advertised that they hired Miami residents. While ostensibly creating a sense of community for locals, the home-labor movement created tension between resident workers and newly arrived workers and between workers and businesses. The result was that the home-labor movement undermined greater chances for worker solidarity by pitting resident against perceived outsiders. As an ever-growing city, worker solidarity would remain a persistent uphill battle in the context of home laborism and employer resistance to unionism. The home labor ethic bubbled to the surface and revealed a serious local concern about the scarcity that threatened workers' lives.

Job hunters coming to Miami could face real difficulty in finding work, but as the city's population continued to grow (from about 29,000 in 1920 to more than 110,000 in 1930), thus creating a stable workforce, some local businesses were sure to embrace localism to foster customer loyalty and demonstrate their concern for workers. Local retail stores emphasized their efforts to hire locally first and thus announced their patriotic localism. The *Miami Daily News* reported in April 1931 that customers, taking advantage of Sears Roebuck's Biscayne Boulevard store's two-dollar-sale days, were welcomed by "familiar faces, those of Miami people. Throughout the store, it was apparent that local people were employed, according to the established Sears, Roebuck policy." Mayor Cliff H. Reeder "and other prominent local men and officials" of the store attended a short ceremony before the day's opening. W. H. Green's campaign "Miamians for Miami jobs," launched in the fall of 1931, gained avid support from Burdine's department store, the largest in the city. Burdine's reportedly had made "a real effort since 1926 to employ only Miamians." In addition to operating a training school to prepare local workers to staff the store, Burdine's made "every effort to discourage any one coming to Miami looking for a job and is plainly advising [out of town] applicants that Miami people will be sufficient to fill their requirements for the coming season." The campaign to hire home labor was prevalent, leading one job hunter to complain in 1931 about the "sectional propaganda" to hire "only Miami help" in the local newspapers and the speakers delivering the same message at Bayfront Park.[18]

In efforts to tackle the problem of unemployment and maintain harmonious class relations, local government and businesses embraced home-labor protectionism. The Miami City Commission passed resolution 6359 in August 1930 urging the federal government to hire local labor in its erection of a new federal building in downtown Miami. Several similar home-labor resolutions that city residents lobbied for were approved through the 1930s.[19] Residents founded various organizations to urge local employers to hire home labor. None seemed long-lasting, but the torch of the home-labor movement passed from organization to organization. Frank G. Roche of the Central Labor Union and Rabbi Jacob Kaplan of the Temple Israel, among others, helped organize Floridians Incorporated in October 1932 (evidently a statewide movement) to encourage the employment of Floridians and the purchase of "Florida-grown and Florida-made products." Two years later, United Floridians formed, and in 1935 the Home Improvement League organized with the same objectives. The Home Improvement League used the union fair-label tactic of rewarding local merchants by advertising their support for the movement, again revealing the influence of organized labor in shaping this grassroots effort.[20]

Workers, businesses, and government leaders came together in apparent harmony of interests, namely, protecting the welfare of Miamians against unemployment by accepting the home-labor initiative. Such public agreements, of course, indicated businesses continued to hire outsiders regardless of the pleas and best efforts of Miami residents. Workers and business could agree on the need to grow the economy while disagreeing on how to protect the local economy from the Depression.

The Hobo Express

The pattern of tourist adventure and labor migration to Miami that had developed during the first half of the twentieth century fostered home-labor protectionism as a response to job scarcity amid a labor market with limited work opportunities. The dichotomy of rich visiting tourists or wealthy winter residents and the working poor helped set the stage for the local government's maltreatment of at least one group of migrants, the "hobo" jobless poor. The transitory unemployed as represented by the hobo jobless worker embodied a threat of scarcity that tapped into the social taboos against poverty. Their influx into the city endangered Miami's dreams of abundance because the transient presence of hoboes reminded rich and poor about the shortcomings of capitalism even while their very existence may have reinforced the cultural importance of the work ethic and the problematic assumption that poverty revealed a moral laxity in the individual. The hobo jobless poor, who appeared to be predominately men, also pressed local resources to accommodate a casual workforce, many of whom were homeless and jobless.[21]

The social tension surrounding hoboes may be traced through the very idea in the word, which had its origins in the late nineteenth century. *Hobo* was widely used by experts as a term to designate homeless, migratory labor. Some hoboes appropriated the term to denote their independence and resistance to mainstream culture and political economy, even though for others *hobo* still had the negative connotations of poverty, homelessness, and dispossession. The sociologist Nels Anderson, who had spent time tramping around in the early part of the twentieth century, revealed in his 1923 study, *The Hobo*, that hoboes of the Midwest and West existed on the outskirts of capitalism, providing casual, temporary labor and existing in perpetual poverty. With a degree of freedom emanating from the liberty to move from place to place, a culture emerged that embraced this varied and unpredictable life on the margins.[22]

By the early years of the Great Depression, when an increasing number took to the road, the term *hobo* often was misused as shorthand to lump together migrants traveling with different intentions. Police authorities in south Florida and the East Coast paid little attention to the differences when arresting "vagrants." Indeed, the term *hobo* was used interchangeably with the terms *undesirables, vagrants, floaters, panhandlers, idlers, bums*, and *tramps*. The reality of a transient unemployed person, often in such a condition because of reasons external to their control, complicated the easy rubric of the degenerate or criminal vagrant as a public nuisance. The term *hobo* served to sensationalize this population and thus helped further ridicule them and justify harsh treatment of them and violations of their civil rights.[23] To many upper- and middle-class citizens, hoboes represented an unworthy unemployed population who siphoned off relief funds from the "worthy unemployed"; to the working class, they represented competition for scarce jobs; for all classes, hoboes challenged the idea of the importance of home, arguably the quintessential symbol of the benefits of abundance and the American Dream.

These migratory jobless and homeless individuals arrived in Miami regularly by the mid-1920s, especially during the winter months, though it is very likely that East Coast hoboes made the city a regular destination even earlier. The increase in job opportunities during the winter tourist season and the comfortable weather probably drew them to south Florida. Karst Hofman of the Young Men's Christian Association noted in a 1928 letter to the *Miami Daily News* that many simply responded "to the alluring advertisements that picture Florida as the land of opportunity." They arrived by rail, on foot, and by hitching rides with travelers heading to Miami.[24] No record exists to indicate what percentage were workers looking for regular jobs, how many were embracing an untethered life on the road and simply seeking warmer weather, and how many were homeless for other reasons. It is also unclear whether any self-identified as the countercultural hobo. What is clear is that government officials deemed them outcasts and viewed them as costly to the city and state, particularly if the migrant did not find work. In addition, states, towns, and cities confronted a moral dilemma when facing the transient problem as it developed during the Great Depression of the 1930s. Whereas unattached men could be treated roughly and contemptuously, the presence of women and children struck a chord of sympathy in the context of the Depression that left local governments in the difficult situation of not being able to provide aid to such increases in the local indigent population.[25]

In the winter season of 1928–29, Miami police began expelling these migrants from the county.[26] The ongoing economic downturn certainly helped put more individuals on the road. L. O. Scarboro, chief Miami detective who initiated the program, recalled in 1958 how it started: "I picked up 15 panhandlers on Flagler Street one Saturday night and that many more blew [fled] before we could catch them." He gained the approval of municipal judge Frank Stoneman. Scarboro told him, "Our tourists and winter visitors don't want to be bummed and panhandled on every block. They [hoboes] come down the highway, and that highway runs both ways." Dubbed first the "hobo special" and soon after the "hobo express," this system of handling transitory migrants operated with national notoriety through the end of the 1930s. Three years later, in 1931, the express started by mid-September, when the police first spotted hoboes arriving earlier than what had been the case. To what extent migrants were trying to circumvent Miami's hobo express by coming earlier is unclear.[27]

This ad hoc, arbitrary, and aggressive measure for controlling population flows into the city emanated from the national practice of settlement law restrictions and Miami's police powers. As enunciated in Miami's 1921 city charter, the local government had the power "to prevent persons with no visible means of support, paupers, and persons who may be dangerous to the peace or safety of the city from" entering or to expel them from Miami if they were found (section 3, part v). This language revealed a change from the 1913 charter (section 27) that had empowered the city to arrest vagrants but did not mandate expulsion as a means of controlling the transitory unemployed (see chapter 1). The adjustment to the charter suggests that the city already had experienced the migration of transitory unemployed and thus sought a legal (though morally and ethically dubious) means of preventing their presence. The police justified such action in the spirit of localism and the protection of the tourist economy. Reinforced by the scarcity of public and private welfare resources, the police sought to reduce crime and protect private property as mandated by the city charter. Their argument undoubtedly was also bolstered by the influx of actual individuals with criminal records or those who engaged in illegal behavior (alcohol consumption during Prohibition, narcotics use, gambling, solicitation of prostitution, for example) and had little means of financial support. This proactive approach of controlling unwanted migrant inflows seems to have predated such measures in other states in the Depression-era United States, and it borrowed from long-standing traditions of strict vagrancy laws and migration restrictions throughout the country.[28]

Accounts of how individuals who were captured and then processed as hoboes are rare. The *Miami Daily News* reported in 1939 that Scarboro took no more than a minute to evaluate whether an individual was a hobo. "One by one the ragged, broke and sometimes hungry men are herded from jail and taken before the detective," who then proceeded to uncover their criminal past or pauper status through his keen, experienced eye. It is not clear how the article arrived at its statistics, which was in no way critical of Scarboro's peculiar and idiosyncratic methods. It asserted "about 40 or 50 per cent" already had police records and thus were either "habitual criminals" or bound to "become criminals" because of their pauperism. Nine of ten men whom Scarboro checked out, according to the article, would fall victim to the express. One revealing 1931 letter written to the *Miami Daily News* by an R. F. Harris related an actual arrest: "Standing on the street was a truck, on it in large letters was Police Patrol, and as the crowd gathered around to look it over, there came out the post-office a policeman, and by his side a young man, thinly clad, with a pale face and holding a letter. . . . The officer opened the door and said: 'Get in.' And in he got, with about 20 or 30 others."[29] No official records reveal the daily operations of the hobo express; it is newspaper reports and other contemporary observations that suggest that the average number of hoboes being arrested or delivered to the county line could range from ten to twenty a day—sometimes even as high as seventy-five, according to Scarboro. As city resources and needs determined, the police reportedly gave hoboes the choice of either expulsion from the county or imprisonment with hard labor.

Such harsh treatment may have deterred hoboes via grapevine communication, at least police officials hoped it would, and it surely surprised many unsuspecting travelers arriving to the city. Miami's growth gave it a big-city veneer, but it continued to have a small-town feel from such police work. Unless trained to live in the difficult Everglades environment, unemployed hoboes were forced to roam the developed areas, apparently simplifying police efforts and exposing the transient poor to intimidation, imprisonment, and expulsion from the county. According to one newspaper police report, some of the transient population engaged in professional begging along Bayfront Park. Tapping into a popular long-standing narrative trope about the immoral entrepreneur beggar, the story related how one transient allegedly was earning $30 a day playing the violin and others were carrying "several hundred dollars in their pockets." Such behavior would not be tolerated in Miami. The newspaper announced that "professional beggars will be given their choice of taking a train out of Miami or being sent north with the daily patrol wagon load of vagrants."[30] Who paid for the train fare is unclear (nor is whether transients were given the choice); the cost of gas was all that was needed in transporting the transient unemployed to the county line.

It did not take long before the other counties in the Gold Coast—the southeast coast of Florida—followed suit and extended a more fully operating hobo express. Indeed, the hobo express's success depended on the cooperation of law enforcement officials along the East Coast. Once these "undesirables" reached the next county, local law enforcement officers would gather them up and take them to the next county to the north. The passing along would continue up to at least Martin County (north of Palm Beach County) and at times even as far north as the Florida-Georgia border. At times the express ran into snags because of strains on local resources and disagreements between police authorities of different counties, but the hobo express served the needs of local businesses interested in keeping up appearances of abundance and gained indirect support from the general populace concerned with the lack of job opportunities, poor wages, and scarcity of relief.[31] Scarboro, for instance, asserted in 1939 and again in 1958 that "the floaters" would drive down the wages of common labor and thus rob "Miami residents of the much needed jobs." It would be hard to swallow Scarboro's nod to home-labor moralism. Apparently, Scarboro had a side construction business and, on at least one occasion in July 1935, he threatened local construction unions when they tried to organize his many building projects. The local labor newspaper reported that he "grew very vociferous and dared [the union business agents] to put one foot on his property[,] . . . very kindly offering to shoot the chairman of the business agents' board."[32]

Scarboro's sentiments, in any case, reflected both the community's larger concern for the welfare of local residents and the social insensitivity born of a small and limited government ill equipped to handle even the most minor disruptions. The hobo express's existence, thus, emerged in locales unable to handle the influx of the poor even while it held out open arms to the better off and certainly the wealthy. Florida governor Doyle E. Carlton feared in 1931 that the state would be flooded with migrants searching for work, an insight, undoubtedly, drawn from reports on the ground. By October 1931, he had joined ten other states in warning unemployed transients not to expect state relief. Cora Bain, secretary of Miami's division of charities, supported the action of Palm Beach County "in placing warning signs at the north county line limits, stating all vagrants will be prosecuted." She believed "every Florida county should take similar action."[33] Others also called for a state-coordinated effort to halt hoboes and poor transients more generally from entering Florida via a border patrol, or at least provide a means of accommodating the transient influx. Progressive Miami commissioner Cliff H. Reeder, who had lost the mayoral seat in June, suggested giving tents to poor transients at the state border, offering them as temporary housing, and making transients work on the state highway, since Florida "has no snow to be removed," a reference to the common work relief programs of the North.[34]

Conditions had improved only slightly for a select few transients in December 1933, when Federal Emergency Relief Administration's (FERA) funds started to pour into Florida and the Dade County Experimental Transient camp's capacity expanded. State officials decided to set up farmwork camps in the cities of Opa Locka (to serve Miami and Dade County), Jacksonville (which had started a camp in December 1932), and Tampa and, if necessary, to extend such camps to Orlando and Pensacola. W. H. Green asked the police to transport transients without criminal records to the Opa Locka camp, ostensibly approving the continuation of the operation of the hobo express. The *Miami Daily News* writer S. S. Matlock highlighted this fact when he reported that "persons who are criminals will be handled by the police in the usual way." Matlock claimed the practice was "humane and practical" as an alternative to an indiscriminate hobo express that apparently did not distinguish between the criminals or idle transients from the down-on-his-luck, unemployed transient. Nonetheless, individuals refusing to join farmwork camps would "be sent away by the police," according to Marcus Fagg, state chair of the Florida Civilian Works Administration (CWA) and FERA. Limited resources also meant many were denied entry into the Opa Locka camp and risked expulsion from the county. Finally, although FERA allocated funds for transients, CWA work relief prohibited transients from participating—a policy that reflected residential fears of transient labor competition.[35]

Miami and Dade County's approach to the transient problem was a hodgepodge method of dealing with the poor that both imposed work discipline as a moral lesson to the lower classes and sustained the system of marginalization and segregation of the down and out. Located north of the municipal airport at Opa Locka, the Dade County Work Camp started operation in the winter of 1933, with help from the Reconstruction Finance Corporation. Florida senator Duncan Fletcher discussed the camp on the Senate floor in February, praising the effort to help the needy. The infusion of more federal dollars allowed it to expand modestly. By late December, seventy-five single men resided in the work camp, and Green expected that four hundred more transients eventually would labor on the farm. The camp paid transient workers 30¢ an hour but charged for the food, clothing, lodging, and recreation (which included horseshoes, a volleyball court, and other activities) furnished by the government, leaving them with about 90¢ left over each week.

Work consisted of farm labor, though it appears that the camp required a cooperative rhythm in which individuals participated in all aspects of the camp's upkeep. Transients faced "semi-military discipline" that entailed fixed hours for rising, working, eating, recreation, and sleeping. Such a regime, Matlock asserted, would safeguard its residents and help teach them a useful occupation. Its laborers used any vegetables and dairy products produced on the farm and any surplus given to the county's needy families. Green and others intended the Dade County Camp to remove transient workers from welfare relief rolls and from the job market.[36]

While a positive and progressive development on the social-welfare terms of the time, this work-relief program appears to have received scant funding, served only a small portion of the transient unemployed, and helped entrench the practice of maltreating hoboes. In early 1934, conditions remained meager, but they expanded with the formation of the local Transient Bureau. The bureau continued to send unattached men to the camp, but it sent unattached women and families to rooming houses "wherever reasonable rates can be obtained." This change reflected the changing demographics of the transient migration, one that increasingly included women, children, and hopeful unemployed skilled male workers searching for work outside their home residency. Transient Blacks, mostly from Georgia, also were apparently on the rise. They were often sent to the Negro Welfare Federation in Overtown.[37]

After the initial effort to assist the transient unemployed through FERA in the winter of 1933–34, President Franklin Roosevelt cut back relief funding for Florida and other states in the fall of 1934. Governor David Sholtz responded by instituting, between 1934 and 1936, a border patrol disallowing the "indigent non-resident" from entering the state by automobile or train and thus implemented what had been imagined for several years. The history of this institution is rather elusive with few extant sources available. It appears to have operated only during the winter season. The Florida division of FERA noted the border patrol's effectiveness in reducing the number of transients entering the state. State police set up guard posts on major highways into the state (and railroad police to inspect trains), stopping suspicious cars carrying individuals "who neither had the funds to keep them while they were in the state nor definite prospects of jobs." The *Atlanta Constitution* reported in December 1934 that hobo jungles were forming along the Florida state border, where transients allegedly waited in hopes that Sholtz's edict would be rescinded. Jungles had been set up off the highways from Brunswick, Georgia, on the east to Dothan, Alabama, on the west. Transients in these camps visited smaller towns to "buy or beg [for] food, but in large part" and were "congregated around rivers and swamps fishing and hunting for their living." Sholtz claimed that more than fifty thousand transients were turned away in the winter seasons of 1934–35 and 1935–36; a report by *New York Times*'s journalist for the Florida winter season, Harris G. Sims (who was based in Lakeland in the center of the peninsula), stated that "more than 25,000 were turned back" in these two seasons. In November 1936, about "2,000 hitchhikers, rod-riding and flivver-driving itinerants" were prevented from entering Florida. When penniless and jobless transients slipped past the border patrols, they still risked being caught by local police and, on the East Coast, including Miami, fell victim to the hobo express. Even when transients escaped capture, the cumulative effect of avoiding the vigilant eyes of the state must have added to the nervous pressures arising out of joblessness, homelessness, and hunger.[38]

The ethic of the hobo express, of passing the burden of relief to other locales, expressed itself on a grander scale in Sholtz's border patrol. The state blockade had no precedent in the country and, in fact, predated other draconian measures in the West. Colorado's governor, Ernest C. Johnson, instituted in April 1936 the only other state executive order in the country blocking entry of "alien laborers from other states," but he rescinded the order a few weeks later because of the impossibility of maintaining the policy. The Los Angeles police in February 1936 stationed a foreign legion at the state border as a "bum blockade" but had to stop when it ran against legal obstacles.[39] The longer history of the hobo express offered Sholtz a model of how to treat unwanted migrants. The inability of private and public welfare agencies to aid more people simply sealed the deal.

The hobo express and state border patrol mirrored anti-immigrant public policies. The politics of exclusion embraced what historian Roger Daniels has called the "likely to become a public charge (LPC) rubric"—a policy framework that sought to exclude from the nation immigrants who would become financial burdens to the state: the diseased, the poor, the criminal, the mentally ill, morally degenerate, politically suspect, and so on. Applied to immigrants before, during (as in the case of Mexican workers), and after the 1930s, it clearly also often applied to poor migrants in interstate travel during the Great Depression, especially in California and Florida. The 1930s great Dust Bowl migration to California, for instance—when Oklahoma, Arkansas, Texas, and Missouri migrants moved in great numbers, made famous by Dorothea Lange's photos and John Steinbeck's *Grapes of Wrath*—witnessed virulent antimigrant campaigns against "Okies." Poor, white, working-class migrants faced marginalization into crude stereotypes during weak economic conditions, when fears existed about limited job and relief opportunities. Similarly, the hobo express and border patrol marginalized the transient poor into the stereotype of hobo or vagrant, especially in light of how city and state officials regularly associated transients with crime. Miami's home-labor protectionism and tourists' preferences (tourists not wanting to be "bummed and panhandled on every block") justified rough treatment of the nonresident unemployed.[40]

The continuous pressure of keeping up appearances and protecting permanent residents' access to jobs and relief received criticism from Miamians and observers from afar. Churches and other individuals protested the hobo express from its inception in 1928. The fall of 1931 witnessed an outpouring of criticism and calls for reform of the "ruthless methods" used by the police. R. F. Harris, a letter writer who recorded a hobo arrest, entitled his letter "What Would Christ Do?" He went on to write, "I realize these pressing times are hard . . . but because a man is poor, or broke, or even a law breaker, we must remember he is still human, and deal justly with him."[41] The conservative populist and columnist Westbrook Pegler took a swipe at Florida's border patrol, observing that the state preferred "soft hands and disposition to loaf and spend" to "calloused hands and a disposition to work and earn." Others pointed out the embarrassing situation of welcoming the affluent and barring the poor, arguing that the border patrols were tantamount to using an "instrument of dictatorship."[42]

Echoing these sentiments, Florida governor Fred Cone ended the border patrols when he came to power in January 1937 on the grounds that it was undemocratic. He restated his anti-border-patrol policy in the fall and protested the hobo express, calling it "absolutely illegal and unconstitutional and against all the laws of the state" (see image 4–1). The transients had the right to a trial, he argued, adding that it was "beyond understanding" how anyone living in a "free country" could be treated with so little regard of their basic civil rights. He ordered county sheriffs to cease aiding the hobo express, but city police chiefs in Miami, Fort Lauderdale, and West Palm Beach vowed to continue arresting vagrants and sending them north or put them in jail or make them work on street gangs. The state border patrol ended in 1937, but the hobo express continued to make regular runs through the end of the decade; it seems to have been discontinued during World War II.[43]

Conclusion

Cone may very well have ended the border patrol because of budgetary issues. His criticism of the hobo express suggests populist sensibilities that may have been influenced by the spirit of the times and that reflected the need to open Florida to more workers for further economic development. The period between the late 1920s and mid-1930s, nonetheless, was a rough one for the unemployed facing limited job opportunities and limited private and public welfare coffers—not that welfare was ever a satisfactory or adequate solution to the poverty endemic to capitalism.

FIGURE 4–1. Hobo express editorial cartoon (*Miami Daily News*, November 1, 1937, 4). Cartoonist Anne Mergen's depiction of the infamous patrol wagon is one of the few extant images of this notorious institution. In 1937 Florida governor Fred Cone criticized this law-and-order enforcement tradition as "illegal and unconstitutional" (*Miami Daily News*, October 29, 1937, 2).

Florida's treatment of the transient unemployed forestalled any greater unemployment movement from arising. The perpetuation of a division between resident and nonresident unemployed may have met short-term relief needs and reduced job competition to some extent, but its myopia hurt the chances of unemployed individuals forming greater bonds of solidarity that ignored localism as a defining characteristic of status and identity. Instead, localism increased a greater sense of community as it reinforced the attractiveness of home-labor protectionism as a job-saving strategy against the threat of scarcity. It was an ironic reality in light of the important role migration played in the population growth of Greater Miami.

Home-labor protectionism existed as a strategy, in part, because of the scarcity framework defining the political economy. With a state unwilling or at least unable to provide better solutions, joined by a private sector equally reluctant, a regime based on arbitrary and harsh exclusionary practices developed and reinforced a culture of appearances. The wealthy visitor found exclusive spaces to keep out the poorer classes, while other vacationing tourists confronted a more diverse and embattled landscape. Residents, from workers to local merchants, struggled to welcome visitors. Workers feared labor competition and so pushed to limit job opportunities to residents. Local merchants wanted to ride this localism to their economic benefit. Kicked out by the shuffle were the poorest transients. Keeping up the appearances of abundance and leisure necessitated the exclusion of the living reminders that the larger political economy, despite the political rhetoric of equal opportunity, produced large numbers of a lower class enduring unemployment and underemployment.

Class-harmony discourse enabled Miami's localism as the resident unemployed struggled to rebalance the economy. Local politics over limited resources necessitated practical solutions for immediate problems, and that meant at the very least tacitly accepting the politics of exclusion. The sustainability of deeper critiques of capitalism and of grassroots insurgency simply was limited amid the pressing problem of immediate scarcities and an entrenched power structure. But harmony discourse lit the light of possibility for reasoned solutions while dissolving the threat of potential chaotic social revolution. Such a framework promised equitable distribution of abundance even while it meekly accepted the nature of power and disallowed greater class solidarities to emerge. The next chapter explores the radical potential of class harmony as it unfolded in the early Great Depression.

CHAPTER 5

Appeals to Harmony

Perrine Palmer and Transcending Scarcity

After experiencing rapid growth from World War I through 1926, bank collapses, real-estate fraud, and rampant land speculation led to an economic downturn that by the mid-1920s left Miami tumbling into the Great Crash and Depression. Capitalism's crippled arm would reach down to the winter playground in spite of all the optimistic boosterism. Growth would continue, but at a slower pace, and the flaws of a local economy dependent on tourism became quite evident. Attempts to diversify the local economy with a larger manufacturing sector largely failed and thus remained small. In the eyes of some, the throngs of the unemployed and the underemployed that filled the landscape threatened Miami's social harmony and perhaps even delayed the promises of abundance. While the inequality between the wealthy and the working class often remained unnoticed or ignored, the increasing number of the hungry, jobless, and homeless indicated that something was awry. The activism of grassroots organizations would help to bring these issues to the foreground.

Exploring how Miami's citizens confronted the issue of unemployment and economic depression, this chapter offers a close reading of the ideas and activism of Perrine Palmer, a regular contributor to the *Miami Daily News* readers' letters forum, a frequent attendee of organized labor's political meetings, and eventually a member and secretary of the Dade County Unemployment Citizens' League (DCUCL). Palmer helped articulate a critical call for social harmony amid the spiraling economic crisis, one that did not embrace corporate welfare as a model. Palmer instead envisioned harmony as promised in the ideal of a cooperative commonwealth, embracing all that modernity offered, especially the promise of abundance. The next chapter will discuss more carefully the social and political history of the DCUCL.

Palmer was a talented individual with a middle-class background who struggled for steady employment in the 1930s. An analysis of the local newspapers highlights Palmer's importance in discussions and actions that sought to alleviate and resolve unemployment in the city. Indeed, it is because of the historical trail that Palmer left behind that a more refined class history for Miami can be written. His articulate letters, reports, and general activism, though forgotten, spoke of the frustrations of many, as well as of their dreams and hopes; they have also left guideposts for the historian to retrace the history of unemployment and class in south Florida during the Great Depression.

Several others joined Palmer in the effort to relieve the plight of the unemployed and underemployed. Charles W. Nicholson, a former organizer and officer in the International Machinist Union, played a critical role in founding the DCUCL, as Palmer and others noted. Nicholson, as an enlightened radical, built on an inclusive tradition of unionism. Years earlier, in 1914, Nicholson stood by striking Cuban and Spanish workers in Ybor City (Tampa), Florida, protesting the rising cost of living. Responding to nativist sentiment, he argued how these cigar workers were critically important to the community. The real foreigners to the city were the capitalists causing the rise in prices. Nicholson stood by the rank and file, arguing that "every movement, organization, or demonstration that functions from the top down instead of the bottom up is absolutely worthless and accomplishes but very little." The praises given to Nicholson at the moment of his sickness in September 1933 and subsequent death in November testified to that democratic spirit.[1]

Other activists were a diverse set of people: Jacob H. Kaplan, rabbi of the progressive Temple Israel, often engaged in local social issues, and would later participate in the 1938 Southern Conference for Human Welfare;[2] Verner Townley, a former store clerk, activist, founding pioneer of the city, and frequent contributor to the *Miami Daily News* letter forum; local labor leaders such as William Wister, John Gavelick, and M. E. Fidler (who named his eldest son Eugene Debs), all DCUCL officials; and several others helped organize a movement for relief, with hopes of economic recovery. The economic depression served as the primary motivation for action, and vast reformist and radical ideologies offered fertile, reasonable ideas to critique the US political economy. In embracing the idea that greater consumption by all would end the economic depression, Palmer and others were in potential opposition to the hierarchy that defined class and Miami's leisure culture.

Consumptionist ideas were only one part of a more visionary perspective. Miami's progressives respected the value of work and its vital role in the political economy, but they were equally disturbed by the lack of power workers possessed. The employment fluctuations faced by workers translated into an insecure world. Palmer and others attempted to reframe how work was imagined, envisioning a world where people would work less and not be defined by their jobs, and where everyone would enjoy the vast resources of the United States, including the available spaces for leisure and recreation.[3] This vision entailed passing judgment on the unequal wealth distribution that defined city life, especially during the tourist season.

At the same time, the consumptionist theoretical framework was limited in its embrace of harmony as the goal of society—that is, while Palmer's ideas were calling for a major shift in how work would be imagined, his appeals to harmony softened the revolutionary potential of his ideas. Unemployment and poverty required immediate practical solutions. The appeals to harmony carried much resonance during the Great Depression even while the structures of the political economy helped limit the radical potential of the unemployment movement. The idea of a cooperative commonwealth entailed harmony, but the realities of power and the limits set by scarcity undermined the appeals of the unemployed.

Both Palmer and the broader grassroots activism are absent from local and state histories. Much of the absence may be explained by the myth of Miami as a frontier land controlled and dominated by heroic pioneers who succeeded in taming a tropical paradise for themselves, for the rich, and for workers and families. The myth presented a whiggish conception of history, seeing progress as inevitable and often ignoring more complex currents of local history.[4] The omission is also a function of what local histories have decided to illuminate. The literature has focused on racism, ethnicity, and urban development, and the majority of these histories offer coverage for the post–World War II period.[5] In addition, the bias in the historiography toward national narratives and more radical responses to capitalism's failures has dominated the histories of this era. The bias is not surprising in the context of the vibrant class activism in the 1930s. The rise of the Congress of Industrial Organizations (CIO), the sit-down strikes, the increase in unionism, an active Communist Party, the Popular Front, and the promises of the New Deal, among other things, attest to such class activism. Miami's absence in the historical literature on this period thus may be attributed to its lack of an industrial economic base, to the absence of leftist intellectuals or a counterpart to Greenwich Village, to the dominance of American Federation of Labor (AFL) craft unions (especially in the construction trades), and to the prevalence of service work—a vital sector in the economy that expanded vastly during the short winter tourist season. Finally, newspapers remain key sources in Miami historiography. With the lack of rich organizational records and the incompleteness or loss of many historical sources such as the early issues of the local Black and labor-union newspapers, historians and others have been unable to get to a more nuanced social history. This chapter and the rest of the book are efforts to continue this conversation.[6]

Perrine Palmer's Early History and Harmony

The story of Perrine Palmer can be traced only in Miami's local newspapers, especially the *Miami Daily News* and the city labor newspaper, though some evidence of his activism appears in a few other extant sources. Through numerous letters to the editor of the *Miami Daily News*, participation in local discussion groups, labor-union political organizing, and activism in the unemployment movement and the local housing crisis, Palmer engaged the early Depression era with calm, focused, but determined civic activism. His civic sensibilities were rooted in his middle-class background; that label, however, only scratches the surface of the complexities of his class consciousness. His sense of his family's heritage, his education, his material experiences, and his moral and intellectual integrity shaped his passion for justice and vision for a sane, equitable, and harmonious society. Recounting his biography prior to the Great Depression will help offer some context and explanation for his civic engagement during the early 1930s.

His story, and particularly his later activism and his written and spoken words, points to a class consciousness comfortable with socialist ideals, and to a determination to establish a new, more humane capitalism. In his mind, capitalists and workers could work together peaceably and for the betterment of society if all agreed that happiness was rooted in expanding consumption. One may argue that his solutions to the economic depression were impractical or that his social and political theories were limited because they lacked sophistication or ideological commitment to revolutionary change, but such criticisms would ignore the power of imagination or at least the significance of challenging the status quo. He envisioned a more egalitarian society that embraced a humane rationality, a moral commitment to economic security for all, and a utopic imagining of the promises of abundance that would offer, at the very least, the opportunity to work for a living wage, indulge in a variety of cultural experiences, and the chance to enjoy the outdoors.

Palmer was born in 1884 in Fernandina, Florida, to Sarah and John D. Palmer. John was a physician and Sarah was a stay-at-home mother who, according to one history, was interested in poetry, Florida history, horticulture, and beautification. According to his 1952 obituary, Perrine was the maternal great-grandson of Dr. Henry Perrine, the famous pioneer horticulturalist who died at the hands of the Seminole at Indian Key in 1840. Henry had been granted a large plot of land by the US government in the 1830s in the southern portion of Dade County, an area that continues to bear his name of Perrine. Sarah inherited a portion of this land in 1897 and moved to the area sometime after the turn of the century. In 1925 Sarah published an article in the *Florida Historical Quarterly* in which she discussed her grandfather's contributions to making Florida the "garden spot of America." In the late 1920s and early 1930s, Sarah lived in the Miami suburb Buena Vista and published occasional letters and poems in the *Miami Daily News*. Besides these details, not much else is known about Perrine Palmer's parents (Sarah was widowed by 1920), his childhood, or what happened to the inherited land.[7]

Perrine Palmer attended the University of the South in Sewanee, Tennessee, an Episcopalian liberal-arts college and theology school, between 1904 and 1908. He likely met his wife Sallie in the area, for the university was not coeducational until 1925 and she was a native of the state. Perrine earned a law degree in 1908 and was an active student at the university. He was a member of the Phi Delta Theta fraternity, Sigma Epsilon Literary Society, and Senior German Club, and he served as vice president in the Senior Law Club. The *Miami Daily News* obituary stated that he entered the lumber industry as a wholesaler dealer in Richmond, Virginia, and worked in it for fifteen years, living there with Sallie and their three children, Perrine Jr. (future mayor of Miami), Albert, and John. Census records and a court case reveal that he actually owned his own small business, the Palmer Lumber Company, though a lost legal suit brought against another company for failure to deliver goods in 1924 may have contributed to financial troubles—much remains unclear. Perhaps as result of this suit, Palmer and his family returned to south Florida sometime in the mid-1920s. He may have been motivated as well by the desire to succeed in a different business. He tried his hand in the real-estate business in Howey-in-the-Hills, a township in central Florida just northwest of Orlando, but he seems to have been unsuccessful. Palmer then moved to Miami. The first evidence of Palmer in Miami was an announcement that he had joined the Florida Historical Society in October 1926; the earliest letters to the *Miami Daily News* that I have located appeared in the fall of 1928. Perrine appears in the 1930 US census for Florida with his family, where he recorded his occupation as an attendant in a filling station. Absent from his 1952 obituary was any account of his 1930s activism.[8]

This narrative shows that Palmer was clearly a talented and fairly social being with a sense of history and his family's heritage, driven to provide for his family, flexible and resourceful enough to find various types of work, and that his move to a new city occurred at an inopportune time. Miami was in the midst of an economic downturn with the end of the great real-estate boom of the early 1920s. His failure to strike success in Howey-in-the-Hills mirrored that of several others who did not get in on the riches promised in the real-estate craze. It is unknown what happened to him and his family in this small central Florida town, envisioned by its founder, William John Howey, as the central point for a citrus empire.[9] What is clear is that the subsequent move to Miami happened at a difficult time in the young city's history, at least difficult for certain classes and certainly for new migrants planning to work regularly. Construction development slowed, the tourist trade decreased, and Miami continued to have a relatively undeveloped manufacturing sector. Not many employment opportunities existed, but that did not stop city boosters from selling the city or even sometimes simply bending the truth to suggest that poor economic conditions were escaping the city. Boosterism often angered local residents because it appeared insensitive to actual conditions of irregular employment. It did not take Palmer long to comment on some of the contradictions he observed in the larger economy and to engage the local problems plaguing the city.

Palmer, in any case, helped transmit a discourse that was critical of the US political economy; he sought, however, to fix capitalism rather than eliminate it. His ideas were not necessarily original. They built on a longer tradition that began to gain even more traction in the New Deal era. The tradition represented the basic outlines of what I call radical harmony discourse: an outlook that sought balance and peace among the social classes, held faith in rational and reasoned discourse, accepted hierarchy and the attainment of individual riches but frowned on greed and a maldistribution of wealth, embraced individual achievement and cooperative association equally, and sought dignity and respect for all social classes through concrete protections of minimal humane living conditions, defined as the right to housing and access to utilities, living wages, fair working conditions, and adequate consumer spending power regardless of occupation or work status (employed, unemployed, or unable to work). Palmer never directly described these ideas as a uniform and conscious ideology. His writing and various public actions, though, reveal an ideology that defined his dream and hope for class harmony or, specifically, a moral economy. Palmer's significance, however, was deeper than simply that he acted and hoped for a better world amid impoverishment and economic depression. His help in engineering a grassroots movement and consistent critical voice of local affairs left a historical trail that has allowed for the uncovering of class-harmony discourse on a local level. I suspect that it was prevalent not only in Miami but likely was embraced in many other parts of the country. Complicating the task of uncovering this class ideology has been the relative fluidity of the ideological context in which Palmer and others in the 1930s operated—a context within which socialist ideals and Marxist theory reinforced critiques of the current political economy then under massive criticism because of the great economic downturn.

The framework of this discourse was often encased by a vibrant and inclusive American patriotism. This fact takes us to a well-trodden path of historiographical debate that embodies the heart of the interpretive struggle for American radicalism. Gary Gerstle, in his work on Woonsocket, Rhode Island, identified Americanism as a malleable term, used by various groups along the political spectrum "to articulate their political beliefs and press their political demands." He took particular issue with Warren Susman's critique of Americanism as essentially pro-capitalist and pro-Fordist and thus too dismissive of genuine, homegrown radicalism. In the case of 1930s Miami, Gerstle's assessment of the malleability of Americanism is an accurate one. Missing from Gerstle's analysis, however, was a closer inspection of how Americanism, even in its radical veins, did embrace the industrial Americanism that Susman critically targeted and that he lamented as the culprit that helped develop a consumerist middle-class culture.[10]

Michael Denning critiqued both Gerstle and Susman in his attempt to rescue Americanism or what he would call the "ballads of Americans." Denning found deeper significance for Americanism than simply Gerstle's "politics of patriotism," and he dismissed Susman's call for a more critical stance of the relationship between culture and political economy. Instead, Denning located crisis and struggle in Americanism over a "pan-ethnic Americanism" and, more specifically, he apparently identified a "constant cultural war" defining America's landscape. His quest to write the history of the "laboring of American culture" took him to the industrial unions of the CIO and the working-class audience taking in the culture productions of the 1930s Popular Front. Denning argued that a "plebian sensibility confident, almost hegemonic," that "was hardly middle class," emerged from the 1930s and, thus, he seemed to drive a dagger into Susman's middle-class monster and, with it, into harmony discourse. He also extended the scope and breadth of Gerstle's Americanism as primarily progressive and nearly hegemonic.[11]

The beat of the industrial machine continued to thump, nonetheless, with the assistance and collusion of the working classes and its leaders. Americanism did entail a conversation between the Fordist state and culture, but it did not necessarily result in Susman's culturally and morally starved middle class or Denning's "pan-ethnic Americanism." Americanism was a political language used to articulate the struggles over political economy often inspired by the various theoretical frameworks of the period. The struggles essentially centered on how to manage the industrial economy's wealth and how to reframe the social contract in the new political economy. A radical class harmony, infused with visions of moral economy, was often embedded in the language of Americanism. That is, the patriotic language of Americanism represented only one part of a larger class-conscious ideological vessel. Radial class-harmony discourse, reflecting the effort to attain a moral economy, however, has been largely ignored in the historiographical struggles over American radicalism and American exceptionalism; or, put in another way, in attempts to answer why there is no socialism in the United States, scholars have been swept away by the currents of exceptionalism and the romanticism of radicalism.

Harmony offered an alternative to classlessness and class-conflict discourses, and it remains relatively unexplored in class analysis literature. It offers a middle road between the dichotomy of classlessness and class conflict that did not buy into the myths of either camp, recognized the need for human cooperation, and valued the contribution of individual effort. Shaped as early as the late nineteenth century and developed more distinctly during the Progressive Era, the push for greater social harmony by intellectuals and progressive reformers energized many, for it bore hope for a better society. As historian Shelton Stromquist has argued for the early Progressive movement and Howard Brick has traced in the twentieth century, the critique of capitalism and desire to reform it ran deep, was visionary, and sought social justice. Palmer's ideas undoubtedly built from the zeitgeist of the era that expressed a faith in modernity's and technology's ability to alleviate economic plight.[12] Combine a small dash of Taylorist faith in efficient production, a pinch of organized labor's vision of expanding and sharing the wealth of the industrial state, and a balanced view of the relationship between freedom and work, and one arrives at Palmer's optimistic brew for a fairer capitalism, a moral economy. Most immediately, he drew from the floating prescriptions that sought to alleviate unemployment and help formulate a more rational and moral economic system: the shorter-hours movement and share-the-work plans and the technocracy movement of the early 1930s.

The shorter-hour work plans emerged from discussions during the era among business, labor, and individuals seeking to increase employment and improve the standard of living. Having roots in the nineteenth century with the movement to reduce the workday so as to create more knowledgeable and active citizens and spread the benefits of employment and leisure, its ideas gained traction as unemployment skyrocketed after 1929.[13] Employers such as Kellogg implemented the six-hour, four-shift workday and increased the number of employees in the company. Along with organized labor, many looked to shorter hours as a solution to unemployment, while others imagined more time for leisure, play, and cultural and spiritual development as humane alternatives to the alienating drudgery of industrial and other forms of work. According to historian Benjamin Hunnicutt, the shorter-hours debates spurred President Franklin Roosevelt's New Deal and its mission to find alternative solutions to unemployment that embraced conservative notions of work over more radical ideas. The victory of the forty-hour over the thirty-hour workweek in federal legislation, for instance, is one concrete manifestation of this debate.[14]

The technocracy movement, existing since at least the early twentieth century, experienced a revival and wide popularity in the fall of 1932. It expressed a faith in the power of technology to increase economic abundance and looked to engineers to figure out how to most efficiently use the vast natural resources in the United States to raise the economic well-being of all individuals. In general, technocrats of this stripe demonstrated impatience with politics, especially the two-party system and the failure of third-party movements, because of their apparent inefficiency, ineffectiveness, and corruption. Technocracy revealed a humane and compassionate commitment to resolving human suffering and seemed to make the most sense to many in the context of the Great Depression. Most important, the technocracy movement invigorated social and political activism throughout the country with the hopefulness of its vision to end scarcity. Advocates of national economic planning and participants and heirs of the experiments and ideas from the Progressive era and World War I embraced the central planning advocated by the technocracy movement and discarded the more radical and technical aspects of its tenets.[15]

The desire to make abundance more available to workers living in a machine age worked hand in hand with a reverence for the idea that people are "endowed by their Creator with certain unalienable rights, that among these are Life, Liberty, and the pursuit of Happiness." Palmer's words and actions helped shape the DCUCL activism in resolving the problems of hunger, homelessness, and joblessness, and, in the process, he succeeded in creating a sense of community. Palmer and the Unemployment Citizens' League's quest for equal opportunity and social justice, and not merely a more adequate social welfare net, were driven by their desire for moral economy in the modern world. Although the DCUCL and Palmer were shaped by the intellectual currents of the time, their concrete connections with the labor movement were indicative of unionism's spirit and symbolism in capitalist America. Radical class-harmony discourse allowed grassroots activists to dissociate from socialism and communism even when their goals for greater equality and social justice overlapped and echoed each other. The balancing act in a red-scare culture was difficult, to be sure, but essential for maintaining political legitimacy in the eyes of the greater public and the local business, religious, and government leaders. Poverty in the midst of economic abundance perplexed many in the early 1930s. Palmer and the DCUCL merely highlighted the need to close the gap and challenge the ideological reverence for scarcity in economic thought. They imagined a world where abundance would provide basic economic security and not bolster greater inequalities and disparities in wealth.

The Palmer Plan

Like many other Americans, Perrine Palmer was often unemployed during the 1930s. His response to economic depression was first to keep trying to find employment and second to try to imagine how society would get out of the crisis. As he shared the plight of the more than 25 percent of America's workforce that was officially unemployed, members of Miami's upper class clung to the power of cheerful boosterism. In January 1931, members of the Chamber of Commerce gathered to listen to Clayton Sedgwick Cooper preach about what Miamians needed in order to get out of the economic depression. Few garnered more legitimacy in the eyes of the business community than Cooper. Writing several didactic books, with a Western-centered, missionary vision, Cooper the world traveler had in 1926 founded the Committee of One Hundred, a millionaires' social club based in Miami Beach that lasted into the late twentieth century. It consisted of wealthy winter visitors interested in spectator sports such as horse racing and polo and individual recreation such as swimming, golf, and yachting. The club also invited speakers to lecture on the topics of the day and other cultural entertainments. Cooper's reputation and status also rested on his early association with the *Miami Tribune* and his many publications. An exemplar of his style was his 1927 book, *The Philosophy of Business*, a collection of optimistic essays he had published in the local newspapers as part of Burdine's department store's advertisement scheme to bolster local morale after the devastating 1926 hurricane hit Miami. Cooper reminded Miami citizens about the greatness of south Florida, "the birthland of health and happiness," and asserted that "the worst form of civic anaemia is negative criticism."[16] He exhorted members of the Chamber of Commerce in a similar vein. Perrine Palmer's encounter with the news of this gathering sparked a response.

Palmer, in a letter to the *Miami Daily News*, related how Cooper told his audience "that what Miami needs is a spirit of optimism and faith in the future of our city." The only problem was that "some 10,000 unemployed wage earners were at home or walking the streets, wondering where their next meal was coming from." Palmer was impatient with and indignant about Cooper's booster optimism in the newspaper amid the Depression. But his concern extended as well to every merchant, businessperson, banker, and professional who wondered "how much longer he can keep his doors open." With a controlled vehemence, Palmer continued: "The preachers might just as well continue to cram creeds and morals down our hungry throats and laws down the thirsty ones as for business and civic leaders to continue to put off the smash they fear with high-sounding words."[17] "Smash" in this context referred to social breakdown and possibly a revolution resulting from the rampant hunger and homelessness.

He demanded action, collective action, and from all groups and individuals in society. Charity offered, at best, temporary relief. "The unemployment and consequent business depression problems," Palmer continued, "will be solved when, and only when, our business, civic and religious leaders face squarely the real cause of these things." The early 1930s identified overproduction as a primary cause of the sluggish economy. Cutting back production and the subsequent reduction in hours and jobs was intended to bring balance to the economy. The National Recovery Administration and Agriculture Adjustment Administration in the summer of 1933 would begin to impose such measures. But the lack of consumption was the key factor in causing and maintaining the economic depression, according to Palmer and other contemporaries. It would not be until the second New Deal (after 1935) that the federal government would identify underconsumption more clearly as a problem and embrace specific policies to encourage consumption.[18] The buying power of "our vast army of wage earners" would far outpace the purchasing power of the concentrated wealth of the rich. The need to "find work that will assure a decent living for [the unemployed] and their dependents" was imperative in order to get out of depression and avoid "the hungry masses" from changing the present form "of government by revolution."[19]

The revolution could be avoided with wise leadership, thought, and a humane vision of reform. Palmer called for the voluntary action of business leaders to reduce the hours of workers, not to reduce production, but rather to distribute employment among the unemployed and thus increase the purchasing potential of the masses. The logic and humaneness of this perspective is both striking and consistent with the larger shorter-hours movement of the period, and with the positions of the American Federation of Labor and many business leaders as well. In this early formulation of his ideas, Palmer already was highlighting the need to tackle technological unemployment and to use the economic and social potential of technology and machines, as he would have put it, for social good and improving the quality of life for everyone. Connecting technology with the need to increase consumption and spread employment so as to lessen the burdens of work and thus improve the quality of life challenged mainstream business thought.[20] Working constructively toward improving the quality of life by using the available technological and natural resources at hand offered a reasoned alternative to revolution and violence.

Just as important, it infused ethics and morality into the questions of political economy. As he wrote: "Blaming overproduction on the machine age is only an admission of defeat. We might just as well say that progress defeats its own purpose: that God's highest law is the survival of the fittest and, in the name of religion, knock some 30,000,000 men, women and children in the head and let it go at that." He was quick to point out that "machines have not been used to shorten man's hours of labor; nor primarily, even to save his back. *They have been used to get rid of him entirely*" (italics added). One may claim that he was overstating the case of technological unemployment, but that would miss the point and the morality. Palmer's argument for greater distribution of abundance implicitly challenged rugged individualism and maintained a deep respect for the drive for individuality. In his deference to the dignity of men, he was ambivalent about charity, not because he feared chiselers taking advantage of being on the dole, but because it damaged one's quest for independence and thus subordinated them as human beings. This clearly related to his struggle to find work to support his family. His attack on the doctrine of survival of the fittest equally carried weight with his audience. Linking God, progress, and the contradictory moral association of religion with a cold, cruel social Darwinism would not have escaped his readers' moral sensibilities. Nor the common sense that "the happiness and well-being of the masses" required that they have the basic means of existence and that an economy and business unable to provide them eventually would collapse. The collective nature of the Depression experience revealed how, out of no fault of their own, a breakdown in economic structure could victimize them despite their most valiant efforts. Palmer's God found unacceptable the moral justifications explaining the Depression and the lack of more effective, creative and humane responses to the economic downturn as well.[21]

This discourse took sharper form over the next year and led eventually to the publication in March 1932 of the Palmer Plan by the *Miami Daily News*, a newspaper that had published several of his letters. It was a full-page article, more than 4,500 words in length. The newspaper introduced Palmer as a representative of the unemployed perspective. The main ideas discussed in February 1931 reappeared in the essay, though the length offered Palmer the opportunity to elaborate on points his two shorter letters could not. The time that elapsed also gave Palmer time to circulate and refine his ideas. Verner Townley, a fifty-year-old Miami pioneer (a resident of the city since 1896), wrote a 1933 retrospective account of the timeline and the crafting of the Palmer Plan. Townley described how Palmer corresponded with his friend Dr. Walter Montgomery, a professor of Latin at the University of Virginia, who asked him what his ideas were on ending the Depression. More notable was his correspondence with John Dewey, famous pragmatist, philosopher of education, and chairman of the League of Independent Political Action. Dewey, who endorsed Palmer's ideas, described him to Townley (also active in local discussions and activism, and perhaps Palmer's biggest supporter), this way: "He has many excellent ideas about the present situation. He has, I think, lost employment, and is not well off in worldly goods, but he has a fine mind and fine ideas, judging from his letter. You might be interested in seeing him." Dewey was responding to Townley's own letter that posed twelve questions on the Depression that echoed Palmer's ideas of nearly a year earlier.[22]

The Palmer Plan's publication occurred after Palmer presented his ideas to a meeting held by Dr. Jacob H. Kaplan in Kaplan Hall in Temple Israel synagogue. Kaplan was a part-time University of Miami faculty member and a respected and active rabbi in the small Jewish community then existing in the city and in Dade County.[23] He endorsed Palmer's thesis and arranged a meeting with the "foremost business men and civic leaders," including former mayor and Chamber of Commerce founder E. G. Sewell, three members of the Committee of One Hundred, and two others, as well as Townley. Once the plan was published, Palmer and Townley distributed hundreds of copies to leading industrialists and the "foremost men in public life." The list included Mayor Frank Murphy of Detroit, Governor Gifford Pinchot of Pennsylvania, Owen D. Young, chair of General Electric, and Governor Franklin D. Roosevelt of New York. According to Townley, Murphy and Pinchot endorsed the plan and Young offered a favorable response. It is unknown how Roosevelt reacted to the plan as governor, but in Townley's view he felt the plan was "identical with the national recovery act." In January 1933 Perrine Palmer sent a copy of the *Miami Daily News* article to president-elect Roosevelt with an attached letter stating that the "forgotten man" or "industrial cannon fodder" was looking to the president "as our only hope." The only response was a warm but formal reply from a Roosevelt secretary. Townley's retrospective highlights the local interest and enthusiasm in Palmer's plan, particularly its embrace of a consumptionist approach to political economy.[24]

The Palmer Plan, as presented in March 1932, now presented a clearer role for the government and elaborated on the idea of an increase in consumption and its significance. The calls for voluntarism as the framework of the plan remained, though Palmer now evoked the patriotism used so effectively during World War I when wide-scale government planning occurred. In the coming months and years, several individuals and New Dealers would point to the war planning as a successful model on which to build.[25] Specifically, Palmer envisioned a presidential proclamation declaring the patriotic duty of businesses to try out voluntarily, and for only a sixty-day period, the plan to increase employment opportunities by reducing hours and offering more jobs. He pointed to the successful implementation of the six-hour-a-day program in the Kellogg Company's Battle Creek, Michigan, factory, which had started the program in December 1930. For Miami and Dade County, however, the reduced-hour program would drop to no more than five hours per worker per day and include all jobs, including agriculture and domestic service. The idea was clearly tailored to Miami's economy. At least one local employer implemented a program of spreading employment. Palmer called for emancipating workers from the drudgery of work and empowering them with the buying power to purchase goods to enjoy their free time. In this way, Palmer viewed the Depression as primarily a social problem and not an economic one. Here is an extended quote that offers his perspective succinctly:

> Our vast army of wage and salary earners, on whose buying power the whole capitalistic system of government must finally stand or fall, would be buying things for which they have never before had any use; because they have never before had time each day to use those things; time each day for the fresh air and sunshine now arbitrarily and foolishly denied them; for the recreational and cultural pursuits so vital for the physical, spiritual, and economic well-being of all nations.

> Did you ever stop to think how many bathing suits, fishing tackles, garden tools, tennis racquets, golf sticks, sport clothes, motor boats, skates, sleds, automobiles, matinee tickets and countless other things that vast army might buy, if they had time each day to use them? How much time has that vast army to buy anything, even when employed?[26]

Absent is the guilt of consuming unneeded goods, a dilemma for many consumptionists of the 1920s. He combined producerist and consumptionist ideas when he highlighted the value of labor as "the thing that constitutes both the supply and demand for all our products." Palmer presented here a conception and outlook that was grounded in the Miami of recreation and leisure. Work was relegated to the status of a vital need but not the only vital need in the pursuit of happiness.

Society's inability to see the connection between work and consumption revealed a moral failure and a misuse of technology. The article pointed to several examples of technological unemployment. One example recounted that recent capitalization in Everglades sugar farming displaced more than five hundred cane cutters. Palmer quoted a passage from a 1931 article by the progressive Colorado senator Edward P. Costigan that reminded its readers that "the unhappy plight of industrial workers, our farm population, and moderate business was treated . . . for the most part with indifference [in the years preceding the 1929 panic]. The steady decrease in employment . . . was noted then forgotten. Diminishing pay rolls were overshadowed by increasing machine production." According to Palmer, machinery had lessened the demand on individuals to labor as long as they once had. The decrease had been ignored because "we have utterly failed to recognize that sound economics, sound religion, good sportsmanship, are all one and the same thing: Inseparable. For it would have indeed been a foolish God who would have decreed an economically unprofitable code of morals." The social order, in other words, should be rational and moral, which of course implied that things had been irrational and immoral. Nothing was necessarily wrong with technology, but because it displaced workers from jobs, society needed to confront the phenomenon and reorder access to abundance. Technological unemployment certainly suggested an irrational path that contradicted the rational and efficient veneer that the modern industrial state promised. The disparity in the standard of living between the rich and ordinary people disrupted social harmony. Workers would revolt when denied access to society's expanding abundance, especially in light of their role in producing the nation's wealth.[27]

The call for balance and fair and equal opportunities to enjoy life had a radical edge even if Palmer was not advocating the equalizing of conditions and abolishing hierarchy. Yet to equate the lives of rich capitalists with those of cooks certainly argued for a radical humanitarianism: "Will you tell me that those great financial and religious leaders, J. P. Morgan and John D. Rockefeller, are entitled each day to fresh air and sunshine, recreation and culture, but that the girls in our stores, the clerks in our office, the cooks in our kitchens, are not?" Palmer wrote. He continued, "And do you think we can promote the wealth of this nation by continuing a system that denies to human beings those gifts of God?" How Palmer's Episcopalianism influenced his thinking is not clear from any extant historical evidence other than that he attended the University of the South. But clearly evoking God and the concern for the physical and spiritual well-being of individuals and the nation promoted a moral world outlook, one that showed concern for each individual's happiness and how that was predicated on the need for economic independence and economic security. That "sound economics, sound religion, and good sportsmanship" were inseparable in Palmer's mind points to the power of radical class harmony and its call for moral economy. While his plan was neither detailed nor permanent, he offered a vision that was hopeful and suggested an alternative capitalism that thus far had not existed or at least only in some quarters. Most concretely, by advocating a "shortage of labor" (or labor scarcity), as opposed to a surplus of labor, he pushed for labor-market conditions favorable to workers that would eventually allow for a fair and moral working of the laws of supply and demand. His view continued an older tradition of moral economy rooted in competency and communalism—and one echoing the persistent demands of organized labor.[28] Finally, the workers highlighted in Palmer's reference reflected Miami's economic landscape. The class juxtaposition of cooks and clerks with wealthy capitalists may hide an equally radical alignment with industrial labor. It is essential, however, to keep this expansive sense of solidarity in focus. Miami's service economy constituted a parallel model to the industrial and had similar though different organizational challenges.

The *Miami Herald* printed a front-page story about the meeting and reported that the business leaders attending Kaplan's meeting found the plan unsound and impractical, leading them to reject it in a minority report. In addition to taking an authoritative stance (they were all employers of labor), they protested Palmer's apparent undiplomatic language, specifically criticizing the plan's opening assertion that apes would be better than humans in finding a remedy for the economic depression. One suspects that Palmer's moral tone struck a discordant chord among these respectable capitalists more accustomed to being on the other end of preaching. E. G. Sewell argued that the state governors meet in conference, agree to increase employment by fifty percent on a designated day, reduce hours to only five a day, and decrease wages accordingly—a refutation of Palmer's demand to maintain high wages. One retailer concurring with this minority report proposed that the road to economic recovery needed to start with retailers. He thought it critical that retailers "remove their bargain signs and by a tempting display of goods inspire optimism among buyers with hoarded money." Apparently, Clayton Sedgwick Cooper's philosophy of positive thinking influenced some people.[29]

The plan was widely discussed in Miami, as in several letters published in the *Miami Daily News* letter forum over the next several weeks. A week later, the newspaper published an alternative plan from "Col. E. R. Thomas of Miami Beach, retired manufacturer and deep student of economic affairs." The plan was not so much a plan, according to Thomas; it was more a call to organizing a nonpolitical advocacy group to promote economic growth and discourage or eliminate speculation. This "retired capitalist"—former manufacturer of bicycles, motorcycles, and automobiles—offered a mostly sprawling response critical of the "profiteering middleman," essentially financiers and "Wall Street bears." He emphasized the critical importance of producers and called for the organizing of a "National Prosperity League" that would advocate for smart progrowth policies that would not injure society's producers (farmers, workers, and businesses "whose prosperity depends upon the prosperity of the masses"). Revealing his nineteenth-century producerist pedigree, he paraphrased the old Knights of Labor ideal and wrote an "injury to one injures all." It was nonresponsive to Palmer's plan.[30]

Edwin Ross Thomas's plan received no reaction or comment, but Palmer's earned enthusiastic reception, largely in part because of its moral economic basis. Several individuals mentioned how they bought many copies of the March 27 *Miami Daily News* issue to distribute to friends and to send to prominent Americans around the country. One reader sent a copy to Gifford Pinchot, Pennsylvania's governor, and then published Pinchot's brief positive response to it. John Phelan, an unemployed former deacon and self-proclaimed communist, criticized the plan because he thought it would maintain capitalism. "There can be no [shared] identity of interest," Phelan noted, since employers always want "labor power to be plentiful so it will be cheap." Perhaps the most interesting response came from Stephen C. Singleton, a house painter and poet. Although he thought it doubtful that a presidential proclamation was possible and was not sure whether shorter hours could help end the depression, Singleton did find Palmer's moral vision important even if he felt that the "law of economics is as fixed and unchangeable as is the law of gravity." His skepticism was fueled by how "government by injunction had undermined liberty," a reference to how the judicial system had impeded successful union organization. Yet, not unlike Phelan, Singleton directed the reader's attention to a more radical perspective: Palmer's moral message that "the Divine law of economics emanates from a source superior to man's wisdom." Much of his letter cited Huey Long's March 22 populist Senate speech, highlighting interestingly Long's biblical references, including "Moreover the profit of the earth is for all" (Ecclesiastes 5:9, KJV). Singleton's point was to align Palmer's and Long's moral messages, noting the latter's concluding statement: "Let us have it understood that it is our purpose to bring the fruits of this land, the wealth of this land, to be enjoyed by 120,000,000 people." Singleton continued, writing that "to the degree that a compass is more reliable in indicating a direction than a wavering finger, to that degree the Divine Plan is superior to the Palmer Plan." The moral power of the Palmer Plan was abundantly evident to Singleton, even though it did not go far enough, and he urged the *Miami Daily News* to publish the entirety of Long's speech. Palmer had clearly captured the public imagination and had since the winter of 1931.[31]

Shorter Hours, Technocracy, and Activism

Palmer's ideas would gain traction in two developments later in 1932: the introduction of the Black bill in the US Senate and the resurgence of the technocracy movement. The American Federation of Labor drafted thirty-hours legislation that Senator Hugo Black introduced to the Seventy-second Congress in December 1932 (introduced as the Connery bill in the House). The bill would "prohibit, in interstate or foreign commerce, all goods produced by establishments where workers were employed more than five days a week or 6 hours a day." The AFL's logic echoed Palmer's Plan to an amazing degree: shortening hours would provide more work and thus offering immediate work relief and, once recovery occurred, as historian Benjamin Hunnicutt pointed out, "labor could bargain effectively for higher wages in a condition of continued labor scarcity." The Black bill represented a break from the AFL's traditional voluntarism and reliance on collective bargaining as the means of improving working conditions and pay because it sought government intervention. Palmer drew attention to the bill in an April 1933 letter.[32]

Palmer argued for the importance of the Black bill, but he felt it did not go far enough. He feared it might be deemed unconstitutional because it singled out businesses involved in interstate or international commerce while leaving workers in local businesses uncovered. Palmer's criticism seemed to suggest a broader reading of the constitution's commerce clause, one that would emerge in Supreme Court case *NLRB v. Jones and Laughlin Steel Corp* 301 US 1 (1937). Palmer believed Miami's locally focused economy, with little interstate and international commerce, would make the bill largely inapplicable in his hometown under the current Supreme Court's narrower reading of the power of the commerce clause. He therefore argued for the principle "equal rights to all, special privileges to none," a hopeful formulation that equated the current bill as "class legislation of the most vicious sort" for not including all commerce. Conditions were unreasonable in the Magic City. As he wrote, "You'll be surprised at the average work hours in Miami, if you'll take the trouble to investigate." Palmer applied the idea of radical class harmony by advocating that all businesses be required to adopt shorter hours and thus offering no group or individual a way of avoiding the law. The merging of the goals of the AFL with those of Palmer rooted the latter in the labor movement nationally and locally.[33] Palmer regularly attended the weekly Labor's Citizenship Committee (organized in 1929), the political and civic arm of the AFL's Central Labor Union of Dade County. Though it is unclear when he began attending, it appears he may have begun as early as 1931, when AFL President William Green spoke on shorter hours in Carpenters Union Hall—a bustling location where the Central Labor Union, Labor's Citizenship Committee, and several other unions held their weekly meetings.

The idea of shorter hours, as it evolved over the 1920s, sought to ameliorate the worst aspects of industrial capitalism and offer the opportunity for greater cultural and personal development. This quest for freedom to attain happiness outside work challenged the industrial order and the power of work over individuals' lives. Citing Edward Sapir, the early-twentieth-century linguist and anthropologist, Benjamin Hunnicutt highlighted the visionary turn of the Progressive agenda in the 1920s. Paraphrasing Sapir, Hunnicutt wrote, "The human standards of the 'harmonious, balanced, and self-satisfactory' society and the 'spiritual primacy of the individual soul' were the bases of 'genuine' progress but were being ignored, since 'part of the time we are dray horses: the rest of the time we are listless consumers of goods which receive not the least impression of our personalities.'"[34] This call for a more ethical society underpinned Palmer's politics. Picking up from this intellectual current and the AFL's embrace of shorter hours, Palmer sought to attain societal harmony by pushing for the spread of abundance through the shortening of the workday and greater democratic cooperation. The elimination of scarcity teased the idea of transcending capitalism.[35]

Palmer's vision also merged and was bolstered by the technocracy movement that developed at the end of the year. Made popular by journalist Wayne Parrish's essays in the *New Outlook*, several Miamians were excited by the scientific-sounding analysis of technocrats who both helped explain the ongoing economic depression and offered hope of a future where economic abundance guaranteed economic security for all. Organized by a group of engineers at Columbia University in the spring of 1932, technocracy sought to rationalize the use of the country's resources and to do so through the efficient and maximum use of technology. It also envisioned the elimination of politics and the distribution of resources to all.[36] Though gaining some press coverage in the summer of 1932, it was not until Parrish's essays, first published in November, that technocracy lit a fire among Miamians. Through the editorial pages of the *Miami Daily News*, Verner Townley, Perrine Palmer, Charles W. Nicholson, and others discussed technocracy as outlined by Parrish. Palmer's letter, "We Must Have Action," deemed Parrish's November essay, "What Is Technocracy?," "the most vital document of our age."[37]

Parrish laid out the ideas of the growing and rejuvenated technocracy movement in this essay but only after outlining the dire economic conditions in the country. Palmer quoted the ominous first sentence of Parrish's article: "The United States is much nearer a complete industrial collapse, as a result of the events of the last three years, than the vast majority of its citizens realize." For Palmer and many others, such a diagnosis rang true and offered an accurate assessment. It highlighted how an appropriate response ought to sidestep politics and offer solutions from experts that were humane and sought a fair distribution of the nation's resources. The outlook echoed the most hopeful aspects of modernity, particularly its faith in technology and its indictment of the current social and political order. It is no surprise that down-and-out workers and other sufferers of Depression conditions would find technocracy appealing. According to technocracy advocates, the biggest cause of unemployment was technology, but the very force that led to such fluctuations in employment and instability in the economy could also liberate the masses with the proper manipulation, guidance, and the abandonment of partisan politics. So, while images and discussions abounded in newspapers, magazines, and other venues about workers being displaced by machines, the cover of journalist Frank Arkright's short book *The ABC of Technocracy* scratched out capitalism, socialism, and communism and wrote in bold letters "technocracy." The title suggested how modernity's promise of abundance discarded the older conceptions of political economy, which was guilty of maintaining scarcity, evoking indirectly the spirit of Edward Bellamy's influential 1888 novel, *Looking Backward*. In scratching out capitalism, socialism, and communism, Arkright's cover highlighted the hopefulness of the moment. Technocratic remedies for societal problems persisted in the century even as technocracy faded in the historical memory.[38]

The technocracy craze lasted for a short period, in part, because it was quickly discredited and ridiculed by economists and other intellectuals. The high expectations its dubious statistics produced, and the hyperbole and egomania of its leader, Howard Scott, helped ruin the nascent movement. Nonetheless, the essence of its ideas lived on in the imagination of many around the country and even sparked a short-lived movement as Scott continued to linger in the shadows.[39]

This movement helped inform the politics of Perrine Palmer and the DCUCL. In July 1933, the Continental Committee on Technocracy held a convention in Estes Park, Colorado, where it issued its *Plan of Plenty*, a fifteen-page pamphlet outlining the political and social vision of the movement. Palmer, on behalf of the DCUCL, referred to the *Plan of Plenty* in an October 1933 letter to President

Roosevelt. He called it a "simple, practical, brief statement" seeking "scientific distribution through constitutional means without doing violence to existing laws or private property rights." The plan, issued on July Fourth—"How insignificant that date, Mr. President," Palmer wrote—challenged the liberal capitalist framework in that it proposed to abolish exploitative labor relations and replace them with a cooperative vision of shared obligations and responsibilities. It called for the intellectual community to "prepare the people for the replacement of the present greed motif by an older and more efficient one, the instinctive desire of all human beings for prestige, for the appreciation of their fellows." The goal of "plenty for all" countered scarcity as an organizing principle, and the Continental Committee on Technocracy stressed that "reason must be allowed to rule, unhampered by anxiety" (i.e., the concerns for "food, shelter or any of the necessities of life"). The call for community cooperation and abundance for all, thus, held its appeal and inspired Palmer and the DCUCL in the hopeful moments of the early New Deal.[40]

Technocracy was only one of the many responses to capitalism's (near) collapse that emerged in the late 1920s and early 1930s and deviated from communism and socialism's more radical approaches. As the historian Donald Miller has argued, a whole array of non-Marxist independent leftists pushed for a democratic socialism or at least a more humane capitalism. Such organizations as John Dewey's League of Independent Political Action, formed in 1928, reflected the frustration with partisan politics shared by so many; this disorganized but vibrant movement pressed to accomplish a progressive solution to economic and social injustice. Alfred Bingham's *Common Sense*, established in November 1932 and linked to Dewey's league, provided one of the platforms on current issues for these independent leftists. Hence, it was by no accident that Palmer and Townley reached out and communicated with John Dewey, a paragon of progressive ideals and pragmatic philosophy.[41]

While the faith in technocracy as a solution to scarcity inspired hope in many, it also increased frustration with the mishandling of the economy. The frustration, and the need for immediate action, was at the core of much activism around the country. Miami's unemployment movement was just one example. In embracing an economics of growth, however, technocracy slipped into a futile, direct competition with capitalism. At least socialists and communists offered more radical alternatives to the corporate economy and the existing power structure. Palmer, and the unemployment movement he was a part of, thus faced the perennial question any political movement faces: to what extent will compromise and tradeoffs sacrifice the goals of the movement?

The similar vision of corporate capitalism and technocracy—an outlook of growth—placed the battle for legitimacy on the terrain of economic convention. Success of the unemployment movement, of course, was not determined by the merits of its arguments for a cooperative commonwealth. The nature of power and its resiliency helped prevent Dewey, other non-Marxist radicals, technocrats, socialists, and communists from cracking the system. The significance of political activism and criticisms of the larger political economy, however, does not rest on the track record of concrete markers of success, as in specific political victories. Influence on the mainstream, while often less obvious, is significant and can be measured only by tracing the activism of such grassroots movements.[42]

Inspired by his own sense of justice and the morality of a cooperative commonwealth and the vision of shared abundance promised by technocracy, Palmer pressed for grassroots activism in Miami and Dade County. Something had to be done that would end the evictions, the cutting of water services, and the miserliness of public and private doles. In the letter "We Must Have Action," Palmer stated, "There is only one thing we can do, and that is to organize the unemployed of our own community for the manning of our surplus tools of production and distribution, not for sale but for use." Evidently, Palmer had already joined Miami's nascent unemployment movement, which joined the efforts of various unemployed self-help groups in the country and the growing activism throughout the country.[43] His idea was consistent with socialist principles, and it anticipated the production-for-use ideas of Upton Sinclair's popular 1934 campaign, End Poverty in California.[44]

Palmer's production-for-use prescription stemmed from a long tradition, pragmatic sensibility, and hopefulness about the possibilities of abundance: technocracy stressed abundant US natural resources. For the unemployed, evicted, and down-and-out, the sight of unused resources must have been frustrating. Even more important, it helped stir the imagination about abundance, frame scarcity as a thing of the past, and reduce economics to questions of production to meet the needs of a consuming public. Palmer called for the local leaders (those with immediate power) to act and thus seemed deferential or possibly even paternalistic. Yet he simultaneously embraced grassroots, democratic organization as a means of enacting change. Palmer targeted his message at institutions of power: local businesses, the mayor, city and county commission, the sheriff, and the courts.[45] He envisioned Miami serving as a model for the rest of the country and thus harked back to the Wisconsin Idea from the Progressive era in which reform at the local and state levels would inform wider progressive change.

Conclusion

Palmer revealed a deep faith in rational discourse and its ability to arrive at reasoned, moral, and ethical solutions to the Great Depression. His humanistic politics drew him to hopeful and optimistic visions of abundance built on the ideals of a cooperative commonwealth. Palmer and others in Miami and across the world were perplexed by the apparent contradiction of the persistence of impoverishment amid abundance. Growing up middle-class, Palmer seems to have been educated to believe in the American dream that hard work would lead to economic success or at least economic security for oneself and one's family. Depressed economic conditions and the lack of opportunities afforded individuals to rise above those depressed conditions struck Palmer and others as evidence that the conservative rhetoric of individualism could not stand up to the overwhelming evidence that the game was rigged. In light of the productive capacities of the modern economy, cooperative democratic engagement seemed to offer the best opportunity to attain social harmony.

Instead of advocating revolution, supporting violent political demonstrations, or embracing a radical political leftist philosophy, he and the DCUCL chose to express their right to freedom of speech and tried to find practical solutions to the unemployment affecting their community. The next chapter will explore the history the DCUCL more carefully. Suffice it to note here that Palmer made no effort to turn to the ideologies or the party organizations of the socialists or communists as solutions to the existing political economy. His perspective, nonetheless, suggested a postcapitalist vision. Palmer's faith in the power of reasoned, rational discourse might be interpreted as reformist, idealistic, or even utopic, the ultimate discrediting accusation that realists employ. Doing so, however, would minimize the significance of his and the DCUCL's activism and reduce one's judgment to condescension or cynicism. We are wise to remember E. P. Thompson's effort to contravene the "enormous condescension of posterity" in judging the significance of the "agency of the working people."[46] One may amend Thompson's call and apply critical analysis of how the contemporary far left or orthodox economists may have assessed Palmer's and the DCUCL's intellectual and political contributions.

A fruitful perspective would be to take David Montgomery's assessment of early-twentieth-century socialism's significance to heart. Montgomery argued that the Socialist Party's success, as little as it may have been in the aggregate, appealed to workers most when it pushed for practical solutions to workers' concerns, as in the Tri-Cities of Rock Island and Moline, Illinois, and Davenport, Iowa, where the party crusaded for setting up kindergartens, improving consumer debt, and tackling home ownership issues. To denigrate those efforts as evidence of the "bourgeois influence on the party" and "sewer socialism" is to ignore the fact that "the bourgeois, and only they, already had good sewers." One should not be distracted by the kinds of demands being made, but rather the real existing human needs. As Montgomery argued about the machinists supporting or at least sympathizing with the Socialist Party, workers took issue with the ethic of competition and greed, particularly when their own economic well-being was threatened. He wrote, "The intellectual dichotomy of reformism versus revolutionary activity obscures, rather than clarifies, the ideology of these workers."[47]

The same may be said of activists in Miami during the 1930s, though with an important caveat: Miami was less exposed to communist and socialist organizing, at least in the first half of the 1930s, and thus never quite established a significant story of radical activism to catch the historian's eye. Reformism may have ruled the discourse, but the various activists were motivated and inspired by a critique of capitalism that did not accept the status quo. Palmer represented one important example. Miamians who analyzed and critiqued the political economy did so in a context where abundance and scarcity were as acute as anywhere else in the country, perhaps even more so. As winter playground for the rich and upper middle class, Miami served as a virtual laboratory of class relations. The discourse of class harmony played a significant role in class relations, offering an alternative worldview that challenged class-conflict discourses.[48] How that was the case is the subject of the next chapter.

CHAPTER 6

Fighting for Social Harmony

Relief, New Deals, and the Unemployed

The opening anecdote of Nels Anderson's 1938 WPA book, *The Right to Work*, serves as a good antidote to the hypocrisy often characteristic of self-interested and aloof theorizing. Anderson, the famous sociologist of hobo culture and homelessness, offered insight on the concrete benefits government investment could have. He related how an economics professor, an avid advocate of laissez-faire at the start of the Great Depression, became a supporter of government intervention after experiencing lost income and joblessness in his own family. Whereas in 1930 he was against relief and argued that the laws of supply and demand would work if given a chance, his blind faith in competition and individualism dissipated in subsequent years as he and his family endured economic hardship. Employment in government jobs for his family and the return of lost teaching assignments helped transform his thinking. He now argued for government to work efficiently, effectively, and with little debt, as any good businessperson would expect of their own venture. Perhaps a didactic anecdote, Anderson's story revealed his own faith in government as director of Labor Relations in the Works Progress Administration. The book was filled with photographs of major public-works projects completed or underway: the iconography of the New Deal filled its pages, images of laboring workers, shared experiences, and collective efforts. It undoubtedly presented the New Deal at its best. Yet the story of the economics professor, while clearly more accepting of government intervention, ends with him expressing concern about the mounting debt and wondering "how are we going to pay the bill?"[1]

Historian Jason Scott Smith reminds us that the question reveals how the New Deal's "public works revolution . . . was a political project not centrally concerned with advancing racial equality, redistribution of wealth, or social democratic ideals." He asserted that New Dealers set out to administer and manage resources efficiently while essentially "preserving the social order." He confirmed indirectly the conservative tendencies of the economics professor that Anderson highlighted and their predominance among many New Dealers. The New Deal adopted "commercial" Keynesianism over a "social" Keynesianism, according to Smith. The reality of a weak welfare state was that professional builders and engineers controlled and ran the various public-works programs, not "experts in solving a crisis in unemployment."[2]

Smith's sobering account of government growth and intervention during the 1930s and after suggests the Herculean if not Sisyphean struggle dreamers of a different world faced—which was perhaps truest of individuals fighting on the local and grassroots level for economic and social justice. In September 1933 Perrine Palmer of the Dade County Unemployment Citizens' League (DCUCL) alerted Harold L. Ickes, secretary of the Interior, who was in charge of the Public Works Administration, "that not a single project yet proposed or sponsored by our local city government has been designed primarily for the protection of the lives, health and happiness of those most vitally interested: the unemployed." He went on to detail the Florida projects then pending or under discussion: the Overseas Highway, Chapman Air Field, the Pan-American exposition building, and harbor improvements. While all are "probably meritorious as business propositions . . . not a single one of them [carries] any provision whatever to engage the full mental and physical participation of the commercially unemployed in a manner that would permit decent housing, proper food, ample water and ample medical care, dental and ocular attention."[3] Palmer was asserting here how the unemployed were often marginalized in the grander visions of development pressed by Florida's and Miami's investors and boosters, confirming Jason Smith's fundamental argument.

This chapter explores the history of the founding of the DCUCL and its refusal to idly wait for things to change. As opposed to the cynical individualists' skepticism about the intervention of government, the league chose to imagine a better world, not as utopian dreamers, but as active and engaged citizens unwilling to accept the existing economic and political structure. It sought to preserve private property as an institution, though they challenged the terms of individualism and called for collective responses to and solutions for the widespread problem of unemployment and scarcity. In this way, the league ran counter to mainstream liberalism. Arguing for production-for-use and economic security for all, the DCUCL offered an alternative vision of how things should be ordered. Advocating the vision meant, of course, fighting on the local front for class harmony and for the goal of a cooperative commonwealth.

The league's history has a historiographic importance; namely, the formation of this unemployed organization, and the unbroken activism of the local labor movement, represents yet another example of the existence of US worker-class consciousness. Where conservative limited-government advocates have argued to assert the New Deal's detrimental effects and have ignored or understated the significance of grassroots activism, and where liberal scholars have argued to assert the benevolent and progressive role government expansion played in society and the economy but who have questioned the soundness and significance of radical voices, the historical evidence suggests an alternative perspective. The breadth and liveliness of grassroots activism reflected in the rise of movements like the DCUCL show that Miami residents in the 1930s developed a robust working-class consciousness, were not merely wage conscious, and embraced communal rather than individualistic solutions to their economic problems. It further illustrates that, although the generally widespread support for the New Deal among working people has clouded the search for a more pervasive working-class consciousness, Miami labor history of this period contradicts the idea of American Exceptionalism, that US workers, unlike their European siblings, never developed class consciousness. Many in the labor movement (broadly conceived) understood the contradictions and inadequacies of New Deal policies, as Palmer's insights suggest. The story of the DCUCL, as with the many other grassroots efforts around the country, indicates that a more fluid dynamic of class existed than scholars usually imagine. When one operates outside the rigid frameworks of Socialist or Communist Party intrigue and internal conflicts, the profoundness of workers' class perspective and the pervasiveness of their disgust about the nature of class relations and power become not only more reasonable but clearer to the historian.

The chapter explores the history of class as it was revealed in the inadequate local, state, and national welfare system, the national and local context that sparked the unemployed into action, and a general outline of the resulting activism. Survival for the down-and-out was the most immediate struggle for the organized unemployed; the more visionary issue at stake was how society would end its regular bouts with scarcity and the persistence of rampant inequality and an unfair distribution of wealth.

Miami Confronts Local Unemployment

Miami's residents faced a frustrating situation created by unequal wealth distribution, limited government agendas, and a holy reverence of the work ethic. The hobo express and state patrol were as much an extension of a cultural bias against public and private welfare as it was a means of protecting home labor and maintaining an idyllic landscape for tourists. The harsh treatment of transients mirrored a nearly equally harsh system of welfare for the poor and unemployed local residents. As the social scientists Frances Fox Piven and Richard Cloward remind us, "The more important function of the relief system was accomplished, not by refusing relief, but by degrading and making outcasts of those few who did get aid." With the continuous problem of seasonal unemployment and the overall increase in the number of unemployed during the Great Depression, the existing welfare system simply failed to accommodate the social need in Miami and elsewhere. Helen C. Mawer, commissioner of the Florida State Board of Public Welfare, claimed that by the middle of 1932 "communities were meeting the problem only by a continuous process of spreading relief," which meant giving less to each welfare case whether it was direct payment or work relief.[4] The unemployment movement reacted to the diminishing economic conditions and the poor welfare system with hope in the possibilities of reform and even a humane capitalism.

Like other local governments overwhelmed by the Great Depression, Florida cities did not offer much assistance to the unemployed and allocated few dollars to its welfare coffers. Paltry mother-aid pensions and a meager county poor relief system defined the state welfare system before the New Deal. Miami, Lakeland and St. Petersburg had city welfare departments staffed by a caseworker, and other cities coordinated public funds for private welfare organizations. Throughout the state local charities, the Salvation Army, YMCA, YWCA, and churches administered welfare programs that included food distribution and other aid in kind. The Dade County commission expended $286,766 in poor relief in 1931, far surpassing any other county in the state, but the average state relief payout was $5.00 per month, per family, and the payment was given only after close scrutiny by county social caseworkers and only after the impoverished resident petitioned the county commission for assistance.[5] Variety in local conditions in such a wide and economically diverse state as Florida led to different responses, with urban areas such as Miami, Jacksonville, St. Petersburg, and Tampa turning to greater government involvement in welfare efforts.

Each area relied on the voluntary charity ethic for organized relief efforts. The social welfare net would not catch the rising numbers of unemployed and offered little help to the impoverished. The Community Chest, a coordinated effort led by prominent local citizens, struggled to maintain steady flows of charity, using newspaper advertisements to solicit contributions from Miamians. One set of advertisements featured workers (from postal to retail) offering testimonials of their small donations in an effort to foster enthusiasm for voluntary charity. Other advertisements featured community leaders, such as Rabbi Jacob Kaplan of Temple Israel and Alexander Orr Jr., a city commissioner, building contractor, and open shopper. These efforts revealed, if nothing else, a commitment to the volunteer ethic and the inability of government to provide economic relief. Despite the well-intentioned efforts of its advocates, its small coffers and enduring cultural taboos toward public welfare limited the Community Chest's effectiveness throughout its existence in late 1920s and early

1930s.[6] Nor was the end-of-year Empty Stocking Fund an adequate measure. Established locally in 1928 by the *Miami Daily News* as a holiday philanthropic effort for the impoverished, it represented a common voluntarist approach that several other cities also practiced for several years. Specifically targeted to improve the Christmas experience of the poor, it continued over the years mainly as a yearly fundraising and entertainment event that occasionally lent its resources to wider relief efforts.[7] The Empty Stocking Fund was at best a momentary and temporary solution to poverty and unemployment as much as was the Community Chest.

In the winter season of 1930–31, Cliff H. Reeder, City of Miami mayor, formed the Committee for the Worthy Unemployed and established an unemployment fund. Reeder was born in 1882 in Tennessee and moved to Miami in 1912. He had worked in the railroad industry as a telegraph operator, switch operator, yardmaster, and train master before coming to Miami, where he worked as a city auditor. After serving in the Twenty-Eighth Engineer Battalion of the American Expeditionary Force in World War I, he returned to Miami and engaged in the real-estate business and later was elected city commissioner in 1927. Reeder seems to have built from his life experience when he initiated the unemployment fund. The fund set out to sidestep the negative baggage of charity through a work-relief program for "able bodied men and women willing to work for the right to eat," an apparent respectable alternative to charity intended to sustain "the morale of hundreds." It was to give temporary employment to bona fide Greater Miami residents, therefore excluding the transient unemployed, in two-week stints and for $2 a day for a full day's work. Directed by the city but building its coffers solely through donations and charity entertainment events, the unemployment fund offered work in "cleaning up unsightly spots and in putting city parks and playgrounds in order."[8]

Reeder and the Unemployment Relief Committee Fund—the label of worthy unemployed was dropped later in the winter season—used a portion of the Empty Stocking Fund in December 1930 for starting the work-relief program; later, horse and dog racing, and other events in Greater Miami, solicited donations. Reeder, noted the *Miami Daily News*, had been "active in soliciting government interest in Miami aviation, in hastening expenditure of public monies for the relief of unemployment, especially government funds, and in behalf of the financial betterment of the city." The revenue raised, however, remained small (a little over $32,000). Perrine Palmer appreciated Reeder's efforts, though he attacked the idea of the "worthy unemployed." While working a two-week stint himself, Palmer claimed in another letter to the newspaper that individuals receiving work relief "would starve rather than accept charity." He celebrated the humanity and work ethic of those turning to the fund, adding the request that the mayor go one step further and "not to let the water company cut off the water on the premises of any of these men who cannot pay for water now." It was a succinct reminder of the fund's inadequate wages and the needs of those out of work.[9]

Reeder's limited approach revealed a progressive liberal instinct. By 1930, several other areas in the country turned to public work relief, but what was innovative in Reeder's effort was its associational spirit in that Reeder had the city government take a lead role in coordinating work-relief efforts while working with private interests, especially in regard to fundraising. It also represented a significant symbol that Miami's mayor took a lead role in the unemployment problem.[10] But the punitive nature of the relief, the understanding of the unemployment fund effort as "rehabilitation, not charity," had its negative drawbacks and explains Palmer's inspiration to comment on the jobless fund. First, the idea of a "worthy unemployed" undoubtedly produced resentment among the unemployed while it satisfied many with its moral measuring stick. It likely also frustrated hard-nosed social Darwinists insensitive to the plight of the down-and-out. Second, single individuals were discouraged, as were the transient unemployed, from applying for aid; (male) heads of households had priority status. In one instance, however, beginning in April 1931, the unemployment committee gave employment to twenty-five women to sew clothing for needy children (a precursor to a later New Deal program). The program paid them $2.50 a day and had the additional function of serving as self-help for the poor.[11] Finally, if this head of household refused the work offered, he would be denied any aid. The first fifty getting work from the fund were all past fifty years old and had "large families to support." The fifty consisted of carpenters, accountants, grocers, "and at least one business man who, a few years ago, was independently wealthy."[12] Even if the phrase "worthy unemployed" represented a delicate political balancing act for politicians handling the crumbling general welfare amid skeptics, such language limited eligible recipients, unburdening the state and private charities from providing relief to a wider population of the unemployed.

Reeder lost his mayoral seat in the 1931 May–June city commissioners' election, even though he received the endorsement of Labor's Citizenship Committee, the political arm of the Central Labor Union, and was the top vote getter in the runoff election. Custom had been and continued to be in subsequent city commissioners' elections that the other commissioners would select the top vote getter as mayor. One suspects that his efforts to relieve the unemployed may not have been appreciated as much by the other city commissioners because he threatened the Miami optimistic, booster tradition that dictated the city's mayor don the cap as south Florida's number-one booster. Palmer argued that "Cliff Reeder is not a politician. He doesn't know how to go after votes, and probably wouldn't if he did. He proved that by the way he spread out the city's unemployment fund. . . . He was making the money he had do the most for the greatest number, let the votes fall where they might." The *Miami Daily*

News reported that the other commissioners aspired to the mayoralty (to which Redmond Gautier was elected), and so perhaps Palmer was correct that Reeder was not a typical politician; he nonetheless remained a commissioner and would later become mayor again in the early 1940s.[13] Persistent economic problems hamstrung local relief efforts and pressed local politicians to seek immediate solutions to the rampant suffering.

In June 1932 Mayor Redmond Gautier joined twenty-eight other US mayors in Detroit "calling upon Congress for a $5,000,000,000 loan to build public works, mobilization of a 'work army,' and authorization for the Reconstruction Finance Corporation to advance credits to cities during the distress." Among the attendees at the conference were Mayors Frank Murphy of Detroit and Jacob S. Coxey of Massillon, Ohio (of 1890s Coxey's Army fame), and the mayors of New York City and Boston.[14] That same month, Miami's City Commission passed resolution 7495 to appropriate all funds collected from issuing drivers' licenses for relief of the unemployed. Gautier estimated the appropriation would amount to about $100,000 for six thousand unemployed, a meager $16.67 for each person if his unemployment figures were accurate. Despite these efforts and others, the unemployment fund dwindled even more in its already very limited effectiveness amid the increasing number of unemployed and the continual resistance to increase welfare coffers. The Miami Realty Board, for example, targeted the license tax as a "gigantic political fund masquerading under the guise of [an] unemployment fund." They labeled any taxing power as essentially a "power to destroy."[15]

The model of providing relief through public works extended to the entire county later in 1932 and early 1933, when Reconstruction Finance Corporation funds became available for states and counties (as in the formation of the Dade County Transient Farm). Helen Mawer stated that 15 to 20 percent of Florida's population in August 1932 was unemployed and not getting enough relief, if any. By January 1933, 28 percent of Floridians were getting some federal relief, but many who needed assistance, "particularly single men and women, were not being reached."[16] With the limited state and city budgets and President Herbert Hoover's administration's reluctance to enact a substantial relief program, local governments were forced to find their own solutions and depended on charity and other voluntary relief efforts. Perhaps inspired by Roosevelt's campaign that promised better times and the possibility of securing greater economic growth and development, as well as more adequate relief, many private citizens chose to organize to get results. It was in this context that the DCUCL emerged.

Origins of Miami's Unemployment Movement

Few histories have been written on the 1930s unemployment movement and fewer exist for the South. In other places around the country, communists played important roles in organizing demonstrations, such as the hunger marches of 1930 and 1931, or in trying to organize grassroots movements after spontaneous actions from the unemployed, as in the community-block mobilizations that prevented evictions. Communist-led unemployed councils popped up in Chicago, Detroit, New York, and elsewhere, but the party remained small even in these hotbeds of activism, and with high member turnover rates. Few Communists were present in Florida in the early 1930s and started to have some limited influence in the labor movement only in the late 1930s and only in a couple of industries.[17] Socialists fared a little better but, again, had only limited influence, especially in Tampa. While socialists operated in Miami and Jacksonville, they were unsuccessful in garnering a significant presence or movement.

A third group described by Roy Rosenzweig was inspired by the ideas of Abraham J. Muste. Students of his from the progressive Brookwood Labor College started in the early thirties to organize Unemployed Citizens' Leagues where they moved (about fourteen different states), but their primary base was in Ohio. The Musteites, shaped by socialist ideas, tended to rely on patriotic rhetoric and looked to US traditions for inspiration and justification for their actions. Some locals gradually became more radical in outlook if they sensed that a revolution was imminent or their frustration compounded with the lack of change and reform of the existing poor economic conditions. All three groups, while moved to unemployed causes for various reasons, eventually relied on bread-and-butter issues as rallying points for organizing. They often turned to the following actions as assistance to the unemployed: serving as advocates for the unemployed struggling with relief agencies, engaging in eviction resistance, starting relief kitchens, lobbying government officials and legislatures, aiding self-help efforts, organizing direct food collection, and taking other immediate actions to solve immediate needs. Communists, socialists, and Musteites struggled to maintain membership and thus fought to survive as organizations. While each group attempted to have national organizations, they failed to establish a unified national presence. The unemployment movement was wholly a local phenomenon.[18]

Miamians joined the wave of national activism after years of inadequate relief and disappointing local government leadership. The Miami unemployment movement appears to have been unaffiliated with the communists, socialists, or Musteites. While no clear connections existed between the three primary groups organizing the unemployed, it does appear that the Musteite Unemployed Citizens' Leagues provided a model for the DCUCL's name, and the DCUCL also resembled them in other ways. Like the Musteites, they embraced a tradition that envisioned a cooperative commonwealth protected by the political principles defined in the Declaration of Independence and the Bill of Rights. The history of the league also demonstrated an equal commitment to peaceful protest, picketing, self-help, and an avoidance of violent tactics to enact change. Its approach, too, was consistent with the philosophy of democratic change through education, grassroots organizing, and general civic engagement that marked the Musteite movement.[19]

Only one report notes the founding of the DCUCL in August 1932. Charles W. Nicholson, the *Miami Herald* reported, stated that the league's immediate objective was "to get under cultivation every acre of tillable soil within the city and as much as possible in the county, with the ultimate objective of getting the unemployed, if not completely, at least nearly, self-sustaining." Aside from articulating an unclear plan about organizing the unemployed by the county's precincts, not much else is reported about the league, nor does another news story on it appear until the following year.[20] It appears the future founders of the league read each other's letters in the readers' forum of the *Miami Daily News* and encountered each other in weekly meetings of Labor's Citizenship Committee (LCC). The activities seem to have gained momentum during the technocracy craze. Palmer had announced in November 1932 the need to organize the unemployed, pointing to Wayne Parrish's analysis of technocracy as a testament of the US economy's capacity to provide for everyone in the country. Technocracy reinforced many of Palmer's insights about political economy as articulated in his letters in 1931 and his 1932 plan to end the economic depression. In addition to Palmer's ample letters, M. E. Fidler (former president of Central Labor Union during World War I), Charles Nicholson, and William Wister—to name three other participants in the league—also published letters in the newspaper. These activists and others benefited from the *Miami Daily News*'s liberal policy of publishing readers' letters, a practice that built on its muckraking tradition of engaged journalism and civic duty to the community. The masthead of the readers' forum reproduces the famous quote supporting the right to freedom of speech: "I wholly disapprove of what you say and will defend to the death your right to say it."[21] Along with the concerned activist citizen Verner Townley, unionists W. J. Fripp (International Typographical Union), and Chas Poore (carpenters' union), and several other vocal citizens, a lively debate filled the letters section of the *Miami Daily News* on unemployment concerns and other relevant issues.

Harry McClurg, president of Miami AFL's Central Labor Union, launched LCC weekly meetings in the latter half of 1929 as the union's "political arm," which offered a physical forum for chance encounters of concerned citizens. John M. Harding, a member of the LCC executive board, wrote in a June 1931 letter that we "have been consistently educating our membership in practical politics and breaking down individualism." Acting on the logic that "whatever benefits labor directly, reacts indirectly for the betterment of all the people," the LCC soon morphed afterward into an ambitious, progressive forum engaging pertinent south Florida and national issues.[22] Held in Carpenters Hall, local politicians running for City Commission and other political offices were sure to give their campaign pitches in front of LCC meetings. Palmer attributed his first meeting with Charles Nicholson to a session of the LCC.[23] The LCC sought to increase citizen participation and awareness of local and national issues of civic concern and encouraged nonunion members to attend its weekly meetings. In presentations from local unionists and other activists and guest lecturers and presenters, the LCC educated and informed the local citizenry. So, when the *American Federationist*, the AFL's monthly journal, issued a vague request in March 1933 to central labor unions around the country to "serve as advocate[s] of the unemployed," helping them organize for relief, and to persuade them to turn to the AFL for leadership, Miami's labor movement had already started reaching out to the larger citizenry. The DCUCL took advantage of such venues to organize and also to gain access to grassroots, community-oriented gatherings.[24]

Another influence in the early development of the DCUCL, working along a similar vein of patriotic leftist activism, was the two-day meeting of the Continental Congress of Workers and Farmers for Economic Reconstruction, held in Washington, DC, May 6–7, 1933. Various progressive groups, including local and state AFL unions, farmer organizations and unions, cooperative societies, unemployed leagues, and the Socialist Party—who were central in organizing the event and who seemed to dominate the event—organized the conference. The Continental Congress sought reform, immediate solutions, and hopes to organize "liberal independent action on state and local levels." Palmer drew attention to the conference in a published letter entitled "The Jobless Organize." Written before the start of the conference on May 5, he apparently had received a copy of the announcement of the meeting, if not an invitation to him, the local Central Labor Union, or to the DCUCL.

The conference did not lead to a national coalition or movement, but members did craft a new declaration of independence reprising many of the themes of the recent technocracy movement and adding a socialist edge in its criticism of the current political economy. Citing the original declaration's call for the right to abolish a destructive government, it targeted monopolistic power, the profit system, the waste of the country's abundant resources, and the maldistribution of wealth, among other things. It called also for "a new economic system based upon the principles of cooperation, public ownership and democratic management, in which the planlessness, the waste, and the exploitation of our present order shall be eliminated and in which the natural resources and the basic industries of the country shall be planned and operated for the common good." The influence of the technocracy discussions was evident, and activists were prepared to organize and act.[25]

Palmer and the DCUCL pressed for larger solutions to the capitalist order—solutions that borrowed freely from the vibrant ideological milieu of the early twentieth century. From its founding, the DCUCL advocated for production for use over profit. They were firm critics of the money system, especially the reliance on "green paper" and "yellow metal" as a system of economic exchange, and thus linked themselves to a longer tradition going back to the late nineteenth century. Palmer emphasized the need to organize and press for production for use to meet immediate needs. In March 1933 he wrote that

> The president can't do it all for us. . . . His leadership will fall flat unless we organize to help him, just as we did during the war [i.e., World War I]. . . . What are all these idle acres, these empty houses, tools of production and distribution for? . . . Are we in Miami and Dade county going to continue to sit idly by and do nothing but talk, while our president works night and day, merely in hope that his efforts will induce some speculator to take a chance and start a buying wave and that chance will bring it our way? Shame on us.[26]

He also supported the shorter-hours movement and found the thirty-hour legislation pending in Congress to be promising. The long hours being worked by Miami workers, according to Palmer, contributed to the general economic plight. The situation was so bad that the 400 barrels of flour the Dade County Red Cross had just received from the federal government fell far short of what was needed. He recommended an increase to 3,700 barrels.[27]

Grassroots, organic intellectuals in the shorter-hours movement, deploying expansive notions of leisure and loose Marxist class-conflict interpretations of the capitalist downturn, called for a change of the status quo through a radical embrace of class harmony. They were not advocates of revolution, or at least not violent revolution. Verner Townley, regular attendee of LCC meetings, argued this point in one letter, "Violent Revolt Unlikely." He called for a change of the current economic order along class-harmony lines, commenting that America had not "developed class consciousness and class hatred as have many of the European countries." Indeed, workers and capitalists could find common ground as the latter slipped into the wage-earning class, making "their economic interest identical" with those of the working class. As important, "the class which is able to contribute to the welfare of the unemployed" needed to work along with the working class for the "economic security of all." Such stretched conceptions of class relations revealed hopeful dreams of cooperation as it also subtly argued for action. Townley's assertion that members of each class "have close relatives and very dear friends in the opposite class" pointed to both the possibilities of economic mobility and the promise of equality. It also supports historian Elizabeth Faue's argument about the subjective nature of class, reinforced by the "sporadic nature of work" and its effects on the reproduction of community.

Her emphasis on the idea "that individuals rework and recreate class relations and location over the life course" is instructive and lends poignancy to class harmony as an ideal amid changing class positions during individual lives.[28]

Speaking perhaps from experience, Townley here tapped into the spirit of American exceptionalism and hopes for class harmony as well. His analysis did not, however, assert that classlessness had been achieved and, in fact, he held out the possibility that revolution could occur amid the Depression. That Townley associated class consciousness with class hatred revealed the power of the Russian revolution. He replaced conflict with common interest and the human need for economic security, but he predicated much on the assumption of American abundance and the inefficiency of wealth distribution. His substitution revealed that Townley's desire for a greater sense of community and social harmony was rooted in the idea that workers had an important role in society. Indeed, he often argued that workers were the producers of the nation's economic wealth.[29]

The DCUCL blended organized labor's goals, socialist ideals, and an Americanism comfortable with pushing the liberal political economy beyond normative conceptions of capitalism into a realm of greater equality and democracy. Palmer's letter, "The Jobless Organize," was a case in point. The Continental Congress of Workers and Farmers, as noted, was a gathering of progressive organizations. In the pamphlet calling for delegates around the country to attend, organizers of the conference pointed to mounting numbers of the unemployed, the foreclosures, the long breadlines, the inadequacy of relief, and the transient poor as evidence of rampant economic plight. It urged action against the "insane economic order," "the greed of the captains of industry," and "the denial of relief by their political leaders." Appended to the pamphlet was a flyer by William Green, president of the AFL, announcing "LABOR IS ON THE MARCH!" A cartoon depicting three workers, two men (one a farmer) and a woman, marching forward toward the US Capitol in Washington, DC, amid scurrying fat black-top-hatted and tuxedoed capitalists getting away with bags of money (see figure 6–1). Green's flyer announced the time had come to wage a battle to end the suffering caused by "the fat enemies of America, who through one device or another, have wrung from the people such a proportion of the fruit of their toil that they are stranded in a motionless sea of unemployment." He continued, "we prefer the council table but we do not shun the battlefield . . . a battle out of which labor expects a new America." Juxtaposed, these images and words pointed to the failure of the economic system and the democratic process. Green appears here as an inspiring and progressive force.[30]

Palmer echoed these progressive voices, and his reading of the Continental Congress pamphlet and Green's flyer suggest how it inspired grassroots movement leaders. He argued that DCUCL was similar to World War I shock troops,

LABOR IS ON THE MARCH!

By William Green

President, American Federation of Labor.

THE American trade union movement has been patient. Our movement has been constructive. But there is no reason for tolerating abuses that have all but wrecked everything that has made America a nation where a man could have a chance in his own right.

WE shall fight with every legitimate weapon at our command. We are in earnest. The measure of our earnestness is the measure of the hunger of those who have no work and no food, of those who are being cast into the streets and driven to the gutters in exhaustion at the end of a long and futile search for work.

WE shall want every friend and every right thinking American to help, but we do not intend to forewarn the money fat enemies of America who, through one device or another, have wrung from the people such a proportion of the fruit of their toil that they are stranded in a motionless sea of unemployment.

FOR we shall soon be on the march. We may fail, we may return more bedraggled than we are, with America more sunk under the crushing weight of injustice than it is, but we shall have fought, and every justice loving American will have had his chance to struggle to guarantee the right to pursue happiness without being hopelessly outdistanced in the race.

WE have come to what we are determined shall be the end of the road of suffering. Here we take a stand and here we fight, perhaps such a battle as no labor movement has ever fought before. We fight a battle for restoration, for happy homes, for great safeguards that shall take from the pillaging band of exploiters the weapons with which they have stricken down our millions.

WE prefer the council table, but we do not shun the battlefield. I am ready to lead the hosts of labor into a battle which we are determined to carry to the last possible ounce of our own strength, not for the sake of conquest but for the sake of justice.

THE die is cast for the battle out of which labor expects a new America.

FIGURE 6–1. *Labor Is on the March!* William Green's 1933 AFL leaflet. (Continental Congress of Workers and Farmers for Economic Reconstruction, Mildred and Mary Hicks Papers, Stuart A. Rose Manuscript and Archives and Rare Books Library, Emory University, box 3, folder 5.)

but, in this context, they were leading the charge against economic depression, fighting for the survival of the unemployed and for the entire community. The insertion of Green into this radical milieu serves as an interesting reminder of how many yearned for improvements in conditions along imaginative and progressive lines that transcended strident political entanglements. Green and the AFL Executive Committee issued a public statement announcing they did not support or sanction the Congress, and they urged national and international unions not to attend. Many AFL locals decided to attend anyway, though none from Miami seemed to have made the trip. Green's action, evidently, reflected the AFL's concern that socialists were playing a leading role in the organizing of the Congress and that its organizers used Green's flyer "Labor Is on the March!" without approval. Green's public statement served to officially dissociate the AFL from more radical organizations and appear mainstream in its public posture while seeming progressive in some circles. Regardless of the public or private political positioning, the AFL continued the long-practiced strategy of political lobbying and trade union organizing.[31]

Palmer quoted in his letter the pamphlet's message of economic security for "ALL men, ALL women, [and] ALL children," adding not only the capital letters but also the phrase "whether they be street cleaners or bank presidents," an idea that framed the goals of the Continental Congress, socialists, the AFL, and the unemployed in their simplest and most visionary terms. He went on to urge Miamians to support the DCUCL and their goal of making production and distribution a function of need and willingness to serve rather than for profit, at least at the level of independent self-help efforts for the down-and-out. Only through covenants "openly arrived at around the council table" could such an adjustment to the economic situation occur. Palmer ventured the idea of using unoccupied property, both land and buildings, for the application of production for use, not profit. His pitch worked within class-harmony logic: "A preliminary conference composed of the city and county commissions, city manager, city and tax assessors, city building inspector, county agricultural agent, sheriff and judges of the courts, together with spokesmen for our business and agricultural interests, organized labor and the Unemployed Citizens' league and the press could accomplish much *with such a high purpose in view*" (italics added). He reiterated these points in a letter written a week later calling for such a meeting and local cooperation in the community.

Palmer premised his call on the idea that civic responsibility necessitated grassroots organizing and local efforts to alleviate the suffering. In this light, the World War I reference in his letter and in earlier ones revealed a faith in collective resolve, drawn from actual experience, to protect individuals, families, and the nation. Class harmony could be achieved in the midst of abundance but only through hard work and vigilant local civic action—a robust participatory democracy. The Continental Congress and Green's vision, as expressed in the flyer, thus merged as a consistent message despite the real-world rift between socialists and the AFL. The high purpose to produce for use rather than profit suggested that socialist ideals shaped the league's vision, while Palmer's call for working around the council table embraced a faith in collective resolution consistent with AFL negotiation practices. It anticipated Upton Sinclair's 1934 End Poverty in California campaign and revealed that even in a touristic setting like Miami such imaginative policies were discussed and inspired a movement to emerge.[32]

The Unemployed Citizens' League in Action

Mirroring the AFL and Unemployed Citizens' Leagues across the country, the DCUCL's larger vision did not prevent them from embracing practical strategies to confront the day-to-day problems that the unemployed faced. This reflected a willingness, however frustrating, to engage local politics. Since its founding in 1932, the DCUCL kept the concerns of the unemployed in the forefront of Miami life advocating for relief of their difficult material conditions. Making regular appearances in the City Commission, announcements in the local mainstream newspapers, organized labor's *Miami News*, and presentations to Labor's Citizenship Committee, the DCUCL made a persistent effort to help meet the material needs of the unemployed.[33]

Through 1935, they had a membership of at least fifteen hundred, holding regular weekly meetings and occasional picnics to educate, organize, strategize, and bolster spirits in the tough economic times. Their membership was as high as six thousand members (May 1934), far surpassing the number of any union local during this period. DCUCL leaders, however, asserted that, according to their own estimates, they represented between twenty and thirty-five thousand nonmember unemployed residing in the city and county. Information about its leadership and the day-to-day operation of the league is incomplete. The sketchy evidence indicates that it was an incorporated organization, having "Inc." appear after its name; it held annual elections of officers, including president, at least one vice president, a secretary and secretary-treasurer; women seemed to have been active participants (a Mrs. John Hunter served as a vice president for at least two consecutive years, 1934–35); it formed committees to tackle specific issues; it appointed an advisory committee, often led by Perrine Palmer; and it reached out regularly to organized labor, especially in its regular attendance of LCC meetings.[34]

The league operated within the mainstream of Miami lobbying, which received tacit support from the government and business interests. Self-help relief efforts received official sanction. Throughout the summer of 1933, the DCUCL placed situation wanted advertisements in the *Miami Daily News* offering workers for skilled and unskilled jobs. The strategy was a response to shady and unfair private employment agencies that required exorbitant fees for work placements, which often was temporary and very exploitative. One *Miami News* columnist noted that, while some of these "privately owned concerns" had disappeared, a few were still "taking in the 50c pieces and getting a cut on the first job the application secures. . . . [which] lasts [no] longer than a week or two—or until the agency gets their commission. The applicant must [then] deposit another 50c, secure another job and help the agency get another commission. And so, on and on."[35] Throughout the 1930s, the City Commission gave the DCUCL permission to conduct tag days—charity drives in which donors were given tags indicating they had donated to the league. Often women members and volunteers would dominate the work of canvassing the city for donations. The DCUCL also lobbied the City Commission for an eight-week charity bazaar in the winter of 1934. The league also conducted a "Repair, Clean-Up, and Paint-Up" campaign, which mirrored an earlier effort in the summer of 1931 when the Chamber of Commerce sponsored a similar drive.[36]

Other fundraising initiatives blended with the accepted practice of organizing charity events as relief efforts, as well as walking in step with common cultural ways of the times and place. Working within the tradition of the unemployment fund's framework of raising funds for relief, the DCUCL organized three social events in the late summer and fall of 1933. The league sponsored at least two minstrel shows in Miami's famous Bayfront Park for two nights in mid-August and mid-September. The proceeds from the first show went to the league's treasury and the second show went toward relief. Presenting minstrel shows were a common practice throughout Miami and Dade County and had been a featured event during the yearly Empty Stocking Fund. Local schools, social clubs (even the Mickey Mouse Club), and some union labor locals—such as the typographers—organized regular blackface minstrel shows.[37] The first show included several vaudeville acts and the second starred the minstrel pair "Duke" Brown and "Dutch" Slawson, as well as Madeline "the Egyptian." The second show added Roland C. McLauglin, a regular performer at the Alcazar, Antilla, and Floridian hotels, and featured the Miami Melody Makers.

The minstrel shows' loaded cultural significance becomes a bit more complicated in the fundraising-for-a-good-cause context. Easily denigrated as a racist cultural artifact, it also was part of a longer evolving history of communal, musical, and comedic styles, intonations, and creative spaces that by the 1930s was near extinction nationally but that remained a conventional entertainment form on the local level. Its appearances as a fundraising tool served a political purpose for the DCUCL, but whether that revealed a racist bent in its members that disallowed cross-racial alliances is less clear. No evidence exists of the

DCUCL turning to the minstrel show for fundraising after September 1933. Indeed, three months later, the league held a charity dance featuring "a 10-act floor show." League members were admitted "without charge by showing their membership cards at the gate." The DCUCL was going to use the proceeds from the show as relief and added, in a rare newspaper advertisement announcing the charity dance, a call for Miamians to give donations "in the form of food, old clothes, or checks" to league headquarters.[38] These strategies to cope with unemployment only served to confirm the benevolent civic profile the DCUCL wished to portray and suggested the conservative nature of the cultural landscape in which they were operating.

The DCUCL maintained a lively civic activism and sense of community, thus creating class solidarity by conducting regular weekly meetings and having occasional picnics while remaining aware of the conservative social and political landscape. On one occasion in the summer of 1934, the DCUCL announced an all-day picnic for the "white unemployed and their families and their friends, whether unemployed or not." Two facts stand out in this announcement: (1) the DCUCL sought to gain a larger class solidarity, one that did not marginalize the unemployed and instead broadened the conception of class beyond employment status; (2) the practice of segregation was not foreign to them. While there is little doubt that they embraced Jim Crow as revealed in the picnic's announcement, it is unclear whether Blacks were disallowed from attending weekly meetings. One can only speculate whether they were, lacking complete extant DCUCL records.

The announcement's statement that whites were invited suggests that Blacks did participate in league activities and that the DCUCL recognized that African Americans also faced the problems of unemployment. Rarely (if ever) would one see such racial parameters stated openly in the newspapers for social events when normal social practice in Jim Crow Miami presumed racial segregation. That is, few advertisements of Black social events ever appeared in the local newspapers and, when they did, they usually included an invitation to whites or simply highlighted that "colored" individuals would participate. Yet, in this picnic affair, league leaders deemed it necessary to invite only whites, which suggests, evoking Booker T. Washington's famous 1895 Atlanta Compromise, that in all things social segregation was the rule, but "in all things essential to mutual progress" whites and Blacks were united. This rare announcement also reflected the very real concern that racial cooperation could be used to bolster accusations that the DCUCL was a radical organization, a practice that was all too common in US history.[39]

The DCUCL's legitimacy stemmed from the conditions of the times as well as the lack of any ties with known radical organizations. Indeed, the City Commission at first gave a room in the old City Hall annex building to serve as the league's headquarters but then discontinued that assistance when the annex was torn down. William Wister, chair of the DCUCL grievance committee, and the league were unhappy with the commission's move, especially since they had made a request for a new space two months prior. In July, when the league made its initial request, Wister and mayor E. G. Sewell indirectly debated the need for an unemployed organization: Sewell asserted his quest for government funding for public-works projects but Wister argued that, "if you get all the projects going here at one time[,] it would leave 10,000 unemployed [and so] there would still be a need for the unemployed headquarters." In September, when their headquarters were finally torn down, the league took issue with Sewell's appointment of two associates of his to two municipal jobs, one of which was a newly created position. Suggesting a misuse of power and political favoritism, if not corruption, Wister pleaded that the DCUCL was "without a roof over its head, must hunt for a meeting place and has members who are in the hospital" (and that included Charles Nicholson). All he asked for was "cooperation." Such exchanges revealed the tension just beneath the surface and the desire for greater class harmony. City commissioner Cliff H. Reeder attempted to ease the tension by noting the commission's continual efforts to obtain federal aid for local relief. The DCUCL's disappointment did not lead to any radical action, though the league did gain access to the central school building, but it is unclear how they gained that access. It was clearly the noble and patriotic efforts of the DCUCL that garnered the support of many.[40]

The league had quickly earned the reputation of being enthusiastic and persistent voices for the unemployed interests by the time of these 1933 City Commission exchanges. In addition to conducting fund drives, the DCUCL had pressed for the protection of unemployed rights to relief coffers and the need to share the work in the government and schools. A heated political battle between the Voters Recall League (formed in May 1933 by realty interests) determined to recall city commissioner Harry Platt and those opposed to the effort spilled over into a controversy over food-relief distribution.[41] Relief clients were approached by recall opponents while in line for food and threatened that they would be refused relief if they did not sign a form letter to remove their names from Platt's recall petition—that is, if they had initially supported it. A conflict of interest did appear when Henry Shaw, chair of the Miami Rate and Traffic Board, and Eli McDonald, an independent citizen, gave Ruth Gaskill of the city welfare agency copies of the letter to distribute to food-relief clients.[42]

The DCUCL protested this real and perceived threat to welfare access. The league called for the City Commission to conduct a thorough investigation of the conflict of interest and political threats, but they did not side with the Voters Recall League's efforts. The DCUCL sought protection of the right to relief and particularly sought to safeguard the unemployed from political intrigue and corruption. The lack of independence resulting from joblessness made the unemployed particularly vulnerable to the changing winds of political squabbles. Therefore, they called for "dismissal of all persons responsible." The realty interests, however, exploited the food distribution controversy as a means of framing their political struggle in starker moral terms, though they were not above using their own questionable strategies. They had first circulated the recall petition at a Red Cross clothing distribution center during their campaign and thus solicited the pro-Platt reaction. The Voters Recall League's interest lay not in the unemployed right to survival, but in bolstering their efforts to influence the city's tax and bond policies and repayment proposals then under consideration. Gaskill herself was an unemployed worker lucky to attain temporary employment in the welfare agency through the city's unemployment fund. The DCUCL stepped into this fray to keep the lifeline that food and other forms of relief free of manipulation and intimidation from either end of the political battle. They never took a public stand on the Platt recall issue.[43]

In another advocacy issue relating to job opportunities and relief efforts, the DCUCL urged the city government to implement a share-the-work relief strategy in local government employment and to increase welfare funds. Both netted unsatisfactory results. The Unemployment Citizens' League found that numerous families had two or more members working for the city government. Calling it "a drive against nepotism," they pressed the City Commission to get the government departments to offer these jobs to "other persons equally qualified" but who were jobless. Their action on what they deemed was fair occurred at an advantageous political moment. The City Commission, led by newly elected commissioners E. G. Sewell, Orville Rigby, A. D. H. (Alexander David Henry) Fossey, and holdovers Reeder and Platt, formed an independent budget committee with the mandate to consolidate departments, equalize salaries, and offer a critical review of the city manager's budget proposal. The pending bond repayment proposals and tax debates led to their action. The commissioners and the budget committee they selected were all businesspeople (construction, real estate, retail, and restaurant or hotel investments). Rigby served as "labor's representative" on the commission on the strength of having served as a business agent for the bricklayers' union, though he was now a building contractor.[44]

Amid the wider mood for budget reform, the DCUCL submitted a questionnaire to the City Commission to be given to each government department head inquiring on the extent of family hires. No record exists indicating whether the inquiry ever occurred. The City Commission either ignored or simply avoided the questionnaire request, a maneuver made easier during the budget reform discussions. In this political context and with continual high rates of unemployment, the league lobbied for a larger budget allocation for unemployment relief, though the request was below what they deemed was the minimum needed.

What they got instead was a consolidation of the various public and private welfare agencies under one Social Services Exchange to avoid "overlapping" cases, save the city money by making it more efficient, and thus maintaining a miserly welfare system in place. The city pinned its hopes on future federal funds entering the region to relieve its welfare burden.[45]

The DCUCL's frustrations with rampant unemployment and an inadequate welfare system compounded in an uphill and controversial struggle over another share-the-work scheme among the public-school teachers. The league lobbied the county school board to not extend contracts to married women with gainfully employed husbands. The jobs, they argued, should go to unemployed widows, single women, and male teachers. The school board, after first deciding not to extend contracts to 287 married teachers if their husbands were employed, reversed their decision after the affected teachers protested and despite protest from the DCUCL. The logic behind the league's actions was consistent with their overall objective: advocate for the unemployed, foster community, and emphasize civic responsibility during the economic crisis.

The married teacher controversy points to long-standing gender discrimination women have had to face. In the context of high unemployment and share-the-work strategies, however, the matter becomes more complicated. The married teacher advocates argued along the lines of professional expertise and work experience; the opponents asserted the need for employment and economic survival. One letter writer to the *Herald*, Mrs. Vella Thomas, advocated the employment of recent women college graduates to the many elementary school jobs (177) and, she insisted, only married teachers in financial need (i.e., having unemployed husbands) should be offered employment. County school superintendent Charles Fisher and the DCUCL eventually asked the married teachers to voluntarily give up their contracts. The resignations apparently never occurred despite the example set by Tampa's married teachers to take this very action or the league's patriotic calls for married teachers (with employed husbands) to "Do your part."[46]

The married school controversy did not reveal a simple right-to-work story, in which women faced second-class citizenship and emerged victorious in a civil-rights battle. The context of economic depression and the centrality of the family ideal inspired a community approach to unemployment. The DCUCL expected government to act in a communitarian manner and not give employment to more than one family member. In the league's simultaneous battle against nepotism in government, they targeted brothers and other relatives and not just marital ties. That married women now faced disapproval for having jobs only exacerbated the nature of their second-class citizenship, but the possibility that younger women teachers might gain these positions revealed the extent of limited job opportunities and the magnitude and diversity of the unemployment problem. The failure of married teachers and the school board to accommodate the league's demands also revealed the limits of communitarian over individualistic strategies. The Florida Supreme Court would rule the following year that a woman's marital status could not bar her from employment as a teacher as long as she passed the certification tests. The league's embrace of share-the-work principles attempted to make unemployment a shared civic experience.[47]

Conclusion

Historian Alex Lichtenstein explored an important historical question about why the Communist Party of the United States and the Congress of Industrial Organizations (CIO) failed to mount any successful campaign in Florida prior to the 1940s. Whereas during World War II the transplanted New York communist Charles Smolikoff succeeded in his CIO organizing drives of shipyard, transport, and laundry workers in Miami and Jacksonville, the party's and CIO's "dismal failure" in the 1930s serves as a notable contrast that Lichtenstein was not quite sure how to explain. He offered several possibilities: that authorities and the Ku Klux Klan threatened and used violence against organizing workers; that culture divided workers, whether it was language, gender, or racial factors; that workers, such as African American dockworkers, attained useful and effective alliance and association with the AFL; and that in the case of the rural proletariat, migratory labor patterns and the combination of an agricultural industrial work regime with a southern plantation mentality isolated workers and created a very unfavorable political economic context not conducive to effective organization. These are all valid explanations. Some such points have already been discussed herein and others are developed more carefully in the next chapter.[48]

Alternative grassroots movements existed that worked within the restrictive context that Lichtenstein described. Class harmony as ideology translated to class organization and coalition. Benefiting from class analysis of socialist ideas, radical class harmony offered a linguistic medium to argue for moral economy. Research in the local archives and the Communist Party records in the Library of Congress, including the *Daily Worker* newspaper, suggests the lack of a Communist Party presence. Review in Socialist Party records yielded similar negligible results. The local craft economy indicated an unfavorable setting as well. Miami was an AFL union city through the 1930s.

It appears that the threat of violence was not enough to frighten people away from left alternatives, at least for short periods. The homegrown grassroots movement that emerged in Florida represented a creative democratic moment. The DCUCL and the efforts of organic intellectuals such as Perrine

Palmer demonstrate that the histories of the Communist and Socialist Parties, while important on their own merits, do not tell the whole story of radicalism in the United States. The history of the DCUCL suggests that historians need to continue to search for the way workers responded to the oppressive and dehumanizing aspects of capitalism.

As important is the resistance that the DCUCL and other critics of the conservative handling of the economic depression faced. The DCUCL sought to create community and share the economic burden of the Depression but, more important, they wanted to prevent the conditions that would allow such hardship to occur again. Individuals such as Palmer sought communal resolution to address what appeared to be a larger systemic breakdown. While motivated by the sweeping generalizations of modern utopic visions such as technocracy, Palmer and others were also keenly aware of the basic contradictions that kept the machine running. The New Deal's poetic and visionary words and images that inspired so many suggested that, collectively, the United States would be that beacon on a hill for the world to see and perhaps mirror. The experiment of the Declaration of Independence, the American Revolution, and the US Constitution would work out and thus create true class harmony and collective security. As with many Americans, Palmer believed that only through grassroots organization—and eventually cross-class unity and collaboration—would a democratic promise come to fruition.

CHAPTER 7

Labor Marches

Class Struggle and the Marginalization of Class

Despite its local grassroots origins, the Dade County Unemployment Citizens' League was viewed with suspicion by most Miami business interests. The league's eventual marginalization to the radical fringes of influence reflected more public perception than any actual adherence to a revolutionary platform. Viewed from another angle, however, the organization's advocacy for the poor outside the philanthropy, charity, and rigid social welfare traditions suggested an association with Marxist political philosophies.

The league's adherence to a radical conception of class harmony sought to reform what Perrine Palmer called in 1935 the "profit-wage-charity system" on the local level, something the federal government through the New Deal was attempting on the national level. The DCUCL worked to make capitalism more humane, however illogical that may have been; members were not necessarily naive, but they did express hope for a progressive interpretation of the US Constitution's preamble phrase, "to promote the general welfare." After 1935, the league evolved from a grassroots activist organization into a volunteer charity outfit. The transformation was precipitous and came for no apparent reason. Perrine Palmer continued to advocate for the homeless and larger economic justice, appearing in Labor's Citizenship Committee meetings through at least 1937. But he too faded away in the historical record, though his son, Perrine Palmer Jr., would become mayor in 1945 as one of the many World War II veterans to enter political office after the war, and he would remain active in local politics into the 1960s.[1]

By 1935–36, the activism of the unemployed, the influx of New Deal monies into the area, and the nationally reenergized labor movement spurred a broader labor and civil-rights movement in south Florida. Historical circumstances made the league impatient and frustrated over time, pushing members to search for wider alliances and more immediate resolution of continuous poverty and joblessness. Extant sources suggests that their radicalization unfolded in three stages.

The *first stage* united the DCUCL with the New Deal and built on Palmer's ideas from the previous three years. The community meeting that Palmer and the league called for in May 1933 never transpired. Embracing the National Recovery Administration as a genuine effort for economic recovery along Palmer's earlier vision, the DCUCL sought consistency and successful implementation of accepted industry codes. Later in 1933, the league embraced the Civil Works Administration's efforts to alleviate joblessness and extreme poverty. Because of the disempowered status of the unemployed and the limitations of the code-writing process, the league worked alongside organized labor and the larger community to see the NRA through in an apparently futile endeavor. An important collaboration, as noted in earlier chapters, had the AFL Central Labor Union and the DCUCL insisting on home labor protectionism as a means of defining fair labor conditions. Their effort ran parallel to the NRA movement, continued a well-worn strategy in controlling the labor market, and was consistent with a progressive version of class harmony. The league's efforts here suggested the possibility of radical inclinations even if embedded in the patriotic rubric of national economic recovery and traditional AFL trade unionism.

The *second stage* developed as the economic depression persisted, the New Deal became mired in conservative quicksand, and the unemployed remained economically insecure and politically frustrated. By the spring of 1934, the DCUCL started seeking to form statewide alliances and articulated with even deeper pathos the plight of the poor and unemployed while pressing for resolutions to immediate problems. The *third stage* saw some of the work of 1933–34 come to fruition but revealed the limitations of class-harmony discourse in a conservative and individualistic context. State and local business interests turned to the tradition of using red-scare culture to protect the economic and political status quo. The tactic further limited the DCUCL as it did other grassroots movements around the country. The league lobbied the Florida legislature in the late spring and summer of 1935 for progressive legislation and eventually orchestrated a mass demonstration at Miami's City Hall, only to be accused in both instances of being motivated by communist ideas.

DCUCL efforts at grassroots organizing were co-opted or undermined by commission politics, business interests, organized labor's adherence to economic growth politics, mainstream social welfare strategies, the lack of federal political will, and an improvement in economic conditions. Each of these developments, combined with the limited resources and power of the unemployed, nearly marginalized the league into oblivion. Perhaps conservatives within the DCUCL blocked an increase activism and prevented the possibility of combining with more radical threads in the unemployment movement across the state and nation; or, simply, political fatigue finally set in after years of struggling on the margins. The lack of historical evidence on the point leads to tentative conclusions about the causes for the demise of Miami's unemployment movement.

The DCUCL would continue operating until at least 1940, but in a much-reduced charity-funding capacity—the heyday of its advocacy long past. Progressive conceptions of class-harmony discourse continued to bubble to the surface after 1935 as calls for harmony, tamer lobbying, an embrace of expertise, and specific New Deal policy initiatives, as in those targeting the housing shortage problem, fused into a buoyant liberalism. A reenergized labor movement, motivated by national initiatives and by local efforts like those sponsored by the DCUCL, helped keep radical conceptions of class harmony alive. The hopefulness of the early New Deal eventually turned into the reality of politics as usual. Harmony fizzled into mere political rhetoric and allowed conservative, paternalistic notions to resurface, particularly during World War II. While the alternative visions Palmer and the DCUCL articulated disappeared from historical memory, their efforts suggest a class perspective beyond class conflict and classlessness, one that envisioned community and civic activism as central in the struggle for economic recovery.[2]

The Unemployed and the New Deal

The DCUCL worked to ensure the success of the NRA production codes in Miami, an effort that showed their commitment to economic recovery and, for a moment, the times must have appeared hopeful for Palmer. The NRA built on voluntarism, patriotism, and collectivism—at least in the sense that the national economic plight necessitated a collective response. Verner Townley thought the NRA program was identical to Palmer's 1932 plan to end the depression.[3] Palmer's plan was more visionary in its embrace of shorter hours, in viewing production as a means of assuring abundance for all, and in raising the standard of living for all workers despite the status of their occupation. The similarities were striking.

Working in the shadow of World War I's War Industries Board and in the framework of President Herbert Hoover's associationalist philosophy, the spirit of the NRA was consistent with Palmer's vision, particularly in its emphasis on increasing general purchasing power, although its simultaneous emphasis on scaling back "overproduction" ran counter to that goal. Employers' continual quest for profit (especially in the major industries) motivated them to reclassify job assignments to ensure lower pay rates, which thus revealed their recalcitrant attitude toward government intervention, their paternalistic attitudes toward workers, and their resistance to organized labor. The proliferation of company unions undermined the cooperative dream and, with it, hopes for radical class harmony. The reality unfolded in the coming weeks and months after the passage of the National Recovery Act.[4]

In July and August 1933, hopes for class harmony were reinforced by the call for civic activism and patriotic duty. General Hugh Johnson, administrator of the NRA, framed the NRA as a proclamation (the President's Reemployment Agreement), as Palmer had envisioned, using an industry code system as the instrument for bringing about economic recovery. Buoyed by President Roosevelt's fireside chat in late July, many in the nation, including Miami's workers, had reason to hope for better days. Johnson's patriotic propaganda scheme for the NRA awarded a Blue Eagle insignia, announcing "We Do Our Part," to businesses that complied with industry codes.[5] The DCUCL pledged its support of the NRA by setting up a code committee "by which the members will be guided," staffed by William U. Wister, Perrine Palmer (who served as its chair), and J. F. Mack.

Even at this early date, more than two dozen complaints flooded the Miami Chamber of Commerce (CC), headquarters of the local NRA, the bulk of which complained of overwork and the "failure to pay minimum wages," and at least one employer risked losing the NRA insignia. The DCUCL and Miami workers more generally embraced the New Deal's intentions, or at least what they perceived them to be. The NRA Legal Division, however, only threatened removal of the Blue Eagle insignia at this nascent moment in its short history. The limitations of the US Constitution, federal law, and the federal court system packed with conservative judges along with bureaucratic disagreements among New Deal lawyers in the NRA and Justice Department and between other agencies made for a slow and weak institution. The large number of complaints across the country created an enormous backlog, further bogged down by the NRA's lack of enforcement power.[6]

The limits of harmony were demonstrated quickly as local employers continued to violate the blanket code regulations (industrywide wage and hours standards) and local NRA leaders acted to reduce the number of complaints. The activities of the league's NRA committee remain unclear. Palmer criticized business, as well as state and local governments, for failing to support the federal government's NRA efforts to shorten hours and pay adequate wages and for organizing "as commercial groups seeking group advantages." Complaints continued to pile up in September about businesses violating code regulations, suggesting that the DCUCL was helping, if not leading, the filing of complaints. The terms of grievance reviews, however, had changed for the worse by this time. While the local NRA continued getting "scores of complaints," they were not "honored unless they [were] delivered in person or signed with the name and address of the complainant," the CC and later the local NRA compliance board asserted. Fears of reprisal from employers also surely created an obstacle for workers to pursue their grievances over hours and wages. The NRA's leadership could not dissociate itself from the local power structure, given its connections with the CC. It is interesting to note a gap in the record of the Miami CC minutes. Missing is the period between May 22, 1933, and May 7, 1934, in an otherwise complete run of their minutes through 1967. The lacuna suggests an inharmonious class context.[7]

The demand for workers to disclose personal information to an institution representing local business interests likely diminished the number and quality of complaints submitted. There was also a threat of being blacklisted. One restaurant employee wrote anonymously to William Farnsworth, NRA assistant counsel, alerting him to the fact that "one must make an affidavit [to the local board] or they do not investigate and you might as well move out of Miami when you do that as no one will hire you." All he asked for was a "living wage and justice."[8] Before any worker acted, common sense dictated he consider the competitive job market, the high unemployment rate, and the possibility of being blacklisted. The local NRA board preferred to orally warn businesses violating the codes to comply, accepting their assurances they would correct the problem. They also pushed for "consumer pledges" to support Blue Eagle establishments, in that way urging code compliance through a loose sense of community pressure.

Getting the NRA to work was clearly turning out to be a difficult task, but workers and the unemployed resorted to various means to help the cause. Workers in numerous trades—restaurant and hotel workers, cigar makers, beauticians, retail clerks, and bakery drivers, for example—organized locals in September as a way to improve job conditions in the city. A renewed urgency to organize emerged in these early days of the New Deal, an effort that would continue to gather steam in the coming months and years.[9] Beginning in late October, local unions also advocated on behalf of workers, organized and unorganized, who had evidence that their employers were violating the NRA codes. Organized labor promised that "the name of the one making the complaint will not be made known to the employer, so one need have no fear of losing his position." Such a complaint, evidently, would be sent to the impotent national NRA officials, though it is unclear how many complaints were given to the local unions and how they used them. The extant copies of NRA responses to workers' complaints advised them to direct their grievances to the local compliance boards. Responses of the kind from the NRA spoke volumes. With the extent of local control and discretion (and the deference to local authorities from the national and regional divisions) and the limited power of the NRA, it is no wonder it failed as recovery, as reform, and as a means of winning greater support from the public for greater government intervention and collectivism.[10]

Another strategy was to educate and appeal to the community to pressure the local NRA board. Labor's Citizenship Committee (LCC) conducted several educational meetings about the NRA. In addition to its weekly discussions and those of the DCUCL, the Building Trades Council, the Central Labor Union, the Dade County Consumers League, and the twenty-seven affiliated locals, the LCC held several evening educational events in local schools in November and December 1933. One meeting at the Glade View School attracted several union leaders, including the LCC chair and member of the electrical workers' union, Frank G. Roche, and Mrs. E. L. Thayer, president of the Consumers League and regular attendee of the LCC, who gave speeches on various aspects of the NRA. Some of the gatherings included musical entertainment.[11] Later, in December 1933, Frank G. Roche and the LCC and DCUCL organized a public NRA discussion in Bayfront Park, where Blackwell Smith, NRA assistant counsel, gave a speech at the well-attended event. The DCUCL had initially introduced the idea of an NRA parade in mid-November, but Roche apparently accommodated local retail merchants by scaling down the plans and conducting a more formal educational event.[12]

The LCC and the DCUCL also turned to local government to help get resident workers back to work. The strategy was to institutionalize a home-labor ideology infused with patriotic localism. They pressed the City Commission in the fall of 1933 to pass a labor ordinance that would require the city to hire resident workers for municipal contract work at prevailing wages and for eight-hour days. Both groups sought to limit, if not prevent, job competition from snowbirds who would enter the area during the upcoming winter tourist season.

In spite of such lobbying efforts, the best the unions and the DCUCL could do was to get the City Commission to pass a resolution requesting that bona fide residents (having lived in Dade County for at least one year) be employed first on city contracts, but the commission took no action on the issue of wages or hours.[13] The *Miami Daily News* reported that employers continued to hire snowbirds willing to accept low wages, some of whom worked only for room and board. Local officials urged workers with cars to make sure they carried Florida license plates in an effort to crack down on snowbird employment.[14] The various strategies, however, offered few immediate results. Union organizing proved to be a protracted struggle, public pressure tactics remained dubious at best, and weak political and patriotic pronouncements marshaled little moral persuasion.

This local context pushed the DCUCL to lobby the City Commission and contact the federal government for assistance. In two letters to the national government—one to Harold Ickes (Secretary or the Interior and public works administrator) in September and the other to President Roosevelt in October—Perrine Palmer expressed frustration at the failures he and the league were witnessing. Palmer emphasized to Ickes the inadequacy of local projects for alleviating poverty and unemployment. Headlined "Consider the Unemployed," the letter argued for the need for a large-scale housing construction endeavor, as well as attention to other immediate welfare needs, such as health, food, and water, instead of huge building projects such as harbor improvements and airfields not intended directly for the unemployed. Palmer urged the City Commission to lobby the federal government for housing construction projects and more direct relief and work opportunities for a diverse workforce. He also suggested that the city, county, and state needed to donate unused land in their possession, especially property gained "through the nonpayment of taxes," to the local government.[15] The City Commission acted on Palmer's request by passing a resolution to pay a full-time lobbyist in Washington, DC. He further informed Ickes that Florida's unemployment had increased between 6 and 7 percent during the past month, according to city commissioner Orville Rigby (former CLU president); county records also revealed that "an average of more than one legal eviction per day for non-payment of rent" had occurred in 1933, adding that "for every legal eviction [however] there are probably ten that do not go through the courts."[16]

The DCUCL's reaction to the NRA operation reflected how Palmer's plan differed from the actual practice of the NRA. "The whole program is failing now," Palmer wrote, "for no other reason on earth than too many exemptions from its obligations and benefits." He expressed a lingering concern that the city, county, and state governments were engaging in "the most flagrant exemptions." He also lobbied the City Commission to get federal support to allow Miami and Dade County to provide "a practical demonstration of the business possibilities of a shorter work day and week by trying out, at the same time, in all lines of economic endeavor, or [*sic*] whatsoever nature, the same number of hours (30 per week) required on public works and relief projects." Until "a shortage of labor is created" that includes everyone simultaneously, the problems of "overproduction and ruinous competition" would not be eliminated. "In no other way is it possible," Palmer insisted, "to do justice to ALL and make increased pay rolls create new business and new business finance increased pay rolls SIMULTANEOUSLY." Palmer's more cooperative vision, it appears, was undercut by the NRA's complicated, inefficient, and ineffective operation, as well as by businesses unwilling to follow the blanket code.[17]

Palmer's letter to Roosevelt expressed a deep frustration with slowness in confronting the unemployment problem. The drastic conditions necessitated radical criticism. In a missive he titled "Flesh and Blood Can Not Wait," Palmer cited that B. R. Kessler, CC secretary, was advising Miami businesspeople to petition "Washington in support of a general demand for exemptions under the national recovery act for this area because of seasonal conditions." Kessler was speaking in front of the newly formed Greater Miami Recovery Association, a business organization representing more than sixty employer groups. The *Herald* reported that the purpose of the association was to "harmonize conflicting interests." That the NRA's plan was being executed so poorly was an indication that a cooperative will was lacking and that such "commercial groups seeking group advantages" undermined the recovery effort. Palmer wrote that the DCUCL had "no quarrel with business for not employing [the unemployed]; nor with the government for not forcing business to do so. But we have a very serious quarrel with both business and government for not permitting us to use the idle means of production and distribution now being denied us . . . because someone else cannot make a profit on our labor."[18]

Palmer revealed a real commitment to cooperation and the elimination of poverty, though he operated within the confines of a radical class harmony. Evoking the passion in the declaration of the Continental Congress of Workers and Farmers for Economic Reconstruction and its criticism of the profit motive, Palmer attacked the tyranny of the small minority "owning and controlling the means of existence of all and thereby dictating the manner in which the majority shall live." "The rights of life, liberty, and happiness" needed to be measured not by profit or wealth but by cooperation and "the mutual and equal protection of ALL." Freedom could be measured no other way, according to Palmer. He referred to the "conservative" Continental Committee on Technocracy's Plan of Plenty as an alternative approach to dealing with the economic depression. Palmer's boldness along one line of reasoning was logically undermined by his support of the current legal system and private property. Only in the context of class harmony, albeit a radical rendition, could such contradictions not seem unreasonable. That is, the current legal system needed radical change, as did private property rights, if his larger vision were to come into fruition.

Palmer and the DCUCL did not go that far, however, even while the league's prescriptions radically challenged the legal and social order. Hope for a cooperative ethic went hand in hand with a vision and expectation that a vibrant civic ethic, with the goal of equality for all, necessitated plenty of vigilance, flexibility, and pragmatism—not conservative ideological economic dogmatism. His postscript revealed the desperate state of things: he had been "discharged from a 91 hour, $15 a-week [state] job. 'We just had another man we had to take care of,' said the state."[19]

Palmer's letters and earlier comments suggest citizens across the country were civically engaged beyond the vote and adherence to "radical" political parties. He, as did others, argued for imaginative progressive solutions that implicitly challenged the status quo.[20] Many of Palmer's letters were published in the local newspapers, several of which appeared only in the local labor newspaper, the *Miami News*. He wrote as an advocate in these letters in a style that contrasted with the supplicant and leader-worshiping citizens commonly highlighted by historians of the period. Palmer and DCUCL's activism suggests a different framework, one not mired in the mud of political cynicism or of tenuous formulations of worker agency. A broader activism existed that stood outside the Socialist Party and Communist Party, that looked to consumption and production as sides of the same coin, and that challenged the status quo. While outside the more traditional sites of radicalism, Palmer and the DCUCL engaged in a participatory democracy that embraced the radical spirit of a moral and liberal humanism. Arguments that would marginalize Palmer or the DCUCL as exceptional would have to ignore or understate the popularity of ideas such as production for use rather than for profit or denigrate it as simple idealism. The political and economic success attained by this activism may have been small and may have missed the headlines or in some cases was never recorded, but the spirit and the humaneness of the vision and effort rises above pedestrian assessments of what the US people wanted or did not want. This progressive outlook, nonetheless, ran up against a rigid power structure set against substantial solutions to unemployment, one that operated at the local, the state, and the national levels.[21]

The Civilian Works Administration and Blue Eagle Picketing

The DCUCL acted in December 1933 to preempt local politics and prevent it from influencing how relief work would be distributed under the short-lived Civilian Works Administration (CWA). The affairs over the summer and the subsequent complications with the NRA colored their perspective. The league supported W. H. Green, the experienced welfare director of Miami, as the local CWA administrator. Fearing a local effort to remove Green as its director, the league sent a letter of support to the City Commission, Dade County Commission, the press, Harry L. Hopkins (the national CWA administrator), and Marcus Fagg (the Florida emergency relief administrator). The league complimented Green's "ability, integrity, human understanding, and kindness," evidently impressed by his earlier administrative efforts running the city's limited unemployment fund. The league feared that a partial business representative or political appointee would hurt the fair and efficient distribution of work in CWA projects. Employer concerns that CWA jobs would lure workers away because of their better pay and better working conditions (as a result of the Davis-Bacon Act—prevailing wage—and the wage and hour stipulations of the CWA) caused the DCUCL to preempt the politicization of the directorship. It sought to prevent a cooptation of the post similar to one that had occurred to the local NRA board. Luckily, from their perspective, Green held onto the post and retained it under the Federal Emergency Relief Administration through July 1935.[22]

The meager allotments to the Florida CWA could not meet the great demand for work and relief, nor did the work projects rescue workers from the state's low-wage economy. Fagg received complaints over lower wages (as for unskilled labor in highway construction, 30¢ instead of 40¢ an hour) and some working past the allowed thirty hours. In some instances, as in the citrus farms and timber and turpentine industry of central Florida, employers complained that the CWA drained their workforces because their workers preferred the higher weekly wage rate ($12 over $9). The *Miami Daily News* argued that, in fact, the "lowness" of these workers (most of whom were Black) made it unwise to pay them high wages. They lacked habits of frugality, not saving any surplus income, preferring instead to shuffle "along year to year with the subsistence to which he his accustomed." "He presents a problem, this fellow, but not one to be solved in the rush of a civil works program. . . . To raise his status [would require] nearer three generations than three months."[23]

Seemingly unswayed by such racist and classist prejudices, Fagg removed workers from relief rolls who allegedly engaged in such defiant acts (as seeking higher wages) so as to provide aid and work to more of the unemployed. Fagg and the government sought to spread the meager relief coffers as far as possible by such means, but they had the effect of subjecting these workers to worse conditions; it also helped reinforce racism in the class structure. The *Miami Daily News* reported in mid-December that the local CWA removed a considerable number of Blacks in Dade County from the eligible unemployed for "refusing work when offered it." The report indicated that the results were that 4,000 of 4,400 eligible unemployed whites were put to work, whereas only 1,500 of 4,300 Blacks attained temporary positions—such as ditch digging and mosquito control. Fagg's policy, though operating in a scarcity framework, also revealed his political awareness by not disturbing Florida's racial status quo.[24]

The bulk of complaints from the unemployed inveighed against the CWA's inability to provide work, citing the scarce resources at the disposal of government bureaucrats. Fagg in January 1934 explained to John Carmody, a CWA engineer, that the work allotments simply did not meet demand: "The real trouble all over Florida is the fact that there are thousands of men out of employment for whom we cannot furnish employment. Somehow it seems impossible for us to get it over to these unemployed the fact that we are specifically and definitely limited to a very small number of people as compared to the tremendous number out of employment." Such contexts revealed how the CWA was unable to accommodate the unemployed or produce adequate and just outcomes. Need simply exceeded the ability of government largesse to ameliorate conditions. As demands whittled away CWA resources over the coming weeks and months (ending on March 31), the anxieties of the unemployed amplified and their activism increased, as Fagg noted in his frustration over the many telegram and letter complaints flooding Washington.[25]

Meanwhile, the DCUCL offered its support in the form of pressing local businesses to back the NRA. The organization used community pressure as its main tactic in combating ongoing employer resistance to the blanket code agreements and against the progressive potential of the NRA. In January 1934, members coordinated picketing of businesses that had their Blue Eagle removed and in March they helped organize a Blue Eagle parade. Restaurants and dry-cleaning businesses, two important local employers, continued to violate blanket code agreements throughout the fall and winter. Organized labor—the CLU, LCC, and the newly organized Hotel and Restaurant Workers Local 133—and the DCUCL got workers to bombard the local compliance board and Washington with complaints about the continual noncompliance. Arthur A. Ungar, chair of the NRA compliance board and owner of the Ungar-Buick automobile dealership, was forced to bring charges against Southern Cafeteria and Sunshine Cleaners as a result of the drive. In a letter to Walter N. Pearce of the US Department of Commerce responsible for the Florida's NRA compliance boards, Ungar noted, "from our [the local board's] point of view [what] has caused 99% of all the troubles we have had in Miami with our restaurant operators and their employees," was the October 1933 publication of the NRA blanket code for restaurant work. The NRA wage and hour code listed the following: fifty-four hours a week for men, forty-eight for women; 24¢ minimum hourly wage for men and women (equivalent to approximately $4.66 in 2020, 82¢ less than Florida's 2020 minimum for tipped workers); gratuities were not to be considered wages; an employee could be charged 25¢ per meal consumed if that had been the practice prior to the NRA code. Apparently, once workers learned of the possibility of better wage and hour conditions, they demanded them. The only reasonable position for workers to take, from Ungar's perspective and the local compliance board, was complete acquiescence to the will of the employer; hence, any effort to challenge managerial prerogative represented a problem.[26]

The employers' labor problem and Ungar's headache represented an opportunity for the DCUCL to push for the larger agenda of spreading employment and improving conditions for workers. J. J. LeVelle, chair of the DCUCL picket committee, and Palmer, chair of the advisory committee, coordinated the picketing four days after the National Compliance Board ordered the removal of the Southern Cafeteria's Blue Eagle on January 9. Palmer and the DCUCL decided to mark their pickets with the Blue Eagle as a sign of their support for NRA's goals, at least as they interpreted them. The Southern Cafeteria, in an attempt to neutralize the patriotism and appearance of authority evoked by the Blue Eagle, complained to the National Compliance Board about the picketers' practice. The board soon pressed Ungar to have the DCUCL end the practice of using Blue Eagles on their picket signs—clearly, patriotism was contested terrain. They were concerned that the wrong message would be sent, namely, that the NRA supported such grassroots action. In the end, the state and local authorities ultimately limited the right to picket. They made their case by arguing about public safety and welfare, as well as the need to protect private property, and cared less about the accuracy of whether the Blue Eagle display indicated the establishment was indeed following NRA production codes.

The NRA Compliance Board did its part, in any case, to douse popular support for the program—the very outcome that both Hugh Johnson and FDR hoped for, at least on some level—by disallowing the use of the Blue Eagle insignia by grassroots mass organizers. Contesting the meaning of this patriotic symbol, the DCUCL sought a larger movement that forced business to implement fairer working conditions and pay and thus allow for a more equitable distribution of wealth to occur. For the National Compliance Board, the Blue Eagle represented a neutral advertising scheme intended to foster popular support for top-down control of production. Economic recovery, the theory went, would be flouted by such manipulation of production, thus balancing the economy and preventing overproduction. Yet the participation of the masses in the power struggle never actually achieved a comfortable equilibrium, particularly in nonindustrial work.

The DCUCL's attempts to shape a progressive meaning of the Blue Eagle thus challenged the top-down approach of power relations. As already noted, Palmer complained to Roosevelt about local businesses' efforts to get NRA code exemptions. B. R. Kessler's actions suggests that the NRA's first year in Miami led to an aggressive countermove to undermine worker organization, which may help to explain the gap in the CC's minutes. Placing the Blue Eagle on worker pickets challenged such power grabs through mass mobilization, or at least the hope of greater grassroots activism. The Southern Cafeteria's complaint about the picketers' use of the Blue Eagle revealed its owners' inherent understanding of the need to undermine the DCUCL's and labor unions' attempt at legitimacy. Bureaucratic entanglements and conservative deference to local power structures hampered the possibility of progressive interpretations of the NRA. The issue of the Blue Eagle highlighted the complicated political web that defined local affairs and the relationship between local and national power.[27]

A radical conception of harmony entailed challenging the paternalism implicit in the employer-employee relationship. Miami workers contended with poor conditions in restaurant work: including low wages (less than 20¢ an hour), employers charging workers for meals whether they consumed restaurant food or not, and the excessively long work hours (fifty-six hours or more—as high as seventy—for men and women).[28] These real-world conditions made conservative and fallacious depictions of harmony all the more contemptible. The DCUCL and organized labor, for example, reacted to the Southern Cafeteria's pathetic attempt to represent itself as a benevolent employer through full-page newspaper advertisements in the *Miami Daily News* and *Miami Herald* on January 10. The Southern Cafeteria claimed that it kept workers on their payrolls during the economically depressed summer of 1933 at a loss of $12,000. The most egregious deception was the claim that workers paid for the advertisement, announcing "We Are Perfectly Satisfied with Our Wages and Treatment by the Executives of the Southern Cafeteria and Restaurant," and, in parenthesis, it stated that a list of employees' names and signatures (ninety of them) were "in the files of the *Miami Herald*." The local Compliance Board's investigation, urged on by the national office that, in turn, was inundated by the local letter campaign, revealed that workers signed the advertisement because they feared losing their jobs; the board did not find any who had contributed to the cost of it. Palmer promised the local newspapers that "pickets will be placed about every concern from which the Blue Eagle is removed," which soon included the Sunshine Cleaners. That establishment's owners physically attacked a picketer and were subsequently fined by the municipal court.[29]

In addition to losing the right to use the Blue Eagle insignia on their picket signs, DCUCL picketers faced a recalcitrant court system committed to protecting individualism, private property, and local businesses against the will of workers. Picketers also confronted insufficiency of funds and ambivalent construction workers' unions (the strongest base of unionism in Miami), or at least a conservative trade union leadership reluctant to offer greater support of the nascent restaurant workers' union (Local 133) and its unemployed allies. Both realities helped curtail greater activism through picketing or other forms of mass assembly. On January 29, the local circuit court placed an injunction on picketing the Sunshine Cleaners. The injunction led to the pulling of pickets from other businesses and a temporary end to such community pressure tactics.[30] The DCUCL, following the conservative logic of Roche and the construction-trade-dominated LCC, sought to preempt any further court actions and to reverse the injunction; unclear, however, is the extent of this effort, whether they were successful in gaining the right to continue picketing at Sunshine Cleaners, and whether they picketed other businesses.

And so, even when the DCUCL's strategy was simply to "call attention to those who violate" the "letter and the spirit" of the NRA through "peaceful and dignified means" and thus "encourage and reward, by patronage, those complying," the organization's efforts did not gain wider support. On the picketing front, it appeared that the more powerful construction unions may have decided against further action or at least continuing their support. The weaker Hotel and Restaurant Workers and the DCUCL dealt with financial limitations that discouraged resistance against the courts. The DCUCL, nonetheless, adopted an old AFL consumer protest strategy of the "unfair list," keeping a list of businesses that practice certain antiunion or antilabor activities and actively discouraging consumer patronage of businesses on the list and encouraging patronage under the union label. In the present case, one need only replace union compliance with NRA compliance.[31]

The Blue Eagle Parade and Harmony

Direct action was complemented with broader community efforts to garner support for the NRA, efforts that evoked the problems of harmony discourse. The histories of the organizing the Blue Eagle parades shows most clearly the countervailing tendencies within harmony. The DCUCL sought to spark a groundswell of support for controlling production, raising wages, spreading work, redistributing income for the greater good, and thus moral economy. This meant getting politicians and local businesses to support their efforts. Palmer argued for a collective class effort to attain meaningful and lasting economic recovery as revealed by his early 1930s activism and his plan to end the depression, the technocracy vision, the organization of the DCUCL, and his letters to the community, Ickes, and Roosevelt. The parades were attempts to get even broader support. Their histories reveal the hopefulness of some about the NRA and the New Deal and ambivalence and resistance among others. All could agree with the dream of class harmony, but the reality of ongoing class struggle persisted behind the facades of parade costumes and floats.

The Blue Eagle Parade committee established in late November 1933 attempted to coordinate a cross section of classes to participate in the event, including business, civic, fraternal, and military organizations. Such plans embraced the essence of the class-harmony ideal and embodied an egalitarian vision in which class cooperation worked to attain greater equality. The strategy to pressure businesses into NRA compliance was not naive about the nature of power. Instead, it revealed a sharp understanding of the role of advertising and boosterism in the city building project. Parades were an extension of existing marketing approaches; the added twist was the well-worn grassroots tactic of using moral persuasion through community pressure tactics—that is, strikes, picketing, parades. The DCUCL introduced the parade idea in an LCC meeting, gaining its and the CLU's support amid the fall labor struggles. In a nod to the power of local unions, Frank Roche and Scott Rhoades (secretary of the LCC) headed the parade committee as chair and vice chair, respectively; DCUCL members Perrine Palmer and William Wister held two of the other three posts (secretaries); George H. Doty, president of the Riverside Improvement Association, served as treasurer.[32]

Class harmony as staged performance meant getting all the groups involved in any proposed boosting event. Cecil Turner, a Dade County commissioner, agreed that the county should cooperate with the parade effort, but he believed it had "no right to appear in the parade" because of the (alleged) NRA restrictions placed on the Dade County government to hire more employees or pay higher wages. Despite this public airing of an elected official's grievance against the NRA, the *Miami Daily News* reported that the parade idea gained support of "virtually every civic, fraternal and business organization in Greater Miami." In addition to organized labor and the DCUCL, several others agreed to participate in the parade, including a few improvement associations, the American Legion, World War I veterans, Shriners, the Greater Miami Auto Maintenance Association, and the City Ice and Fuel Company. Conspicuously missing were the newly formed Greater Miami National Recovery Association, the Greater Miami Board of Trade, the CC, the Greater Miami Hotel Association, and the Greater Miami Restaurants Association. These business organizations had already made extensive efforts to exempt south Florida from NRA blanket code minimum requirements. The Greater Miami Retail Merchants Association and the Miami Avenue Merchants Association tepidly agreed to support the Bayfront meeting, but they were silent about participating in a parade.[33]

The results of these organizing efforts were mixed. While the Blue Eagle Parade Committee succeeded in luring an NRA official to visit Miami to observe the proceedings and give a speech, they were unlucky in not being able to bring their first choice. The committee wanted General Hugh Johnson, head of the NRA, but instead got a promise from Donald Richberg, the NRA general counsel, who then sent the rising young attorney Blackwell Smith, assistant general counsel and head of the NRA's Legal Division. In the end, the parade was canceled. All that remained was a short talk by Florida congressperson J. Mark Wilcox and a speech by Blackwell Smith, who read prepared remarks at Bayfront Park after being introduced by Mayor E. G. Sewell. Approximately fifteen thousand attended, filling "every available seat" and extending "around the edges of the park seats." The cancelation was reportedly the result of the "shortness of the time and the nearness of Christmas," with downtown retail merchants apparently afraid that parade traffic would reduce sales. Ongoing class struggles over the implementation of the NRA likely undermined the initiative as well.[34]

The hierarchal and corporatist strands of the NRA vision of class harmony, as Blackwell Smith iterated them, appealed to the conservative *Miami Herald* but received a neutral reception from the *Miami Daily News* and earned a mixed reaction from the *Miami News*, the city's labor newspaper. Smith argued that the NRA sought to eliminate strikes but remained committed to improving pay and working conditions; the gist of his speech, nevertheless, emphasized the leading role business would have in crafting a solution. Cooperation through group resolutions was a key expectation. Smith emphasized that the NRA did not want to resolve commercial disagreements and conflicts via the courts but preferred "intelligence" and "administrative technique" to attain compliance. The *Miami News* agreed with the need "to bring about amicable adjustments . . . whenever possible." They argued, however, that, "after failure of such efforts within a reasonable length of time, *and it is clearly indicated that certain interests or concerns have no intention of complying with its provisions but are merely sparring for time*, then the law should be made to show its teeth for the benefit of those concerns which are honestly complying with its requirements" (italics added). The tension surrounding the first parade attempt constituted the background of the Blue Eagle struggles. Though the first parade short-circuited, ongoing grassroots activism pressed for more vigilant compliance, and the DCUCL and organized labor successfully coordinated a second parade in spring 1934.[35]

The DCUCL's quest to reframe class harmony so that workers would have a larger role in determining the outlines of equity and fairness, in specifically local circumstances, challenged employers' power in the workplace. Employer resistance to radical conceptions of class harmony prevented NRA success. Invigorated perhaps by the direct-action tactic of picketing, the DCUCL pushed the LCC to organize a Blue Eagle Parade on the George Washington birthday holiday, February 22, 1934. The planned date of the parade represented a clear attempt to gain authority and legitimacy for the workers' place in shaping the political economy: it demonstrated the DCUCL's patriotic intentions and support of FDR. The DCUCL's activism benefited from the Communist Unemployed Councils' and Socialists' hard work across the country for the down and out. The Communist and Socialist Parties' coordination of rent strikes and other mass demonstrations fueled the public imagination and motivated politicians to seek reformist solutions to quell the potential for unrest. Indeed, Blackwell Smith stated as much in his Bayfront Park speech when he highlighted how one of the main objectives (out of his enumerated eleven) of the New Deal was to reduce and relieve unemployment so as to kill "the threat of violent revolution." Whether the times were ripe for revolution was not important; talk of revolution stirred action and appeared plausible in light of labor strikes and other mass demonstrations. Grassroots organizing threatened to reorder the nature of local power in concrete ways and, for a short moment, the national government teased the imagination that it would aid such an effort. And, like the Communist Party, the DCUCL's objective was broader than just dealing with the suffering and uncertainty of unemployment. It continuously operated as a coalition institution as it reached out to unions through the LCC and worked within a political framework conducive to cooperative activism: a radical conception of class harmony.[36]

The spring parade embodied the class-harmony spirit. The committee was essentially the same as the December parade committee (Roche, Rhoades, Palmer, and Wister and Doty). They succeeded not only in conducting an actual parade—though not until March 12 because of various delays[37]—but also included a large contingent of the working class even when the parade was moved from a Friday to a Monday evening; and again, they reached out to business interests to participate.[38] The mayors and city commissioners of Miami, Miami Beach, and Hialeah, county officials, and others reviewed the parade from a stand erected on East Flagler Street and Third Avenue. No photos of the parade or of the subsequent Bayfront Park speeches or the movies that were shown at the end of these speeches have survived. The *Miami News* claimed that organized labor, consisting of around ten thousand unionists in the county who marched behind the banner of the Central Labor Union, had the best showing, but the newspaper did not give the number of participants. It also claimed that the parade attained a 100 percent showing of Dade teachers and CWA workers, the latter turning out between two and six thousand; the unemployed had a membership of five to six thousand, by far larger than any single union local. The number of workers, who were accompanied by thirty-nine floats and five bands, possibly exceeded fifteen thousand (see table 7–1 for the parade alignment) in a county with a total population somewhere between one hundred forty and one hundred eighty thousand. The local newspapers estimated that close to fifty thousand spectators watched the parade move down East Flagler Street toward Bayfront Park.[39]

The parade embraced an ebullient patriotism, and the designated speakers personified justice and class harmony. In addition to representation from veterans' groups, the local American Legion chapter, and the National Guard, the Bricklayers, Masons, and Plasters International Union marched with large American flags. In light of the cutbacks and looming end of the CWA program, the large contingent of marching CWA and CCC workers added a powerful reminder of the positive role government played in lifting the unemployed and in economic recovery. At Bayfront Park, the speakers did not include any labor leader, though Frank Roche, chair of the LCC, served as chair of the proceedings. The local papers reported that Mrs. E. L. Thayer of the Consumers League stressed the importance of cooperating with Roosevelt's plan, as the NRA was often described. The *Miami Daily News* noted that she reminded the audience to "remember those who fly the Blue Eagle [when] they do their shopping." This echoed a familiar message she made in LCC meetings that urged consumers to buy "only those products made under real N.R.A. conditions." All the other speakers were religious leaders: J. C. Simms, pastor of the Riverside Baptist church; reverend P. J. Roche, pastor of St. Mary's Catholic Church, Little River;

TABLE 7–1. March 12, 1934, NRA parade alignment

Division I: Organizations
Police escort, National Guard band, National Guard troops, veterans' organizations, Riverside Military Academy, American Legion Drum and Bugle Corps, and Women 's Auxiliary American Legion
Division II: Civil Works Administration Workers
Section 1: CWA Projects 13–1 to 13–100 Workers
Section 2: Junior Chamber of Commerce Drum and Bugle Corps
CWA Projects 13–101 to 13–200 Workers
Section 3: Junior Chamber of Commerce Harmonics Band
CWA Projects 13–201 to 13–500
Section 4: Dade County unemployed
Division III: Uniformed Units
Mahi Shrine Band and Mahi Shrine Patrol
Miami High Band and Pep Girls
Ida Fisher Pep Girls
Miami Edison High Band and Pep Girls
Dade County School Teachers
NRA Hotel
Restaurant employees and allies
Post office band and federal employees
Civilian Conservation Corps Motor 1304
Division IV: Uniformed Bodies
Central Labor Union Organization (headed by the Miami Musicians Federation band)
Building Trades Council
Division V: Uniformed Bodies
Decorated floats
Division VI: Uniformed Bodies
The CWA String Band
Commercial organizations' decorated automobiles and floats

Source: *Miami Daily News*, March 11, 1934, 5.

and Rabbi Jacob Kaplan of Temple Israel. Only snippets remain of their speeches. All three argued against rugged individualism, greedy self-interest, and for the implementation of the Golden Rule and utilitarian principles in politics and government—while a humane perspective, it hardly represented a radical tone or a systematic analysis of the political economic context. Father Roche commented that "the worker has a right to live up to the dignity of a human being. Life was never intended to be a struggle against the wolf at the door." Kaplan elaborated: "every human being has the right to have his needs considered by the government. This can be done and must be done. . . . We want justice and won't lose sight of the end." After the speeches, the Motion Picture Operators local showed films in support of the NRA.[40]

The parade offered organized labor and the DCUCL an opportunity to increase support for the NRA and its progressive potential. The ongoing labor organizing both in skilled and unskilled work entailed an uphill battle with recalcitrant employers set on maintaining a low-wage economy. The struggle by restaurant workers, cleaners, and other workers, for example, to gain recognition and for the unemployed to attain greater and more consistent relief revealed the need for expanding government involvement in the economy. They, no doubt, were also inspired by the recent pronouncements of the Roosevelt administration. President Roosevelt, in a recent NRA conference (March 5) in Washington that included industry heads, had argued for employers to pay "purchasing wages" (an awkward version of the idea of a living wage). NRA director Hugh Johnson, speaking a few days later at the same conference, urged business leaders to allow workers to choose their own representation and thus follow section 7A of the National Industrial Recovery Administration. Indeed, he argued, "company unions in 99 out of 100 cases involve illegal 'interposition' by employers."[41]

The prevalence of company unions in Miami is unknown from the historical record. But organized labor and the unemployed knew economic conditions were tough in Miami despite all the ballyhoo of a better economy and a great tourist season. Indeed, Roche noted in an LCC meeting that many visitors to the city thought Miami "to be the most backward N.R.A. city in the country, but he expected a real showing [in the parade] on labor's side of the question." The appearance of harmonious class relations hid the enduring struggle, but the spirit of a progressive class harmony remained alive.[42]

Some business interests chose to ignore the symbolic and progressive significance of the parade and interpret it in paternalistic, sympathetic terms. The *Herald* celebrated Miami's apparent class harmony in a postparade editorial entitled "Labor Marches." The editorial's condescending tone and silence on the poor pay and working conditions offered only a partial picture of Miami's labor relations. Whereas "labor riots" and "bloodshed" characterized the conditions in other countries and strikes in other US states and cities, Miami's peaceful, docile workers marched in a parade. Some were wearing "their only suit of clothes, garments that showed the effects of long usage" and "in the faces of some were evidence of hunger, seriousness of purpose." The "gayety and the brilliance of the parade," the *Herald* reminded us, only hid their desperate desire to find steady work and satisfy that "American urge for self-support, for a chance to do and be." The editorial stated the obvious: many of Miami's permanent residents needed steady employment. It lamely suggested, however, that employment opportunities "should not wait upon Washington nor an NRA or CWA but upon ourselves, our own voluntary efforts toward co-operation, helping one another, providing work, patronizing the local interests, spending money at home."[43]

Such references to laissez-faire voluntarism, encased in a weak concoction of home labor ideology, could be offered in the context of continual business resistance to complying with and adhering to NRA code provisions. The condescension shown to workers made sense when employer-employee relations operated in a paternal framework. The *Herald* paid its highest compliment to US workers when it characterized them in exceptionalism rhetoric as ambitious, rising, middle-class folk—in essence, they were aspiring employers and businesspeople.

This excursion into the mind of the worker was indeed quite remarkable. Like any distorted analysis of the *other*, assumptions abounded. Paternalism defined a neat social order filled with generalities and playful caricatures. Take this passage as a succinct example of the distortion: "American workers are patient; generally they are eager to serve. They seldom engage in riots, except as pushed by violent organizations, backed by agitators, radicals, Communists. Labor as a whole is sound and safe and willing to abide by reason. Real Americans have no use for the regimentation of the Soviet or Fascism. They are not slaves to be driven into certain ruts and kept there. Most of them are ambitious; most of them hope to climb up and out of their classification to win a fortunate turn of the cards and become somebody. This, they know, can only be accomplished through the old American system of democracy and freedom."[44]

The *Herald* spoke for workers here without reference to the long and ongoing struggles of restaurant employees, cleaners, and the DCUCL. The newspaper interpreted the absence of worker militancy in Miami and elsewhere as a sign of US workers' patience and desire to climb the ladder of success; where militancy did occur, one could follow the circular logic: violent organizations, agitators, radicals, and Communists were clearly at fault. In order to accept the newspaper's clairvoyance into the worker, one must ignore the *Herald*'s own indirect support of the Southern Cafeteria's intimidation of its workforce, for example, by publishing the restaurant's coerced affidavit (their advertisement) claiming workers had no grievances. Workers avoided speaking up or protesting, let alone engaging in militancy, because they feared losing their livelihood. Fear of reprisal, not a conservative class harmony, explained the conditions at Southern Cafeteria. This incident was likely the tip of an iceberg of more widespread economic precarity given the evidence of worker complaints to the NRA and their concerns about being blacklisted. The editorial's reference to slavery highlighted the *Herald*'s class hierarchy logic: it condemned the labor of the working class as a condition of a lower social order and thus justified the workers' low wages and poor working conditions. Those who were unemployed, poor, or working in low-wage and difficult jobs had yet to become "somebody."[45]

The effort to express empathy and even celebrate the lives of workers was undermined by the editorial's condescension and passive-aggressive attitude toward their class status, unions (and their supporters), and the implicit negative characterization of certain types of work. Its celebratory tone and apparent empathy for the worker hid cultural judgments and the true nature of power relations. Vacuous clichés celebrating the American spirit took the place of deeper, closer reporting and investigation of local conditions. The article's leger-demain deceived the reader into believing workers to be essentially passive and their employers to be innocent, hardworking "somebodies." The Committee of One Hundred's didactic lectures could not have expressed a hokier message in the exclusive confines of their Miami Beach clubhouse. The *Miami News* had no direct response to the editorial. It did, however, send a message to recalcitrant employers who resisted improving wages and hours when it published side by side three articles on its front page in support of the NRA: "[William] Green Charges N.R.A. Labor Section Is Violated: Predicts Labor War Unless Anti-union Employers Are Compelled to Obey Law and Stop Illegal Activities against Workers Organizing"; "Humanity before Profits" (quoting extensively Roosevelt's March 5 NRA code conference speech); and "Labor's 30-Hour Week Bill before Congress" (discussing the Connery bill).[46]

Class Harmony and Red Scares

Class-harmony discourse disabled more effective critiques of capitalism even in its most progressive renditions. In part, the disabling was the result of a resilient power structure that refused genuine or lasting experimentation with progressive cooperative economic initiatives. Contentment with the status quo prejudiced those in power, particularly conservatives, and made them reluctant to address the pressing problems of unemployment and dire economic need in creative or redistributive ways. The often less-than-swift resolutions angered those most in need and the leaders of their organizations, which led to desperate attempts by unemployment movement leaders to make coalitions with business and government leaders to help resolve immediate issues. At times, the threat or actual manifestation of mass protest helped gain quicker solutions, however inadequate they may have been. The surface revealed real attempts by workers and the unemployed to gain greater cooperation from government and business for their benefit and thus logically for the larger community. In this way, class harmony echoed moral economy, translating into a progressive and potentially radical challenge to paternalism and top-down approaches to governing and leadership.

The specter of communist influence haunted grassroots organizations. Outside skeptics of movement intentions were prepared to red-bait, delegitimize, and therefore undermine their efforts. The insiders of the unemployment movement dealt with the immediate problems of hunger, homelessness, and other hardships and were not deterred by radical ideas. Openness to critical ideas about capitalism and the political system defined the DCUCL and other workers' organizations. Their inspiration usually derived from progressive readings of the US Constitution and Declaration of Independence, aided by progressive or populist politicians such as Vito Marcantonio, Huey Long, Hugo Black, William Connery, Robert Wagner, or Bronson Cutting and leftist writers such as Norman Thomas, A. J. Muste, and Stuart Chase, or local writers such as the autodidact Verner Townley and his many letters to the *Miami Daily News* and presentations to Labor's Citizenship Committee. In January 1934 and again in June 1935, socialists Frank J. Manning of New Jersey and Covington Hall spoke before the LCC and the local socialist chapter. They may have also presented before the DCUCL, especially because socialists such as Manning organized the unemployed throughout the country.[47]

The various activists, politicians, writers, and educators questioned the humanness of the free market system. Defenders of the system, the status quo, resorted to narrow conceptions of patriotism to choke off competing ideas. The remainder of this chapter will explore how the initial novelty of the DCUCL's advocacy turned into a public nuisance for local officials concerned with the potential radicalization of the unemployed and with continuing the optimistic boosting of local economic growth and opportunity. The conservative political context, an improvement in economic conditions, a resurgent local labor movement, and the waning resources of the DCUCL contributed to the organization's marginalization and disappearance.

Just about six weeks after the apparent display of class harmony shown in the NRA parade, the DCUCL sent a delegation to the first Florida State Federation of Workers' Leagues convention in an attempt to connect with a statewide effort to combat unemployment. Interest in expanding the workers unemployment movement, while facing several obstacles, evidently did not prevent these unemployed Floridians from widening their organizational networking. It is unclear, however, how these various groups remained in contact or coordinated with each other. Among the other nine cities that sent forty delegates to the two-day convention in Tampa were Clearwater, St. Petersburg, Lakeland, Orlando, and Jacksonville. Perrine Palmer, M. E. Fidler (the socialist who named his eldest son Eugene Debs), Joe Shepard, Charles Laughinghouse, and Merrill C. Meade represented the DCUCL at the convention.

Showing how the booster spirit seldom discriminated against economic opportunities, the *Miami Daily News* and *Miami Herald* reported how the delegates would seek to bring the convention to Miami in 1935. In addition, their brief report of the upcoming meeting noted that the "purpose of the state federation is to obtain more federal funds for federal emergency relief administration work and other government projects" and help from other sources. The local newspapers spun the potential opportunities for economic development. How the meeting unfolded and then was reported revealed the political limitations that the DCUCL and other worker organizations faced when organizing and advocating for greater distribution of wealth and greater human dignity in the United States, Florida, or individual cities such as Miami.[48]

On April 30, 1934, the *Tampa Morning Tribune* announced the formation of the Florida State Federation of Workers' Leagues, listing its elected officers and some of the convention's adopted resolutions. Eugene F. Poulnot, president of Hillsborough County Unemployed Brotherhood, was elected president; O. M. Alfonso of Tampa, first vice president; G. B. Jackson of Orlando second vice president; and D. M. Benson of Tampa, secretary-treasurer. The resolutions passed included "opposing capitalistic wars and fascism," "favoring a three-year moratorium on mortgage and tax foreclosures," support for the "workers' unemployed insurance already introduced in congress," and "that relief administration funds be turned over to the unemployed for distribution." Another resolution that passed that called for "free rent, water, lights, and clothing for the needy." The resolutions revealed a dislike for means-testing, a concern for the livelihood and dignity of the unemployed, and an anxiety that current relief allocations were being misused because of local political squabbles and corruption. Socialist organizers were likely active participants in this meeting. Later in May, socialist Covington Hall gave a lecture in the St. Petersburg's Workers' League's Industrial Hall. The *Miami Daily News* reported on May 2 that members of the DCUCL found the convention "too red for us—even the badges were red . . . so we, to the displeasure of the delegates of the convention, wore small American flags over them. After a half day's listening, we decided the ideas were red, too, so we came home." Perrine Palmer denied any of the DCUCL delegates made any such comment in a report of the meeting entitled "Scream of the Eagle," appearing in the *Miami News*.[49]

Palmer contested the *Daily News*'s claim of communistic radicalism by asserting a radical Americanism. He sarcastically pointed out that the flags worn by the Miami delegates were made in Japan and were "the same as those worn in the late N.R.A. parade in Miami." While the men and women attending the convention were nearly penniless and could not afford "red flags," they did collectively chip in to purchase three big US flags that were "draped behind the speaker's platform, and a fourth which they proceeded to choke down the throats of skeptics who doubted their knowledge of what that flag means." Palmer related an exchange between two officers of the convention that evoked the right to assembly and free speech. He wrote, "A young man, evidently of Latin birth, bearing the unfurled American flag, stepped before [the chair] and asked,

> "Mr. Chairman, under what article of the United States Constitution does this convention open?
>
> "Article one of the Bill of Rights," responded the chairman.

"What does the article say," asked the Latin. To which the chair replied:

"Congress shall make no law respecting an establishment of religion or prohibiting the free exercise thereof; or abridging the freedom of speech, or the press; or the right of the people to peaceably assemble, and petition the government for a redress of grievances."

"Does that apply to us," continued the interrogator.

"Yes."

"Then," concluded the flag-bearer, "we will continue to fight for those rights and for all other rights guaranteed to us by the Constitution, and, if need be, die for them."[50]

Palmer added that "there are some other passages in the Constitution, and in the American Declaration of Independence, that the 'reds' might have included in their ritual, but I guess that they are too hot even for reds. You will find some of them in one of the resolutions offered by the 'conservatives' from Dade." Successfully contradicting the *Daily News* in Americanist terms, Palmer suggested that communism was not a bad option and certainly preferable to fascism. He worried that the country suffered from "a touch of fascism" and this made him "immensely sick." "But why worry about names," Palmer insisted. "Why not take our natural wealth, the genius and willingness of our own people and our own United States Constitution and have real DEMOCRACY?"

Political economy and moral economy: the clarity of the problem and the solution were crystal clear to Palmer. D. M. Benson, the secretary-treasurer, attended with his father and sister, which, according to Palmer, was an inspiring sight "to watch those three fight side by side for the things which they believe." The DCUCL contributed to formulating at least one of the convention's resolutions, though it is unclear which one. The "hand-painted signs" on display at the convention proclaimed the causes of the gathering: "We can't sell our Labor"; "We must have relief"; "We want our rent paid, or will forcibly resist evictions"; "We refuse to starve amid plenty"; "Give us Relief—while you have Peace"; "No cutting water"; and "To hell with PROSPERITY, we must have SECURITY." The drive to organize, despite the dire conditions of the unemployed, revealed an idealistic and practical faith in grassroots democracy, inspiring Palmer to evoke the memories of Patrick Henry, Thomas Jefferson, and George Washington as examples of homegrown patriotic fighters for justice and freedom. The delegates at the convention believed in the idea of democracy and the practical necessity to assemble and petition the government for relief during an economic crisis when more than one-fifth of US workers were unemployed, many more underemployed, and plenty who were underpaid. Most important, the act of organizing and meeting to discuss their grievances and real, concrete needs demonstrated the hope they placed in nonviolent action. Palmer repeatedly announced that the DCUCL and now the delegates to the State Federation of

Workers' Leagues wanted to avoid revolution and thus violence, yet they were obligated as active, critical citizens to demonstrate their outrage against the existing unjust conditions and their right to live with dignity.[51]

The government had an obligation to provide for the common welfare, not simply to help a few benefit at the cost of the many. In March, Palmer recommended to the readers of the letter forum of the *Daily News* to read Republican Senator Bronson Cutting's essay, "Is Private Banking Doomed?" Cutting supported the expansion of relief efforts and the nationalization of banks; he regretted that Roosevelt had not taken that action in the first hundred days of his presidency. As Palmer and many others had done since the early 1930s, he charged technological unemployment as a major factor in the current crisis. As powerful was Cutting's connection to the plight of the unemployed: "Yet practically and morally these unemployed workers must be cared for. If purchasing power is to reach its ultimate high, they must have work and income to spend. Morally, they must have their chance to live like human beings. And when industry cannot care for them, then it becomes government's duty."[52]

On May 1, a day after the state convention, Palmer, as a representative of the DCUCL, sent FDR a telegram complaining about the end of the CWA and "the humiliating and slow method of certification under [the] social service system." Palmer highlighted how the delegates at the state convention were "fast losing hope" in the current system and that the unemployed and "those subsisting on [NRA] minimum code wages" hoped that the president would live up to his words in the March 5 speech: shorten work hours, increase wages, and get people to work. If not, Palmer argued, workers' "only recourse will be to take by force the equal privileges and immunities guaranteed them by the constitution, the same as did those who made that sacred instrument." As threatening as his words may have been, it was not nearly as radical a statement as another in the telegram, one Palmer had written and uttered before and that repeated the spirit of the Florida State Federation of Workers' Leagues: "To deny men the right to live in peace and decency merely because someone else cannot make a profit on their labor is contrary to the basic law of our land, and of the God who created it." Palmer outlined here the boundary between moral economy and, in effect, immoral usury. The profit system should not be "paramount to human life," argued the DCUCL leader. And this idea struck at the heart of capitalism.[53]

How then would the unemployed and their allies fight for their welfare? In addition to low relief payments, unemployment movement leaders feared welfare officials would undercount the number in need by prejudiced means-testing or simply overlooking cases. After the hit from CWA layoffs and eventual end of the program in March and early April, the total federal relief allotment (direct and work relief) to Miami's district fell from $101,748 in April to $78,119 in May, right when Miamians faced the regular seasonal unemployment and when federal relief spending started to be cut back more generally. Tampa's district also faced a reduction, as did all of Florida's eleven districts, but it continued to get $201,740 in May (from $444,760 in April). Palmer and the DCUCL spent a lot of energy in the rest of 1934 and 1935 to change perceptions and demonstrate that Miami in fact still had a large number of down-and-out folks despite the ballyhoo that conditions were good. Their preference was to work with city and county business and government leaders to fix conditions. There were, however, other approaches.[54]

The last comment Palmer made in his "Scream of the Eagle" report at the state convention laid out the difference between Tampa's relief allotment and Miami's. He wrote, "Miami has had no demonstrations by the unemployed yet. Tampa has and Tampa got $225,000 for relief this month [by May 17]. Miami got $63,000." Palmer was referring to the organized protests of Poulnot and the Unemployed Brotherhood on May 9 and 10 against Tampa relief officials' suspension of free school lunches for low-income students. Poulnot had been a welfare activist since the early 1930s and had been marked as a radical and inaccurately a communist by local Tampa officials because of his advocacy for the poor. He did join the Socialist Party at some point during this time. His egalitarian views likely motivated his membership. In the successful May rally, which helped restore free-lunch relief, Poulnot rallied parents and children to protest the sudden cut. Fewer than 500 of 1,100 students showed up at school and fewer than 100 showed up after lunch time. Poulnot spoke to at least 700 unemployed people when he stated, "If they don't give us the relief we want let's go open a warehouse and take what we need." His efforts to gather an organized mob led to his arrest, but authorities did act on the protest and its expressions of moral outrage and called for immediate restitution of the hunger program. The St. Petersburg *Evening Independent* also reported that Poulnot "denounced any discrimination between white or black, or married or single" relief recipients. Demonstrating cross-county solidarity, the St. Petersburg Workers' League collected funds to help with the legal fees incurred by Poulnot's case. The league reminded the public that their and the Florida State Federation Workers' League's primary objectives were to gain "direct control of all relief administration, convenient food distribution centers, [and] immediate increase of relief to adequately care for all unemployed." Poulnot and Palmer were driven by the goal of relieving conditions for the poor, which necessitated cooperation from all sectors of society; neither wanted to turn to violence and the problems that could result from such action, whether it was injury or death.[55]

To this end, Palmer and the DCUCL succeeded in organizing the Dade County Emergency Welfare Council in June 1934, a cooperative organization that included Labor's Citizenship Committee, the Central Labor Union, the Consumers' Council of Dade County, the Riverside Improvement Association, the county and city government, the CC, and other leaders of greater Miami. The idea of the organization emanated from yet another DCUCL initiative and revealed a moment of progressive class harmony attempting to unfold in reality. The DCUCL gained support from the CLU, LCC, and Consumers' Council to seek local government assistance in increasing federal aid to the area. The *Miami Daily News* reported that the citizens of these groups approached civil-court judge A. B. Small in his office to help their effort for a larger community movement. They were concerned that "a successful winter season here and prosperous conditions in building and real estate activities seem to have made federal government officials believe Dade County does not need as much emergency relief funds as other sections." Lorena Hickok of the Federal Emergency Relief Administration reported as much in January 1934 when she wrote Harry Hopkins about the celebratory newspaper stories announcing Miami's successful season.[56]

This pattern of boosting south Florida had a long tradition. The Welfare Council sought to correct these false perceptions—at least the Welfare Council's grassroots organizers did. According to Florida's Emergency Relief Administration statistics, a greater gap did exist between Tampa's allocation and its needs than in Miami's, to take just one example. Tampa suffered only a 11 percent gap between cases needing aid and those actually getting the paltry assistance in May and June, but it decreased to 8.1 percent in July and 5.1 percent in August; the disparity in Miami was horrendous: 50 percent in May and 51.2 percent in June, though improving slightly to 42 percent in July and 43 percent in August. The Welfare Council attempted to gather support through voluntary efforts and financial contributions, but the Welfare Council effort seems to have petered out by August despite the best hopes of the DCUCL.[57]

The terrible living conditions endured by the unemployed and poor were insufficiently improved with the paltry payments received either from work or direct relief. Palmer pointed out in a July 1934 letter to the local newspapers how dire conditions were for those getting assistance. The 263 relief cases, consisting of 533 adults and 551 children, received an average of $5 per month per person when the average monthly housing rental rate was $8.50. "Judge for yourself," Palmer wrote, "what those quarters must be [like] and how even that low figure leaves for food alone, *to say nothing of eyes, teeth, illness, recreation, transportation, clothes, education.—And death*" (italics added). He pointed to a government report that revealed 105 eviction cases in Miami during May. The Florida Emergency Relief Administration noted an increase in food prices in the state as well as an increase in unemployment, a decrease in economic activity, and an increase in the number of those needing relief. These patterns especially marked the conditions for the major state counties: Pinellas (St. Petersburg), Hillsborough (Tampa), Duval (Jacksonville), and Dade (Miami). Before the disappearance of the Welfare Council, Palmer pleaded with the public to donate money to help fund the expenses for an office with a full-time stenographer ($15 weekly pay). He also reported how the Welfare Council—one imagines driven by the DCUCL—was attempting to set up committees on housing, electricity, water, medical, dental, vision care, and legislation on the local, state, and national level. The DCUCL sent another desperate telegram to Harry Hopkins, Federal Emergency Relief Administration head, and Governor Dave Sholtz, as well as a letter to Julius Stone, the FERA state administrator, in August 1934 asking for an increase in appropriations for Dade and Broward Counties (District 10 of Florida's eleven relief zones).[58]

Conditions would get no better over the next year. The *Miami News* warned in September 1934 of the gross miscalculations of the local grocery bills that the Federal Emergency Relief Administration estimated a family of four or five had to pay: $283.24 annually or $5.44 per week or $1 per person of a five-person family. Miami's food expenses were the highest in the state, and the FERA analysis underestimated the true costs. The newspaper's insight paints a powerful picture:

> Did you ever stop to think, or try to live on an expenditure for a family of four or five persons, an average of $5.44 a week for YOUR family[?] Here might be a sample menu. . . . Breakfast: toast and coffee; maybe a little mush or rolled oats for a change. Lunch, a couple of avocado pears. . . . Supper. . . . grits, grunts, coffee: possibly beef stew now and then. **Then they wonder why you see so many people out with fishing poles on the causeway.** (emphasis added).[59]

The labor newspaper took issue with the judgment that people were not living within their means. It echoed Palmer's long-standing argument and a growing national consensus that called for increasing the purchasing power of the masses who represented 80 percent of the country's consumers. The newspaper argued that "skilled craftsmen and even common laborers" deserved a "living wage" and certainly more than what they were getting. "'Don't do as I do, but do as I say,' seems to be the motto of that class" of employers and government officials criticizing workers and the unemployed for asking for higher wages and relief. Calling for increases in federal intervention in the economy and attacking critics who advocate federal expansion, the *Miami News* stated, "the day had passed when the laborer can be regarded as a chattel who thankfully accept the morsels from his master's table for his wage." The *Herald*, "the morning newspaper," took issue with the *Miami News*'s calculations, but the labor newspaper shot back with a detailed account of the high grocery costs in the area and the low standard workers were expected to accept. Miami's labor and unemployment movement, despite the *Herald*'s rosy "Labor Marches" outlook, resented the condescension and distortion of what they knew to be the true conditions for many of the city's workers. Walter Hoyt, president of the CLU, would later write a rebuttal that disproved a *Herald* article that accused union picketers of the Seven Seas restaurant to be the work of labor racketeers. He assured the public that unionists sought "the betterment of our wonderful city" and found it unfortunate that the morning newspaper published misleading articles.[60]

To the DCUCL's chagrin, FDR and the US Congress continued to extend insufficient funds to the unemployed and remained biased against enlarging government relief any further. By the fall of 1934, Palmer started working for the Florida Emergency Relief Administration, where he conducted a housing survey of Miami and Dade County. I have only been able to uncover a short excerpt of the report. Palmer reported the horrendous conditions plaguing "Colored Town," namely its overcrowding and congestion, the shoddy conditions of many of the homes (e.g., defective roofs, windows, door screens), and poor sewage system. Most residents were renters, and the insufficiency of the housing to accommodate the demand led to greater overcrowded conditions.

Through the fall and for the next two years, Palmer would campaign for better housing for the poor and unemployed, giving regular presentations to the DCUCL and the LCC. In November 1934 he visited the office of John C. Gramling, a major coordinator of the Public Works Administration housing project in Liberty City, to find out what the Emergency Division of Public Works could do to alleviate the housing problems of Miami. Gramling informed Palmer that the PWA would entertain only housing projects "that were self-liquidating." In other words, the poor and unemployed were out of luck if they could not pay enough rent to pay off the cost of construction (that is, through rental payments over time). Gramling added in his letter to Horatio B. Hackett, director of the PWA Housing Division, that "the condition is really appalling" and that the city, county and state failed to build any new homes for the needy. "The unemployed have nowhere to go," relaying Palmer's fieldwork, "and rents have soared to such an extent that those working for a salary cannot pay the rents demanded. I do not know what to do about it." Palmer later returned to Gramling's office to call attention to the need for housing for "about 3,500 families in Miami." Gramling suggested seeking government support to tap into unused land in the county so as to set up 3,500 army tents. These discussions, no doubt, demonstrated the need for housing assistance, both for Blacks and whites, and likely were the first conversations that would eventually lead to the "white" Edison Housing projects erected in 1939.[61]

The league, with Palmer's assistance, continued to lobby the federal government while embracing more self-help solutions to the housing and food problems. In December 1934, Palmer, on behalf of the LCC, DCUCL, and United Floridians (a home-labor advocacy group), sent yet another telegram to President Roosevelt, saying,

> We appeal to you to end immediately the wholesale eviction, imprisonment and threats of imprisonment of destitute families here. More than 1,700 white families on federal relief roles alone facing eviction or jail, or both, because of inability to pay rent, which Florida law permits. Situation among negroes even worse. Six hundred families without running water. Over 100 with no water at all. Nine hundred families living under leaky roofs. We have repeatedly appealed to our city, county and state governments, but in vain. . . . They acknowledge this condition but admit inability to deal adequately with it. Is there nothing left for these people but to take the law into their own hands and protect themselves as best they can?[62]

If residents of sunny tourist Miami managed to craft such a telegram, one must wonder how many more of this kind of message reached Roosevelt and his administration from the rest of the country. Palmer lobbied the City Commission in late 1934 to secure housing for the poor and unemployed. The examples of eviction victims told of the harrowing poverty the poor faced: one widow with three children was living on $14 per week (about $272 in 2020); a man in another family earned $25.20 per month (about $490 in 2020) while his wife suffered from tuberculosis, had a ten-day-old baby, and two other children three and four years old; another family of seven earned only $33.60 per month (about $653 in 2020). Urged by Palmer, the City Commission called a special meeting to discuss the issues, but plans to obtain lumber to build houses in northwest Dade fell apart.

In February 1935, the DCUCL purchased its own tents after the City Commission failed again to help them: tents to shelter the destitute and unemployed—a reflection of hard economic times and the lack of political will. The DCUCL was able to purchase six army tents after raising money through donations, erecting them at Viney's Tourist Camps, 807 SW 32 Avenue. The league noted how fifty-seven families faced eviction in January. They called for further help "to all who can assist in meeting the emergency" whether through donations of rooming space, more tents, building materials, plumbing, furniture, or the use of land.[63]

Years of economic crisis led to mounting frustration. Again in March 1935, Palmer warned the City Commission that only $2,100 remained of federal funds to assist ten thousand individuals on the relief rolls. He notified the commissioners that the DCUCL had sent a delegate to Washington "to tell federal officials there is still great need in Miami in spite of the unprecedented tourist season." Several Miami citizens collected signatures to nominate Palmer for city commissioner, but he rejected the request in a letter to the *Miami Daily News*, claiming that Federal Emergency Relief Administration rules prohibited its employees to run for office. Self-identifying as a labor leader, Palmer insisted that citizens, including businesspeople and labor leaders, were not doing enough to change things. His radical egalitarianism and consumerist perspective revealed his hopes for social harmony, a view predicated on the notion of the interconnectedness of society. He articulated his vision of moral economy in radical class-harmony terms. Palmer noted that "street cleaners and farm hands are more vital to democracy than millionaires. Which could you get along without? . . . [The] very numbers [of the] wage-earning masses make them the only possible adequate customers for business. . . . [But] we are still turning pregnant mothers and children into the streets or herding them into tents, tool houses, old bus bodies, condemned shacks and other unsanitary conditions (I can give you instances, if you desire)." The opportunity was certainly ripe for more radical action.[64]

Fever-pitch tension arrived by the spring of 1935. The increasing number of evictions, some resulting from the high winter rental rates of the 1935 tourist season, set the context for the purchase of the army tents. The looming summer promised the usual high rates of unemployment as well. In response, the local and state unemployment movement sought to lobby the state legislature for greater relief.

With an average of ten weekly evictions and more than 1,800 Miami families facing possible eviction in May 1935, Dade unemployment movement representatives attending the session of the state legislature warned that revolution would result if the dire economic conditions did not receive immediate attention by the legislature. The local newspapers claimed they were delegates of the Florida Council of Unemployed Leagues (FCUL) that had just formed in Jacksonville in May and had sent them as a lobbying group to the state's capital. Miami's delegates to Tallahassee—whether or not they were indeed connected to the FCUL—included M. E. Fidler and Sam Stodel and DCUCL officers John Gavelick, John Burke, and George Maurer.[65] The delegates, according to the *Miami Daily News* and the *Herald*, supported a legislative platform that included the abolition of the poll tax, the placing of minority parties on the ballot, adequate old-age pensions, worker's compensation, and a criticism of the amendment on the pending social welfare bill that, according to the *Herald*, "makes subject to arrest anyone unemployed who refuse to accept work at prevailing rates of wages." The *Daily Worker*, the Communist Party newspaper, labeled it the "forced labor bill"; a vagrancy clause in the bill was eventually stricken. The *Daily Worker* reported that Dave Sholtz, in a press conference, denounced the FCUL, labeling their presence a "communist invasion on the capital."[66]

The DCUCL, in any case, telegraphed Governor Sholtz that it had not authorized this delegation to represent it; the telegraph was a desperate political move to create distance from itself and the red tinge surrounding the delegation. Fidler's and the DCUCL officers' presence, Palmer's earlier advocacy of ending the poll tax in 1932 and 1933, and the LCC and State Federation of Labor's support of the worker's compensation bill then in the legislature, suggests that the DCUCL supported the delegation's proposals. Fidler's statements, quoted in the *Miami Daily News*, echoed much of what Palmer had been writing about for years: the warning of revolution, the lack of sufficient relief, and the poor inadequate pay workers got. He emphasized that employers reduced the wages of unskilled workers from 40¢ to 20¢ because of the labor market was glutted and consisted of "men clamoring for jobs." "You'll either give us relief or you will have to feed us in jail or shoot us," Fidler warned. Much of the DCUCL's NRA activism focused on similar issues of pay and oversupplied labor markets (calls for shorter hours, spreading work).

The DCUCL's rushed telegram revealed how much they feared the *Daily News*'s and *Herald*'s red baiting. The articles appeared on May 15 and the telegraph was sent the very next day at 7:02 a.m. Its timing revealed the panic among DCUCL leadership back at home. Later in the summer, a second unemployment organization appeared, calling itself the Unemployed Relief Association, but it appears to have been a front organization, for its leaders had been part of the DCUCL leadership and they held their weekly meetings in the same place and time as the league.[67]

The FCUL's emergence and the DCUCL's telegram reveal a history of grassroots division in a hostile political environment. It is unclear whatever happened to the State Federation of Workers' Leagues formed in April 1934, but it did seem connected with a broader national movement. The workers' leagues appear to have been led by socialists and later evolved into a branch of the socialist Workers Alliance, but the histories of each locale that sent delegates to Tampa in April 1934 are not clear. As suggested by Palmer's account of the 1934 convention, various groups likely took part including the DCUCL.

Communist organizers in Florida claimed to have only a "faction" in the FCUL, and so they were far from dominating the group despite their high hopes. The FCUL likely had passing travelers or others who simply wanted to align with the movement's goals. Neither the workers' leagues nor the FCUL could claim a monopoly over the unemployed. Palmer had a point when he wrote pragmatically, "why worry about names," when the means existed to resolve the existing problem of workers overworked, underpaid, and near complete destitution.[68]

The FCUL's membership was likely politically diverse. The Tallahassee delegation, allegedly representing the FCUL, embraced a platform widely supported by organizations like the DCUCL, the socialist-led Tampa Unemployed Brotherhood, St. Petersburg Workers' Leagues, and state Workers Alliance, as well as communists. Grassroots movements in Florida required the formation of coalitions, like that of the DCUCL and AFL unions; the activism and intellectual climate of grassroots movements gave them a popular front feel.

The historian Michael Denning argued that a "powerful social democratic movement," a "popular front," emerged in the 1930s and lasted for three decades. Calling the period the age of the Congress of Industrial Organizations (CIO), Denning emphasized the importance of the progressive and egalitarian strands within the CIO and the larger culture. He further made a point of decentering the importance of the Communist Party in encouraging such a "radical social-democratic movement." We can see how the movement evolved as Denning described in south Florida, for the context predated the CIO and existed outside the Communist and even the Socialist Party. The fluidity of ideas, the commonness of living in degraded conditions, and the existence of abundant wealth stirred many to question the logic and morality of existing institutions.[69]

Grassroots progressive movements had reason to fear being marginalized out of existence. Red-scare tactics, as proven after World War I, were a useful means to disempower them. Persistent advocacy for the employed and unemployed workers between 1932 and 1935 by groups such as Tampa's Unemployed Brotherhood and Miami's DCUCL raised suspicions because they stood outside traditional, conservative charity and philanthropic approaches to poverty. The DCUCL already confronted a subtle stab at them in the *Daily News* in the May 1934 story. The minimum influence of Florida's Communist Party, District 25, only offered an assist to conservative forces in the state. The *Daily Worker* noted how Florida's agricultural interests were "probably the most conservative in the country," and cities such as Miami, Tampa, and Jacksonville were "controlled by land barons, the bond holders and commercial pirates." Despite the *Daily Worker*'s trenchant and sharp analysis of Florida's exploitative economy, the Communist Party's presence helped to undermine the already tenuous situation the state's many grassroots progressive organizations faced.[70] Florida's restrictive political landscape disabled free speech and broader political discourse, which had the effect of crushing organic activist movements.

Communism-obsessed, Governor Dave Sholtz began beating the drum for a more conservative patriotism in 1934–35. In July 1934, Edward R. Hayes, the national American Legion commander, addressing the National Education Association in Washington, DC, had warned of creeping communism in US schools, universities, and churches and even among peace advocates. Building on this speech in an October 1934 speech to the national American Legion convention in Miami, Sholtz claimed that the nation under Roosevelt was "engaged in a peaceful rebellion against communism and anarchy" through his administration's efforts to improve economic conditions in the country.[71]

By January, Sholtz was able to identify the presence of District 25 in Florida and, though unsure of their goals ("I do not believe they know themselves what they want"), he warned that all they care to do is destroy the US government. After confronting the FCUL delegates, including communist members, in May

1935, Sholtz told American Legionnaires they had a "'job to do' in stamping out organized communism in the state." The District 25 delegates, he claimed, "demanded action" and threatened to use force to get what they wanted. Wearing the American Legion uniform as he spoke before the seventeenth convention of the state American Legion in June, the governor warned that thousands of communists were in the South "plotting the overthrow of the government," including at least three thousand members in one unnamed Florida county alone. Sholtz did not explain how he arrived at his number, but he did find it necessary to mention that "white and negro men and women attended" one recent Jacksonville communist meeting. His choice of the old racist tactic of linking radicalism to miscegenation—thereby threats to segregation and race hierarchy—demonstrated the nature of his fear. Sholtz cited communist atheism and ordered legionnaires to fight communism in the school and at home and to "combat 'street-corner critics' of government officials."[72]

Fred J. Manning of the Miami Harvey Seeds post of the American Legion told the LCC in July 1935 about the "ravages of communism" and later wrote in the *Daily News* that "the movement against American traditions is widespread." Repeating much of what the national American Legion and Dave Sholtz espoused over the past year, he added, "We hear the demand for a 'new social order,' for the 'redistribution of wealth,' for the 'production for use and not for profit,' and for numberless other radically inspired sentiments, all old, tired, and found wanting, but which have been shouted so loudly and so continuously as almost to submerge the mighty truths that our Constitution still lives, still holds power to correct our errors, and to right any injustices which may have crept into the national life."[73]

One imagines that the members of the DCUCL and Palmer would have had heated discussions with Manning and the American Legion's mystified perspective on the meaning of the Constitution and the Declaration of Independence. Evidence soon began to appear that Sholtz may have been onto something. A civic club in St. Petersburg uncovered "four paid workers of the Third Internationale of the Russian Soviet government" who were working in Florida. The Communist Party issued the leaflet "An Open Letter to Unemployed Workers of Florida" that denounced Sholtz's claims, emphasized the coalition nature of the FCUL, and restated its goals for "real relief," such as its support of the social security bill in the US Congress. The minutes of the Building Trades Council records Frank Roche giving a talk on communistic activities in Miami, where he read a "circular given out by Communists"—likely the open letter.[74]

Federal funds for direct relief were scheduled to end July 1 amid this red scare. The DCUCL lobbied both the county and city governments yet again for the need for assistance in late June; for the first time, the Unemployed Relief Association (URA) appeared in the historical record, lobbying the city government in early July for more relief. The DCUCL announced to a joint meeting of city, county, and federal officials on July 12 that "it was with the 'greatest difficulty' they were restraining their members from rioting and raiding stores dispensing foodstuffs." City Manager L. L. Lee warned that dependent-relief recipients faced the possibility of "actual starvation" and that the small emergency city allotment of $7,500 issued the previous week for the rest of the month of July would be exhausted within four days. William H. Green, federal relief administrator, pointed out that the government-allotted $40,000 for the area translated to "only about one day of work a week for men on relief." He reminded the officials at the meeting that the new federal work-relief program would help only those who could actually contribute to government projects. This meant that workers without the appropriate skills, aged persons, and ill persons would be left unassisted. In fact, the burden for direct relief now fell on the shoulders of city, county, and state governments. Bobo Dean of the national employment service office (and former owner of the *Miami Metropolis*) stated that, while there was plenty of work for skilled mechanics, none could be found for "common labor, white collar workers, and those in similar brackets": 3,500 Blacks and 10,000 "white persons" had filed applications with him. Exploring this issue of the difficulty of finding work, the *Daily News* ran a special investigative report the following week (July 16, 17) in which two of its journalists uncovered that it was indeed hard to find a job in Miami, eliciting at least one response from a reader.[75]

Three days later, after the government meeting, the URA invited the public and the affected to attend their upcoming weekly Monday meeting in Miami's Lummus Park. There is little evidence to suggest that the URA was indeed a separate organization, especially because their meetings occurred on the same day and place as the DCUCL's. The URA, in a letter to the *Daily News*, reported that its battle with local authorities was encountering little success: "The failure of the FERA to fill the need and the slowness of our local officials to take time to study and visualize for themselves the terrific need of adequate aid has forced our hands to the wheel. . . . The time for action has come. . . . Rise to your feet prepared for definite decision and action! We have starved and underfed our children too long now. Be a man! Act!" The planning for the biggest class demonstration in Miami's history likely originated at this meeting.[76]

On July 31, 1,500 unemployed men, women, and children gathered at a City Commission meeting to protest conditions and demand immediate relief. The local newspapers did not comment on the racial makeup of the unemployed; evidently the vast majority were white. According to communist observers on the ground, however, the "Negro unemployed" participated. Demonstrators filled the council chamber and overflowed into the courthouse lobby where the meeting was held and down the steps to Flagler Street.[77]

By all accounts, the demonstration was orderly and disciplined; the only tense moment occurred when commissioner and ex-mayor E. G. Sewell shouted, "Don't you scalawags start anything here," an alleged response to two men telling him to sit down when he rose to speak during the commission meeting. John F. Gavelick, described by the local newspapers as the treasurer of the URA, spoke sympathetically of the small local government coffers but insisted that something needed to be done. Recent government cutbacks left many individuals and families in a tough spot. Gavelick pointed out that "thousands of men, women, and children in Miami are starving and we look to the city to feed them." Furthermore, he argued, the charges made by the government that the "men will not work when work is available . . . is a lie. Men in our league have wallowed in mud and water up to their waists for the pitiful sum of $2 a day." He continued, "the government has seen fit in recent months, while it still gave direct relief, to consider $1.87 a week sufficient to feed a family of four. Our people do not ask for charity. We want work, work which will permit us to support our wives and children in a decent manner." Gavelick spoke with passion, demanding justice as "dozens of people in rags, shoeless and hungry" stood behind him.[78]

The speech flowed with a focused class perspective that questioned the way power organized itself in the city. Gavelick noted that the newspapers reported that no poverty existed in Miami, "consequently thousands have flocked here to look for work and eventually to take their place in the bread lines. . . . Secretary Kessler [of the CC] has broadcast stories that Miami has no bread lines. I'll show him plenty of breadlines in Miami." Continuing in this vein, Gavelick went for the power structure's jugular: "The merchants are responsible for the conditions that now exist" in blocking the city's plans "to levy new taxes that would have provided food for our families. It's all right with the merchants when the city spends thousands of dollars to bring tourists here [referring to the city's publicity funds]. They benefit from that."[79]

Mayor A. D. H. Fossey and the other city commissioners agreed to form an advisory committee. The committee consisted of thirty-seven representatives, including eight city newspaper owners, three members of the URA (John Burke, John Gavelick, and Joseph Shepard), one representative of labor (Herbert Edgecombe, chair of the LCC), and twenty-five business and civic leaders; absent from the group were any African American leaders. The size of the committee made it unwieldy, though the mayor shrank it down to nine members five days later, keeping Gavelick and Edgecombe as two of the nine. Mayor Fossey was not against establishing a sales tax to raise city revenue, but he was adamant that "they'll only increase the real estate tax over my dead body." The ethic of protecting private property, in this case, overrode the interest of the unemployed. Palmer, however, argued that "unless you meet the situation and meet it quickly you will find all law breaking down." He recommended that an emergency be declared and a 1 percent sales tax be imposed to meet the needs of the unemployed. Gavelick added to Palmer's insight that a larger mass of unemployed would march to City Hall if something was not done soon, but he added that this remark was not meant as a threat.[80]

What unfolded in the next several weeks recapitulated the uphill battle the unemployed had faced for years. None of the newspapers writing on the events of the July 31, 1935, mass demonstration and subsequent discussions over what to do with the "deserving unemployables" referred to the history of Miami's unemployment movement.[81] Even the recent advocacy of the unemployed in June and early July 1935 fell below the journalistic radar of local coverage. The press failed to highlight S. Bobo Dean's comment on how skilled construction workers were the only ones able to find work or W. H. Green's parallel warning that only workers with the necessary skills (mostly in the construction trades) would be able to find jobs.[82]

The *Miami Daily News*'s own July investigative reports on the lack of work (confirming Dean's findings) went unmentioned. The most egregious omission, of course, was the silence about the history of the local unemployment movement. Unemployment movement leaders repeated over and over to local, state, and national government officials and business leaders the facts of the inadequate living conditions endured by the poor. The failed community effort of the summer of 1934 (Dade County Emergency Welfare Council), for example, had led to yet another uncovering of the impoverished conditions of the unemployed and poor, as the account in the CLU's *Miami News* of the grossly inadequate food budgets so vividly revealed. The steady rate of evictions told a powerful tale of impoverishment punctuated by such events as the erection of tents to house the evicted. Silence about this longer history marked the discussions in the press for August and the subsequent months. In addition to the historical amnesia and well-worn practice of just ignoring their demands, the poor and unemployed now earned the right to further marginalization of their class interests through charges of corruption and communist affiliations.

The efforts of local officials were disappointing and minimalist at best. The *Miami Daily News* and retail businesses protested any talk of raising sales or excise taxes. Real-estate interests were adamantly against raising property taxes. Talk of balancing budgets, cutting unnecessary spending, and promoting volunteer and charity-led fundraising dominated the discussions about relief funding. The city arranged an opportunity for the more than six thousand unemployed heads of household to work on the city's Opa Locka farm: single unemployed men would work one day a week, men with families with fewer than two children would work two days a week, those with more would work three, and all would earn $2 for a day's worth of work; Blacks would work only during "bean-picking time" and "would receive vegetables instead of cash." In the effort to feed the children, officials arranged for milk donations to provide free milk to needy families. Mayor Fossey's special subcommittee sought to attain maximum efficiency and accountability. The president of the First National Bank and former mayor, E. C. Romfh, successfully lobbied for a requirement that applicants "swear to the true circumstances of their condition" so as to risk perjury charges if shown at a later time to have lied. The committee wanted to ensure they weeded out "chiselers," and so in their extra vigilance they required applicants to be photographed and fingerprinted. Assistance would come with the sting of being stigmatized. Apparently, dehumanizing those in need was a necessary component of the welfare system.[83]

Finally, the spirit of class harmony flourished when 120 employers signed the Home Employment pledge of the recently formed Home Improvement League. It represented a goodwill promise to hire permanent residents whenever possible. The idea emerged as a result of the subcommittee meetings and was pushed forward by the Democratic Party leadership, though the idea of hiring home labor had long been a local grassroots demand. Added to the home-labor twist were calls to remove "negro aliens" from Miami, referring to the Bahamian migrant workers living in the city. As easy as targeting radical class arguments, the case against immigrant laborers revealed a lazy and uncreative approach to the scarcity of jobs. It is unclear how many Bahamian immigrant workers were ever deported. No organized systematic effort seems to ever have occurred, but Bahamians who had evaded immigration laws faced imprisonment and deportation if caught.[84]

The unemployed movement leadership remained frustrated with these minimalist approaches. While the step toward hiring home labor certainly was a sound moral one, the safeguarding of the austere welfare apparatus was not. Gavelick protested the requirement for sworn affidavits and photographs. He asked that unemployment movement leaders have power over the distribution of relief in order to avoid the humiliating experience of being evaluated by social workers. Wister of the DCUCL declared that the $200,000 estimate for relief made by the mayor and others was insufficient for the more than 14,000 unemployed in the city (as of early August).

Perrine Palmer's recommendations to increase welfare revenues were coupled with his call for employers to pay living wages. He also continued to advocate for the homeless and those on the verge of being evicted, insisting on the need for immediate action. The problem of low wages, leaving workers to pay up to 40 to 60 percent of their income on rent, led to the evictions; the more than 18,800 unemployed as of September 1935 were even in worse condition. In addition, the average wage earner could not afford to "pay the two, three, and sometimes four month advance rent" landlords often required. None of this advocacy or efforts to educate the public was new or communist-led. All the authorities agreed that the July 31 demonstration was orderly. Local officials did become nervous, however, when Gavelick warned that twenty thousand people might descend on City Hall for relief of their grievances. The unemployment movement may have finally reached its ultimate limits with this threat of greater protest.[85]

Accusations of local political corruption and radical communist politics helped silence the URA and DCUCL. A movement began to recall several city commissioners who were indicted for questionable city purchases of park lands (none was removed from office). The corruption led to a precarious political context. The rabble-rousing *Miami Daily Tribune* was prominent in the recall effort, and they sought to get the URA to join them in their campaign. The URA rebuked the *Tribune* and paid a price for doing so. The URA's activism, building on the DCUCL (and likely constituting the same organization), unfortunately occurred at the same time that the Communist Party was making a membership push in Florida. Communists did have a very small presence in Miami, but their newspapers indicate it was insignificant. Likely worsening their impact was how their organizers, as revealed by the Communist Party papers, demonstrated a lack of understanding of the local conditions and history of Miami's unemployment movement.

Newspaper stories emerged in August reporting communist activity, including one report of copies being circulating of the June leaflet criticizing Dave Sholtz and also of copies of the communist newspaper, the *Daily Worker*. On August 14, Jacksonville experienced its own unemployed movement demonstration.[86] Finally, the fluid nature of intellectual discourse experienced for years among workers and the unemployed now became a potential liability. Dave Sholtz's and the American Legion's anticommunist activism indicated which direction the political winds were blowing. All these developments combined to give the *Daily Tribune* enough fodder to accuse the URA and its leaders of being racketeers and communists. URA leaders declared they were not communists and, while getting paid for relief work, were working hard in the interests of the unemployed. They also proudly asserted that their organization was nonpartisan and did not discriminate against any party. Such declarations made them suspect to the red-baiting *Daily Tribune*. The lackluster local relief initiatives continued the practices of half-hearted welfare policies; the suggestion that the often-ignored unemployment movement might have turned slightly red only encouraged further marginalization of the underclass and of service and unskilled workers. The URA disappeared from the historical record after this heated month, and the DCUCL continued through the rest of the 1930s but only as a shadow of its former self.[87]

Conclusion

The history of DCUCL demonstrates that a lively grassroots unemployment movement existed in Miami, even though it was limited by, among other things, red scares, small city coffers, and business and civic leaders who pressed for economic growth and believed an undeserving class of poor existed. The movement was not only local; it encompassed other major cities in Florida as well, such as Jacksonville, Orlando, St. Petersburg, Tampa, and West Palm Beach and garnered support from the poor farm laborers across the state. The New Deal helped inspire this nascent movement in south Florida by highlighting the poor conditions workers endured.

Initial hopes for the success of the NRA and CWA may have faded quickly, but workers' desire for change, better working conditions, and equitable pay set the groundwork for further grassroots organizing. Organized labor supported the unemployed, among their own ranks as well as among white-collar and unskilled workers. And, as demonstrated by the picketing of the Southern Cafeteria and Sunshine Cleaners in January 1934, the DCUCL aided workers—as the Lucas County Unemployed League in Toledo, Ohio, would do in a much more dramatic fashion in April of the same year. Mass picketing of the Electric Auto-Life Company there by the AFL Federal Local #18384 and the Unemployed League eventually led to a bloody confrontation but a successful contract negotiation for its workers.[88] Miami's picketing did not result in such open conflict, but it nevertheless represented an impassioned statement for better conditions.

The grassroots unemployment movement and the populism of the New Deal helped create a vibrant context that challenged the status quo of power. Calls to end the poll tax resonated among African Americans long denied the vote as well as among poor white workers and the unemployed.[89] Activism among the least privileged would later help encourage the local labor movement to organize unskilled common laborers. Organized labor pulled back in the summer of 1935 from more active support of the unemployed, perhaps because jobs became more abundant in the skilled construction trades, but Labor's Citizenship Committee continued to sponsor engaged speeches, such as Perrine Palmer's several presentations between 1935 and 1937 on the city and county housing problems. In addition, the LCC, the CLU, and the Building Trades Council ended up supporting the organizing drives of laundry workers, dockworkers, construction laborers, taxi drivers, and other workers through the early 1940s. The construction trade unions mounted their own renewed organizing drives, as when they reconstituted their Building Trades Council in the summer of 1935 and geared up for a push to raise work standards and working conditions, as well as pay.

The precipitous fall of the unemployment movement mirrored the apparent disappearance of Palmer. Few of his letters appeared in the *Miami Daily News* or *Miami News* after 1935. A typed March 1937 letter to Franklin Roosevelt entitled "Is the Money-Saving Habit Destroying the Profit System?" had a circled handwritten note on top stating "From one of your former relief workers out of a job again." Palmer was around fifty-three years old at this point, college educated, and evidently still struggling to find steady employment. He made consumerist arguments in this letter similar to those he had made many times over the years: "each man, woman and child in America willing to do their part, whatever that part may be" deserved "sufficient purchasing power to meet their needs EVERY DAY IN THE YEAR." One of the last entries in the labor newspaper the *Miami News* that noted Palmer occurred in September 1937 when he lectured Labor's Citizenship Committee that wages should be based on need and not production; he warned that "democracy is doomed to destruction" if such an economic system did not emerge.[90] Mass impoverishment jeopardized a smooth-running democracy by making too many dependent on a powerful few. Palmer's argument represented a long-standing criticism that would have continued relevance throughout the twentieth century.

Epilogue

When the city's labor newspaper, the *Miami News*, changed its name to the *Miami Citizen* in November 1937, it sought to end any confusion between its name and the *Miami Daily News*, but, more important, it reflected the newspaper's broader objectives of standing up for citizens' fundamental right to a moral economy. To attain it would require persistent and continuous effort, particularly in the context of the complexity of modern society. The newspaper's very existence was predicated on achieving this goal. It expressed this perspective in the issue announcing the change and asserted that it

> has stood for clean things, both in the labor movement and the general life of the city, for the upbuilding of Miami into a better place in which to live and work. Believing that the worker is worthy of his hire and is a most vital force in community character and development, it has consistently advocated the payment of living wages to all classes of labor, whether members of a union or not, and has fought for the highest standards possible. At the same time it has urged that these things be obtained not by radical methods but by recognition of the rights of all parties concerned.[1]

This passage embodied radical class-harmony discourse. Workers felt a deep connection to the significance of their work and how it contributed to local and state development. Their work signified a sincere effort to live dignified lives for the larger purpose of individual human happiness and the health and well-being of the larger community. Yet the newspaper had to write defensively by stating it was for "clean things" and "the highest standards possible." Organized labor often had to fend off implicit and sometimes explicit charges of their lack of morality, whether as inefficient workers or as obstacles to the free market because they insisted on a moral economy. The *Miami News* was correct to state that labor represented a "vital force in community character and development" as it argued a living wage be paid to all classes of labor. Regardless of its warmth and beautiful setting, to live and work in Miami was no easy challenge, particularly when seasonal work, low wages, long hours, and unsafe and difficult working conditions persisted. To be critical of such conditions and to act toward changing them was to advocate for a radical sense of class harmony. Although its calls for community and moral economy recognized "the rights of all parties concerned," a clear nod to the employing class, such strategies revealed the power imbalance between employer and employee, as well as an understanding of how the changing urban landscape in a constant state of growth and change posed a real challenge to effective organization and the sharing of power.

Florida workers had some success with organizing in the interwar years (especially in the urban areas) in spite of the flows of migrants and fluctuating economy. They certainly tried to organize, and there was potential for more. Employers learned that workers reacted positively, but against apparent employer interest, when they had national sanction for organizing, as in section 7A of the National Industrial Recovery Act in the years 1933–35 and the National Labor Relations Act after 1935. The American Federation of Labor's national membership increased by 30 percent between 1933 and 1935. Even the minimal improvements the National Recovery Administration's production codes promised could help motivate workers to action if they were not met, as noted in the restaurant, retail, and dry-cleaning sectors. The Blue Eagle picketing controversy and the effort to get local businesses to follow the wage and hour provisions in 1933 and 1934, as discussed in chapter 7, revealed that unemployed and employed workers could unite for a common cause even if it did not lead to a widespread unionizing drive. Even though the Dade County Unemployment Citizens' League began in August 1932, it particularly grew in the early New Deal period. Local 133 of the restaurant workers' union, along with several other unions (retail, streetcar operators, and bus drivers), formed in the fall of 1933. Organizing stirred up as the promise of equal opportunity seemed to lie in democratic and collective action. Continual attempts to organize farmworkers in Florida and elsewhere, years of the unemployed agitating and demanding more, the rise of the Congress of Industrial Organizations (CIO), and a motivated American Federation of Labor (AFL) demonstrated quite clearly to business interests that an inspired public represented a challenge to their power and the possibilities of maintaining a low-wage, high-profit economy.[2] Employers did what they could to douse the flames of democratic enthusiasm by fostering distrust and encouraging cynicism. Their efforts included in various industries and places around the country undermining the progressive potential of the NRA, section 7A, and later the Wagner Act. They usurped control of NRA production boards, initiated employer-dominated company unions, organized public-relations attacks on unionization, used or threatened to use force, including loss of employment, and challenged emerging labor laws through legal and political means.

Perceptive business interests had good reason to believe that their fiefdoms were threatened. Politicians started to tap into the democratic spirit of the time. In 1936, within a year after the 1935 mass unemployment movement demonstration in Miami, Earnest Graham ran for state senator from Dade County with a political platform that included an anti-poll-tax plank. Graham won the election and made good on his promise, helping to abolish the tax in 1937. One suspects the groundswell from below supported his pro–New Deal politics and the progressive anti-poll-tax idea. Perrine Palmer, among others, had long criticized the tax. Grassroots activism had helped to keep the undemocratic nature of the poll tax in the public's eye. In a brilliant move in the summer of the 1937, Graham and John R. Beacham of West Palm Beach, seat of another active labor movement, added a pet bill abolishing the tax in that year's state legislative session. The bill immediately passed, in part, because there was a continuation of a $1 head tax to support county schools, thereby undermining arguments about shrinking government revenue. Nevertheless, disconnecting the franchise from one's ability to pay a tax was certainly a step to expanding democracy.[3]

Black workers also sought to enact change. Dockworkers, an occupation long dominated by Blacks in the city, organized a local in 1936 and soon went on strike that summer. Earlier efforts to organize a union in the mid-1920s, as noted in chapter 1, failed even though such activism led to temporary wage increases at the time. This time, they gained support from the white-dominated Central Labor Union as well as white dockworkers. White and Black locals of the longshoremen's union (1421 and 1416, respectively) organized in the spring of 1936 and soon were involved in summer and fall labor strikes; another occurred in 1937. Because the vast majority of dockworkers were Black, this biracial organizational structure was likely an accommodation of Miami's and the South's segregationist racial system. The longshoremen's union, in any case, would remain an active local for the rest of the century.[4] Soon after this successful interracial movement and clearly reacting to the CIO insurgency, the AFL sought to hold onto ground and therefore encouraged state federations of labor and local central labor unions to actively organize workers of all skilled types. Labor's *Miami News* editorials in the spring and summer of 1937 attacked the CIO and asserted Miami's loyalty to the AFL. The change in name from the *Miami News* to *Miami Citizen* was likely also a response to the apparent threat of the CIO.[5]

Miami's CLU benefited from years of grassroots activism and the popularity of Franklin Roosevelt's New Deal state. Several groups of service and construction workers made concerted organizing drives: restaurant workers, retail clerks, laundry workers, dry-cleaning workers, tile setter helpers, glaziers, bakery and confectionary workers, and automobile painters (among others). In the spring of 1937, Miami's white tile setters' union and bricklayers' union helped get the biracial Tile Setters Helpers Union Local 100 recognized by local contractors and gain a wage increase for them. D. V. Godard, secretary of the contractors' negotiation committee, asserted that there had "never been a union of helpers south of the Mason-Dixon line" in which much of the help "comes from negroes." The contractors noted how it "would set a unique precedent." It apparently did, because the local was recognized and gained a wage increase.[6]

Another example of trying to organize the unorganized occurred when the Building Trades Council supported the April 1937 effort of white and Black laborers to form a biracial union. It consisted of six hundred black and two hundred white members. The Building Trades Council, a white organization, with a history of excluding Blacks from skilled construction jobs (at least in the white sections of segregated Miami) backed the laborers' efforts for union recognition in the fall of 1937. A local newspaper reported that Peter McCabe, spokesperson for the Building Trades Council, and various organizers "vigorously contended that the constitution of the United States allowed the negro the same rights of whites." Yet the newspaper also asserted that they were not motivated by any radical racial liberalism. They simply hoped "to better [the] working conditions for unskilled labor in general." In an unusual moment of class and racial solidarity in Miami's history, skilled white workers refused to cross picket lines while the laborers struck a construction worksite. They even threatened a general strike. After a few days, the construction company gave in and recognized the union. Things certainly seemed to have changed since the fall of 1919.[7]

Clearly, racism could be an obstacle to greater worker solidarity, and ingenious methods to circumvent its constricting limitations were required. The organizing of dry-cleaning workers, common laborers, tile setter helpers, and dockworkers reveals that local biracial collective efforts to improve the labor market conditions of workers, at least "unskilled," occurred. The point here, however, is not to suggest that a secret history of racial liberalism exists and has yet to be told, even though such stories have intriguing potential. Rather, workers' efforts to organize faced various difficulties, none more challenging than employer resistance. The effort just to mount collective responses represented a success of worker agency and empowerment. Worker conversations and commitment (and possibly even risk) to attend meetings, to picket, and to imagine improving a collective economic situation revealed a moral effort to limit and possibly overcome the enslaving aspects of capitalism. The push for higher wages, better working conditions, and shorter hours all pointed to that goal.

These sorts of struggles had long been part of Miami's landscape. The World War I period saw white and Black drivers clash over access and control of jobs, particularly with the short tourist season. For a short moment, white skilled workers supported Black common laborers' efforts to organize, but such opportunities all but disappeared in the 1920s. The continual open-shop struggles, seasonal ebbs and flows of the economy, and the population growth and circulation of visitors and workers that shaped much of this period made working-class survival challenging and unionization difficult. While the white skilled unionists' exclusionary policies certainly were rooted in racist ideas, they also reflected the very nature of worker precarity and vulnerability. An active local AFL presence (even more motivated after 1935 with the possibility of CIO competition), an unemployment movement, and the New Deal regime all merged to offer a context filled with possibilities for successful organization despite the many odds. The political economic context of a tourist-based economy and a pervasive red-scare culture did not prevent social movements from emerging. Radical class-harmony discourse articulated a moral economic vision in these collective struggles in spite of racism and cultural intolerance.

Once the mobilization for World War II started, conditions changed in Miami and new opportunities emerged for the working class, as did new attacks on class-centered critiques of the power structure. Persistent employer intransigence would continue to be an impediment to successful organizing across groups. Beginning in 1939 with unsuccessful efforts to pass antiunion labor laws and culminating in 1943 and 1944 with the passage of antilabor legislation, including the nation's first right-to-work law (an amendment added to the Florida state constitution), Florida business interests sought to defy the New Deal labor regime. The new virulent World War II employer antiunion campaign and effort to turn public opinion against unionization would negatively transform the historical context and potential of fostering economic and political opportunities for the working class. Victories on the labor front would continue in the postwar period, perhaps with none more important and symbolic than Miami Beach's hotel workers enjoying a big win in the mid-1950s after a twenty-month strike. They gained recognition and a master contract with the Miami Beach Hotel Association, which encompassed 180 hotels.[8] Yet the roots of more restrictive restraints were just being established in the late 1930s and during World War II. A union-dominated city still remained a possibility in the mid-twentieth century, though darker days were certainly not far ahead.

APPENDIX

Miami Occupation Distribution

Data for the following tables comes from the US Bureau of the Census, *Fifteenth Census of the United States: 1930*, vol. 4, *Occupations* (Washington, DC: GPO, 1932), 358–61; *Sixteenth Census of the United States: 1940, Population*, vol. 3, *The Labor Force: Occupation, Industry, Employment, and Income*, pt. 2, Alabama–Indiana (Washington, DC:GPO, 1943), 660–65. Note that totals do not add up in the tables. Not all occupations listed in the census compilations are included in the totals here. In an effort to produce a clearer picture of Miami's occupational distribution I summarized data from the cited census publications using subsets of occupations with significant numbers to avoid reproducing the elaborate and sometimes confusing details in the census compilations. I culled and aggregated data from the pages noted here in this citation. Please refer to the census publications cited here.

Female occupations, 1930

Aggregate categories[A]	Total	White	Black
Total	15,567	8,148	7,416
Manufacturing and mechanical	886	707	179
Domestic, personal services	8,956	2,076	6,789
Clerical and sales[B]	4,065	3,827	138
Professional (teacher, etc.)	1,570	1,399	173
Occupation focus 1930, women	**Total**	**White**	**Black**
Laundresses	1,997	43	1,954
Laundry operatives	685	161	524
Dressmakers (not in factory)	413	342	71
Servants	4,338	355	3,983
Waitresses	558	513	45
Saleswoman and clerks in stores[C]	1,309	1,247	62
Stenographers, typists, bookkeepers, clerks, cashiers, telegraph, telephone	2,264	2,248	16[D]
Barbers, hairdressers, manicurists	229	190	39
Teachers	690	574	116
Trained nurses	396	357	39

(A) White collapses foreign (720) and native (7,428); (B) includes telegraph and telephone operators, as well as retail dealers who likely were managers; (C) includes retail dealers who likely were managers; (D) there were no black telephone or telegraph operators.

Female occupations, 1940

Aggregate categories[A]	Total	White	Black
Total[B]	25,316	15,746	9,566
Operatives/kindred workers	2,154	1,294	860
Domestic/personal services	7,112	814	6,297
Service workers[C]	5,213	3,353	1,860
Clerical and sales	6,513	6,390	121
Professional/semiprofessional	2,491	2,252	239
Proprietors/managers/officials	1,326	1,252	73
Occupation focus 1940, women	**Total**	**White**	**Black**
Laundry operatives and laundresses (excluding private families)	1,044	365	679
Domestic and personal services[D]	7,112	814	6,297
Dressmakers (not in factory)	576	494	82
Servants (except private families)	1,597	350	1,247
Waitresses and bartenders	1,691	1,564	127
Saleswomen	1,910	1,862	48
Stenographers, typists, bookkeepers, clerks, cashiers, ticket agents, operators[E]	3,362	3,325	37
Barbers, beauticians, and manicurists	604	489	115
Teachers	1,033	857	176
Trained nurses	735	705	30

(A) Only 143 craft workers (133 whites, 10 Blacks); (B) totals do not add up, small counts excluded; (C) 1,247 servants (Black) excluding private family; (D) includes servants and laundresses for private families but specific numbers not listed; (E) there were no Black telephone or telegraph operators.

Male occupations, 1930

Aggregate categories[A]	Total	White	Black
Total	35,304	27,454	7,802
Manufacturing/mechanical[B]	11,238	8,892	2,343
Clerical, etc., and sales[C]	10,930	10,094	824
Transportation/communication[D]	3,808	2,524	1,283
Domestic and personal services	4,032	1,947	2,079
Professional and public services[E]	3,553	3,179	374
Occupation focus 1930, men	**Total**	**White**	**Black**
Police officers, firefighters, mail carriers	557	557	0
Professions[F]	878	865	13
Teachers	95	81	14
Clergymen	145	91	54
Salesmen, clerks in stores, retail	5,526	5,274	252
Real-estate agents	950	939	11
Skilled construction	5,056	4,791	265
Chauffeurs, truck and tractor drivers	1,341	913	428
Dockworkers	221	4	217
Laundry operatives	181	89	92
Servants, porters, janitors[G]	1,709	549	1,160
Laborers[H]	3,502	754	2,748

(A) White collapses foreign (3,570) and native (23,884); (B) includes skilled construction workers; (C) excludes mail carriers; (D) combines categories of clerical and sales (324 were Black laborers); (E) includes mail carriers; (F) includes lawyers and judges (1 Black), physicians, (8 Black) dentists (3 Black), engineers (1 B); (G) 16 white porters, 401 white and 237 Black janitors; (H) includes all laborer categories (e.g., 657 Blacks and 188 whites in construction).

Male occupations, 1940

Aggregate categories[A]	Total	White	Black
Total	50,005	39,043	10,881
Craftsmen and kindred workers	8,149	7,607	542
Operatives and kindred workers	7,112	5,566	1,529
Clerical and sales[B]	9,659	9,382	270
Service workers	6,569	3,283	3,246
Domestic and personal services	646	130	506
Laborers (except farm)	5,595	1,468	4,126
Professional/semiprofessional[C]	4,833	4,637	191
Occupation focus, men	**Total**	**White**	**Black**
Police officers, firefighters, mail carriers, misc. gov't[D]	1,401	1,387	13
Professions[E]	1,012	994	18
Clergymen	153	106	47
Sales[F]	5,421	5,245	164
Clerical[G]	3,201	3,148	53
Skilled construction	4,410	4,173	237
Laborers, construction	2,140	443	1,696
Chauffeurs, truck drivers, deliverymen	3,167	2,491	670
Attendants, filling station, parking lot, airport	569	406	163
Manufacturing operatives	677	542	154
Laundry operatives	235	114	121
Janitors and porters	1,942	198	1,743
Cooks (except in private families)[H]	984	665	296
Dockworkers	359	11	348
Laborers (excluding farm/construction/dockworkers)	3,096	1,014	2,082

(A) Not listing other races (total = 81); (B) includes protective workers/mailmen/gov't; (C) excludes letter carriers; (D) includes watchmen/guards (10 Black, 278 white) and only one Black police officer, fire fighter, or letter carrier; (E) includes lawyers and judges (2), engineers (0 Blacks), physicians 12 (Black), dentists (4 Black); (F) includes salesmen/other sales agent/real estate/insurance brokers; (G) includes bookkeepers, accountants, cashiers, ticket agents, other clerical and kindred workers; (H) includes 23 other races.

Notes

Abbreviations

MDN	*Miami Daily News*
MH	*Miami Herald*
MM	*Miami Metropolis*
MN	*Miami [Labor] News*
MT	*Miami Tribune*
NYT	*New York Times*

Introduction

1. Andrew Frank, *Before the Pioneers: Indians, Settlers, Slaves, and the Founding of Miami* (Gainesville: University Press of Florida, 2017).

2. *MH*, May 30, 1919, 3; June 18, 1922, 1A; September 10, 1923, 9; December 21, 1923, 6 (advertisement about Miami Cigars); May 18, 1924, 2B; *MM*, June 28, 1922, sec. 2: 1; June 26, 1923, 16; August 6, 1923, 3 (Miami Maid Cigar Company advertisement); *MDN*, June 24, 1934, 5; Miami Chamber of Commerce, *Minutes of the Board of Directors Meetings*, October 13, 1924 (quotes), HistoryMiami Museum; December 18, 1922 (a J. A. S. Cigar Company claimed that they were hiring only "Americans"); April 23, 1923; Gary Mormino and George Pozzetta, *The Immigrant World of Ybor City: Italians and Their Latin Neighbors, 1885–1985* (Gainesville: University Press of Florida, 1998).

3. See the *Miami Metropolis* editorial, "Tourists Merely a Sideline" (February 19, 1918, 6) that engaged the tension between tourism and the need to diversify the economy. A flurry of tourist letters and a CC resolution condemned the editorial's argument that pressed for year-round prosperity. Examples include February 22 and 26–28 (February 26 reports a CC resolution), and March 2 and 4, 1918.

4. The problem that shallow waters, narrow shipping channels, and the lack of an adequate deepwater harbor represented was best symbolized when the *Prins Valdemar*

grounded in January 1926 at the head of the channel to Miami Harbor—playing its role in hurting the real-estate and building boom of mid-1920s south Florida. Chronicler Kenneth Ballinger wrote in his book, *Miami Millions: The Dance of Dollars in the Great Florida Land Boom of 1925* (Miami: Franklin, 1936), 139, that "ships grounding in the channel were regarded as ordinary hazards until new federal dredging could start." Helen Muir, *Miami U.S.A.* (Gainesville: University Press of Florida, 2000), 3–13 and 143–45 (lack of deepwater harbor accommodations and *Prins Valdemar*); Tracy Hollingsworth, *History of Dade County, Florida* (Miami: Miami Post, 1936), 70–71 (on harbor development).

5. Michael Grunwald, *The Swamp: The Everglades, Florida, and the Politics of Paradise* (New York: Simon and Schuster, 2006).

6. *Planning Your Vacation in Florida: Miami and Dade County including Miami Beach and Coral Gables, American Guide Series* (Northport, NY: Bacon, Percy, and Daggett, 1941), 74–78, for a quick overview of agricultural in Dade County. See also Paul S. George, *A Journey through Time: A Pictorial History of South Dade* (Virginia Beach, VA: Donning, 1995); Cindy Hahamovitch, *The Fruits of Their Labor: Atlantic Coast Farmworkers and the Making of Migrant Poverty, 1870–1945* (Chapel Hill: University of North Carolina Press, 1997), ch. 5 and 6.

7. "Miami Beach Adopts Fingerprinting Law," *Evening Independent* (St. Petersburg, FL), November 5, 1936, 1. The article stated that "the Beach regulation applies to all employes of night clubs, any place that handles liquor or beer, amusement houses, hotels, apartment houses, delivery services, restaurants and bath houses and to special policemen, newspaper boys, golf caddies, taxi drivers, charter boat operators and domestics." Miami Beach police had fingerprinted various employees from at least 1933 and a standard of surveillance of the working class existed from the earliest days.

8. *MDN*, May 28, 1958, 1A (crime in Miami Beach); January 16, 1930, 1 (detectives); March 14, 1933, 12; December 29, 1937, 11A (Pinkertons in Miami). A "foreign legion" of northern detectives apparently descended on the area each tourist season: *MDN*, September 20, 1936, 1. Polly Redford, *Billion-Dollar Sandbar: A Biography of Miami Beach* (New York: E. P. Dutton, 1970), 221–24 (on exclusion of Blacks and Jews).

9. Gary Mormino, *Land of Sunshine, State of Dreams: A Social History of Modern Florida* (Gainesville: University Press of Florida, 2005), 83, 236–41.

10. Examples of this tendency include Ethan V. Blackman, *Miami and Dade County, Florida: Its Settlement, Progress and Achievement* (Washington, DC: Victor Rainbolt, 1921); Isidor Cohen, *Historical Sketches and Sidelights of Miami, Florida* (Miami: self-pub., 1925); Hollingsworth, *History of Dade County*; John Sewell, *Miami Memoirs: A New Pictorial Edition of John Sewell's Own Story*, ed. Arva Moore Parks (Miami: Arva Parks, 1987); Jane Fisher, *Fabulous Hoosier: A Story of American Achievement* (New York: Robert M. McBride, 1947); Arva Moore Parks, *Miami: The Magic City* (Miami: Centennial, 1991) and Thelma Peters, *Biscayne Country, 1870–1926* (Miami: Banyan, 1981).

11. *MM*, December 8, 1917, 1.

12. *MDN*, December 9, 1928, 6.

13. *MM*, September 28, 1920, 4. *Miami News-Metropolis* (1923–24), *Miami Daily News and Metropolis* (1924–30), and *Miami Daily News* (1930–57), and finally the *Miami News*.

14. *MM*, September 20, 1915, 1, 6 (quotes); September 15, 1915, 1, 2; Metropolitan Dade County Office of Community and Economic Development, Historic Preservation Division, *From Wilderness to Metropolis: The History and Architecture of Dade County, Florida* (Miami: Metropolitan Dade County, 1982), 56–57; Donald W. Curl, "The Florida Architecture of F. Burrall Hoffman Jr., 1882–1980," *Florida Historical Quarterly* 76, no. 4 (1998): 399–416.

15. *MM*, February 14, 1917, 7 (quote from real-estate developer E. E. Dammers).

16. Louis Hartz, *The Liberal Tradition in America* (New York: Harcourt Brace, 1955). For a discussion of the liberal roots of equal opportunity discourse and the problems it represented to actual social equality, see Claire Goldstene, *The Struggle for America's Promise: Equal Opportunity at the Dawn of Corporate Capital* (Jackson: University Press of Mississippi, 2014). For the biases found in exceptionalism discourse that has shaped strands of US labor history, see Reeve Vanneman and Lynn Weber Cannon, *The American Perception of Class* (Philadelphia: Temple University Press, 1987), 1–52. Labor historians would support Vanneman and Cannon's observation that "Americans have a collective amnesia about their history of labor conflict" (28). See also David Montgomery, *The Fall of the House of Labor: The Workplace, the State, and American Labor Activism, 1865–1925* (New York: Cambridge University Press, 1987).

17. Melanie Shell-Weiss, *Coming to Miami: A Social History* (Gainesville: University Press of Florida, 2009).

18. For a useful reassessment of the American Federation of Labor (AFL), see Dorothy Sue Cobble, "Pure and Simple Radicalism: Putting the Progressive Era AFL in Its Time," *Labor: Studies in Working-Class History*, 10, no. 4 (Winter 2013): 61–87. See the critical reviews of Melvyn Dubofsky, Andrew Wender Cohen, Donna T. Haverty-Stacke, Julie Greene, and Cobble's response in the same issue. For an important study that explores the dynamic of craft unionism operating sometimes in progressive and also limiting ways, see Cobble's *Dishing It Out: Waitresses and Their Unions in the Twentieth Century* (Urbana: University of Illinois Press, 1991). Andrew Wender Cohen's discussion of Chicago's craft economy offers useful insight into Miami's economic context: *The Racketeer's Progress: Chicago and the Struggle for Modern Economy, 1900–1940* (Cambridge: Cambridge University Press, 2004).

19. Jacquelyn Down Hall, James Leloudis, Robert Korstad, Mary Murphy, Lu Ann Jones, and Christopher B. Daly, *Like a Family: The Making of a Southern Cotton Mill World* (New York: W. W. Norton, 1987); Lizabeth Cohen, *Making a New Deal: Industrial Workers in Chicago, 1919–1939* (New York: Cambridge University Press, 1990).

20. Lizabeth Cohen, *A Consumers Republic: The Politics of Mass Consumption in Postwar America* (New York: Alfred A. Knopf, 2003); Meg Jacobs, *Pocketbook Politics: Economic Citizenship in Twentieth Century America* (Princeton, NJ: Princeton University Press, 2004); John Commons, David J. Saposs, Helen J. Sumner, E. B. Mittelman, H. E. Hoagland, John B. Andrews, and Selig Perlman, *History of Labour in the United States* (New York: Macmillan, 1918); Selig Perlman, *A Theory of the Labor Movement* (1928; repr., New York: Augustus M. Kelley, 1949); Selig Perlman and Philip Taft, *Labor Movements*, vol. 4 of *History of Labor in the United States, 1896–1932* (New York: Macmillan, 1935).

21. The literature on the consistent employer resistance to unionization is vast. A great reminder of the importance this theme has is the collection edited by Rosemary Feurer and Chad Pearson, *Against Labor: How U.S. Employers Organized to Defeat Union Activism* (Urbana: University of Illinois Press, 2017). See also Chad Pearson, *Reform or Repression: Organizing America's Anti-union Movement* (Philadelphia: University of Pennsylvania Press, 2016).

22. For a useful introduction, see the "dossier on moral economy" in *Humanity* 11, no. 2 (Summer 2020): 187–254. Authors include historians Jeremy Adelman, Joel Isaac, Emilio Kourí, Samuel Moyn, Tim Rogan, and Francesca Trivellato; sociologists Didier Fassin, Margaret R. Sommer, and Marion Fourcade. Important origin points of moral economy discussions include E. P. Thompson's seminal article, "The Moral Economy of the English Crowd in the Eighteenth Century," *Past and Present* 50 (February 1971): 76–136, and Karl Polyani, *The Great Transformation: The Political and Economic Origins of Our Time* (1944; repr., Boston: Beacon, 2001).

23. Benjamin Kline Hunnicutt, *Free Time: The Forgotten American Dream* (Philadelphia: Temple University Press, 2013). See also Tobias Higbie's *Labor's Mind: A History of Working-Class Intellectual Life* (Urbana: University of Illinois Press, 2019).

24. Cobble suggests this meaning in her argument about the AFL, "Pure and Simple Radicalism," 75. She engages as essential works Lawrence Glickman, *A Living Wage: American Workers and the Making of Consumer Society* (Ithaca, NY: Cornell University Press, 1997); Rosanne Currarino, *The Labor Question in America: Economic Democracy in the Gilded Age* (Urbana: University of Illinois Press, 2011); Philip S. Foner and David R. Roediger, *Our Own Time: A History of American Labor and the Working Day* (New York: Verso, 1989). Susan Porter Benson's *Household Accounts: Working-Class Family Economies in the Interwar United States* (Ithaca, NY: Cornell University Press, 2007) offers a rich exploration of how constant economic struggle in the interwar years made the benefits of mass consumerism unattainable for so many.

25. Cedric Robinson, *Black Marxism: The Making of the Black Radical Tradition* (Chapel Hill: University of North Carolina Press, 2000). Gregory Meyerson, "Rethinking Black Marxism: Reflections on Cedric Robinson and Others," *Cultural Logic*, 6, no. 1 (2000): https://doi.org/10.14288/clogic.v6i0.192628. Examples of whiteness studies abound; see, for example, John Munro, "Roots of Whiteness," *Labour/Le Travail* 54 (fall 2004): 175–92; and David Roediger, *Working toward Whiteness: How America's Immigrants Became White* (New York: Basic Books, 2005). See also Eric Arnesen, "Whiteness and the Historians' Imagination," *International Labor and Working Class History* no. 60 (Fall 2001): 3–32 (see also the responses to Arnesen and his rejoinder in that issue) and Touré Reed's *Toward Freedom: The Case against Race Reductionism* (London: Verso, 2020). See also Cedric Johnson's many interventions, including "The Wages of Roediger: Why Three Decades of Whiteness Studies Has Not Produced the Left We Need," *Nonsite.org* (September 2019), https://nonsite.org/the-wages-of-roediger-why-three-decades-of-whiteness-studies-has-not-produced-the-left-we-need/.

26. George Lipsitz, *The Possessive Investment in Whiteness: How White People Profit from Identity Politics* (Philadelphia: Temple University Press, 2006), is emblematic of this practice.

27. Ellen Meiksins Wood, *The Retreat from Class: A New 'True' Socialism* (New York: Verso, 1998). Another useful primer is Adolph Reed Jr., *Class Notes: Posing as Politics and Other Thoughts on the American Scene* (New York: New Press, 2000).

28. W. E. B. Du Bois, *Black Reconstruction in America, 1860–1880* (1935; repr., New York: Free Press, 1992). For insightful analysis of the meaning of Du Bois's use of the term *psychological wage*, see Adolph Reed Jr.'s "Du Bois and the 'Wages of Whiteness': What He Meant, What He Didn't, and, Besides, It Shouldn't Matter for Our Politics Anyway," *NonSite.org* (June 29, 2017), https://nonsite.org/editorial/du-bois-and-the-wages-of-whiteness.

29. Munro, "Roots of Whiteness," 192. Robin D. G. Kelley, *Hammer and Hoe: Alabama Communists during the Great Depression* (Chapel Hill: University of North Carolina Press, 1990); Robert Rodgers Korstad, *Civil Rights Unionism: Tobacco Workers and the Struggle for Democracy in the Mid-twentieth South* (Chapel Hill: University of North Carolina Press, 2003).

30. Barbara J. Fields, "Ideology and Race in American History," *Region, Race, and Reconstruction: Essays in Honor of C. Vann Woodward*, ed. J. Morgan Kousser and James M. McPherson (New York: Oxford University Press, 1982), 150–51. See also E. P. Thompson, *The Making of the English Working Class* (New York: Vintage, 1966); Herbert Gutman, *Power and Culture: Essays on the American Working Class*, ed. Ira Berlin (New York: New Press, 1987); Montgomery, *Fall of the House of Labor*; Eric Arnesen, *Waterfront Workers of New Orleans: Race, Class and Politics, 1863–1923* (Urbana: University of Illinois Press, 1994); Arnesen, *Brotherhoods of Color: Black Railroad Workers and the Struggle for Equality* (Cambridge, MA: Harvard University Press, 2001); Alex Lichtenstein, *Twice the Work of Free Labor: The Political Economy of Convict Labor in the New South* (London: Verso, 1996); Brian Kelly, *Race, Class, and Power in the Alabama Coalfields* (Urbana: University of Illinois Press, 2001).

31. Fields, "Ideology and Race," 149.

Chapter 1. Class and Race in the Interwar Years

1. *MM*, February 14, 1913, 4 (Watson); May 24, 1916, 6 (call for vigilance toward "white loafers"); *MM*, May 23, 1916, 4, and May 26, 1916, 2 (whites paying tax); August 27, 1915, 3. $3 = $76 in 2019 dollars.

2. *MM*, August 7, 1917, 8 (Black impersonator); September 20, 1916, 8 (receipt); July 3, 191, 2 (Haiti); February 14, 1913, 4, August 5, 1918, 2, August 17, 1918, 2, and November 4, 1918, 1 (shooting incident; acquittal and paid legal fees); August 6, 1918, 1 (Black leaders protest street tax); August 27, 1915, 3, and August 6, 1918, 3 (complaints).

3. Florida Department of Agriculture and Nathan Mayo, *The Seventh Census of the State of Florida*, 1945 (Tallahassee: Florida Department of Agriculture, 1946), https://stars.library.ucf.edu/floridaheritage/79, 84 (for Miami), 11 (for Dade). Population numbers through 1945 were culled from earlier federal census data (compared by author with earlier census compilations): US Bureau of the Census, *Census of the Population, 1950*, vol. 2, pt. 10: Florida (Washington, DC: US GPO, 1952), 27, 29. Raymond Mohl, "Miami, Florida," *An Encyclopedia of Urban History*, vol. 2, ed. David Goldfield (Thousand Oaks, CA: Sage, 2007), 467 (population percent increase).

4. Christina Abreu, *Rhythms of Race: Cuban Musicians and the Making of Latino New York City and Miami, 1940–1960* (Chapel Hill: University of North Carolina Press, 2015), 193–95, and ch. 6; Louis Perez, *On Becoming Cuban: Identity, Nationality and Culture* (New York: Eco, 1999), 432–44; Melanie Shell-Weiss, *Coming to Miami: A Social History* (Gainesville: University Press of Florida, 2009).

5. US Bureau of the Census, *Fourteenth Census of the United States, 1920*, vol. 2, *Population* (Washington, DC: US GPO, 1922), 760, 795 (Bahamian immigrants); *Census of the Population, 1950*, vol. 2, pt. 10: Florida, xxx.

6. James Gregory, *The Southern Diaspora: How the Great Migrations of Black and White Southerners Transformed America* (Chapel Hill: University of Carolina Press, 2005), 9.

7. Raymond Mohl, "Black Immigrants: Bahamians in Early Twentieth-Century Miami," *Florida Historical Quarterly*, 65, no. 3 (1987): 284; Melanie Shell-Weiss, "Coming North to the South: Migration, Labor, and City Building," *FHQ*, 84, No. 1 (2005): 88–91. Shell-Weiss notes that in 1910, in one precinct, about 12 percent of the 382 households contained intermarriages between Bahamians and southern Blacks; Mohl notes one 1910 Bahamian household with Florida-born children.

8. Florida Department of Agriculture and Nathan Mayo, *The Seventh Census of the State of Florida, 1945* (Tallahassee: Florida Department of Agriculture, 1946), https://stars.library.ucf.edu/floridaheritage/79, 13 (Dade figures), 93 (white nativity); US Bureau of the Census, *Sixteenth Census of the United States: 1940, Population*, vol. 2, 73 (numbers for Central Europe for 1940); E. P. Hutchinson, *Immigrants and Their Children, 1850–1950* (New York: John Wiley and Sons, 1956), 32–33; US Bureau of the Census, *1950 Census of Population*, vol. 3, *Census Tract Statistics, Miami, Chapter 31* (Washington, DC: US Bureau of the Census, 1952), 7.

9. 1921 Miami City Charter, http://dpanther.fiu.edu/dpService/dpPurlService/purl/FI00007784/00001; 1913 Miami City Charter, http://dpanther.fiu.edu/dpService/dpPurlService/purl/FI00300419/00001.

10. Stuart Ewen and Elizabeth Ewen, *Typecasting: On the Arts and Sciences of Human Inequality* (New York: Seven Stories, 2008); Scott Sandage, *Born Losers: A History of Failure in America* (Cambridge, MA: Harvard University Press, 2005).

11. *MDN*, October 10, 1924, 12 (poor migrants warned not to come; "negro loafers" rounded up to work on farms); April 24, 1927, Society sec., 10; December 31, 1928, 12; August 2, 1925, sec. 2, 2.

12. Frank Tobias Higbie, *Indispensable Outcasts: Hobo Workers and Community in the American Midwest, 1880–1930* (Urbana: University of Illinois Press, 2003), 100 and 116–18; Mark Pittenger, *Class Unknown: Undercover Investigations of American Work and Poverty from the Progressive Era to the Present* (New York: New York University Press, 2012), 3–4, 59, 90–93 (quote on 93); Nancy Isenberg, *White Trash: The 400-Year Untold History of Class in America* (New York: Viking, 2016), 193–230; Ewen and Ewen, *Typecasting*; Chris Maisano, "The New 'Culture of Poverty,'" *Catalyst* 1, no. 2 (Summer 2017): 195–208.

13. Peter Linebaugh and Marcus Rediker, *The Many-Headed Hydra: Sailors, Slaves, Commoners, and the Hidden History of the Revolutionary Atlantic* (Boston: Beacon, 2000), 42; Karen Fields and Barbara Fields, *Racecraft: The Soul of Inequality in American Life*

(London: Verso, 2012), 11–12; Judith Stein, "Defining the Race, 1890–1930," in *The Invention of Ethnicity*, ed. Werner Sollors (New York: Oxford University Press, 1988): 77–104.

14. Research Center, HistoryMiami Museum, *Highlights of Greater Miami, Hollywood and Fort Lauderdale* (Miami: J. C. Mills, 1952). John Sewell, *Miami Memoirs: A New Pictorial Edition of John Sewell Story*, ed. Arva Moore Parks (1933; repr., Arva Parks, 1987), 17–20, 145–52, and 168–69 (city incorporation and use of Black workers for vote), and 52–59 and 159–169 (street work, etc.).

15. Excellent histories of Miami include Arva Moore Parks, *Miami: The Magic City* (Miami: Centennial, 1991). Paul George and Raymond Mohl have contributed many foundational studies on Miami's history, for example: George, "Policing Miami's Black Community, 1896–1930," *Florida Historical Quarterly* 47, no. 4 (April 1979): 434–50; George, Colored Town: Miami's Black Community, 1896–1930," *Florida Historical Quarterly* 56, no. 4 (April 1976): 434–50; Mohl, "Black Immigrants"; Mohl, "Trouble in Paradise: Race and Housing in Mimi during the New Deal Era," *Prologue: Journal of the National Archives*, 19, no. 1 (Spring 1987): 7–21. See also Marvin Dunn, *Black Miami in the Twentieth Century* (Gainesville: University Press of Florida, 1997); Shell-Weiss, *Coming to Miami*; N. D. B. Connolly, *A World More Concrete: Real Estate and the Remaking of Jim Crow South Florida* (Chicago: University of Chicago Press, 2014); Chanelle N. Rose, *The Struggle for Black Freedom in Miami: Civil Rights and America's Tourist Paradise, 1896–1968* (Baton Rouge: Louisiana State University Press, 2015); Gregory Bush, *White Sand, Black Beach: Civil Rights, Public Space, and Virginia Key* (Gainesville: University Press of Florida, 2016); Julio Capó's *Welcome to Fairyland: Queer Miami before 1940* (Chapel Hill: University of North Carolina Press, 2017).

16. Historian Judith Stein stated that "to understand the behavior of white groups towards blacks, and blacks towards whites, one must understand the larger forces at work and the structures of power in the society. By reifying and isolating race consciousness and racism, these relationships are ignored" ("'Of Mr. Booker T. Washington and Others': The Political Economy of Racism in the United States," *Science and Society*, 38, No. 4 [Winter, 1974—75]: 463).

17. US Bureau of the Census, *Sixteenth Census of the United States: 1940, Population*, vol. 3, *The Labor Force: Occupation, Industry, Employment, and Income*, pt. 2, Alabama–Indiana (Washington DC: GPO, 1943), 660–65; Myra B. Young, "*Lord, Please Don't Take Me in August": African Americans in Newport and Saratoga Springs, 1870–1930* (Urbana: University of Illinois Press, 1999), 63–71.

18. The drop reflected the rise of the airline industry: the census listed 162 of the 430 workers in transportation other than railroad were Black (no category yet existed for airline labor).

19. US Bureau of the Census, *Fifteenth Census of the United States: 1930*, vol. 4, *Occupations* (Washington DC: GPO, 1932), 358–61; US Bureau of the Census, *Sixteenth Census of the United States: 1940*, vol. 3, *Population*, 660–65; *Census of the Population: 1950*, vol. 2, *Characteristics of the Population*, pt. 10, "Florida" (Washington DC: GPO, 1952), 238–40; *Census of the Population: 1960*, vol. 1, *Characteristics of the Population*, pt. 11, "Florida" (Washington DC: GPO, 1963), 478–80; for the 1970 census, please refer to the following web link, http://www2.census.gov/prod2/decennial/documents/42189395v7_TOC.pdf.

20. Gregory Bush, "'Playground of the USA': Miami and the Promotion of Spectacle," *Pacific Historical Review* 68, no. 2 (May 1999): 153–72.

21. Michael Zweig, *The Working Class Majority: America's Best Kept Secret* (Ithaca, NY: Cornell University Press, 2000), 13.

22. Mohl, "Black Immigrants," 271–97; Howard Johnson, "Late Migration and Early Twentieth Century Labour Migration to Florida," *Bahamians in Slavery and Freedom* (Kingston, Jamaica: Ian Randle, 1991); Jerrel Shofner, "Florida and the Black Migration," *Florida Historical Quarterly*, 57, no. 3 (1979): 267–88; Shofner, "The Legacy of Racial Slavery: Free Enterprise and Forced Labor in Florida in the 1940s," *Journal of Southern History* 47, no. 3 (1981): 411–26; Shell-Weiss, "Coming North," 79–99.

23. *MDN*, October 10, 1924, 12 (vagrants); see the *Papers of the NAACP*, pt. 10, "Peonage, Labor, and the New Deal, 1913–1939," reels 10, 16, and 20, University Publications of America, Frederick, MD, for coverage of the 1926 Great Miami Hurricane and conscription.

24. *MDN*, September 26, 1925, 7; *MT*, August 1925, 1; *MDN*, July 8, 1926, 22. See especially the summer and fall coverage in the *MDN*, *MH*, and *MT*. Important study for waterfront workers in the South, see Eric Arnesen's *Waterfront Workers of New Orleans: Race, Class, and Politics, 1863–1923* (Urbana: University of Illinois Press, 1991).

25. *Planning Your Vacation in Florida: Miami and Dade County, including Miami Beach and Coral Gables* (Northport, NY: Bacon, Percy, and Daggett, 1941), 4 and 5; for estimates of greater influxes of African American workers, see Gary W. McDonough, *The Florida Negro: A Federal Writers' Legacy* (Jackson: University of Mississippi Press, 1993), 39–40, and Young, *"Lord, Please,"* 63–71.

26. Thelma Peters, *Lemon City: Pioneering on Biscayne Bay, 1850–1925* (Miami: Banyan, 1976), 232–36; Dunn, *Black Miami*, 30–44 and 165; Enid Pinkney, "Brownsville," *Miami's Historic Neighborhoods: A History of Community*, ed. Becky Roper Matkov (San Antonio, TX: Historic Publishing, 2001), 72; *MDN*, August 29, 1925, 17 (naming of Liberty City and its description); September 28, 1926, 12 (devastation of hurricane).

27. For a series of newspaper reports on Colored Town's dilapidated conditions, see *the Miami Herald*'s coverage in September 1934. See the Dade County Grand Jury reports from the 1930s through the 1940s in the Florida Collection, Dade County Public Library, in downtown Miami. Grand Jury Reports, Miami-Dade County, reel 1: November 24, 1919, through May 1956, Reports 1–2350, Helen Muir Florida Collection at Miami-Dade Public Library System (thanks to Giselle Alonso, librarian from the Florida Collection, for tracking the citation for me). On Grand Jury reports, the *Miami Herald* reported in 1941 that "again a grand jury has paid an official visit to Miami's negro section. Again unsanitary conditions have been noted. Slum filth and degraded housing have been commented upon. . . . Grand jury after grand jury has been making similar visits, turning in the same comments, noting the same appalling conditions." *MH*, November 26, 1941, 6; highlighted again in the *MH*, October 24, 1946, 6.

28. *MDN*, November 21, 1935, 2 (tuberculosis); December 16, 1928, 10 (bus lines); December 7, 1939, 1A (transportation limitations/social control); on negro jitneys to Miami Beach; see also Polly Redford, *Billion Dollar Sandbar: A Biography of Miami Beach* (New York: E. P. Dutton, 1970), 223. See also Miami Chamber of Commerce, *Minutes of*

the Board of Directors Meeting, April 24, 1922 (African American shopping), and May 2, 1921, where Dr. J. M. Jackson complained about how difficult it was "to obtain and keep servants on account of no transportation, to the south side of Miami" (race of servant not indicated), HistoryMiami Museum; see also the letter from John Gramling (white attorney advocate for the Liberty City housing project) to Horatio Hackett of the Emergency Housing Division, September 20, 1934, Records of the Public Housing Administration, Record Group 196, National Archives, Washington, DC [hereafter PHA-RG 196], box 298. Gramling noted that "at the present time the negroes are dependent upon the street car line and negro hacks. In the majority of cases the street cars do not operate near where the negroes work, therefore the negroes are dependent upon negro hacks to haul them to work. . . . There are no colored bus lines and *negroes are not permitted to ride on many of the white bus lines*" (emphasis added).

29. *MM*, April 15, 1919, 2; *MDN*, September 14, 1925, 28; *MDN*, December 9, 1928, 12; *MDN*, December 16, 1928, 10.

30. *MM*, April 15, 1919, 2; *MDN*, September 14, 1925, 28; *MDN*, December 9, 1928, 12; *MDN*, December 16, 1928, 10; *MM*, October 26, 1920, 1 (on Black colony); Fisher to Pancoast and Schilling, August 25, 1919, box 7, folder 9, and box 13, folder 10, Carl Fisher Papers, 1896–1956, Research Center, HistoryMiami Museum [hereafter CGF Papers]; Redford, *Billion-Dollar Sandbar*, 223; Enid Pinkney, Miami Stories, HistoryMiami Museum, https://www.historymiami.org/miami-stories/enid-pinkney/; Joann Biondi, ed., *Miami Beach Memories: A Nostalgic Chronicle of Days Gone By* (Guilford, CT: Globe Pequot, 2007), 23 (memory of Stella Stuberman on Smith Cottages); *MDN*, October 27, 1950, 1B and July 5, 1951, 9C (razing of shacks).

31. *MM*, March 19, 1918, 11; June 12, 1923, 2; for Fisher advertisement, see *MDN*, January 6, 1929, 35; *MDN*, March 28, 1929, 18 (for Coral Gables).

32. Miami Chamber of Commerce, *Minutes*, June 15, July 7 and 13, and September 18, 1925 (on Black workers); September 1, October 1, October 12, November 9, 1925, and December 27, 1926 (on worker accommodations). *MDN*, August 2, 1925, 1, and September 11, 1925, 34; and *MT*, July 16, 1925, 12 (request for waiving fire ordinances); September 11, 1925, 10A (Burdine's). A *Miami Tribune* advertisement noted an Okeechobee "Portable Housing Factory" was opening (*MT*, October 3, 1925, 2B). See also Nicholas N. Patricios, "Phineas Paist and the Architecture of Coral Gables, Florida," *Tequesta* 64 (2004): 17 (San Sebastian); *MT*, September 16, 1925, 4 (Gables tent city); *MDN*, August 19, 1925, sec. 2, 2 (tent cities). See Joanne Pearcy's oral history in Miami Stories, HistoryMiami Museum, which mentions her grandparents living in a tent city, https://www.historymiami.org/miami-stories/joanne-pearcy/.

33. See chapter 1 of my dissertation "Laboring in the Magic City: Class Struggle in Miami, 1914–1941 (PhD diss., University of Maryland, 2011) for a discussion of the production of southern nostalgia and other cultural products, including sports entertainment and minstrel shows.

34. Bush, "'Playground of the USA,'" 155; Paul George, "Passage to the New Eden: Tourism in Miami through Everest G. Sewell," *Florid Historical Quarterly*, 59, no. 4 (April 1981): 440–63; Capó, *Welcome to Fairyland*.

35. George, "Passage to the New Eden," 450–51; *MDN*, March 4, 1919, 1.

36. *Highlights of Greater Miami, Hollywood and Fort Lauderdale*; "This Week in Greater Miami: What to See; What to Do," 2, no. 2 (December 11, 1937), Pamphlets Collection, Research Center, HistoryMiami Museum (guidebook distributed free from leading hotels). Alligator wrestling, along with staged Indian weddings, "cooking, sewing patchwork garments, or carving canoes and the like," created a safe, anthropological tourist experience of the exotic (Harry A. Kersey Jr., *The Florida Seminoles and the New Deal, 1933–1942* [Boca Raton: Florida Atlantic University Press, 1989], 38–41, quote on 38). See also "Musa Isle Village Interesting Place," *MDN*, June 27, 1934, 6 (Indian life); and "Gator Wrestling Is Daily Feature," *MDN*, December 7, 1929, 9, which wrote, "Nowhere, perhaps, is Florida life so characteristic of the primitive that obtained before the coming of the white man." For images of the themed village, see Musa Isle Indian Village, http://www.pbase.com/image/81114049, and the pictures in the Everglades Digital Library.

37. *MH*, August 9, 1925, 5D; *MT*, October 8, 1925, 1; Harold Dorn, "Mango Growing around Early Miami," *Tequesta* 16 (1956): 37–53. See the many postcards for Miami and Miami Beach in two excellent collections: Patricia Kennedy, *Miami in Vintage Postcards* (Charleston, SC: Arcadia, 2000), and Kennedy, *Miami Beach in Vintage Postcards* (Charleston, SC: Arcadia, 2000). In addition to the many images of sport, fun, and recreation, the marketing of the palm tree as a signifier of leisure is quite evident. See for example, Anne O'Hare McCormick, "Adventuring in Our Tropical Empire," *NYT*, March 15, 1925.

38. *MDN*, July 26, 1936, 11; fortieth anniversary section; "Inventing Antiquity: The Art and Craft of Mediterranean Revival Architecture," in "Florida Theme Issue," special issue, *Journal of Decorative and Propaganda Arts* 23 (1998): 195–96.

39. Metropolitan Dade County Office of Community and Economic Development, Historic Preservation Division, *From Wilderness to Metropolis: The History and Architecture of Dade County, Florida, 1825–1940* (Miami: Metropolitan Dade County, 1982), 41–43, 70–73, and 86–87; US Bureau of Labor Statistics, "Building Permits in the Principal Cities of the United States," *Bulletin of the United States Bureau of Labor Statistics*, no. 449 (Washington, DC: US GPO, 1927), 29–30 and 36. Statistics are not available for subsequent years, though the number of new housing units built dropped drastically between 1927 and 1935 even while the population continued to increase (US Department of Commerce, *Housing Construction Statistics: 1889 to 1964* (Washington, DC: US GPO, 1966), 156.

40. Connolly indirectly suggests that Allapattah, initially an exclusive white neighborhood, evolved from a white worker enclave (Connolly, *World More Concrete*, 144–45). See also Michel-Rolph Trouillot's important discussion about narratives and history in *Silencing the Past: Power and the Production of History* (Boston: Beacon, 1995), 22–30.

41. George Merrick, *Coral Gables, Miami Rivera* (Coral Gables, FL: G. E. Merrick, 1920); Marjory Stoneman Douglas, *Coral Gables, Miami Rivera an Interpretation* (n.p., n.p., 1925).

42. A jump in residential house construction occurred between 1936 and 1941 after a decade of little development (1935 witnessed a jump to 919 issued permits from the 1934 total of 282) (US Department of Commerce, *Housing Construction Statistics*, 156); Raleigh Barlowe, "Homestead Tax Exemption: A Tenure Improvement Measure?," *Jour-*

nal of Land and Public Utility Economics," 23, no. 4 [November 1947]: 360–70). For the further institutionalization of segregation via redlining, see Raymond Mohl, "Trouble in Paradise: Race and Housing in Miami during the New Deal Era," *Prologue* (Spring 1987): 7–21; John A. Stuart, "Constructing Identity: Building and Place in New Deal South Florida," in *The New Deal in South Florida: Design, Policy, and Community Building, 1933–1940*, ed. John A. Stuart and John F. Stack Jr. (Gainesville: University Press of Florida, 2008), 40 and 64 (south Florida tourism becoming accessible to middle and working classes). See also Mary Wood's chapter, "Migrants, Millionaires, and Tourists," in the same collection.

43. See Kennedy, *Miami in Vintage Postcards* and *Miami Beach in Vintage Postcards*, for tourist imagery; *MDN*, July 26, 1936, sec. 2, 9 (Lummus Park Recreation Center). The sports pages of the *MDN* and *MH* abound in descriptions of local sports activity; see the social pages and amusement sections for leisure activities. Bush, *White Sand, Black Beach*, offers more context of nonaccess to beaches for Blacks; see chapter 1 of Thomas A. Castillo's "Laboring in the Magic City: Workers in Miami, 1914–1941," PhD diss., University of Maryland, 2011, for a deeper discussion of Miami entertainment and leisure in the interwar years.

44. Stephen Cochran Singleton, "My Florida" (Winter Park, FL: Angel Alley, 1930). Singleton's poem was recited widely (*MDN*, October 26, 1930, 2, society section). Miami Junior Women's Club chose it as their song. Benjamin Kline Hunnicutt, *Free Time: The Forgotten American Dream* (Philadelphia: Temple University Press, 2013), discusses the idea of "higher progress," of living full, meaningful lives, as the forgotten American Dream (see pp. 2–11, for example). See also Tobias Higbie, *Labor's Mind: A History of Working-Class Intellectual Life* (Urbana: University of Illinois Press, 2019).

45. *MDN*, June 16, 1923, 4 (Ward sermon); July 19, 1921, 1 (Irwin sermon); *St. Petersburg Times*, July 30, 1924, 11 (marble inscription); *MDN*, June 17, 1929, 1 (De Priest).

Chapter 2. Driving and Chauffeuring in Miami

This chapter is a revised and expanded version of an earlier publication, "Chauffeuring in a White Man's Town: Black Service Work, Movement, and Segregation in Early Miami," in *Florida's Working-Class Past: Current Perspectives on Labor, Race, and Gender from Spanish Florida to the New Immigration*, edited by Robert Cassanello and Melanie Shell-Weiss (Gainesville: University Press of Florida, 2009).

1. Paul S. George, "Colored Town: Miami's Black Community, 1896–1930," *Florida Historical Quarterly* 56, no. 4 (April 1978): 435–36, 442; Raymond Mohl, "Black Immigrants: Bahamians in Early Twentieth-Century Miami," *Florida Historical Quarterly* 65, no. 3 (January 1987): 281; Marvin Dunn, *Black Miami in the Twentieth Century* (Gainesville: University Press of Florida, 1997).

2. Edward Ayers, *The Promise of the New South: Life after Reconstruction* (New York: Oxford University Press, 1992), 132–59, 426–37; Grace Hale, *Making Whiteness: The Culture of Segregation in the South, 1890–1940* (New York: Pantheon, 1998), 85–197; August Meier and Elliot Rudwick, "The Boycott Movement against Jim Crow Streetcars in the South, 1900–1906," *Journal of American History* 55, no. 4 (March 1969): 756–75.

3. *MM*, October 4, 1915, 6. George, "Colored Town," 433; Dunn, *Black Miami*, 94–95. Rayford W. Logan, *Betrayal of the Negro: From Rutherford B. Hayes to Woodrow Wilson* (New York: Collier, 1965). Leon F. Litwack, *Trouble in Mind: Black Southerners in the Age of Jim Crow* (New York: Alfred A. Knopf, 1998).

4. *MDN*, October 9, 1931, 8; November 29, 1931, 7 (hotel training); *Miami* (Labor) *News*, July 19, 1935 (organized labor lobbying for the school and for home labor).

5. *MDN*, September 13, 1931, 2 (Burdine's). See also Susan Porter Benson, *Counter Cultures: Saleswomen, Managers, and Customers in American Department Stores, 1890–1940* (Urbana: University of Illinois Press, 1986), 150–53. Jack Kassewitz, "Adults Also Suffer in Space Pinch," *Miami News* (*MDN*, Blue Streak Edition), September 19, 1968, 1A. The vocational school eventually became the main office of the Dade County School Board, named after Coca-Cola bottle magnate Lindsey Hopkins, who had purchased the unfinished building, formerly named the Roosevelt Hotel. The original owner of it, Frederick Rand, envisioned making the hotel a featured place of Second Avenue, which he hoped would become the Fifth Avenue of Miami (*MDN*: August 29, 1965, Miami Magazine Section, 9).

6. Thomas Castillo, "Miami's Hidden Labor History," *Florida Historical Quarterly*, 82, no. 4 (Spring 2004): 438–67. Car rental advertisements appear in the newspaper throughout the period. Councilor and unionist John T. Blackman argued in that local taxicab drivers ought to be given the best taxicab stands in the city (*MM*, November 11, 1917, 1). "Situation wanted" advertisements placed by chauffeurs would sometimes indicate mastery and the ability to drive in the city or country (*MM*, October 1, 1915, 11).

7. Individuals who transported people or goods by rail or ship were identified separately in the US Census during this period.

8. US Bureau of the Census, 1920 census schedules for Miami and Dade County, rolls 215 and 216. I recorded all drivers appearing in the 1920 census. The labels indicated whether the drivers drew a wage or were paid a salary and whether they were self-employed and drove a vehicle for hire or whether they were employees of a particular establishment. The categories used to describe drivers included chauffeur/driver (drives car and transports people), driver of jitney buses, domestic chauffeur, hackman and carriage (transport of people not clear), deliverymen, caddying, teamster, drayman, driver (transports of goods), driver of construction materials, and driver of truck (not clear what they transport). On the challenges of identifying occupations that involved driving during this period, see Kevin Borg, "The 'Chauffeur Problem' in Early Auto Era: Structuration Theory and the Users of Technology," *Technology and Culture* 40, no. 4 (1999): 797–832 (see especially 83n70); Rachel Moshkowitz, "When the Drive Lasts All Day: Taxidrivers and Chauffeurs," *Occupational Outlook Quarterly* 37 no. 2 (1993): 32–36. The plethora of union locals for drivers in major cities like Chicago further indicates the diversity of this sector (Sterling F. Rigg, "The Chicago Teamsters Unions," *Journal of Political Economy* 34, no. 1 [1926]: 13–36).

9. 1920 census rolls for Miami, reels 215 and 216.

10. 1930 census rolls for Miami, reels 308–10; US Bureau of the Census, *Fifteenth Census of the United States, 1930*, vol. 4, *Occupations* (Washington, DC: US GPO, 1932), 359.

11. Julian Street, "The Passing of the Old-School Chauffeur," *Collier's, Automobile Supplement*, January 1912, 46, 48; Lorenzo J. Greene and Carter G. Woodson, *The Negro Wage Earner* (Washington, DC: Association for the Study of Negro Life and History, 1930), 111–12; Gorman Gilbert and Robert E. Samuels, *The Taxicab: An Urban Transportation Survivor* (Chapel Hill: University of North Carolina, 1982), 63, 65–66, 95; Paul S. George, "Traffic Control in Early Miami," *Tequesta* 37 (1977): 3–18.

12. *MM*, January 6, 1915, 9; January 2, 1915, 19; Street, "Passing," 46 (quote); Jacqueline Jones, *American Work: Four Centuries of Black and White Labor* (New York: W. W. Norton, 1998), 322; Lorenzo J. Greene and Carter G. Woodson, *Negro Wage Earner* (Washington, DC: Association for the Study of Negro Life and History, 1930), 111–12; Borg, "Chauffeur Problem," 822; US Bureau of the Census, *Thirteenth Census of the United States, 1910*, vol. 4, *Population, Occupation Statistics* (Washington, DC: US GPO, 1914), 414–15; US Bureau of the Census, *Fourteenth Census of the Population, 1920*, vol. 4, *Occupations* (Washington, DC: US GPO, 1922), 350–51.

13. *MM*, January 2, 1915, 19 (ad quotes; "make own repairs" was a common phrase in ads for chauffeur positions); Borg, "Chauffeur Problem," 809–11, 821; Street, "Passing," 46, 48; "The Reform of Chauffeurs," *Literary Digest*, February 10, 1912, 273–74; T. H. Parker, "The Worth of a Good Chauffeur," *Harper's Weekly*, April 6, 1912, 14.

14. Street, "Passing," 46, 48; Parker, "The Worth of a Good Chauffeur," 14 (for exchange on high-priced chauffeur); "A Word for Chauffeurs and Garages," *Literary Digest*, June 8, 1912, 1215–16; *MM*, December 30, 1915, 7 ("no bad habits"); *MM*, January 17, 1919, 15 (married, reliable chauffeur); *MM*, January 22, 1919, 14; and Borg, "Chauffeur Problem," 809–11, 821. The white chauffeur arguments here echo David Montgomery's insights in *Worker's Control in America: Studies in the History of Work, Technology, and Labor Struggles* (Cambridge: Cambridge University Press, 1979).

15. *MH*, February 28, 1915, 5; *MM*, March 1, 1915, 2.

16. See front page letter to the *MM* on August 5, 1915, 1 and 8, which argued that blacks were natural servants and how southern whites were accustomed to this; hence, exclusion seemed hypocritical.

17. *MM*, July 29, 1915, 4. An *MH* editorial took issue with northern criticism of Miami's chauffeuring segregation rule, noting that it was just like any "other" community "custom" that had "obtained something of the sanction of law. . . . The people here believe that those who come down from the north should conform to our customs" (*MH*, March 17, 1915, 4).

18. *MM*, July 29, 1915, 4. For images of Blacks and the shaping of segregation custom and law, see George M. Fredrickson, *The Black Image in the White Mind: The Debate on Afro-American Character and Destiny, 1817–1914* (New York: Harper and Row, 1971); Joel Williamson, *The Crucible of Race: Black White Relations in the American South since Emancipation* (New York: Oxford University, 1984); Hale, *Making Whiteness*, 85–197; Litwack, *Trouble in Mind*.

19. Howard Kleinberg, "History of the *Miami News*, 1896–1987," *Tequesta* 57 (1987), 14–16 (quote on 16); Ethan V. Blackman, *Miami and Dade County, Florida: Its Settlement, Progress, and Achievement* (Washington, DC: Victor Rainbolt, 1921), 116; *MDN*, March 24, 1945, 1 and 4; *MH*, March 25, 1945, 10-A; Nixon Smiley, *Knights of the Fourth Estate:*

The Story of the Miami Herald (Miami: E. A. Seemann, 1974), 27–29; Jeanne Bellamy, "Newspapers of America's Last Frontier," *Tequesta* 7 (1952): 7–10. Dean established the *Weekly Lake Worth News* in 1894. He then began the *Daily Lake Worth News*, later renamed the *Palm Beach Daily News* (Kleinberg, "History," 14).

20. *MH*, March 17, 1915, 4.

21. *MM*, June 29, 1915, 4; June 30, 1915; August 3, 1915, 1; August 4, 1915, 1; August 6, 1915, 1; *MH*, July 31, 1915, 8; August 5, 1915, 8; August 8, 1915, 4, 8; August 6, 1915, 4 ("burning question").

22. *MM*, June 30, 1915, 2 (Okell letter); August 5, 1915, 1 (McNeil). On links between a living wage and exclusion of Blacks, see Lawrence Glickman, *A Living Wage: American Workers and the Making of Consumer Society* (Ithaca, NY: Cornell University Press, 1997).

23. *MH*, August 6, 1915.

24. *MM*, August 5, 1915, 8 (Ryan letter); 1920 census rolls for Miami, reels 215 and 216 (Ryan's occupation); *MH*, August 6, 1915; Litwack, *Trouble in Mind*, 181. See also Randy Roberts's *Papa Jack: Jack Johnson and the Era White Hopes* (New York: Free Press, 1983). On manliness and racial dominance, see Gail Bederman, *Manliness and Civilization: A Cultural History of Gender and Race in the United States, 1880–1917* (Chicago: University of Chicago, 1995).

25. *MM*, August 5, 1915, 1, 8 (Sheeler letter). Another letter by Sheeler offered a sharper attack on organized labor: "Can we afford . . . that the Chauffeurs unions or nay other Unions dictate the policies of conduct of our city affairs?" (*MM*, October 4, 1915, 1). See Borg, "Chauffeur Problem," for class dynamic in regulating chauffeur profession.

26. The directory listed only one chauffeur; categorization issues also plagued directory entries.

27. *MM*, August 6, 1915, 1, 3 (Moore and McNeil comments); *MM*, August 7, 1915, 6 (editorial). *MM*, August 4, 1915, 3 (Black competency); *Miami City Directory* (Jacksonville, FL: R. L. Polk, 1913–15). Not much is written about Black chauffeurs in the early automobile years. A few references point to fluidity being the rule and attempts that some whites made to place restrictions (John Dittmer, *Black Georgia in the Progressive Era, 1900–1920* [Urbana: University of Illinois, 1977], 21; Neil R. McMillen, *Dark Journey: Black Mississippians in the Age of Jim Crow* [Urbana: University of Illinois, 1990], 8, 11; Litwack, *Trouble in Mind*, 336).

28. On the continued debate, see *MM*, September 9, 1915, 2; September 22 1915, 7; September 25, 1915, 1; October 4, 1915, 6; October 15, 1915, 10 (Highland quote); November 18, 1915, 2 (first reported chauffeur incident); January 4, 1916, 3; *MH*, December 1, 1915, 5; *MM*, August 6, 1915, 1, 3; *MH*, August 7, 1915, 4 (free service).

29. *MM*, July 9, 1917, 5; July 11, 1917, 2; July 12, 1917, 1; July 23, 1917, 2; *Carpenter*, August 1917. Biographical information on Andrews is drawn from the census rolls for 1920, reel 216, and World War I draft registration cards (accessed through Ancestry .com). Andrews had signed up at the local draft board on June 6. No extant records give his view on the war. Earlier in the year, *MH* reported a tourist accepting Miami's segregation policy without incident (*MH*, January 14, 1917, 1).

30. *MM*, July 14, 1917, 2 (all quotes are from this letter). In May 1915, Blacks had

sought approval from the city council to open a garage in Colored Town but seemed to have been ignored. The effort to expand driving rights represented a shift in tactics (going to the public), as well as a change in the context of the tourist economics (*MM*, May 8, 1915, 4; *MH*, May 7, 1915, 6).

31. *MM*, July 14, 1917, 2.

32. *MM*, July 16, 1917, 1; Paul George, "Policing Miami's Black Community, 1896–1930," *Florida Historical Quarterly* 47, no. 4 (April 1979): 441; Dorothy J. Fields, "Black Entertainment, 1908–1919," *Update* 2, no. 1 (December 1974): 11. For more insight on Black businesses in the South, see Walter B. Weare, *Black Business in the New South: A Social History of the North Carolina Mutual Life Insurance Company* (Urbana: University of Illinois, 1973).

33. *MM*, July 16, 1917, 1 (quotes); July 17, 1917, 1, 2.

34. *MM*, July 16, 1917, 12.

35. *MM*, July 16, 1917, 12.

36. *MM*, July 16, 1917, 12; Elliot Rudwick, *Race Relations at East St. Louis, July 2, 1917* (Carbondale: Southern Illinois University Press, 1964); George B. Tindall, *The Emergence of the New South, 1913–1945* (Baton Rouge: Louisiana State University Press, 1967), 150; Kevin Gaines, *Uplifting the Race: Black Leadership, Politics, and Culture in the Twentieth Century* (Chapel Hill: University of North Carolina Press, 1996); Mark Ellis, *Race, War, and Surveillance: African Americans and the United States Government* (Bloomington: Indiana University Press, 2001).

37. Jerrell Shofner, "Florida and the Black Migration," *Florida Historical Quarterly* 57, no. 3 (January 1979): 267. On growing anxiety of Black migration, see *MH*, June 8, 9, 10, 14, 15, 17, 1917 (last date on enticement trial on Dade recruitment efforts); on Bryant and 1889 enticement law, see *MM*, June 9, 1917, 1, 2; *MM*, July 16, 1917, 12 (Black leaders).

38. *MM*, July 16, 1917, 1.

39. *MM*, July 16, 1917, 6.

40. The white committee consisted of (as listed in the paper, *MM*, July 16, 1917, 1, 12) F. M. Hudson, Dr. James M. Jackson, Frank B. Love, J. M. Berecegeay, A. H. Adams, J. I. Conklin, and Frank S. White. Black members at the conference were Reverend S. H. Travis, Allan Stokes, R. A. Powers, H. S. Braggs, K. L. Pharr, Reverend J. W. Drake, and Dr. William. B. Sawyer.

41. *MM*, July 17, 1917, 1; July 23, 1917, 2 (report of arrests for violation of curfew).

42. *MM*, July 18, 1917, 1; July 21, 1917, 6.

43. White chauffeurs agreed to let tourists choose their drivers. Councilor John Blackman insisted on reserving the best hacking stands to local labor (*MM*, November 9, 1917, 1; *MH*, November 9, 1917, 2).

44. *MM*, November 12, 1917, 9 (Black chauffeur ad); *MM*, January 11, 1918, 9 (Black chauffeur ad and white listing race).

45. *MM*, September 25, 1917, 8; November 16, 1917, 2.

46. *MM*, December 21, 1917, section 2, 1 (contains the full exchange).

47. *MM*, December 21, 1917, section 2, 1 (all quotes are taken from this article).

48. *MM*, December 21, 1917, section 2, 1; January 11, 1918, 16; January 25, 1918, 4; March 15, 1918, 2.

49. *MM*, January 18, 1919, 5; February 7, 1919, 6; March 7, 1919, 12.

50. *MM*, November 3, 1919, 6.

51. *MM*, November 3, 1919, 6.

52. *MM*, November 5, 1919, 3.

53. Miami Chamber of Commerce, *Minutes of the Board of Directors Meetings*, November 3, 1919, 12–13, HistoryMiami Museum; *MM*, November 20, 1917, 8. For Hill and Frazier, see 1920 census rolls, and *MM*, November 5, 1919, 3 (Hill listed as business agent).

54. *MM*, November 6, 1919, 1, 2 (chamber of commerce resolution and affidavit), 6 (letter to editor), and 13 (Calloway story).

55. *MM*, November 7, 1919, 1.

56. *MM*, November 7, 1919, 1 (May Smith quotes); November 5, 1919, 3 (chauffeur quotes); November 11, 1919, 6 (editorial).

57. *MM*, November 5, 1919, 3.

58. Beth Thompson Bates, *Pullman Porters and the Rise of Protest Politics in Black America, 1925–1945* (Chapel Hill: University of North Carolina, 2001), 17–39; Doug Bristol, "From Outposts to Enclaves: A Social History of Black Barbers, 1750–1915," (PhD diss., University of Maryland, 2002); Hale, *Making Whiteness*, 85–197; W. E. B. Du Bois, *Darkwater: Voices from Within the Veil* (1921; Millwood, NY: Kraus-Thomson, 1975), 109–21.

59. Robin Kelley, "'We Are Not What We Seem': Rethinking Black Working-Class Opposition in the Jim Crow South," *Journal of American History* 80, no. 1 (1993): 75–112; James Scott, *Domination and the Arts of Resistance: Hidden Transcripts* (New Haven, CT: Yale University Press, 1990); Kenneth W. Goings and Gerald L. Smith, "'Unhidden' Transcripts: Memphis and African American Agency, 1862–1920," *Journal of Urban History* 21, no. 3 (1995): 372–94. See also Robert Cassanello, "Violence, Racial Etiquette, and African American Working-Class *Infrapolitics* in Jacksonville during World War I," *Florida Historical Quarterly* 82, no. 2 (Fall 2003): 155–69.

60. Clara G. Stillman, "Florida: The Desert and the Rose," *The Nation*, October 31, 1923, 485–87. The *Afro-American*, Baltimore's Black newspaper (July 3, 1926, 14), noted in passing that "white elements" were against Black chauffeurs operating in Miami suggesting the ongoing danger Blacks faced when driving years after apparent the resolution.

61. US Bureau of the Census, *Fifteenth Census of the United States, 1930*, vol. 4, *Population* (Washington, DC: GPO, 1932), 359; *Miami* [Labor] *News*, June 18, 1936, 6; 1930 census rolls for Miami, reel 309; *MT*, January 12, 1957, 3; Polly Redford, *Billion-Dollar Sandbar: A Biography of Miami Beach* (New York: E. P. Dutton, 1970), 211, 223–24; Gary W. McDonough, *The Florida Negro: A Federal Writers' Project Legacy* (Jackson: University of Mississippi, 1993), 40; *MH*, June 4, 1936, 1.

62. See Richard Wright, "The Ethics of Jim Crow," in *Uncle Tom's Children* (1936; repr., New York: Harper Perennial, 1993), discussing the limitation of Black movement in white neighborhoods to workers at designated times.

Chapter 3. Fighting the Open Shop

1. *MH*, September 2, 1919, 1; *MM*, September 2, 1919, 1 (formation of GMA); *MH*, September 7, 1919, 1; *MM*, September 8, 1919 (GMA-BTC labor conference); *MM*, October 28, 1919, 1 (hod carriers' walk-off); *MM*, August 19, 1919, 1; August 21, 1919, 4; September 3, 1919, 1 (hod-carrier unionization and the cross-racial solidarity). *Proceedings of the Nineteenth Annual Convention of the Florida State Federation of Labor*, St. Augustine, Florida, April 1920, 16–24, 29–30 (statement for industrial security). The convention location changed year to year. The proceedings are held in various libraries such as University of Florida Smathers Library, Gainesville, and State Library of Florida, Tallahassee.

2. The term *closed shop* was a contested one. "Closed shop" meant joining the union was a condition of employment and nonnegotiable. For the unions, this meant everyone covered by their bargaining was a dues-paying member. Workers' control was a critical component. Unions argued for the right to bargain not only over wages but also over the nature of work: from intensity to issues of skill training and competency. Employers used the term to stigmatize the practice as undemocratic, restricting individual free choice and managerial prerogatives in hiring. For unions, the open shop allowed free riders to enjoy the benefits resulting from the union as their bargaining agent without having to join or contribute dues toward those negotiating efforts.

3. NAM president George Pope's speech, New York City, Wednesday, May 26, 1915, *Proceedings of the Twentieth Annual Convention of the National Association of Manufacturers* (New York: Secretary's Office, 1915), 269. Pope reminded the audience of the open-shop principles in the 1903 NAM Declaration of Principles, stating that "we maintain them as strongly as the time they were announced . . . *equal rights to all*, and the right of every man to earn a living" (269, from *Proceedings*, italics added); (*MM*, September 2, 1919, 1; *MH* September 2, 1919, 1). "Equal rights to all" is sometimes also written as "equal rights *for* all" in these reports announcing the formation of the GMA. See also *MM*, September 4, 1919, 1 (*MM* taking responsibility for introducing the term "open shop"). David Brian Robertson discusses how the 1902 anthracite coal strike and the strike commission's refusal to endorse the closed shop was the context in which the NAM Declaration of Principles was composed (Robertson, *Capital, Labor, and State: The Battle of American Labor Markets, from the Civil War to the New Deal* [New York: Rowman and Littlefield, 2000], 122.)

4. Michael Kazin, *Barons of Labor: The San Francisco Building Trades and Union Power in the Progressive Era* (Urbana: University of Illinois Press, 1987), 5; Andrew Wender Cohen, *The Racketeer's Progress: Chicago and the Struggle for Modern Economy, 1900–1940* (Cambridge: Cambridge University Press, 2004); Grace Palladino, *Skilled Hands, Strong Spirits: A Century of Building Trades History* (Ithaca, NY: Cornell University Press, 2005); William Haber, *Industrial Relations in the Building Industry* (1930; repr., New York: Arno and New York Times, 1971). Focus on industrial unions characterizes Joseph A. McCartin's *Labor's Great War: The Struggle for Industrial Democracy and the Origins of Modern American Labor Relations, 1912–1921* (Chapel Hill: University of North Carolina Press, 1997).

5. General overviews of southern labor history include Gary M. Fink and Merl E. Reed, eds., *Race, Class, and Community in Southern Labor History* (Tuscaloosa: University of Alabama Press, 1994); Robert Zieger, ed., *Southern Labor History in Transition, 1940–1995* (Knoxville: University of Tennessee Press, 1997). The literature on the various industries and occupations include Tera Hunter, *To 'Joy My Freedom: Southern Black Women's Lives and Labor after the Civil War* (Cambridge, MA: Harvard University Press, 1997); Robin Kelley, *Hammer and Hoe: Alabama Communists during the Great Depression* (Chapel Hill: University of North Carolina Press, 1990); Bryant Simon, *A Fabric of Defeat: The Politics of South Carolina Millhands, 1910–1948* (Chapel Hill: University of North Carolina Press, 1998).

6. On segregation of locals, see Minutes of the United Brotherhood of Carpenters and Joiners of America, Local 993, July 31, 1914, August 7, 1914, September 4, 1914, August 8, 1919, October 17, 1919, December 5, 1919, February 27, 1920, *U.B.C. Local 125 Records*, Otto G. Richter Library Archives and Special Collections, University of Miami [hereafter, *Min-L993-UBCJA*], box 4.

7. Thomas Castillo, "Miami's Hidden Labor History," *Florida Historical Quarterly* 82, no. 4 (Spring 2004): 438–67; *Carpenter*, August 1916, August 1917, August 1919, and August 1925; *MM*, September 25, 1919, 8; September 26, 1926, 2. On overtime pay, see *MM*, November 14, 1917, 1, and 1931 by-laws, Local 993, United Brotherhood of Carpenters and Joiners of America (UBCJA) Records, Special Collections and University Archives, University of Maryland. College Park [hereafter, UMD-UBCJA], series 1, box 8, folder 28. Time-and-a-half became the rule by 1935 (1935 by-laws).

8. *Carpenter*, January 1914, 44; *Proceedings of the Fifteenth Annual Convention of the Florida State Federation of Labor*, Miami, Florida, January 1915, 5 (establishment of East Coast District Council and its coverage); *Carpenter*, October 1931, 19 (date of founding of Local 993). A 1925 letter from the East Coast District Council indicated that the region was 85 percent organized (*Carpenter*, December 1925, 52). See *Miami City Directory* (Jacksonville, FL: R. L. Polk, 1904–25), for a list of labor unions.

9. Trustees' Report of Local 993, *U.B.C. Local 125 Records*, Otto G. Richter Library Archives and Special Collections, University of Miami, box 3; US Bureau of the Census, *Fourteenth Census of the Population, 1920*, vol. 4, *Occupations* (Washington, DC: US GPO, 1922), 288.

10. *MH*, May 19, 1919, 8; *MH*, June 2, 1919, 5; *MM*, September 13, 1919, 1 (hod-carrier wages).

11. *MM*, April 17, 1917, 8; July 19, 1917, 11 (MBCA incorporates). The newspapers sometimes also called them the Masters Building or Miami Contractors Association and, later, in 1926, the Building Exchange.

12. Herbert Hill, "The Racial Practices of Organized Labor—the Age of Gompers and After," in Arthur M. Ross and Herbert Hill, eds., *Employment, Race, and Poverty* (New York: Harcourt, Brace and World, 1967). Among the many examples of the recent resurgence, see Paul Frymer, *Black and Blue: African Americans, the Labor Movement, and the Decline of the Democratic Party* (Princeton, NJ: Princeton University Press, 2008).

13. David Roediger and Elizabeth Esch, *The Production of Difference: Race and the Management of Labor in U.S. History* (New York: Oxford University Press, 2012); see

also Eric Arnesen's useful analysis of the whiteness-study school of thought, "Whiteness and the Historians' Imagination," *International Labor and Working-Class History* no. 60 (Fall 2001): 3–32.

14. Karl Polyani, *The Great Transformation: The Political and Economic Origins of Our Time* (Boston: Beacon Press, 1991), 185–86. He reminded readers that "the employers' demand for mobility of labor and flexibility of wages really means . . . a market in which human labor is a commodity."

15. AFL, Executive Council Records, Vote Books, reel 13, frames 627–29, AFL Records, http://www.gompers.umd.edu/SG%20Clayton%20defense%201915.htm; International Labour Office, International Labour Organization, *Labour Provisions of the Peace Treaties* (Geneva: International Labour Office, 1920), https://www.ilo.org/public/libdoc/ilo/1920/20B09_18_engl.pdf; "American Labor Endorses Peace Treaty and Covenant," *American Legislative Review* 9 (1919): 320–21 (Furuseth quote); Stein Evju, "Labour Is Not a Commodity: Reappraising the Origins of the Maxim," *European Labour Journal* 4, no. 3 (2013): 222–29; Paul O'Higgins, "'Labour Is Not a Commodity'—an Irish Contribution to International Labour Law," *Industrial Law Journal* 26, no. 3 (September 1997): 225–34

16. *Min-L993-UBCJA*, May 18, 1917; August 10, 1917.

17. *MH*, November 29, 1917, 15 (Miami a "One Hundred per Cent Union Town"); *MM*, February 19, 1918, 1.

18. *MH*, March 13, 1917, 5; *MM*, May 4, 1917, 1 (building boom prospects); *MM*, May 2, 1917, 6; May 4, 1917, 6; May 16, 1917, 6 (noted the newspaper would "protest against the increased cost of food supplies"); April 9, 1917, 9 (home economics); May 1, 1917, 3 (Union Label League and Buyers Association); May 3, 1917, 5 (high school home economics).

19. *MM*, May 7, 1917, 5 (Cook quote); May 8, 1917, 1; May 9, 1917, 2; *MH*, May 9, 1917, 3.

20. *MM*, April 2, 1917, 5 (buy-at-home initiative); *MM*, March 26, 1918, 7 (Cook, food administrator, quotes); March 30, 1918, 7; April 9, 1918, 7; April 12, 1918, 1; April 16, 1918, 1; April 17, 1918, 1 (on opening and success of the Curb Market); July 26, 1918, 3 (city ordinance passes, allowing the Curb Market). The *Miami Metropolis* announced that "only those who grow products will be entitled to use the market [eliminating] all competition with the hucksters who buy produce from other counties to sell in Miami" (*MM*, July 26, 1918, 3). Writers' Program, Work Projects Administration, *Miami and Dade County including Miami Beach and Coral Gables*, American Guide series (Northport, NY: Bacon, Percy and Daggett, 1941), 130 (referencing the Curb Market). After having several homes, by 1941, the City Curb Market was located on SW Second Avenue at the Miami River, housed in a "white building with red tile roof and open on all sides."

21. "Buy-at-Home Campaign Starts Tomorrow," *MH*, April 1, 1917, 2; April 2, 1917, 5; 9, 16, 23; April 30, 1917; 7, 14, 21; May 28, 1917; June 4, 1917 (dates of full-page advertisements).

22. *MH*, April 18, 1917, 4 (letter dated April 4). Blackman's name was often misspelled as Blackmon.

23. *MM*, March 7, 1917, 2; *MH*, March 8, 1917, 2 (initial effort to organize clerks); *MM*, February 5, 1919, 8 (Burdine's *Enthusiast*); *MM*, July 19, 1917, 1 (clerk agreement);

July 20, 1917, 5 (clerks, Union Label League); *MM*, June 21, 1917, 1; *MM*, September 1, 1917, 2. *MH*, November 29, 1917, 7 (twenty-four labor unions in Miami).

24. *MM*, January 7, 1915, 7; January 15, 1915, 1, 3; *MH*, January 15, 1915, 1, 3; *Min-L993-UBCJA*, January 22, 1915. Castillo, "Miami's Hidden Labor History," engages more closely Local 993's history than this chapter does.

25. Cindy Hahamovich, *The Fruits of Their Labor: Atlantic Coast Farmworkers and the Making of Migrant Poverty, 1870–1945* (Chapel Hill: University of North Carolina Press, 1997); Frank Tobias Higbie, *Indispensable Outcasts: Hobo Workers and Community in the American Midwest, 1880–1930* (Urbana: University of Illinois Press, 2003); Jacqueline Jones, *The Dispossessed: America's Underclasses from the Civil War to the Present* (New York: Basic Books, 1992). See William P. Jones's brilliant analysis of how this trope of movement was used to undercut Black timber workers in *The Tribes of Black Ulysses: African American Lumber Workers in the Jim Crow South* (Urbana: University of Illinois Press, 2005).

26. Castillo, "Miami's Hidden Labor History"; *Carpenter*, August 1915; *Min-L993-UBCJA*, July 2, 1915; Walter Galenson, *The United Brotherhood of Carpenters: The First Hundred Years* (Cambridge, MA: Harvard University Press, 1983), 135–36 (on stay-away notices), 162–63 (on clearance cards, which allowed carpenters to get work). As applied to waitressing, see Dorothy Sue Cobble, *Dishing It Out: Waitresses and Their Unions in the Twentieth Century* (Urbana: University of Illinois Press, 1991), 138–39.

27. Both the *MM* and *MH* carried the lathers' union's employer notices between January and March. See, for example, *MM*, January 18, 1917, 6 (*Lathers*, November 1915, 21). The *Min-L993-UBCJA* and the *Carpenter* contain an active record of the reading and sending of correspondence between various locals across the country. The discussion between locals was often related to traveling carpenters, and so I suspect labor conditions were a consistent topic, but the letters were not kept by the local.

28. *Min-L993-UBCJA*, December 22, 1916 (meeting with contractors favoring wage demand), December 29, 1916 (plan to publish in both newspapers); *MM*, January 16, 1917, 2; *MH*, January 16, 1917, 8; *MM*, January 23, 1917, 4 (Blackman letter); *MH*, March 13, 1917, 5; *MM*, April 26, 1917, 2 (Local 1149).

29. *MM*, June 23, 1917, 1; *MH*, June 24, 1917 (painters' wage demand); "Contractors Not Willing to Pay Lathers $8 a Day," *MM*, July 16, 1917, 1; *MH*, April 28, 1917, 8 (wage scales).

30. 1931 by-laws, Local 993, UMD-UBCJA, box 180.

31. An insert on the front page of the August 6, 1917, the *Miami Metropolis* announced, "No Compromise Made by Painters Union." It discussed a letter the painters published in the *Miami Herald* that indicated that they were forcing contractors to pay their new wage rate on old and new contracts. The *Miami Herald* article itself is not extant (the month of July 1917 is missing in the archival record).

32. *Lathers*, September 1917, 18; *MM*, July 16, 1917, 1; August 6, 1917, 1; August 7, 1917, 1; August 8, 1917, 1; August 9, 1917, 1.

33. *MM*, July 16, 1917, 1 (wage rates). The calculation is as follows: 350¢ ÷ 1000 laths = .35¢ per lath. To figure how one could earn $6, simply divide 600¢ by .35 = 1,714. Divide this by 8 to get the per-hour production and then divide that by 60 minutes to get the per-minute productivity.

34. The calculation is as follows: 400¢ ($22 = $4 per day and $2 on a Saturday half-day) ÷ .35 (per nailed lath) = 1,142.857143 per 8-hour day; divided by 8 hours = 142.8571 per hour (*MM*, July 17, 1917, 8. Wadsworth comment in *MM*, August 6, 1917, 1.

35. *MM*, July 17, 1917, 8 (quotes); *MM*, July 16, 1917, 1 (*MM* initial article). The calculation is as follows: 1,142 × .40 (per lath unit price at $4 for 1,000 rate) = 456.8 ÷ 100¢ = $4.568 daily wage.

36. *MM*, July 17, 1917, 8; *MM*, July 16, 1917, 1.

37. *MM*, May 22, 1917, 1. The carpenters' union investigated Comer's worksites for potential violations of wage and hour standards (*Min-L993-UBCJA*, April 27, 1917) and later brought charges that a union rule was violated when one of their own worked with scab labor, which may have meant working with African Americans doing skilled work in this instance (*Min-L993-UBCJA*, October 26, 1917).

38. *MM*, August 6, 1917, 1 (Wadsworth); August 7, 1917, 1; August 8, 1917, 1 (Shaw); *MM*, August 9, 1917, 1. *Lathers*, November 1914, 5 (on lathing bosses).

39. *MM*, August 7, 1917, 2 (italics added).

40. *MM*, July 24, 1917 (chamber of commerce quotes), 1; July 27, 1917, 4 (quotes about union labor); August 7, 1917, 4 (*MM* not supporting wage reduction); August 11, 1917, 6 (*MM* editorial continuing theme incompetent labor).

41. *MM*, August 7, 1917, 4 (quotes); *MM*, August 11, 1917, 6 (demand for higher back wages).

42. *MM*, November 14, 1917, 1, November 15, 1917, 1 (overtime); December 24, 1917, 1; December 26, 1917, 2; December 29, 1917, 1; December 31, 1917, 1 (Richardson Company); January 7, 1918, 1; January 10, 1918, 1; January 11, 1918, 2; January 16, 1918, 2 (painters).

43. *MM*, January 17, 1918, 1; January 19, 1918, 1; January 22, 1918, 1.

44. *MM*, January 19, 1918, 1; *MH*, January 20, 1918, 16 (BTC letter); *MM*, January 19, 1918, 12 (IBEW letter); January 17, 1918, 1 (Red Cross quotes).

45. Labor union business agents in the construction industry were union representatives who traveled to jobsites ensuring that unionists were hired, union wages paid, and union job rules followed. Employers took issue with these representatives because of their challenge of employer managerial prerogative.

46. *MM*, July 14, 1917, 2 (home guard); January 19, 1918, 12 (announcing purchase of liberty bonds); January 18, 1918, 1; January 19, 1918, 12 (City Day Care Nursery); February 2, 1918, 1; *MH*, February 2, 1918, 1 (description of Columbia painting); *MM*, February 2, 1918, 2; February 8, 1918, 16 (armory); February 13, 1918, 3 (full-page war savings stamps advertisement); April 8, 1918, 1 (Liberty parade); February 9, 1918, 1 (ultimatum); February 12, 1918, 1; February 13, 1918, 1; February 14, 1918, 1; February 15, 1918, 1 (labor's rejection).

47. *Min-L993-UBCJA*, February 18, 1918; March 1, 1918 (agreement noted but no details offered); *MM*, March 5, 1918, 1; March 13, 1918, 1 (report agreements reached); February 9, 1918, 1 (MBCA statement); February 11, 1918, 1 (Fidler comment); *MH*, March 8, 1918 (Bridges's letter).

48. Soldiering means underworking. Soldiering was a term used by employers and it was made famous by Frederick Winslow Taylor at the beginning of the twentieth century. Taylor considered it "the greatest evil," and he identified two forms: natural (individual tendency "to take it easy") and systematic (pressure from coworkers). An-

tiunion employers made this charge against organized labor (Taylor, *The Principles of Scientific Management* [1911; repr., Mineola, NY: Dover, 1998], 3–10).

49. *MM*, July 17, 1917, 12; January 19, 1918, 12; *MH*, February 12, 1918, 5 (Hansen letter); *MM*, January 28, 1918, 1 (Hendrick's comments; meeting called by F. H. Davis of the Good Government League "for the purpose of showing the patriotism of the laboring men of Miami"); *MM*, November 26, 1915, 2 ("former drinking man"); *MM*, February 12, 1918, 4; January 28, 1918, 1 (working-class percentage).

50. Small sample of the evidence: *MM*, August 20, 1917, 2; September 22, 1917, 1; October 15, 1917, 1 (agriculture); August 6, 1918, 1 (temporary waiving of literacy to begin in October); January 25, 1918, 4 (aviation field, Arcadia, Florida); October 27, 1917, 3 (government cantonment, Jacksonville, Florida); October 24, 1918, 2 (Penniman, Virginia). On Charleston: *MM*, September 9, 1918, 7; October 7, 1918, 7 (skilled workers); August 10, 1918, 1; August 13, 1918, 2; August 14, 1918, 1 (Bahamian workers); *MM*, October 11, 1918, 8 (wage demands).

51. J. R. Livingston, "Twenty-Five Years of Service to Labor and Our Community," *Miami Citizen*, April 15, 1943. The *Miami Central News* changed its name to the *Miami News* soon after its founding, then again in 1937 to the *Miami Citizen*, then later in the 1940s to the *Miami Labor Citizen*, until finally to the *South Florida Labor Tribune* by the 1960s. Extant copies first begin in September 1933.

52. Kazin, *Barons of Labor*, ch. 8. See also "Retail Prices, 1913 to December 1923," *Bulletin of the United States Bureau of Labor Statistics*, No. 366 (Washington, DC: US GPO, 1925), 7.

53. *MM*, May 1, 1919, 1; May 3, 1919, 1; *MH*, June 1, 1919, 12 (Blackman quote and comments); *MM*, August 14, 1919, 14; August 18, 1919, 1; August 26, 1919, 2 (on painters); August 25, 1919, 1 (chauffeur wage hike); *MM*, August 22, 1919, 1 (high cost of living).

54. *MM*, October 24, 1919, 6 ("square deal city"). For the second string of labor conflict in mid-October till the first ten days in November, only the *Miami Metropolis* has extant copies between October and December. See also Greater Miami Employers' Association, *One Year of Open Shop in Miami, Florida* (Miami: Greater Miami Employers' Association, 1920).

55. Greater Miami Employers' Association, *One Year of Open Shop*, 3. Castillo, "Miami's Hidden Labor History," 447, 466. On the issue of union corruption, see David Witwer, *Corruption and Reform in the Teamsters Union* (Urbana: University of Illinois Press, 2003); Witwer, *Shadow of the Racketeer: Scandal in Organized Labor* (Urbana: University of Illinois Press, 2009).

56. *Carpenter*, December 1920, 39; *Proceedings of the Twenty-First Annual Convention of the Florida State Federation of Labor*, West Palm Beach, Florida, 1921, 25–26; The literature on the open shop is vast; see Sidney Fine, *"Without Blare of Trumpets": Walter Drew, the National Erectors' Association, and the Open Shop Movement, 1903–57* (Ann Arbor: University of Michigan Press, 1995); Chad Pearson, *Reform or Repression: Organizing America's Anti-union Movement* (Philadelphia: University of Pennsylvania Press, 2016); Rosemary Feurer and Chad Pearson, *Against Labor: How U.S. Employers Organized to Defeat Union Activism* (Urbana: University of Illinois Press, 2017).

57. *MM*, June 16, 1921, 1.

58. *MM*, June 16, 1921, 10; *MM*, April 10, 1920, 8 (GMEA advertisement).

59. *MM*, September 17, 1923, 6 (women); September 20, 21, 1923, sec. 2, 1; September 29, 1923, 12 (advertisement: "The Workers Future Depends upon the Route"); *Sheet Metal Workers Journal*, October 12, 1923, sec. 2, 1; October 15, 1923, 12.

60. *MM*, January 7, 1924, 17 (first of the advertising campaign); January 9, 1924, 5A (explanation of the campaign); February 11, 1924, 17 (platform); March 11, 1924, 2 (commodity); June 22, 1924, 2 (last of the campaign).

61. William Leiserson, "Closed Shop and Open Shop," *Encyclopedia of the Social Sciences* (New York: Macmillan, 1930), 3, 568–70. Leiserson highlighted that "trade unionists frankly defend the principle of the closed shop although in practice, because of the active opposition of employers and through considerations of expediency, they consent to open and preferential shops" (569).

62. *MM*, June 7, 1921, 4 (Jennings residency); January 26, 1922, 1 (Jennings speech); 1921 Charter of the City of Miami, Florida, http://dpanther.fiu.edu/dpanther/items/itemdetail?bibid=FI00007784&vid=00001.

63. *MDN* (*MM* changed to *Miami Daily News*), July 9, 1927, 2; July 11, 1927, 20 (McClurg quote); July 12, 1927, 15; "Miami Unions Cut Their Pay Scales," *MDN*, September 4, 1928, 1.

Chapter 4. Winter Playground Blues

1. *MDN*: March 5, 1933, sec. 2, 8 (Larus); February 27, 1933, 14 (Ade). The booster practice of publishing visitors' testimonials witnessing the good times in Miami was a steadfast tradition. During the Depression, this advertising scheme sought to illustrate how the economic downturn escaped south Florida. See the 1931–32 winter *MDN*'s advertisement series, "Miami Prosperity as Others See It" (e.g., November 9, 1931, 1).

2. *MDN*, March 1, 1933, 1, 16, 18 (Albreicht, fish, and charities); March 2, 1933, 9 (sample charitable event).

3. *Miami* [Labor] *News* [hereafter *MN*], April 15, 1937. The newspaper changed its name later in the year to the *Miami Citizen*. It started in April 1919 and continued to the mid-1960s, changing its name a few more times.

4. US Census Bureau, *Fifteenth Census of the United States: 1930; Unemployment*, vol. 1, *General Report* (Washington, DC: US Government Printing Office, 1932), 5–7, 235, 236, 252, 253. See Alexander Keyssar, *Out of Work: The First Century of Unemployment in Massachusetts* (Cambridge: Cambridge University Press, 1986) for unemployment before the 1920s; see chapter 3 and especially appendix B (342–58) about issues with unemployment statistics before 1940, such as the "gainful worker" concept.

5. US Census Bureau, *Fifteenth Census*, 1: 236. See also Susan Porter Benson's *Household Accounts: Working-Class Family Economies in the Interwar United States* (Ithaca, NY: Cornell University Press, 2007) for a discussion of family survival strategies during interwar years.

6. John D. Biggers, *Census of Partial Employment, Unemployment, and Occupations: 1937*, vol. 1 (Washington DC: GPO, 1938), ix–xi, 463, 477 (unemployment statistics);

Nathan Mayo, *Sixth Census of the State of Florida: 1935* (Winter Park, FL: Orange, 1936), 91 (population numbers).

7. *Census of Partial Employment*, ix–xi, 463, 477 (1937 statistics); US Bureau of the Census, *Sixteenth Census of the United States: 1940; Population*, vol. 3, *The Labor Force: Occupation, Industry, Employment, and Income*, pt. 2, Alabama–Indiana (Washington, DC: US GPO, 1943), 629; Eric Beecroft and Seymour Janow, "Toward a National Policy for Migration," *Social Forces* 16, no. 4 (May 1938): 476n6. The total number of unemployed in 1937 increased for both Blacks (from 2,557 to 3,241) and whites (from 3,935 to 5,939). White women, though, experienced the greatest increase, from 574 to 2,095 (2,465 if one adds partially unemployed). In 1940, 8.5 percent of whites were unemployed (men = 9% and women = 7.3%) and 11.2% of Blacks were (men = 11% and women = 11.4%), according to the census.

8. *MDN*, February 9, 1931, 4 (Perrine Palmer letter).

9. *Congressional Record*, 72 cong., 1st sess., February 2, 1932, 3118.

10. *MN*, September 28, 1933 (Palmer); October 26, 1933 (Palmer); July 26, 1934 (Palmer); May 8, 1935, August 8, 1935, August 15, 1935, August 22, 1935.

11. Bernice Sawyer, "Tell the Story," interview by Stephanie Wanza, October 25, 1997, 8–9, the Black Archives, History and Research Foundation of South Florida.

12. The histories of both these institutions (and other exclusive clubs, such as the Surf and Bath Clubs) have not been written. The Committee of 100 started after the hurricane of 1926 and Miami Beach builder Carl Fisher and two partners started the Cocolobo Cay Club in 1916. Jennifer Browne Leynes and David Cullison, *Biscayne National Park: A Historical Resource Study* (Atlanta: National Park Service, 2008), 23–24, http://dpanther.fiu.edu/dpService/dpPurlService/purl/FIGO000057/00001, mentions the Cocolobo Cay Club. *MDN* (December 14, 1930, 11) reported that "the clubhouse is on a 60-acre island, facing Biscayne Bay to the west, Caesar's Creek to the south, and the ocean to the east. The only means of access to the island is by boat or airplane," and that the average wealth of members was $15 million (more than $229 million in 2019 dollars). See chapter 1 of Thomas A. Castillo's "Laboring in the Magic City: Workers in Miami, 1914–1941," Ph.D. diss. (University of Maryland, 2011) for more on the Committee of One Hundred.

13. Helen Muir, *Miami, U.S.A.* (1953; repr., Gainesville: University Press of Florida, 2000), 163–68 (on Al Capone); *MDN*, May 16, 1930, 20 (ordinance discussed); *MH*, May 15, 1930, 1, 2 (ordinance).

14. *MDN*, November 11, 1933 (Miami Beach fingerprinting), 5; *Miami Tribune*, November 15, 1934, 3 (Miami Beach); *MH*, January 26, 1935, 10; *Miami Tribune*, January 29, 1935, 2 (Miami adopts fingerprinting law for all bar and night-club workers); *Evening Independent* (St. Petersburg, FL), November 5, 1936, 1 (Miami Beach fingerprinting law). See introduction of this book for a brief discussion of the hiring of private detectives during the tourist season.

15. *MH*, May 15, 1930, 1, 2 (labor rep observation); May 20, 1930, 1, 2; May 23, 1930, 1; *MDN*, May 16, 1930, 20; May 23, 1930, 1 (quote from commissioner).

16. *MDN*, March 8, 1930, 16 (Lemon City Improvement Association, labor competition, and unsightly comment). For letters discussing tourist camps, see *MDN*, November 11, 1930, 6 (Lemon City Improvement Association); *MDN*, November 14, 1930, 4 (tourist

camp owner); for editorial that triggered this exchange, see *MDN*, November 7, 1930, 6. See also Chamber of Commerce, *Minutes of the Board of Directors Meetings*, September 16, 1929, HistoryMiami Museum (on petition to remove a tourist camp in Lemon City). On tin-can tourists, see *NYT*, December 31, 1922, 82; *NYT*, October 27, 1935, 21; *MDN*, October 18, 1937, 4; *MDN*, January 10, 1937, 1D (number of tourist-camp trailers); Warren James Belasco, *Americans on the Road: From Autocamp to Motel, 1910–1945* (Cambridge, MA: MIT Press, 1979), 56, 111–22.

17. *Planning Your Vacation in Florida: Miami and Dade County, including Miami Beach and Coral Gables* (Northport, NY: Bacon, Percy, and Daggett, 1941), 4, 5; Gary W. McDonough, *The Florida Negro: A Federal Writers' Legacy* (Jackson: University Press of Mississippi, 1993), 39–40; *MDN*, November 29, 1939, 13A (snowbirds); December 5, 1932, 4 (home labor effort).

18. *MDN*, April 21, 1931, 4 (Sears); September 13, 1931, 8 (Burdine's and Miami for Miamians); October 21, 1931, 4 (job hunter).

19. Miami Office of the City Clerk, Resolutions and Minutes of the City Commission, Florida State Archives, Tallahassee, Res. 6359, August 18, 1930; Res. 8129, June 28, 1933; Res. 9347, September 28, 1934; *MDN*, June 29, 1933, 1; September 28, 1934, 1, 11.

20. *MDN*, November 22, 1932, 14 (home labor); November 23, 1932, 5 (home labor); December 5, 1932, 4 (Floridians Incorporated); December 9, 1932, 6 (home labor); December 11, 1932, 2 (Kaplan); *MN*, December 13, 1934 (Palmer); *MDN*, December 8, 1935, 8 (home-labor employers).

21. John N. Webb, *The Transient Unemployed* (Washington, DC: Works Progress Administration, 1935), 24–42.

22. Nels Anderson, *The Hobo: The Sociology of the Homeless Man* (Chicago: University of Chicago Press, 1923); Nels Anderson, *On Hobos and Homelessness*, ed. Raffaele Rauty (Chicago: University of Chicago Press, 1998); Todd Depastino, *Citizen Hobo: How a Century of Homelessness Shaped America* (Chicago: University of Chicago Press, 2003); Frank Tobias Higbie, *Indispensable Outcasts: Hobo Workers and Community in the American Midwest, 1880–1930* (Urbana: University of Illinois Press, 2003); Kenneth L. Kusmer, *Down and Out, on the Road: The Homeless in American History* (New York: Oxford University Press, 2002), 169–237. A relative silence remains for the East Coast phenomenon. Critically important texts for these migrations include Cindy Hahamovich, *The Fruits of Their Labor: Atlantic Coast Farmworkers and the Making of Migrant Poverty, 1870–1945* (Chapel Hill: University of North Carolina Press, 1997); Jones, *The Dispossessed*. Jeffery S. Cole, "'Hopeful People on the Move': The Urban South and the Transient Problem during the Great Depression," in *The New Deal and Beyond: Social Welfare in the South since 1930*, ed. Elna C. Green, 47–70 (Athens: University of Georgia Press, 2003.

23. Joan M. Crouse, *The Homeless Transient in the Great Depression: New York State, 1929–1941* (Albany: State University of New York Press, 1986), 94–123; Mark Pittenger, *Class Unknown: Undercover Investigations of American Work and Poverty from the Progressive Era to the Present* (New York: New York University Press, 2012), 9–113; Depastino, *Citizen Hobo*, 195–220; Beecroft and Janow, "Toward a National Policy," 478 (esp. note 15 on Los Angeles police and unemployed). For later civil-rights efforts for transients, see Risa Goluboff, *Vagrant Nation: Police Power, Constitutional Change, and the Mak-*

ing of the 1960s (New York: Oxford University Press, 2016). I will use the term *hobo* interchangeably with *transient unemployed* to highlight the historical context and the condescension and marginalization faced by this diverse group of migrants.

24. *MDN*, December 1, 1928, 4 (Hofman letter); December 8, 1929, 8; December 8, 1931, 4 (for an example of one hitchhiker relating their experience and thoughts about the hobo express); November 27, 1932, 2; September 27, 1934, 1.

25. The National Association of Travelers Aid Societies, *A Brief Report on Transient Families in Florida* (Washington, DC: President's Organization on Unemployment Relief, 1931); "Transient Families in Arizona and Florida," *Monthly Labor Review* 33, no. 6 (December 1931): 1363–65; Helen C. Mawer, *Organization and Activities of the State Board of Public Welfare, January 1, 1931, to January 1, 1933* (Tallahassee, FL: State Board of Public Welfare, 1933), 47–48.

26. L. O. Scarboro, chief city detective, claimed in 1958 that the hobo express had started in 1927, which is not unlikely. I found no evidence, however, to indicate that it was the case. The first reference I discovered to the hobo express was in the fall of 1928; the coverage and newspaper description suggests that was the hobo express's inaugural run. Jane Wood, "In Days When Jobless Drifted South, Miami Ran a Unique 'Hobo Express,'" *Miami News* (name had changed from the *MDN*), February 23, 1958, 5B (informal journalistic history); *MDN*, October 30, 1928, 4; *MDN*, December 21, 1928, 1.

27. *Planning Your Vacation in Florida*, 6; *MDN*, February 23, 1958, 5B; December 21, 1928, 1; December 3, 1929; December 1, 1931, 15; December 2, 1931, 7.

28. Sidney L. Harring, *Policing a Class Society: The Experience of American Cities, 1865–1915* (New Brunswick, NJ: Rutgers University Press, 1983), 201–23; Edward L. Ayers, *The Promise of the New South: Life after Reconstruction* (New York: Oxford University Press, 1992), 154; Kusmer, *Down and Out*, 66–69.

29. *MDN*, November 29, 1939, 13A; December 12, 1931, 4 (Harris).

30. *MDN*, February 12, 1931, 1 (beggars Bayfront Park); October 1, 1931, 3 (another example of similar effort).

31. *MDN*, September 22, 1931, 1; November 26, 1931; November 27, 1932, 2; December 7, 1931. The November 27 article mentioned that in 1931 a hobo jungle formed in the woods of Hallandale (south Broward, just north of the Dade border), "menacing isolated homes," because of the lack of Broward County cooperation.

32. *MDN*, November 29, 1939, 13A; February 23, 1958, 5B; labor's *Miami News*, July 18, 25, 1935.

33. *MDN*, September 21, 1931, 2 (Cora Bain quote); Harry Hopkins, *Spending and Saving: The Complete Story of Relief* (1936; repr., Seattle: University of Washington Press, 1972), 19; *NYT*, October 9, 1931, 13 (Carlton fear of flooding migrants). The ten other states were New York, Rhode Island, Indiana, Michigan, Connecticut, Illinois, California, West Virginia, Delaware, and Missouri.

34. *MDN*, December 6, 1931, 4 (Reeder); Keyssar, *Out of Work*, 159, 253–62, 272.

35. *MDN*, December 17, 1933 (Green), 1; December 19, 1933, 1 (Fagg); December 24, 1933, 16 (Matlock article); December 30, 1934, 8; Cole, "Hopeful People," 53–54.

36. *MDN*, December 24, 1933, 16 (Matlock article).

37. *Congressional Record*, 72 cong., 2nd sess., February 20, 1933, 4503–4 (Florida

senator discussing the camp in Congress); *MDN*, April 25, 1933, 8; December 24, 1933, 16; December 5, 1934, 4; December 30, 1934, 8. For a general overview of poverty and welfare, see Michael Katz, *In the Shadow of the Poorhouse: A Social History of Welfare in America* (New York: Basic Books, 1986).

38. *MDN*, December 5, 1934, 1; October 11, 1935, 2; October 8, 1936, 11; Florida Emergency Relief Administration, Department of Research and Statistics, *Review of Relief and Economic Statistics* 32, no. 2 (March 1935): 9–11; *Atlanta Constitution*, December 18, 1934, 10; *Atlanta Constitution*, December 19, 1934, 8; *Atlanta Constitution*, December 21, 1934, 6; *Atlanta Constitution*, October 8, 1936, 22; *NYT*, October 25, 1936, E10; *NYT*, November 20, 1936, 13; Beecroft and Janow, "Toward a National Policy" 479n25).

39. *NYT*, April 10, 1936, 3; *NYT*, February 5, 1936, 2; *NYT*, February 15, 1936, 17; Beecroft and Janow, "Toward a National Policy," 478–80; Walter J. Stein, *California and the Dust Bowl Migration* (Westport, CT: Greenwood, 1973), 73–75.

40. Roger Daniels, *Coming to America: A History of Immigration and Ethnicity in American Life* (Princeton, NJ: Perennial, 2002), 274; James Gregory, *American Exodus: The Dust Migration and Okie Culture in California* (New York: Oxford University Press, 1989), 78–113; Francisco E. Balderrama and Raymond Rodriguez, *Decade of Betrayal: Mexican Repatriation in the 1930s*, rev. ed. (Albuquerque: University of New Mexico, 2006).

41. *MDN*, December 30, 1928, 4; December 8, 1929, 8; December 12, 1931, 4 (R. F. Harris letter). Examples of firsthand accounts of the hobo express include the following letters: *MDN*, November 10, 1931, 4; December 3, 1931, 4; December 8, 1931, 4.

42. *Chicago Tribune*, December 3, 1931, 13; *Atlanta Constitution*, December 18, 1934, 6 (Pegler); "Sunny Florida: America's Winter Playground Bars the Indigent, Welcomes the Affluent," *Literary Digest*, November 7, 1937, 6–7; *NYT*, October 25, 1936, E10; *NYT*, December 20, 1936, E7.

43. *Washington Post*, January 16, 1937, 14 (Cone ends border patrol); *NYT*, September 11, 1937, 4 (Cone reasserts policy); October 3, 1937, C7 (border patrol not to be reinstituted); *MDN*, October 29, 1937, 1, 2 (Cone protest against hobo express); October 30, 1937, 1 (hobo express); October 31, 1937, H6 (hobo express to continue).

Chapter 5. Appeals to Harmony

1. *Tampa Daily Times*, February 2, 1914; February 9, 1914; September 3, 1933, 4 (Palmer letter); *MDN*, September 8, 1933, 6 (Townley letter on Nicholson); MH, November 5, 1933, 28, and MDN, November 6, 1933, 12 (Nicholson obituaries). Nicholson had lived in Miami for ten years. He was survived by his wife Martha, and his body was sent to Albany, New York, where his brother Fredrick lived.

2. *Report of the Proceedings of the Southern Conference for Human Welfare*, Birmingham, Alabama, November 20–23, 1938, 31 (located in several libraries).

3. Lizabeth Cohen, *Making a New Deal: Industrial Workers in Chicago, 1919–1939* (New York: Cambridge University Press, 1990); Meg Jacobs, *Pocketbook Politics: Economic Citizenship in Twentieth Century America* (Princeton, NJ: Princeton University Press, 2004).

4. Ethan V. Blackman, *Miami and Dade County, Florida: Its Settlement, Progress and Achievement* (Washington, DC: Victor Rainbolt, 1921); Isidor Cohen, *Historical Sketches and Sidelights of Miami, Florida* (Miami: self-pub., 1925); Tracy Hollingsworth, *History of Dade County, Florida* (Miami: Miami Post, 1936); Thelma Peters, *Biscayne Country, 1870–1926* (Miami: Banyan, 1981); Arva Moore Parks, *Miami: The Magic City* (Miami: Centennial, 1991).

5. See, for example, Raymond Mohl, "Black Immigrants: Bahamians in Early Twentieth-Century Miami," *Florida Historical Quarterly* 65, no. 3 (1987): 271–97; Mohl, "Trouble in Paradise: Race and Housing in Miami During the New Deal Era," *Prologue: Journal of the National Archives* 19, no. 1 (Spring 1987): 7–21 ; Paul George, "Passage to the New Eden: Tourism in Miami through Everest G. Sewell," *Florid Historical Quarterly* 59, no. 4 (April 1981): 440–63; Melanie Shell-Weiss, *Coming to Miami: A Social History* (Gainesville: University Press of Florida, 2009).

6. See my discussion in chapter 1; Alex Lichtenstein, "'We at Last Are Industrializing the Whole Ding-Busted Party': The Communist Party and Florida Workers in Depression and War," in *Florida's Working-Class Past: Current Perspectives on Labor, Race, and Gender from Spanish Florida to New Immigration*, ed. Robert Cassanello and Melanie Shell-Weiss (Gainesville: University Press of Florida, 2009).

7. *MDN*, May 27, 28, 1952 (obituary); Arva Moore Parks and Gregory W. Bush, *Miami: The American Crossroads, A Centennial Journey, 1896–1996* (Coral Gables, FL: Simon and Schuster Custom, 1996), 48 (reference to Sarah Palmer and Palmer's son, Perrine Palmer Jr.; the text is silent on Palmer Sr.); Michael G. Schene, "Indian Key," *Tequesta* 36 (1976): 3–27; Sarah R. W. Palmer, "Henry Perrine, Pioneer Botanist and Horticulturalist," *Florida Historical Quarterly* 5, no. 2 (October 1926): 112–16. US Bureau of the Census, 1920 Census Schedules for Miami and Dade County, 1900, 1910, 1920, and 1930.

8. *MDN*, May 27, 28, 1952; "New Mills and Equipment," *American Lumberman*, January 20, 1917, 69 (announcement of lumber company, Palmer, and English); Parks and Bush, *Miami*, 48; census schedules, 1900, 1910, 1920, 1930. College information is from the student records of the Archives and Special Collections at Jesse du Pont Library, University of the South, Sewanee, Tennessee; *Palmer v. C. E. Frosst & Co.*, 139 Va. 239; *MDN*, September 27, 1928, 4; October 29, 1928, 4; Palmer was listed as a new member of the Florida Historical Society in "Notes and Comments," *Florida Historical Quarterly* 5, no. 2 (October 1926): 120.

9. Town of Howey-in-the-Hills, Florida, website, accessed May 22, 2020, https://www.howey.org/community/page/clone-history-howey-hills.

10. Gary Gerstle, *Working-Class Americanism: The Politics of Labor in a Textile City, 1914–1960* (Princeton, NJ: Princeton University Press, 1989), 5–15, 153–95.

11. Gerstle, *Working-Class Americanism*, 5–15, 153–195; Warren Susman, *Culture as History: The Transformation of American Society in the Twentieth Century* (Washington, DC: Smithsonian Institution, 1973), 75–85; Michael Denning, *The Cultural Front: The Laboring of American Culture in the Twentieth Century* (London: Verso, 1997), 124–36, 152.

12. Charles Maier, "Between Taylorism and Technocracy: European Ideologies and the Vision of Industrial Productivity in the 1920s," *Journal of Contemporary History* 5,

no. 2 (1970): 29–34; Howard Brick, *Transcending Capitalism: Visions of a New Society in Modern American Thought* (Ithaca, NY: Cornell University Press, 2006), 1–151; Shelton Stromquist, *Reinventing "The People": The Progressive Movement, the Class Problem, and the Origins of Modern Liberalism* (Urbana: University of Illinois Press, 2006), 1–11, 21–24.

13. David Montgomery, *Beyond Equality: Labor and the Radical Republicans, 1862–1872* (1967; repr., Urbana: University of Illinois Press, 1981); Roy Rosenzweig, *Eight Hours for What We Will: Workers and Leisure in an Industrial City, 1870–1920* (New York: Cambridge University Press, 1983 (New York:); Philip S. Foner and David R. Roediger, *Our Own Time: A History of American Labor and the Working Day* (London: Verso, 1989).

14. Benjamin Kline Hunnicutt, *Work without End: Abandoning Shorter Hours for the Right to Work* (Philadelphia: Temple University Press, 1988); Hunnicutt, *Kellogg's Six-Hour Day* (Philadelphia: Temple University Press, 1996).

15. Henry Elsner Jr., *The Technocrats: Prophets of Automation* (Syracuse, NY: Syracuse University Press, 1967); William E. Akin, *Technocracy and the American Dream: The Technocrat Movement, 1900–1941* (Berkeley: University of California Press, 1977); Patrick D. Reagan, *Designing a New America: The Origins of New Deal Planning, 1890–1943* (Amherst: University of Massachusetts Press, 1999).

16. *MDN*, January 31, 1931, 2 (Cooper and Chamber); Clayton Sedgwick Cooper, *The Philosophy of Business* (Miami: Burdine's, 1927), 10; Cooper, *College Men and the Bible* (New York: Association Press, 1911); Cooper, *The Modernizing of the Orient* (New York: McBride, Nast, 1914); Cooper, *Latin America: Men and Markets* (New York: Ginn, 1927).

17. "Millionaires' Talk," *Time*, October 14, 1935, 68–69 (discussing origin of the Committee of One Hundred); *MDN*, February 9, 1931, 4 (quotes); February 12, 1931, 6 (Palmer's continued discussion from February 9); February 17, 1931 (reader reacts positively to Palmer's letters).

18. Jacobs, *Pocketbook Politics*, 94–135; Hunnicutt, *Work without End*, 67–108; Steven Fraser, *Labor Will Rule: Sidney Hillman and the Rise of American Labor* (Ithaca, NY: Cornell University Press, 1991): 259–67. Roland Marchand, *Advertising the American Dream: Making Way for Modernity, 1920–1940* (Los Angeles: University of California Press, 1985): 117–63.

19. *MDN*, February 9, 1931, 4 (quotes); February 12, 1931, 6; April 6, 1931, 4 (another example of Palmer discussion of unemployment).

20. Hunnicutt, *Work without End*, 147–90; Hunnicutt, *Kellogg's Six-Hour Day*, 1–84.

21. *MDN*, February 9, 1931, 4; February 13, 1931, 6; February 17, 1931, 6; April 12, 1931, 4; May 8, 1931, 4 (M. E. Fidler, former CLU president and future president of the DCUCL).

22. Verner Townley, "Dr. John Dewey's Reply," *MDN*, January 8, 1932, 6 (quotes taken from this letter; also available in the John Dewey Collection, Special Collections, Morris Library, Southern Illinois University, Dewey VFM 79); *MDN*, January 27, 1932, 6 (other letter by Townley discussing Dewey exchange); March 3, 1932, 4 (Palmer).

23. Carlton W. Tebeau, *Synagogue in the Central City: Temple Israel of Greater Miami, 1922–1972* (Coral Gables, FL: University of Miami Press, 1972), 84–98.

24. *MDN*, March 27, 1932, Society Section, 8; March 19, 1932, 4 (meeting was held

on March 16); *MDN*, August 8, 1933 (Townley's history of Palmer Plan), 4; Palmer to Roosevelt, January 2, 1933, and February 10, 1933, FDR Presidential Library. In his letter "Communism No Remedy" (*MDN*, December 23, 1931, 6), Palmer published two letters he received responding to his own letters over the year. One was a solicitation from the local Communist Party organizer to join the party and the other was a notice he would be evicted. Palmer noted that "neither one of those letters, Mr. Editor, can be answered without answering both of them; not for me, but for the millions. . . . I will be glad to furnish you with copies of my answers to both, provided you will publish them in full, regardless of whose toes they may step on. Will you?" There is no record of any responses, and so one is left to wonder about the extent of Palmer's radicalism.

25. William Leuchtenburg, "The New Deal and the Analogue of War," in *Change and Continuity in the Twentieth Century America*, ed. John Braeman, Robert J. Brenner, and Everett Walters (Columbus: Ohio State University, 1964).

26. "The 'Palmer Plan,'" *MDN*, March 27, 1932, society section, 8.

27. "The 'Palmer Plan,'" *MDN*, March 27, 1932, Society Section, 8; Edward P. Costigan, "A National Political Armistice?" *Atlantic Monthly*, February 1931, 258–67 (quote on 262).

28. "Palmer Plan." For reactions to Palmer, see *MDN*, April 1, 1932, 4; April 11, 1932, 4.

29. *MH*, March 24, 1932, 1. Here are Palmer's objectionable words: "Are we apes or are we men? To admit that there is no simple immediate and permanent remedy, at least in America, for the social disease now epidemic all over the world, is to admit ourselves of a lower order of intelligence" ("Palmer Plan"). Positive thinking may have clouded these entrepreneurs' mind a bit. On positive thinking and business, see William Leach, *Land of Desire: Merchants, Power, and the Rise of a New American Culture* (New York: Vintage, 1994), 225–60.

30. *MDN*, April 3, 1932, sec. 2, 5.

31. *MDN*, April 25, 1932, 4 (Pinchot reference); "A Communist's View," *MDN*, April 6, 1932, 4 (Phelan wrote a letter on his destitution entitled "A Story of Hunger," *MDN*, November 29, 1931, 4); *MDN*, April 10, 1932, 4 (Singleton); Huey Long speech, *Congressional Record* 75, 72nd cong., 1st sess. (March 21, 1932): 6539–45. Singleton urged the *MDN* to publish Long's entire speech. The newspaper had been receiving so much mail, including reaction to the earlier, shorter versions of the extended Palmer Plan publication. See "The Forum" (*MDN*, March 18, 1932, 6), where the newspaper noted that it was impossible to print the enormous number of worthy letters it had been receiving. On government by injunction, see William Forbath, *Law and the Shaping of the American Labor Movement* (Cambridge, MA: Harvard University Press, 1991).

32. Hunnicutt, *Work without End*, 150–51; *MDN*, April 16, 1933, 4 (Palmer letter on Black bill). The AFL executive committee, in a January 1931 meeting in Miami, discussed the shorter-hour and share-the-work plan: The *MDN* quoted the AFL's William Green as saying, "I believe the five-day work week is the most important issue with the seven-hour working day next in importance. . . . [It would put] the nation back on a spending basis." *MDN*, January 13, 1931, 1, 2. The newspaper reported Green saying at Carpenters Union Hall that "Reduction of working hours a week, so all labor would share in the

benefits, is necessary because of the increase in the use of machinery" (*MDN*, January 18, 1931, 5).

33. *Report of the Proceedings of the American Federation of Labor, 1931*, 278–81; *Report of the Proceedings of the American Federation of Labor, 1932*, 284–97; *Report of the Proceedings of the American Federation of Labor, 1933*, 362–69, all in United Brotherhood of Carpenters and Joiners of America (UBCJA) Records, Special Collections and University Archives, University of Maryland [hereafter, UMD-UBCJA], series IV, subseries 2, box 8; Hunnicutt, *Work without End*, 76–84, 148–53, 186–87; Foner and Roediger, *Our Own Time*, 243–56; *MDN*, April 16, 1933, 4; January 13, 1931, 1, 2; January 18, 1931, 5.

34. Hunnicutt, *Work without End*, 105; Brick, *Transcending Capitalism*, 86–117.

35. Karl Marx, *Capital* (1976; repr., London: Penguin, 1990), 1: 375–89, esp., 381, on profit drive and its relation to the worker and workday: "*Après moi le déluge!* is the watchword of every capitalist and of every capitalist nation. Capital . . . takes no account of the health and the length of life of the worker, unless society forces it to do so" (381). For a discussion on how intellectuals engaged capitalism and its reforms, see Brick, *Transcending Capitalism*, 38–43.

36. Wayne W. Parrish, "What Is Technocracy?" *New Outlook* (November 1932): 13–18; Parrish, "Technocracy's Question," *New Outlook* (December 1932): 13–17; Parrish, "Technocracy's Challenge," *New Outlook* (January 1933): 13–16; Elsner, *Technocrats*; Akin, *Technocracy*; Robert Westbrook, "Tribune of the Technocratic Structure: The Popular Economics of Stuart Chase," *American Quarterly* 31, no. 4 (Autumn 1980): 387–408. For more another example of the literature and discussion in the period on technocracy, see Harold Loeb, *Life in a Technocracy: What It Might Be Like* (1933; repr., Syracuse, NY: Syracuse University Press, 1996).

37. *MDN*, November 22, 1932, 4 (Fripp); November 27, 1932, 4 (Townley); November 29, 1932, 4 (Palmer); November 30, 1932, 4; December 3, 1932, 4 (Nicholson); December 11, 1932, 4 (another letter engaging technocracy). The *MDN* published six articles (December 20–25) by syndicated journalist Pat Harrison of the News Enterprise Association on technocracy.

38. Parrish, "What Is Technocracy?" 13–18; *MDN*, November 29, 1932, 4; December 13, 1932, 4 (pictures a robot with the label "the industrial machine" standing above a soup kitchen and, just above the robot, "A Giant Surveys His Work," indicating the costs of technological unemployment). See also Amy Bix, *Inventing Ourselves Out of Jobs: America's Debate over Technological Unemployment, 1929–1981* (Baltimore, MD: Johns Hopkins University Press, 2000), for a larger history of technological employment; see further Frank Arkright, *The ABC of Technocracy* (London: Hamish Hamilton, 1930), for a contemporary articulation of technocracy.

39. Elsner, *Technocrats*, 44–97; Akin, *Technocracy*, 116–70.

40. *MN*, October 26, 1933 (Palmer letter); Harold Loeb, Felix Frazer, Carle Whitehead, and L. G. Sherer, *Technocracy*, "Plan of Plenty," July 4, 1933, Bear Lake, Estes Park, Colorado [location of the conference], Special Collections, Morris Library, Southern Illinois University, Carbondale; Elsner, *Technocrats*, 52–56.

41. Donald L. Miller, *The American Radicalism: Alfred M. Bingham and Non-Marxian Insurgency in the New Deal Era* (Port Washington, NY: Kennikat, 1979), 3–8; Edward J.

Bordeau, "John Dewey's Ideas and the Great Depression," *Journal of the History of Ideas* 32, no. 1 (1971): 67–84; Robert B. Westbrook, *John Dewey and American Democracy* (Ithaca, NY: Cornell University Press, 1991), 443–58.

42. Frank A. Warren, *An Alternative Vision: The Socialist Party in the 1930s* (Bloomington: Indiana University Press, 1974), 109–20, offers a fruitful discussion on how to not to judge the political and moral significance of a movement by the record of its "success."

43. *MDN*, November 29, 1932, 4 (Palmer); Roy Rosenzweig, "Radicals and the Jobless: The Musteites and the Unemployed Leagues, 1932–1936," *Labor History* 16, no. 1 (Winter 1975): 52–77; Rosenzweig, "Organizing the Unemployed: The Early Years of the Great Depression, 1929–1933," *Radical America* 10, no. 4 (July 1976): 37–61; Rosenzweig, "'Socialism in Our Time': The Socialist Party and the Unemployed, 1929–1936," *Labor History* 20, no. 4 (Fall 1979): 485–509.

44. Kevin Starr, *Endangered Dreams: The Great Depression in California* (New York: Oxford University Press, 1996), 121–55; George E. Rising, "An Epic Encounter: Upton Sinclair's 1934 California Campaign," *Southern California Quarterly* 79, no. 1 (Spring 1997): 101–24. On socialism and production for use, see Warren, *Alternative Vision*, 62–68.

45. *MDN*, November 29, 1932, 4. Palmer will echo this call seven months later in *MDN*, May 8, 1933, 4.

46. E. P. Thompson, *The Making of the English Working Class* (New York: Vintage, 1966), 12–13.

47. David Montgomery, *The Fall of the House of Labor: The Workplace, the State, and American Labor Activism, 1865–1925* (New York: Cambridge University Press, 1987), 282–88 (quotes on 286, 288). For a thoughtful reminder about the hope and power of utopian thought (and how it fell out fashion), see Russell Jacoby's *Picture Imperfect: Utopian Thought in an Anti-utopian Age* (New York: Columbia University Press, 2005). Jacoby notes that "utopianism demands boldness," as well as the ability to connect its vision to practical politics (148–49).

48. Warren, *Alternative Vision*, 109–20. Michel-Rolph Trouillot, *Silencing the Past: Power and the Production of History* (Boston: Beacon, 1995), reminds us, "History is the fruit of power, but power itself is never so transparent that its analysis becomes superfluous. The ultimate mark of power may be its invisibility; the ultimate challenge, the exposition of its roots" (xix).

Chapter 6. Fighting for Social Harmony

1. Nels Anderson, *The Right to Work* (1938; repr., Westport, CT: Greenwood, 1973), 3–5.

2. Jason Scott Smith, *Building New Deal Liberalism: The Political Economy of Public Works, 1933–1956* (Cambridge: Cambridge University Press, 2006), 263; Bonnie Fox Schwartz, *The Civil Works Administration, 1933–1934: The Business of Emergency Employment in the New Deal* (Princeton, NJ: Princeton University Press, 1984).

3. *MN*, October 5, 1933.

4. Frances Fox Piven and Richard A. Cloward, *Poor People's Movements: Why They Succeed, How They Fail* (New York: Vintage, 1979), 42; Helen C. Mawer, *Organization and Activities of the State Board of Public Welfare, January 1, 1931, to January 1, 1933* (Tallahassee, FL: State Board of Public Welfare, 1933), 7; Michael B. Katz, *In the Shadow of the Poor House of Welfare in America* (New York: Basic Books, 1986), 206–24.

5. Mawer, *Organization and Activities*, 32–33.

6. *MDN*, January 29, 1932, 1; *MDN*, February 26, 1933, sec. 2, 12.

7. *MDN*, December 21, 1928; December 19, 1930, 1; December 23, 1933, 1.

8. *MDN*, April 27, 1931, 3.

9. *MDN*, December 29, 1930, 2, 4; February 1, 1931, 2 (worthy unemployed); March 14, 1931, 2; April 6, 1931, 4 (Palmer quotes); April 10, 1931, 1; April 27, 1931, 3 (MDN quotes about Reeder); May 27, 1931, 1, 14.

10. *MDN*, December 29, 1930, 4; Udo Sautter, *Three Cheers for the Unemployed: Government and Unemployment before the New* Deal (New York: Cambridge University Press, 1991), 94–110, 268–318; Alexander Keyssar, *Out of Work: The First Century of Unemployment in Massachusetts* (Cambridge: Cambridge University Press, 1986), 286–98.

11. *MDN*, March 30, 1931, 1 (women sewing); April 6, 1931, 1; April 10, 1931, 5 (women sewing).

12. *MDN*, February 2, 1931, 1.

13. *MDN*, June 3, 1931, 1, 2; June 9, 1931, 4; *MH*, June 16, 1931, 1 (Gautier's election as mayor); *MDN*, May 27, 1931, 1, 14 (CLU endorsement of Reeder); May 28, 1931, 1 (Labor and Reeder); June 1, 1931, 4 (Palmer). The City Commission minutes were silent on the contested mayoralty (Miami Office of the City Clerk, Resolutions and Minutes of the City Commission, Florida State Archives, Tallahassee [hereafter *CityMin*]). Reeder won reelection to the mayoralty in 1941.

14. *Conference of Mayors of the United States, Detroit, Michigan, June 1, 1932*, reel 98, pp. 42, 120–21, Frank Murphy Papers, Bentley Historical Library (Gautier support for relief plan). The conference's accepted resolution called for a "prosperity loan" for "the employment of millions of men . . . for our jobless, redistribute purchasing power and thereby stimulate industry" (101); *NYT*, June 2, 1932, 1.

15. *NYT*, June 8, 1932, 28 (license tax); *CityMin*, May 25, 1932; June 8, 1932; *MH*, June 3, 1932, 6; "Cities Beg," *MH*, June 7, 1932, 4 (Detroit meeting, call for balanced budgets, skepticism of local government); June 10, 1932, 10 (realty board).

16. Mawer, *Organization and Activities*, 28–29.

17. Alex Lichtenstein, "'We at Last Are Industrializing the Whole Ding-Busted Party': The Communist Party and Florida Workers in Depression and War," in *Florida's Working-Class Past: Current Perspectives on Labor, Race, and Gender from Spanish Florida to New Immigration*, ed. Robert Cassanello and Melanie Shell-Weiss, 168–97 (Gainesville: University Press of Florida, 2009).

18. Roy Rosenzweig, "Radicals and the Jobless: The Musteites and the Unemployed Leagues, 1932–1936," *Labor History* 16, no. 1 (Winter 1975): 52–77; Rosenzweig, "Organizing the Unemployed: The Early Years of the Great Depression, 1929–1933," *Radical America* 10, no. 4 (July 1976): 37–61; Rosenzweig, "'Socialism in Our Time': The Socialist Party and the Unemployed, 1929–1936," *Labor History* 20, no. 4 (Fall 1979): 485–509; and sev-

eral studies by James Lorence, including *The Unemployment People's Movement: Leftists, Liberals, and Labor in Georgia, 1929–1941* (Athens: University of Georgia Press, 2009).

19. Rosenzweig, "Radicals and the Jobless," 52–64.

20. *MH*, August 28, 1932, 2; *MDN*, July 10, 1932, 4.

21. *MDN*, November 29, 1932, 4 (Palmer letter); Burdette Kinne, "Voltaire Never Said It!," *Modern Language Notes* 58, no. 7 (November 1943): 534–35.

22. *MN*, March 5, 1936 (LCC influence); *MDN*, June 2, 1931, 4 (Harding letter).

23. *MDN*, September 3, 1933, 4 (Palmer referencing Nicholson). Verner Townley followed up on Palmer's discussion a few days later praising Nicholson's intellect and labor activism (*MDN*, September 8, 1933, 6 (Townley letter to the *MDN* on Nicholson). The story of his support of Tampa's workers in 1914 (discussed in chapter five) was mentioned by Townley (though he incorrectly identified the date as 1912).

24. "Central Labor Unions and Our Unemployed," *American Federationist* 4, no. 3 (March 1933): 234–35; *MN*, March 5, 1936.

25. *MDN*, May 8, 1933, 4 (Palmer); "The Continental Congress," *World Tomorrow* 16, no. 17. (May 1933): 388; Devere Allen, "A New Declaration of Independence," *World Tomorrow* 16, no. 18 (June 1933): 416–17; Donald W. Whisenhunt, "Continental Congress of Workers and Farmers, 1933," *Studies in History and Society* 6, no. 1 (1974): 1–14; David A. Shannon, *The Socialist Party of America: A History* (Chicago: Quadrangle, 1955), 227–28; Donald R. McCoy, *Angry Voices: Left-of-Center Politics in the New Deal Era* (1958; repr., Port Washington, NY: Kennikat, 1971), 30.

26. *MDN*, March 11, 1933, 4.

27. *MDN*, March 11, 1933, 4; April 16, 1933, 4.

28. *MDN*, May 4, 1933, 4 (Townley); Elizabeth Faue, "Retooling the Class Factory: United States Labour History after Marx, Montgomery, and Postmodernism," *Labour History* 82 (May 2002): 109–19.

29. *MDN*, May 4, 1933, 4. Townley argued that "wealth is not produced at the top of society but is produced by labor power in mines, mills, factories, workshops, farms, and only labor power gives it value" (*MDN*, January 5, 1932, 6). Townley's engagement with class was not just a theoretical idea. In one letter, he related an occasion when he assisted striking workers (*MN*, August 2, 1934).

30. The Continental Congress of Workers and Farmers pamphlet is kept in numerous archives. See the "Socialist Party" folder in the National Association for the Advancement for Colored People Papers, Library of Congress, Administrative File, Socialist Party, part 1, C399 [hereafter NAACP Papers], or "The Continental Congress of Workers and Farmers," box 3, folder 5, Mildred and Mary Hicks Papers, Stuart A. Rose Manuscript and Rare Book Library, Emory University, Atlanta, Georgia [hereafter Hicks Papers].

31. *MDN*, May 8, 1933, 4; Continental Congress pamphlet, NAACP Papers and Hicks Papers; "A. F. of L. Executive Committee Council Places Ban on Congress of Farmers and Workers," *Journal of Labor*, May 5, 1933, Hicks Papers; article originally published in AFL, Weekly News Service, April 29, 1933; AFL Minutes of the Executive Council, Washington, DC, April 20–May 2, 1933, United Brotherhood of Carpenters and Joiners of America Records, Special Collections and University Archives, University of Maryland, series IV, subseries 1, box 2.

32. *MDN*, May 8, 1933, 4; May 16, 1933, 4 (Palmer letters); Continental Congress pamphlet; Whisenhunt, "Continental Congress," 5; William Leuchtenburg, "The New Deal and the Analogue of War," in *Change and Continuity in the Twentieth Century America*, ed. John Braeman, Robert J. Brenner, and Everett Walters (Columbus: Ohio State University Press, 1964).

33. Labor's *Miami News* started in 1919, as noted in chapter 1. The first extant issues, however, start in September 1933. My discussion in this paragraph represents an overview of my findings developed later in this chapter and in the next.

34. *MN*, October 5, 1933; December 22, 1933, 11; January16, 1934, 2; May 10, 1934; *MN*, July 5, 1934 (election of officers); *MDN*, November 1, 1933, 4.

35. The Papoose, "On and Off the Reservation," *MN*, February 8, 1934.

36. *CityMin*, June 26, 1933, February 7, 1934, April 18, 25, 1934; Miami Chamber of Commerce, *Minutes of the Board of Directors Meetings*, June 22, 1931, August 14, 1931, August 28, 1931, HistoryMiami Museum (Paint-Up and Clean-Up initiative); *MDN*, July 31, 1933, September 8, 11, 1933, 9 (want ads); January 7, 1938, 8 (tag day).

37. MDN, December 1932, 20 (Mickey Mouse Club, which had been around since 1930). See Thomas A. Castillo's "Laboring in the Magic City: Workers in Miami, 1914–1941," PhD diss., University of Maryland, 2011, on Miami's minstrel history (especially chapter 1).

38. *MDN*, August 10, 1933, 1; September 15, 1933; December 21, 1933, 11 (minstrel shows); December 22, 1933, 11 (dance). See also Castillo's "Laboring in the Magic City."

39. *MN*, August 16, 1934 (picnic); Booker T. Washington, *Up from Slavery*, in *Three Negro Classics* (New York: Avon, 1965), 148.

40. *MH*, July 13, 1933, 6 (headquarters); *MDN*, September 14, 1933 (Sewell).

41. Platt was a native of New Orleans, Louisiana, a Miami resident since 1920, and owner of Platt and Tingle Paint Company (Platt & Tingle Paint Co."Life Sketches of Candidates for City Commission—No. 3," *MDN*, April 25, 1931, 3.); "Platt Recall Move Started," *MDN*, April 30, 1933, 1.

42. On Platt recall, see *MDN*, April 30, 1933, 1; May 6, 1933, 1; May 20, 1933, 1; June 15, 1933, 1; June 16, 1933, 1.

43. *MDN*, June 18, 1933, 1; June 19, 1933, 1; June 20, 1933, 1; June 21, 1933, 1–2; June 22, 1933, 1–2 (DCUCL quote). Shaw's position was dissolved a few weeks later amid budget cuts and the food distribution–Platt recall controversy (*MDN*, July 8, 1933, 1). City manager L. L. Lee reassigned Gaskill to another relief program job, who was judged prejudicially for her gender. Her job was given to a man, whom the City Commission ordered have a "diplomatic manner and enough business ability to handle this office in such a way that a matter of this kind will not again occur" (Miami Chamber of Commerce, Resolution 8145, July 8, 1933).

44. Fossey had been president of the Miami Board of Realtors. Paul George, "Passage to the New Eden," 440–63; Stuart B. McIver, *The Greatest Sale on Earth: The Story of the Miami Board of Realtors* (Miami, FL: E. A. Seemann, 1980), 50, 100, 108, 112 (on connections between city commissioners and Miami Board of Realtors).

45. *MDN*, June 29, 1933, 15 (nepotism); June 30, 1933, 10; July 9, 1933, 7; *MH*, July 13, 1933, 6; July 18, 1933, 3 (consolidation); July 18, 1933, 4; Resolution 8237, Miami Chamber of Commerce, August 30, 1933.

46. *MH*, July 8, 1933, 1; July 13, 1933, 1–2; July 13, 1933, 6 (Vella Thomas); July 14, 1933, 1–2; *MDN*, July 8, 1933, 5; July 15, 1933, 1, 4 (letter in favor of married teachers); July 18, 1933, 4 (letter supporting married teachers); July 20, 1933, 14 (married teacher rule); July 24, 1933, 4; September 7, 1933, 4 (Wister letters); September 11, 1933, 1 (John Rigby letter).

47. *MDN*, September 17, 1933, 1; September 7, 1934, 1 (Florida Supreme Court case). On restricting married women's employment, see Robert S. McElvaine, *The Great Depression: America, 1929–1941* (New York: Three Rivers, 1993), 182–87; Alice Kessler-Harris, *In Pursuit of Equity: Women, Men, and the Quest for Economic Citizenship in 20th Century America* (New York: Oxford University Press, 2001), 58–60.

48. Lichtenstein, "We at Last Are Industrializing," 167–97; Jerrell Shofner, "Communists, Klansmen, and the CIO in the Florida Citrus Industry," *Florida Historical Quarterly* 71, no. 3 (January 1993): 300–309.

Chapter 7. Labor Marches

1. *MDN*, March 31, 1935, 7.

2. On grassroots community organizing, see Staughton Lynd, ed., *"We Are All Leaders": The Alternative Unionism of the Early 1930s* (Urbana: University of Illinois Press, 1996); Frank A. Warren, *An Alternative Vision: The Socialist Party in the 1930s* (Bloomington: Indiana University Press, 1974).

3. *MDN*, August 8, 1933, 4.

4. David Kennedy, *Freedom from Fear: The American People in Depression and War, 1929–1945* (New York: Oxford University Press, 1999), 177–89; Ellis Hawley, *The New Deal and the Problem of Monopoly* (Princeton, NJ: Princeton University Press, 1966), 19–146.

5. Kennedy, *Freedom from Fear*, 183–84; Hugh Johnson, *The Blue Eagle from Egg to Earth* (1935; repr., New York: Greenwood, 1968), 250–70.

6. *MDN*, August 15, 1933, 1 (worker's complaints). Peter Irons, *The New Deal Lawyers* (Princeton, NJ: Princeton University Press, 1982), 17–107 (for a history NRA implementation), 35–57. The NRA's weakness as an institution was revealed, as Peter Irons notes, in its "non-litigious approach to enforcement" (35) and its reluctance to test the codes in court (35–57).

7. *MDN*, September 11, 1933, 1 (violation complaints); September 19, 1933, 4 (Palmer's criticism of business). I was unsuccessful in my search for these specific complaints, but letters to Hugh Johnson, Franklin and Eleanor Roosevelt, and others are in the Records of the National Recovery Administration, Compliance Division, PRA Complaints, July 1933–February 1934, Record Group 9 [hereafter RG 9], box 6, entry 109, National Archives, College Park, MD. A thick folder titled "Miami" was filled with letters and short replies. Most of them comment on the really poor working conditions and wages that was the common practice in the restaurant industry in Miami.

8. Anonymous letter to William F. Farnsworth (assistant counsel, Blue Eagle Division, NRA), October 22, 1933, RG 9, box 6, entry 109.

9. *MN*, September 28, 1933 (forming unions); October 12, 1933 (restaurant workers); November 2, 1933.

10. *MN*, October 26, 1933, and November 2, 1933 (union support of complaints); November 2, 1933 (compliance board). See RG 9, box 6, entry 109, for examples.

11. *MN*, November 23, 1933 (Glade View). The *Miami News* provided reports on the local union meetings, including the Building Trades Council, the CLU, and the LCC. Reports for 1933–34 reveal labor union activism.

12. *MN*, November 16, 1933 (DCUCL, parade idea in LCC, and meeting on NRA); November 23, 1933; November 30, 1933 (Hugh Johnson invitation); December 7, 1933 (NRA parade); December 14, 1933; December 21, 1933; February 15, 1934 (parade moved to March 2).

13. See *Miami News* issues for September–December 1933, for home labor activism and prevailing wage-hour efforts. Miami Office of the City Clerk, Resolutions and Minutes of the City Commission, Florida State Archives, Tallahassee [hereafter, *Miami-City-Min*], Res. 8129, June 28, 1933; Res. 8372, October 26, 1933 (reaffirmed earlier action by the commission); *MDN*, June 29, 1933, 1; September 13, 1933, 1, 4 (J. J. Bridge letter); September 15, 1933, 4 (W. J. Fripp letter); September 16, 1933, 4 (Wister response to Bridges); September 18, 1933, 4. The 1933 candidates for city commissioner pledged support for home labor in their meetings with the LCC at Carpenters Hall in April and May.

14. *MDN*, October 27, 1933, 1, and October 31, 1933, 1 (transient unemployed); November 3, 1933, 3 (license tags).

15. Stuart B. McIver, *The Greatest Sale on Earth: The Story of the Miami Board of Realtors* (Miami: E. A. Seemann, 1980), 112, writes, "People who had bought property in the heady days of the twenties were unable to raise even enough money to pay their taxes. . . . The total number of tax delinquencies was staggering. Printed in the Sunday newspaper, the list of delinquencies once ran to forty-one pages, of small type." (McIver failed to provide a date.)

16. *MN*, October 5, 1933 (Palmer letter). Palmer reacted to an Ickes speech in *NYT*, September 24, 1933, 32; *Miami-City-Min*, Res. 8312, September 27, 1933.

17. *MN*, September 5, 1933 (Palmer complaint of lack of government cooperation); October 5, 1933. Hawley, *New Deal*, 19–146 (esp. 130–46 for insight into main players in NRA implementation: business planners and associationists, national economic planners, and the antitrusters). Suggestive of how small and medium-sized businesses favored the NRA or at least some version of it is Donald R. Brand, *Corporatism and the Rule of Law: A Study of the National Recovery Administration* (Ithaca, NY: Cornell University Press, 1989), 125–74. Small and medium-sized businesses complained about the high costs of wage and hour provisions during the early period of NRA implementation (Bland, *Corporatism*, 150–57; Johnson, *Blue Eagle*, 274–82). Small and medium-sized businesses dominated the situation in Miami as well.

18. *MN*, October 26, 1933 (Palmer letter sent October 8, signed as a DCUCL representative and as chair of the NRA Committee); *MH*, September 20, 1933, 1; *MDN*, October 4, 1933, 4 (reported Greater Miami Recovery Association meeting); *MN*, September 19, 1933 (on commercial groups).

19. *MN*, October 26, 1933 (Palmer letter).

20. Robert S. McElvaine, *Down and Out in the Great Depression: Letters from the "Forgotten Man"* (Chapel Hill: University of North Carolina Press, 1983); Elna C. Green, *Looking for the New Deal: Florida Women's Letters during the Great Depression* (Columbia, SC: University of South Carolina Press, 2007). I was informed by Virginia Lewick, archivist at the Franklin D. Roosevelt Presidential Library and Museum, that the correspondence record to the president was far from complete (approx. 2% of the correspondence was retained) (email, January 8, 2007). The shrinking of the evidentiary base has removed from the historical record correspondence that is relevant to local social histories. Palmer's many letters were absent from the National Archive collection. Their publication in the *Miami News* and *Miami Daily News* saved them for posterity.

21. Lizabeth Cohen, *Making a New Deal: Industrial Workers in Chicago, 1919–1939* (New York: Cambridge University Press, 1990); McElvaine, *Down and Out*, 170–95; Anthony J. Badger, *The New Deal: The Depression Years, 1933–1940* (Chicago: Ivan R. Dee, 2002); Warren, *Alternative Vision*, 109–33, offers important insight on how to judge failure.

22. *MN*, December 28, 1933 (DCUCL and Green); Records of the Works Projects Administration, Civil Works Administration, RG 69, National Archives, College Park, MD [hereafter RG 69], box 13.

23. Fagg to John Carmody, December 6, 1933 (regarding roadwork); notes of telephone conversation, Frank Bane (federal CWA) and Fagg, December 15, 1933 (citrus fruit growers), RG 69, box 12; *MDN*, November 28, 1933, 4 (quote); December 14 1933, 1.

24. *MDN*, November 28, 1933, 4; December 14, 1933, 1; Fagg to John Carmody, December 6, 1933 (regarding roadwork); notes of telephone conversation, Frank Bane (federal CWA) and Fagg, December 15, 1933 (citrus fruit growers), RG 69, box 12.

25. Fagg to Carmody, January 8, 1934 (quote), RG 69, box 12.

26. Ungar was a member of the University of Miami Athletic Association, served on its board of trustees (1937–65), and also served on the Orange Bowl Committee (University of Miami, "Named Buildings History, Coral Gables Campus," 86, last updated spring 2013, https://studylib.net/doc/7540338/university-of-miami; Kenneth Ballinger, *Miami Millions: The Dance of the Dollars in the Great Florida Land Boom of 1925* [Miami: Franklin, 1936], 38; E. L. Allsworth, vice chair, Miami Compliance Board, to Walter N. Pearce, Florida District compliance director, November 17, 1933, RG 9, box 6, entry 109; William Farnsworth to Ungar, October 12, 1933 [contained copy of news article, "Wage Scale Set for Restaurants"]).

27. *MN*, January 11, 1934 (Blue Eagle removed); *MDN*, January 13, 1934, 1 (jobless picketing); *MDN*, January 19, 1934, 1; "Minutes of the Meeting of the National Compliance Board Held January 9, 1934," RG 9, box 2, entry 125; telegram from W. M. Galvin (legal assistant, Compliance Division, NRA) to Arthur Ungar, January 17, 1934, RG 9, box 6, entry 109 (regarding DCUCL and picketing with Blue Eagle insignia); loose note, January 18, 1934 (Galvin notes telephone conversation with Ungar, picket sign issue). Ungar asked Galvin to pay for their long-distance conversation (the charges amounted to $19.20, January 18, 1934). On Palmer letter referring to Kessler's efforts, see *MN*, October 26, 1933.

28. Anonymous letter to Farnsworth, October 22, 1933, RG 9, box 6, entry 109, which stated the poor working conditions; other testimonies include Mrs. A. T. Hodges to Hugh Johnson, December 26, 1933, RG 9, box 6, entry 109; and Miss Effie Cheatwood to Hugh Johnson, September 21, 1933, RG 9, box 6, entry 109 (letters were often written to President Roosevelt or heads of department but then answered by the relevant bureaucrat); W. M. Galvin note on restaurant situation in Miami to National Compliance Board, January 19, 1934, RG 9, box 6, entry 109; *MN*, January 18, 1934 (cafeteria workers and compliance board); *MH*, January 10, 1934, 12.

29. W. M. Galvin note on restaurant situation in Miami to National Compliance Board, January 19, 1934, RG 9, box 6, entry 109. (Galvin found the *Miami Herald* "unsympathetic with [the] NRA"); Southern Cafeteria full-page announcement published in *MH*, January 10, 1934, 7, and in *MDN*, January 10, 1934, 16; *MH*, January 10, 1934, 1; *MDN*, January 10, 1934, 17 (loss of Blue Eagle); *MH*, January 10, 1934, 12 (employees oppose exemptions); *MN*, January 11, 1934 (NRA investigation); *MDN*, January 17, 1934, 1 (Palmer quote); *MN*, January 18, 1934; *MDN*, January 21, 1934, 4, and *MN*, January 25, 1934 (picketing); MDN, January 26, 1934, 1 (physical assault by Sunshine Cleaners on picketer).

30. Newspaper coverage, mainstream or the AFL press, was selective and incomplete; it is not unlikely that the DCUCL persisted in alerting anyone they could about code violations. See, for example, *MDN*, January 30, 1934, 4, and *MN*, February 1, 1934 (picketing blocked). The culinary workers and beverage dispensers' union organized in October 1933 (*25th Anniversary, 1933–1958, Metropolitan Miami Local 133, Club and Restaurant Employees and Bartenders Union, AFL-CIO*, Wirtz Library, Washington, DC). See also *MH*, October 1, 1933, 2, for how streetcar operators, bus drivers, and retail clerks were organizing; and *MH*, October 9, 1933, 2, which also mentions Local 133 of Restaurant Workers Union.

31. *MDN*, January 21, 1934, 4; Frank Roche, chair of the LCC and electrical worker unionist, noted "that steps will be taken to have the temporary injunction set aside, if possible" (*MN*, February 1, 1934). No record exists if any effort was made.

32. *MN*, November 16, 1933 (Wister-DCUCL, parade idea, LCC meeting); *MDN*, November 24, 1933, 4, food section; November 26, 1933, 8 (parade officers).

33. *MDN*, November 28, 1933, 1; November 30, 1933, 17 (quote); November 12, 1933, 1 (café owners and NRA); November 27, 1933 (hotel owners and NRA); December 1, 1933, 1; December 12, 1933, 4 (merchants and parade).

34. *MN*, November 30, 1933 (on Johnson); December 7, 1933 (on parade); *MDN*, December 8, 1933; December 12, 1933, 8 (change in parade plans); *MN*, December 14, 1933; February 15, 1934 (parade change). Roche explained Smith's read speech by saying that "it had been prepared at Washington by the [NRA] in order to make it authoritative" (*MN*, December 21, 1933).

35. *MH*, December 14, 1933, 1 (Smith speech); *MDN*, December 14, 1933, 1; *MN*, December 14, 1933.

36. *MH*, December 14, 1933, 1 (Smith quote); *MDN*, January 28, 1934, 2 (DCUCL-led parade); *Miami-City-Min*, February 7, 1934; *MN*, February 8, 1934 (citizen support of NRA).

37. The director of public safety changed the February date because of tourist season traffic; two more delays then occurred because of rain (Friday, March 2) and a conflict with events at Bayfront Park (Friday, March 9).

38. *MDN*, March 6, 1934, 2 (Retail Merchants Association cooperated but did not actually participate).

39. *MDN*, March 11, 1934, 5; March 13, 1934, 20; *MH*, March 12, 1934, 1; March 13, 1934, 1; *MN*, March 15, 1934, 4. E. J. Close, administrator of works for Dade County CWA projects, was elected as a marshal; he promised six thousand CWA workers would march (*MDN*, February 11, 1934, 4). Palmer, in *MN*, October 26, 1933, estimated that 140,000 lived in the county, and the 1935 state census conducted in April 1935 listed 180,998 for the county—127,600 in Miami. See also Nathan Mayo, *The Sixth Census of the State of Florida*, 1935 (Winter Park, FL: Orange, 1935), 13, 87.

40. *MN*, March 8, 1934 (Thayer LCC quote); March 15, 1934, 4; *MH*, March 12, 1934, 1 (parade coverage); for participate quotes, see *MDN*, March 13, 1934, 20, and *MH*, March 13, 1934, 1, 4.

41. *MDN*, March 5, 1934, 1, 10 (FDR speech); March 8, 1934, 1 (Johnson quote).

42. *MDN*, March 5, 1934, 1, 10 (FDR speech); March 7, 1934, 1 (claimed this was the best season since the boom); March 8, 1934, 1; *MN*, March 1, 1934 (Roche quote); March 15, 1934. On economic statistics, see, for example, *MH*, December 1, 1933, 1; *MDN*, December 3, 1933, 2; "1,500,000 Visitors in Florida during the Tourist Season," *Evening Independent* (St. Petersburg), April 1, 1934, 1.

43. *MH*, March 14, 1934, 6.

44. *MH*, March 14, 1934, 6.

45. *MH*, March 14, 1934, 6.

46. *MH*, March 14, 1934, 6; *MN*, March 15, 1934. The Connery Bill (sponsored by Massachusetts Representative William B. Connery) sought to reform the NRA and called for a thirty-hour maximum workweek and prohibiting reduction in wages or salaries, among other provisions. It never passed.

47. *MN*, January 18, 1934 (Manning's speech); June 27, 1935 (Hall).

48. *MDN*, April 25, 1934, 11; *MH*, April 25, 1925, 2; *Tampa Morning Tribune*, April 29, 1934, 9 (Florida federation formed).

49. *Tampa Daily Tribune*, April 30, 1934, 7; *Evening Independent*, May 11, 1934, 6 (Hall); *MDN*, May 2, 1934, 1 (red-baiting quotes); *MN*, May 17, 1934 (Palmer); Elna Green, "Hidden in Plain View: Eugene Poulnot and the History of Southern Radicalism," *Florida Historical Quarterly* 84, no. 3 (Winter 2006): 358 (per 358n41, a military intelligence report labeled the workers' leagues a radical organization).

50. *MN*, May 17, 1934.

51. *MN*, May 17, 1934 (all quotes); Stéphane Hessel, "Indignez-Vous!," *The Nation*, no. 292 (March 7–14, 2011): 15–19.

52. *MDN*, March 23, 1934, 6 (Palmer article); Cutting, "Is Private Banking Doomed?," *Liberty*, March 21, 1934, 7–10.

53. *MN*, May 10, 1934 (Palmer DCUCL telegram); *MH*, May 12, 1934, 4; *MN*, March 15, 1934.

54. Florida Emergency Relief Administration, *Review of Relief* 1, no. 1 (August 1934): 11; *Review of Relief* 1, no. 2 (September 1934): 5–6, 13.

55. *MN*, May 17, 1934; *Evening Independent*, May 11, 1934, 1; May 21, 1934, 2; *St. Petersburg Times*, May 10, 1934, 1; May 11, 1934, 1; Green, "Hidden," 357–59; Robert P. Ingalls, "The Tampa Flogging Case, Urban Vigilantism," *Florida Historical Quarterly* 56, no. 1 (July 1977): 13–27 (Poulnot quote on 20); Ingalls, *Urban Vigilantes in the New South: Tampa, 1882–1936* (Knoxville: University of Tennessee Press, 1988), 180–81.

56. *MDN*, June 11, 1954, 15A (brief retrospective of welfare council as larger community); June 12, 1934, 2 (quoted material); July 26, 1934; Richard Lowitt and Maurine Beasley, eds., *One Third of a Nation: Lorena Hickok Reports on the Great Depression* (Urbana: University of Illinois Press, 1981), 167–70.

57. Florida Emergency Relief Administration, *Review of Relief* 1, no. 3 (October 1934): 17.

58. *MN*, July 26, 1934 (Palmer letter, also published in MDN, July 26, 1934, 7); Florida Emergency Relief Administration, *Review of Relief* 1, no. 1 (August 1934): 6, 8–10; *Review of Relief* 1, no. 3 (October 1934): 13, 16; *MDN*, August 12, 1934, 4 (report of DCUCL telegram).

59. *MN*, September 13, 1934.

60. Florida Emergency Relief Administration, *Review of Relief* 1, no. 1 (August 1934): 6, 8–10; *Review of Relief* 1, no. 3 (October 1934): 13, 16; *MDN*, September 7, 1934, 1 (Miami bill highest in Florida); *MN*, September 13, 1934 (grocery budget); September 27, 1934 (*MN* response to *MH*); *MH*, September 20, 1934, 6; December 19, 1934, 1; *MDN*, December 22, 1934, 7 (Hoyt rebuttal).

61. "Perrine Palmer's Housing Report [inc]," September 1934, Public Housing Administration, RG 196, box 302; Gramling to Horatio Hackett, November 8, 1934, Public Housing Administration, RG 196, box 297; Gramling to A. B. Clas, Housing Director, November 20, 1934, PHA-RG 196, box 297. For Palmer's advocacy, see *MN*, October 4, 11, and 18, 1934; January 3, February 7, 14, August 8, 15, 22, and September 26, 1935; February 13, 20, 1936; June 8, 24, 30, 1937 (asks for LCC support of Wagner-Steagall low-rent housing bill). See also Jason Scott Smith, *Building New Deal Liberalism: The Political Economy of Public Works, 1933–1956* (Cambridge: Cambridge University Press, 2006), 263.

62. *MDN*, December 14, 1934, 9.

63. *Miami-City-Min*, November 28, 1934; December 6, 19, 1934; March 6, 1935 (housing in Opa Locka); *MDN*, December 7, 1934; *MN*, December 13, 1934, and *MDN*, December 9, 1934, 7 (Palmer article); *MDN*, December 16, 1934, and *MN*, February 14, 1935 (Palmer).

64. *MDN*, March 13, 1935, 1, 12 (federal funding); March 10, 1935, 1, and March 24, 1935, 5 (petitioning for Palmer candidacy); March 31, 1935, 7 (Palmer's denial of candidacy and Palmer's quotes).

65. Sam Stodel was labeled a New York economist by the *Miami News* (June 6, 1935) and a dentist by the *Miami Daily News* (May 15, 1935, 10); he had been an Industrial Workers of the World activist and an organizer of unemployed workers. See *Putnam County Courier*, March 20 and April 10, 1908 (Stodel); the *Oswego Daily Palladine*, February 3, 1915, 6 (IWW and Stodel). *MN*, April 11, 1935 (Gavelick, treasurer; Maurer and Burke, trustees). Burke later helped organize white and Black hod carriers in Miami.

66. *MDN*, May 15, 1935, 10 (Fidler quotes), 15; May 16, 1935, 1; *MH*, May 15, 1935, 10a;

Evening Independent, May 15, 1935, 1; *Daily Worker*, May 16, 1935, 3 (communist invasion).

67. *MDN*, May 15, 1935, 10 (Fidler quotes), 15; May 16, 1935, 1; *MH*, May 15, 1935, 10a; *Evening Independent*, May 15, 1935, 1; Dade County Unemployment Citizens' League to Governor Dave Sholtz, Florida, May 16, 1935, series 278, box 28, folder 6, Correspondence of Governor Sholtz, 1933–1937, Florida State Archives, Tallahassee; *Daily Worker*, May 16, 1935, 3; District Buro to all sections and units, June 10, 1935, Records of the Communist Party of the United States of America, Russian State Archive of Socio-Political History, Library of Congress [hereafter RGASPI], reel 298, delo 3900; *MDN*, May 1, 1932, 6 (Palmer); November 1, 1933, 4 (on poll tax); the *MDN* advocated abolishing the poll tax (e.g., October 20, 1933, 4).

68. Letter dated September 30, 1935, RGASPI, reel 298, delo 3900 (faction quote); *MN*, May 17, 1934 (Palmer "why worry").

69. Letter dated February 25, 1935 (plan for April conference and representative of National Unemployed Council traveling the state); letter dated June 10, 1935; letter dated October 28, 1935; letter dated December 17, 1935, RGASPI, reel 298, delo 3900; *MN*, May 17, 1934. See also Michael Denning, *The Cultural Front: The Laboring of American Culture in the Twentieth Century* (London: Verso, 1997), xvii–xviii, 22–24.

70. *Daily Worker*, May 3, 1935, 3.

71. *MDN*, July 6, 1934, 9 (Hayes); *MDN*, October 22, 1934, 18 (Sholtz).

72. *Sarasota Herald Tribune*, January 6, 1935, 6; *Daily Worker*, May 16, 1935, 3 (Sholtz attack on FCUCL); *MDN*, June 7, 1935, 14 (street corner critics); *MH*, June 7, 1935, 1; *Palm Beach Post-Times*, January 5, 1935, 9.

73. LCC Minutes, *MN*, July 4, 1935; *MDN*, July 28, 1935, 6 (Manning).

74. *MDN*, July 6, 1934, 9; October 22, 1934, 18; June 7, 1935, 14; July 14, 1935, 6; July 28, 1935, 6 (Manning); *Palm Beach Post-Times*, January 5, 1935, 9; *Sarasota Herald Tribune*, January 6, 1935, 6; *Daily Worker*, May 16, 1935, 3; *MH*, June 7, 1935, 1; *Palm Beach Post*, June 7, 1935, 9; LCC Minutes, *MN*, July 4, 1935; August 1, 1935; *Evening Independent*, July 11, 1935, 1; *St. Petersburg Times*, July 12, 1935, 6; Open Letter to Unemployed, RGASPI, reel 298, delo 3900.

75. *MDN*, July 3, 1935, 2 (URA); July 12, 1935, 1 (DCUCL, Lee, Dean, and Green); *Sarasota Herald*, July 12, 1935, 1 (Miami riot threats); *MDN*, July 14, 1935, 7 (K. H. Brown of URA). For *MDN* special investigative report, see MDN, July 16, 1935, 1, 8 (Dave Harris job search); July 17, 1935, 1, 2 (Helen Hansl job search); July 28, 1935, 7 (letter from "Disillusioned" job hunter).

76. *MDN*, June 28, 1935, 5 (DCUCL and county commission); July 12, 1935, 1, 13 (only DCUCL mentioned; July 14, 1935, 7 (URA quotes). A technical shift in language begins to appear in the summer of 1935: the unemployed start being labeled *unemployables* (see *MN*, June 27, 1935, first appearance I found in the labor paper).

77. *MDN*, July 31, 1935, 1; August 5, 1935, 1; *MH*, August 1, 1935, 1; *Daily Tribune*, August 1, 1935, 1; *MN*, August 1, 1935; *Baltimore Sun*, August 1, 1935, 10; District Buro to Comrade Brown, September 30, 1935, RGASPI, reel 298, delo 3900 (communist observer).

78. Quotes culled from newspaper coverage: *MDN*, July 31, 1935, 1; August 5, 1935, 1; *MH*, August 1, 1935, 1; *Daily Tribune*, August 1, 1935, 1; *MN*, August 1, 1935.

79. *MDN*, July 31, 1935, 1; August 5, 1935, 1; *MH*, August 1, 1935, 1; *Daily Tribune*, August 1, 1935, 1; *MN*, August 1, 1935; *Baltimore Sun*, August 1, 1935, 10; District Buro to Comrade Brown, September 30, 1935, RGASPI, reel 298, delo 3900.

80. *MDN*, July 31, 1935, 1; August 2, 1935, 1; *MH*, August 6, 1935, 1, 5 (Fossey quote, Palmer quote, Gavelick indirect quote).

81. *MDN*, August 20, 1935, 4.

82. *MDN*, July 12, 1935, 1 (Dean and Green); Smith, *Building New Deal Liberalism*, 263.

83. *MDN*, August 1, 1935, 4 (against tax raises); August 5, 1935, 1; August 6, 1935, 1; August 7, 1935, and August 17, 1935, 1, 2 (farming plan); August 18, 1935, 1 (city employee payroll discussion); *MT*, August 13, 1935, 3 (photographs and fingerprints).

84. *MH*, August 6, 1935, 5; *MDN*, August 20, 1935, 5; *Daily Tribune*, August 29, 1935, 16; *MN*, October 10, 1935 (home labor). On aliens, see *MN*, August 15, 1935, and *MDN*, August 21, 1935, 1. On Bahamian alien arrest and deportation, see *MT*, March 10, 1936, 6, and April 24, 1936, 5; Raymond Mohl, "Black Immigrants: Bahamians in Early Twentieth-Century Miami," *Florida Historical Quarterly* 65, no. 3 (1987): 292–93.

85. *MDN*, August 5, 1935, 1; August 14, 1935, 1; *Daily Tribune*, August 6, 1935, 1, 15 (Palmer, taxes); August 15, 1935, 20; August 18, 1935, 3; *MH*, August 6, 1935, 5; *MN*, August 15, 1935 (Palmer, living wage). For Palmer on landlords, see *MN*, September 26, 1935, and *MDN*, September 29, 1935, 5.

86. *MDN*, August 2, 1935, 1; August 5, 1935, 4; August 6, 1935, 2; August 15, 1935, 1 (federal agents in Miami investigating communism activity); September 1, 1935, 1; District Buro to Comrade Brown, September 30, 1935, RGASPI, reel 298, delo 3900; *Baltimore Sun*, August 2, 1935, and *MDN*, August 15, 1935, 1 (Jacksonville protest).

87. *MN*, August 29, 1935; *Daily Tribune*, August 15, 1935, 20; August 22, 1935, 1; August 23, 1935, 1; August 24, 1935; August 25, 1935, 1; August 25, 1935, 6; August 27, 1935, 1.

88. Roy Rosenzweig, "Radicals and the Jobless: The Musteites and the Unemployed Leagues, 1932–1936," *Labor History* 16, no. 1 (Winter 1975): 66–68; Irving Bernstein, *The Turbulent Years: The History of the American Worker, 1933–1941* (Boston: Houghton Mifflin, 1971), 218–27.

89. Frederic D. Ogden, *The Poll Tax in the South* (Birmingham: University of Alabama Press, 1958), 182–85; *MN*, June 3, 1937, 1 (poll tax); June 10, 1937, 1.

90. Palmer to Roosevelt, April 13, 1937, alphabetical file, 1933–1945, series 1937–1941, Franklin D. Roosevelt Presidential Library and Museum, Hyde Park, New York; *MN*, September 22, 1937; Palmer, "Adequate Income for Fall," *MH*, January 8, 1939, 2 (editorial section).

Epilogue

1. "Old Policies to Continue under New Name," *Miami News*, November 11, 1937; the first issue with the name *Miami Citizen* had this headline on its front cover: "Laundry Help Need Boost, Too: Labor Believes Underpaid Workers Entitled to Same Consideration as Dry Cleaners and Laundry Bosses," *Miami Citizen*, November 18, 1937.

2. *MH*, October 1, 1933, October 2, 9, 1933, 2. US Department of Commerce, Bureau of the Census, *Historical Statistics of the United States, 1789–1945* (Washington, DC: US

GPO, 1949), 72–73; Robert H. Zeiger, *The CIO, 1935–1945* (Chapel Hill: University of North Carolina Press, 1995), 17; Irving Bernstein, *The Turbulent Years: A History of the American Worker, 1933–1940* (1969; repr., Chicago: Haymarket, 37–171, 684–87; Stuart Jamison, *Labor Unionism in Agriculture*, US Department of Labor, Bureau of Labor Statistics, Bulletin no. 836 (Washington, DC: US GPO, 1945), 18, 23, 27, 327–42. By the end of 1933, the United Citrus Workers had organized thirty thousand workers (18); several AFL federal locals were chartered by 1935 (23); United Citrus Workers' initial stimulus from the NRA (330). For the significance of AFL unionizing in the 1930s, see Christopher Tomlins, "AFL Unions in the 1930s: Their Performance in Historical Perspective," *Journal of American History* 65, no. 4 (March 1979): 1021–42; on use of federal locals, see Dorothy Sue Cobble, "Lost Ways of Organizing: Reviving the AFL's Affiliate Strategy," *Industrial Relations* 36, no. 3 (July 1997): 278–301.

3. Frederic D. Ogden, *The Poll Tax in the South* (Birmingham: University of Alabama Press, 1958), 182–85; "Poll Tax Ends on January 1," *Miami News* June 3, 1937, 1; "Special Session of Legislature Called Unlikely," *Miami News*, June 10, 1937, 1.

4. See the local Miami newspapers on this early history, along with labor's *Miami News*. Also useful are the US Federal Mediation and Conciliation Service, Record Group 280, National Archives, College Park, Maryland. A 2021 *Miami Herald* article offered a recent bootstrap narrative of Local 1416: Taylor Davlon, "After 85 Years of Building Miami's Black Middle Class," *MH*, February 27, 2021.

5. William Green, AFL president, wrote to state, city, and other labor bodies in mid-February asking that they "renew their pledge of loyalty and devotion to the American Federation of Labor" (Bernstein, *Turbulent Years*, 686). Miami's Central Labor Union and Building Trades Council noted in their published minutes that they received this message (*Miami News*, March 4, 1937). The *Miami News* editorials begin to appear soon after: "Florida Labor Loyal to A. F. of L." (April 8, 1937); "The Truth about Sit-Down Strikes" (May 6, 1937); "Danger of the C.I.O. to the Greater Miami Area" (May 20, 1937); "Cooperation Is Necessary" (July 1, 1937); Tomlins, "AFL Unions," 1021–42.

6. *MN*, May 20, 1937; June 8, 1937; June 10, 1937 (unionization and new locals); *MT*, May 18, 1937, 3; May 26, 1937, 3; June 9, 1937, 3. Joseph E. Dames, "Tell the Story," interviewed by Electra Ford, August 21, 1997, 1, 8, the Black Archives, History and Research Foundation of South Florida, the Historical Lyric Theater, Miami, Florida, relates how his father, a Black Bahamian, was a tile setter helper in the 1930s and was one of the first Black presidents of the local. Dames's interview is part of larger collection available at the Black Archives and the Samuel Proctor Oral History Program, George Smathers Library, University of Florida, https://ufdc.ufl.edu/oral/results/?t=overtown&t=overtown.

7. "General Building Walkout Feared in Kress Strike," *MT*, October 3, 1937, 3; "AFL Unions Support Laborers' Demands of Full Recognition," *MT*, October 14, 1937, 1, 33 (quote).

8. "In Labor: End of Hotel Strike," *Business Week*, January 26, 1957, 104; Maria Jurkovic, "Picketing in Paradise: The Garment, Laundry, and Hotel Workers Union in 1950s Miami," master's thesis, Florida Atlantic University, 1995.

Index

THOMAS A. CASTILLO is an assistant professor of history at Coastal Carolina University.

The Working Class in American History

Worker City, Company Town: Iron and Cotton-Worker Protest in Troy and Cohoes, New York, 1855–84 *Daniel J. Walkowitz*

Life, Work, and Rebellion in the Coal Fields: The Southern West Virginia Miners, 1880–1922 *David Alan Corbin*

Women and American Socialism, 1870–1920 *Mari Jo Buhle*

Lives of Their Own: Blacks, Italians, and Poles in Pittsburgh, 1900–1960 *John Bodnar, Roger Simon, and Michael P. Weber*

Working-Class America: Essays on Labor, Community, and American Society *Edited by Michael H. Frisch and Daniel J. Walkowitz*

Eugene V. Debs: Citizen and Socialist *Nick Salvatore*

American Labor and Immigration History, 1877–1920s: Recent European Research *Edited by Dirk Hoerder*

Workingmen's Democracy: The Knights of Labor and American Politics *Leon Fink*

The Electrical Workers: A History of Labor at General Electric and Westinghouse, 1923–60 *Ronald W. Schatz*

The Mechanics of Baltimore: Workers and Politics in the Age of Revolution, 1763–1812 *Charles G. Steffen*

The Practice of Solidarity: American Hat Finishers in the Nineteenth Century *David Bensman*

The Labor History Reader *Edited by Daniel J. Leab*

Solidarity and Fragmentation: Working People and Class Consciousness in Detroit, 1875–1900 *Richard Oestreicher*

Counter Cultures: Saleswomen, Managers, and Customers in American Department Stores, 1890–1940 *Susan Porter Benson*

The New England Working Class and the New Labor History *Edited by Herbert G. Gutman and Donald H. Bell*

Labor Leaders in America *Edited by Melvyn Dubofsky and Warren Van Tine*

Barons of Labor: The San Francisco Building Trades and Union Power in the Progressive Era *Michael Kazin*

Gender at Work: The Dynamics of Job Segregation by Sex during World War II *Ruth Milkman*

Once a Cigar Maker: Men, Women, and Work Culture in American Cigar Factories, 1900–1919 *Patricia A. Cooper*

A Generation of Boomers: The Pattern of Railroad Labor Conflict in Nineteenth-Century America *Shelton Stromquist*

Work and Community in the Jungle: Chicago's Packinghouse Workers, 1894–1922 *James R. Barrett*

Workers, Managers, and Welfare Capitalism: The Shoeworkers and Tanners of Endicott Johnson, 1890–1950 *Gerald Zahavi*

Men, Women, and Work: Class, Gender, and Protest in the New England Shoe Industry, 1780–1910 *Mary Blewett*

Workers on the Waterfront: Seamen, Longshoremen, and Unionism in the 1930s *Bruce Nelson*

German Workers in Chicago: A Documentary History of Working-Class Culture from 1850 to World War I *Edited by Hartmut Keil and John B. Jentz*

On the Line: Essays in the History of Auto Work *Edited by Nelson Lichtenstein and Stephen Meyer III*

Labor's Flaming Youth: Telephone Operators and Worker Militancy, 1878–1923 *Stephen H. Norwood*

Another Civil War: Labor, Capital, and the State in the Anthracite Regions of Pennsylvania, 1840–68 *Grace Palladino*

Coal, Class, and Color: Blacks in Southern West Virginia, 1915–32 *Joe William Trotter Jr.*

For Democracy, Workers, and God: Labor Song-Poems and Labor Protest, 1865–95 *Clark D. Halker*

Dishing It Out: Waitresses and Their Unions in the Twentieth Century *Dorothy Sue Cobble*

The Spirit of 1848: German Immigrants, Labor Conflict, and the Coming of the Civil War *Bruce Levine*

Working Women of Collar City: Gender, Class, and Community in Troy, New York, 1864–86 *Carole Turbin*

Southern Labor and Black Civil Rights: Organizing Memphis Workers *Michael K. Honey*

Radicals of the Worst Sort: Laboring Women in Lawrence, Massachusetts, 1860–1912 *Ardis Cameron*

Producers, Proletarians, and Politicians: Workers and Party Politics in Evansville and New Albany, Indiana, 1850–87 *Lawrence M. Lipin*

The New Left and Labor in the 1960s *Peter B. Levy*

The Making of Western Labor Radicalism: Denver's Organized Workers, 1878–1905 *David Brundage*

In Search of the Working Class: Essays in American Labor History and Political Culture *Leon Fink*

Lawyers against Labor: From Individual Rights to Corporate Liberalism *Daniel R. Ernst*

"We Are All Leaders": The Alternative Unionism of the Early 1930s *Edited by Staughton Lynd*

The Female Economy: The Millinery and Dressmaking Trades, 1860–1930 *Wendy Gamber*

"Negro and White, Unite and Fight!": A Social History of Industrial Unionism in Meatpacking, 1930–90 *Roger Horowitz*

Power at Odds: The 1922 National Railroad Shopmen's Strike *Colin J. Davis*

The Common Ground of Womanhood: Class, Gender, and Working Girls' Clubs, 1884–1928 *Priscilla Murolo*

Marching Together: Women of the Brotherhood of Sleeping Car Porters *Melinda Chateauvert*

Down on the Killing Floor: Black and White Workers in Chicago's Packinghouses, 1904–54 *Rick Halpern*
Labor and Urban Politics: Class Conflict and the Origins of Modern Liberalism in Chicago, 1864–97 *Richard Schneirov*
All That Glitters: Class, Conflict, and Community in Cripple Creek *Elizabeth Jameson*
Waterfront Workers: New Perspectives on Race and Class *Edited by Calvin Winslow*
Labor Histories: Class, Politics, and the Working-Class Experience *Edited by Eric Arnesen, Julie Greene, and Bruce Laurie*
The Pullman Strike and the Crisis of the 1890s: Essays on Labor and Politics *Edited by Richard Schneirov, Shelton Stromquist, and Nick Salvatore*
AlabamaNorth: African-American Migrants, Community, and Working-Class Activism in Cleveland, 1914–45 *Kimberley L. Phillips*
Imagining Internationalism in American and British Labor, 1939–49 *Victor Silverman*
William Z. Foster and the Tragedy of American Radicalism *James R. Barrett*
Colliers across the Sea: A Comparative Study of Class Formation in Scotland and the American Midwest, 1830–1924 *John H. M. Laslett*
"Rights, Not Roses": Unions and the Rise of Working-Class Feminism, 1945–80 *Dennis A. Deslippe*
Testing the New Deal: The General Textile Strike of 1934 in the American South *Janet Irons*
Hard Work: The Making of Labor History *Melvyn Dubofsky*
Southern Workers and the Search for Community: Spartanburg County, South Carolina *G. C. Waldrep III*
We Shall Be All: A History of the Industrial Workers of the World (abridged edition) *Melvyn Dubofsky, ed. Joseph A. McCartin*
Race, Class, and Power in the Alabama Coalfields, 1908–21 *Brian Kelly*
Duquesne and the Rise of Steel Unionism *James D. Rose*
Anaconda: Labor, Community, and Culture in Montana's Smelter City *Laurie Mercier*
Bridgeport's Socialist New Deal, 1915–36 *Cecelia Bucki*
Indispensable Outcasts: Hobo Workers and Community in the American Midwest, 1880–1930 *Frank Tobias Higbie*
After the Strike: A Century of Labor Struggle at Pullman *Susan Eleanor Hirsch*
Corruption and Reform in the Teamsters Union *David Witwer*
Waterfront Revolts: New York and London Dockworkers, 1946–61 *Colin J. Davis*
Black Workers' Struggle for Equality in Birmingham *Horace Huntley and David Montgomery*
The Tribe of Black Ulysses: African American Men in the Industrial South *William P. Jones*
City of Clerks: Office and Sales Workers in Philadelphia, 1870–1920 *Jerome P. Bjelopera*

Reinventing "The People": The Progressive Movement, the Class Problem, and the Origins of Modern Liberalism *Shelton Stromquist*
Radical Unionism in the Midwest, 1900–1950 *Rosemary Feurer*
Gendering Labor History *Alice Kessler-Harris*
James P. Cannon and the Origins of the American Revolutionary Left, 1890–1928 *Bryan D. Palmer*
Glass Towns: Industry, Labor, and Political Economy in Appalachia, 1890–1930s *Ken Fones-Wolf*
Workers and the Wild: Conservation, Consumerism, and Labor in Oregon, 1910–30 *Lawrence M. Lipin*
Wobblies on the Waterfront: Interracial Unionism in Progressive-Era Philadelphia *Peter Cole*
Red Chicago: American Communism at Its Grassroots, 1928–35 *Randi Storch*
Labor's Cold War: Local Politics in a Global Context *Edited by Shelton Stromquist*
Bessie Abramowitz Hillman and the Making of the Amalgamated Clothing Workers of America *Karen Pastorello*
The Great Strikes of 1877 *Edited by David O. Stowell*
Union-Free America: Workers and Antiunion Culture *Lawrence Richards*
Race against Liberalism: Black Workers and the UAW in Detroit *David M. Lewis-Colman*
Teachers and Reform: Chicago Public Education, 1929–70 *John F. Lyons*
Upheaval in the Quiet Zone: 1199/SEIU and the Politics of Healthcare Unionism *Leon Fink and Brian Greenberg*
Shadow of the Racketeer: Scandal in Organized Labor *David Witwer*
Sweet Tyranny: Migrant Labor, Industrial Agriculture, and Imperial Politics *Kathleen Mapes*
Staley: The Fight for a New American Labor Movement *Steven K. Ashby and C. J. Hawking*
On the Ground: Labor Struggles in the American Airline Industry *Liesl Miller Orenic*
NAFTA and Labor in North America *Norman Caulfield*
Making Capitalism Safe: Work Safety and Health Regulation in America, 1880–1940 *Donald W. Rogers*
Good, Reliable, White Men: Railroad Brotherhoods, 1877–1917 *Paul Michel Taillon*
Spirit of Rebellion: Labor and Religion in the New Cotton South *Jarod Roll*
The Labor Question in America: Economic Democracy in the Gilded Age *Rosanne Currarino*
Banded Together: Economic Democratization in the Brass Valley *Jeremy Brecher*
The Gospel of the Working Class: Labor's Southern Prophets in New Deal America *Erik Gellman and Jarod Roll*
Guest Workers and Resistance to U.S. Corporate Despotism *Immanuel Ness*
Gleanings of Freedom: Free and Slave Labor along the Mason-Dixon Line, 1790–1860 *Max Grivno*

Chicago in the Age of Capital: Class, Politics, and Democracy during the Civil War and Reconstruction *John B. Jentz and Richard Schneirov*

Child Care in Black and White: Working Parents and the History of Orphanages *Jessie B. Ramey*

The Haymarket Conspiracy: Transatlantic Anarchist Networks *Timothy Messer-Kruse*

Detroit's Cold War: The Origins of Postwar Conservatism *Colleen Doody*

A Renegade Union: Interracial Organizing and Labor Radicalism *Lisa Phillips*

Palomino: Clinton Jencks and Mexican-American Unionism in the American Southwest *James J. Lorence*

Latin American Migrations to the U.S. Heartland: Changing Cultural Landscapes in Middle America *Edited by Linda Allegro and Andrew Grant Wood*

Man of Fire: Selected Writings *Ernesto Galarza, ed. Armando Ibarra and Rodolfo D. Torres*

A Contest of Ideas: Capital, Politics, and Labor *Nelson Lichtenstein*

Making the World Safe for Workers: Labor, the Left, and Wilsonian Internationalism *Elizabeth McKillen*

The Rise of the Chicago Police Department: Class and Conflict, 1850–1894 *Sam Mitrani*

Workers in Hard Times: A Long View of Economic Crises *Edited by Leon Fink, Joseph A. McCartin, and Joan Sangster*

Redeeming Time: Protestantism and Chicago's Eight-Hour Movement, 1866–1912 *William A. Mirola*

Struggle for the Soul of the Postwar South: White Evangelical Protestants and Operation Dixie *Elizabeth Fones-Wolf and Ken Fones-Wolf*

Free Labor: The Civil War and the Making of an American Working Class *Mark A. Lause*

Death and Dying in the Working Class, 1865–1920 *Michael K. Rosenow*

Immigrants against the State: Yiddish and Italian Anarchism in America *Kenyon Zimmer*

Fighting for Total Person Unionism: Harold Gibbons, Ernest Calloway, and Working-Class Citizenship *Robert Bussel*

Smokestacks in the Hills: Rural-Industrial Workers in West Virginia *Louis Martin*

Disaster Citizenship: Survivors, Solidarity, and Power in the Progressive Era *Jacob A. C. Remes*

The Pew and the Picket Line: Christianity and the American Working Class *Edited by Christopher D. Cantwell, Heath W. Carter, and Janine Giordano Drake*

Conservative Counterrevolution: Challenging Liberalism in 1950s Milwaukee *Tula A. Connell*

Manhood on the Line: Working-Class Masculinities in the American Heartland *Steve Meyer*

On Gender, Labor, and Inequality *Ruth Milkman*

The Making of Working-Class Religion *Matthew Pehl*

Civic Labors: Scholar Activism and Working-Class Studies *Edited by Dennis Deslippe, Eric Fure-Slocum, and John W. McKerley*
Victor Arnautoff and the Politics of Art *Robert W. Cherny*
Against Labor: How U.S. Employers Organized to Defeat Union Activism *Edited by Rosemary Feurer and Chad Pearson*
Teacher Strike! Public Education and the Making of a New American Political Order *Jon Shelton*
Hillbilly Hellraisers: Federal Power and Populist Defiance in the Ozarks *J. Blake Perkins*
Sewing the Fabric of Statehood: Garment Unions, American Labor, and the Establishment of the State of Israel *Adam Howard*
Labor and Justice across the America *Edited by Leon Fink and Juan Manuel Palacio*
Frontiers of Labor: Comparative Histories of the United States and Australia *Edited by Greg Patmore and Shelton Stromquist*
Women Have Always Worked: A Concise History, Second Edition *Alice Kessler-Harris*
Remembering Lattimer: Labor, Migration, and Race in Pennsylvania Anthracite Country *Paul A. Shackel*
Disruption in Detroit: Autoworkers and the Elusive Postwar Boom *Daniel J. Clark*
To Live Here, You Have to Fight: How Women Led Appalachian Movements for Social Justice *Jessica Wilkerson*
Dockworker Power: Race and Activism in Durban and the San Francisco Bay Area *Peter Cole*
Labor's Mind: A History of Working-Class Intellectual Life *Tobias Higbie*
The World in a City: Multiethnic Radicalism in Early Twentieth-Century Los Angeles *David M. Struthers*
Death to Fascism: Louis Adamic's Fight for Democracy *John P. Enyeart*
Upon the Altar of Work: Child Labor and the Rise of a New American Sectionalism *Betsy Wood*
Workers against the City: The Fight for Free Speech in *Hague v. CIO* *Donald W. Rogers*
Union Renegades: Miners, Capitalism, and Organizing in the Gilded Age *Dana M. Caldemeyer*
The Labor Board Crew: Remaking Worker-Employer Relations from Pearl Harbor to the Reagan Era *Ronald W. Schatz*
Grand Army of Labor: Workers, Veterans, and the Meaning of the Civil War *Matthew E. Stanley*
A Matter of Moral Justice: Black Women Laundry Workers and the Fight for Justice *Jenny Carson*
Labor's End: How the Promise of Automation Degraded Work *Jason Resnikoff*
Toward a Cooperative Commonwealth: The Transplanted Roots of Farmer-Labor Radicalism in Texas *Thomas Alter II*
Working in the Magic City: Moral Economy in Early Twentieth-Century Miami *Thomas A. Castillo*

The University of Illinois Press
is a founding member of the
Association of University Presses.

University of Illinois Press
1325 South Oak Street
Champaign, IL 61820-6903
www.press.uillinois.edu